Girls, Boys, Books, Toys

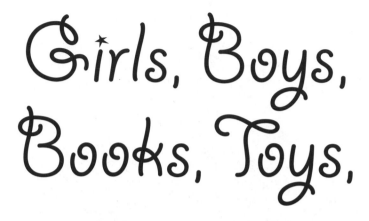

Girls, Boys, Books, Toys,

Gender in Children's Literature and Culture

EDITED BY

Beverly Lyon Clark
and
Margaret R. Higonnet

The Johns Hopkins University Press
BALTIMORE AND LONDON

© 1999 The Johns Hopkins University Press
All rights reserved. Published 1999
Printed in the United States of America on acid-free paper

2   4   6   8   9   7   5   3   1

The Johns Hopkins University Press
2715 North Charles Street
Baltimore, Maryland 21218-4363
www.press.jhu.edu

Library of Congress Cataloging-in-Publication Data will be
found at the end of this book.
A catalog record for this book is available from
the British Library.

ISBN 0-8018-6053-9

Contents

Acknowledgments

We gratefully acknowledge the assistance of Katharine Capshaw Smith and Kristine A. Byron, who worked very long hours in order to meet deadlines at several phases of the project.

Girls, Boys, Books, Toys

Introduction

Beverly Lyon Clark

If children's literature dawned in the 1740s, as most historians of it suggest, then perhaps it began in 1742, when Mary Cooper published *The Child's New Play-Thing*, a rhyming alphabet book that invited young readers to cut out its letters. Two years later, John Newbery published *A Little Pretty Pocket-Book*, accompanied by ball and pincushion (children stuck pins in it to record good and bad actions), to delight and instruct "little Master Tommy, and pretty Miss Polly." Girls and boys, books and toys. From the start, children's literature was imbricated with material culture, and reading and play were seen through the lens of gender. Adults were already constructing age and gender categories through children's culture. These issues continue to resonate for the contributors to this book, who focus on feminist theory's engagement with children's literature and other aspects of children's culture (henceforth "children's literature and culture"). Like feminist thinkers in other areas, critics of children's literature and culture have discovered powerful new ways of seeing and thinking from the margins. Study of children's literature and culture raises important questions about the definition of high culture, the social construction of childhood, a text's construction of its readers or a commodity's construction of its consumers, censorship and self-censorship, textual structures in mixed media, and the core texts that carry a culture's values.

To date, British and American criticism of children's literature has centered on literary history and social context or on reader response. Literary histories have moved well beyond the annotated bibliography in paragraph form that once constituted criticism in the field. In his recent *Audacious Kids*, Jerry Griswold sketches the American character by examining its canonical children's texts, fusing literary history with cultural and psychoanalytic critique. In *American Childhood,* Anne Scott MacLeod reads American children and culture, from Horatio Alger to recent censorship debates, in light of each other. In numerous essays, Mitzi Myers explores the literary, philosophical, and social contexts of women writers in the late eighteenth and early nineteenth centuries, especially Maria Edgeworth. In *When Toys Come Alive,* Lois Kuznets traces the typology of toy narratives through shifting adumbrations of anxiety, desire, power, and nostalgia. In their new historical accounts, these authors grapple with such theoretical issues as the position of the child in culture: Is the child a blank slate upon which culture is to be inscribed? Is the child the symbol of all that a culture aspires to?

Other socially inflected readings of children's culture have been informed by Marxist and postcolonial theorizing. In *The Empire's Old Clothes,* Ariel Dorfman explores the global impacts of such figures as Babar and Donald Duck. Jeffrey Richards collects postcolonial criticism of Victorian books, especially boys' books, in *Imperialism and Juvenile Literature.* Jack Zipes's Marxist readings of fairy tales appear in volumes ranging from *Breaking the Magic Spell* to *Happily Ever After.*

Children's literature also invites a reader-response approach, for its authors and critics are almost never members of the presumed audience—a gap that makes children's literature theoretically unique. John Stephens does a poststructuralist unraveling of this gap in *Language and Ideology in Children's Fiction.* Michael Steig stresses the importance of affect and the reader's construction of the author in *Stories of Reading.* Another humanist exploration, in this case limning the possibilities for a childist criticism, appears in Peter Hunt's *Criticism, Theory, and Children's Literature;* Hunt's work has been particularly important in making us rethink what a "child" is.

Much of this recent work on children's literature and culture addresses issues of gender. Feminist thinking, in one form or another, has long been implicated in and by children's literature, which has been a venue receptive to women writers, especially during the twentieth century. Women are well represented among those who write, edit, buy, read, and teach children's literature. It is no accident that 69 percent of the recipients of the Newbery Medal for outstanding work in American children's literature have been women, whereas women have won only 34 percent of the Pulitzer Prizes for fiction and 9 percent of the Nobel Prizes in Literature.

Feminist criticism of English-language children's literature has evolved in parallel with British and American feminist criticism—what can be called mainstream criticism—of works for adults. In the 1970s, Kate Millett was critiquing the "sexual politics" of Mailer and Miller, and Judith Fetterley was a "resisting reader" of Hawthorne and Hemingway. Feminist critics and social scientists such as Lenore Weitzman were likewise examining the images and gender roles of women and girls in children's media, including literature. Fairy tales came under attack for fostering passive Sleeping Beauties and helpless Snow Whites. Picture books were criticized not only for portraying feminine passivity but for vastly underrepresenting females.[1]

By the late 1970s, mainstream feminist scholars were increasingly attending to literature by women, usually to celebrate it. Elaine Showalter was tracing the history of "a literature of their own." Sandra M. Gilbert and Susan Gubar were exploring the recurring eruptions of "the madwoman in the attic." For these critics, literature by women was a lost continent of literature for adults.

In children's literature, too, there have been lost traditions—not just children's literature itself (overlooked by feminist and other mainstream critics) but also children's literature by women (lost to many critics of children's literature). The authors and editors of "classic" nineteenth-century children's literature tended to be men: the Grimm brothers, Mark Twain, Lewis Carroll, Kenneth Grahame, Jules Verne, Heinrich Hoffmann, Wilhelm Busch, Carlos Collodi. One trend in feminist criticism of children's literature has been to reclaim women authors who have been undervalued. The author who has received the greatest attention in this regard is Louisa May Alcott, but such English-language authors as Frances Hodgson Burnett, Maria Edgeworth, and L. M. Montgomery have not gone unnoticed.[2] A related venture, begun in the late 1980s, is the republication of lost works by women writers, including Evelyn Sharp's *Making of a Schoolgirl* and the stories collected in Nina Auerbach and U. C. Knoepflmacher's *Forbidden Journeys*. Reclaiming such neglected authors leads to rethinking critical norms. A figure like Alcott can be rescued from consignment to insipidity and hence dismissal if we acknowledge that she created communities of women; that her children's texts often cloak subversive energies; and that fairy tales, fantasy, and adventure stories are not the only important traditions in children's literature.

Several other developments have helped push feminist criticism of children's literature beyond its initial "images of girls" approach. One is French feminism, including the work of Hélène Cixous, who celebrates women's writing, emphasizing *jouissance* in *l'écriture féminine*, and that of Julia Kristeva, who points to the contradictory multiplicity of response and desire and revalues gaps, disjunctions, and uncertainty. These French feminists and also American feminists have rethought the construction of gender, acknowledging the interplay between masculinity and femininity within individuals and cultures.

Not all women and girls enact a single, biologically determined way of writing or responding—gender is not essential but rather is constructed in contradictory ways both in different people and within individuals.

In the Anglo-Saxon world Jacqueline Rose has explored children's literature most fully from a French psychoanalytic perspective: the necessary rupture between writer and audience leads her to examine how, in constructing childhood through children's literature, adults often conflate the origins of language, sexuality, and childhood. Other critics inspired by the play of gender include Claudia Nelson, who has rethought the meanings of masculinity—whether "boys will be girls"—in Victorian children's literature, and Claudia Marquis, who has explored the Lacanian pleasures of *The Secret Garden*.

In the 1980s, scholarship on race started to converge with that on gender in the study of children's literature, as elsewhere in feminist criticism. Feminists were exploring not just "differences within" but "differences between." Not all women and girls are oppressed in the same ways or subject to the same desires. African-American scholar Rudine Sims, for instance, undertook a case study of the reading choices of a girl who favored "strong black girls." Nancy Armstrong, primarily a critic of literature for adults, explored the traces of imperialist thinking in such cultural artifacts as *Alice's Adventures in Wonderland*.

In the same decade, scholars of cultural studies, long interested in the relationship between youth and culture, began paying more attention to gender. Cultural studies has encouraged scholarship devoted not just to literature-with-a-capital-L but also to other aspects of culture that address children, such as comic books, rock music, films, and fashions.[3] Angela McRobbie has pioneered work in this area in Britain, exploring, for instance, how popular magazines that target teenage girls construct femininity. In North America, Susan Willis has explored a broad range of the presumably trivial—including Barbie, He-Man, and MTV—to deepen our understanding of immersion in capitalist culture. Linda Christian-Smith has pointed out how teen romance novels can both induce conformity to stereotyped images of femininity and foster oppositional practices. Lynne Vallone and Sally Mitchell have extended this work by tracing historical constructions of girls' culture, whether their focus is on eighteenth- and nineteenth-century institutions and the attendant "disciplines of virtue" or on the eventual emergence of "the new girl."

Despite these convergences, however, mainstream feminist critics have not been eager to embrace children's literature.[4] Sometimes they attempt to appropriate what could be considered literature for adolescents, as Jane Tompkins has done in *Sensational Designs*, trying to save Susan Warner's *Wide, Wide World* from associations with juvenility. Critics of children's literature, however, such as Shirley Foster and Judy Simons, acknowledge Warner's participation in traditions of literature for young people. Both literature for young children and literature for adolescents reveal a culture's attitude toward the young and its cultural construction of youth, not to mention its key values; the materials we address in this book include culture created for both young children and adolescents, both animal picture books and Riot Grrrl music.

In any case, what mainstream feminist critics can't appropriate they ignore. Accounts of women writers in the nineteenth century routinely neglect works of children's literature. Theorists of marginality rarely extend their parameters beyond gender, race, class, sexual orientation, and types of "disability" to age. When they do, they mean thereby to acknowledge the positioning of the elderly, not the young. On the rare occasion when mainstream critics do address children's literature, they often approach it as if it too were a "child"—a blank slate—assuming that no one else has ever discussed the work in question and indeed that children's literature has never been theorized.

Nor has all criticism of children's literature been duly attentive to feminist thought. Feminist thinking has so far had the strongest impact in the study of fairy tales and Victorian children's literature. Most studies with other foci have paid little attention to gender. Hunt's *Children's Literature,* a 1990 collection of previously published essays, includes a single instance of feminist criticism, Lissa Paul's frequently cited "Enigma Variations." In the introduction to his 1992 collection, *Literature for Children,* Hunt points out that although 92 percent of those teaching children's literature at the college level are women, only 10 percent of them are full professors. As a way of excusing the "sexual imbalance" of his book, he suggests that women may be working more in areas of practice than in theory. Yet it should be clear by now that many scholars of children's literature have in fact been doing feminist thinking, both practical and theoretical.

Important milestones in this engagement include the 1987 essay by Paul, in which she argues that women's and children's literatures share a content (enclosure and entrapment) and a language (of otherness and deceit). Developing this parallel, Perry Nodelman argues in a 1988 editorial that children's literature, regardless of the sex of the author, resembles women's writing because it responds to repression by finding alternative ways of describing reality, ways that are often nonlinear and contradictory. More recently, Margaret Higonnet points out that much as feminist critics ask how women's texts reflect and deflect their relationship to the dominant masculine culture, critics of children's texts question the way our representations of children inscribe the dominant adult culture: each group has been treated as Other. Literature by women and that for children share common threads, the fiction reflecting the "real" yet also revealing that the "real" is a fiction we construct. Their narrative structures are often double voiced, simultaneously conforming and rebelling. But the common threads should not blind us to important differences both within and between the two, differences that play out in, for instance, debates over issues of censorship.[5]

Feminist approaches, in this book and elsewhere, have begun to extend beyond fairy tales and Victorian literature, even as feminists continue to work these rich veins. Some feminist critics continue to map the "images of girls." Others seek female traditions, within both children's literature and the broader culture. Some deconstruct binary thinking and give play to the preoedipal semiotic, in the liminal space provided by our culture's construction of childhood. Some question the boundaries and chart the slippages between male and female, rethinking not just femininity but also masculinity. Others query the boundaries between adult and child, including that buffer zone called adolescence. In short, some feminist critics of children's literature and culture expose the politics of marginalization by extending the triumvirate of race, class, and gender to include age, exploring the confluence of these nodes of difference in texts, genres, or culture.

Girls, Boys, Books, Toys is a sampler of such approaches, a reader that gathers theoretically informed new feminist criticism of children's literature and culture. Like feminism itself, it is a coat of many colors. Although our focus is on children's literature and culture in the English-speaking world, contributors come from around the globe. And the essays are written in a range of styles. Several, in keeping with one current in feminism, can be considered personal essays. Many of the essays are illustrated: some subordinate the pictures to the text; others function more like photographic essays—or picture books—with the pictures and text in counterpoint. Some essays address broad theoretical issues; others focus on particular works, but in ways that resonate with larger theoretical and methodological issues. All are short essays that take suggestive positions rather than cover the field.

It is a truism (usually honored in the breach) that feminist scholarship should be interdisciplinary; approaches to children's literature and culture need, if anything, to be more so. We have therefore sought specialists outside traditional literary criticism. A team composed of two sociologists and a psychologist reminds literary critics that children and their culture are shaped not just by individual texts but by the aggregate impact of all children's literature, especially the most popular or most recommended works. Other scholars—experts in American studies, cultural studies, history, and photography—

variously illuminate films, dinosaurs, comic strips, and boys' toys, and their exciting approaches to cultural texts suggest new approaches to literary texts as well.

This rich diversity is balanced by recurring themes in the essays. Home, a Victorian trope for the mother country, is that which can be romanced by a colonial writer of adventure stories; for a postcolonial writer, however, it must be earned. Traditionally a site of comfort in literature for young children, likewise a figure for the self, the domesticity that "home" enshrines is both attractive and dangerous for women. The private sphere it circumscribes is, nevertheless, not so private, as yet other contributors remind us: the literature of the private sphere can be highly political, whether a story encodes startling commentary on Irish or Middle Eastern politics or portrays schoolgirls or nannies mediating the two spheres. Then of course it is not just girls who are socially constructed but also boys, whether through literature such as adventure stories or through material culture such as toys. White, middle-class, Western norms are constructs too, as scholars here remind us by exploring what happens when the center colonizes the margin or the margin impinges on the center or by examining non-Western culture on its own terms.

The essays are grouped into sections entitled History, Theory, and Culture. These clusters, which point to broad trends in the field, are intended to be suggestive rather than mutually exclusive. History, for example, always mobilizes theoretical categories, however unconsciously. Because the most theoretically informed previous work in children's literature, feminist or otherwise, has generally delved into historical contexts, traditional critics of children's literature are likely to feel most at home with work in the History section, whether an essay traces the gendering of Sleeping Beauty over time or particularizes the contexts for Maria Edgeworth's work, the girls' school story, or the boys' adventure story. The Theory section opens up the critical conversation to a broad array of theoretical perspectives. A metatheoretical reading of research on children's literature in sociology and psychology reveals that such work has gone beyond counting aprons and puppy dogs' tails to converge with work by literary critics on race as well as gender. Other readings are postcolonial, Jungian, narratological, or Certeauvian, as critics variously read poetry, fiction, nonfiction, and picture books. The final part, Culture, takes theory and criticism beyond literature narrowly defined. Contributors explore the impact of mass culture on children and children's own constructions of culture. How, for instance, does the political climate shape the construction of dinosaurs—and how do children respond? How does a Syrian comic strip challenge Western assumptions about the dominance of certain genres and the way gender functions in Third

World cultures? How can viewing a Disney film offer a critique of unitary "identification" or of the uniform reception of "messages"?

This final essay on Disney brings us back to where we began, for it returns us to a text of children's literature, even as the first essay in the History section ends by invoking Disney. From literature to film and back again, from schoolgirls to mill girls to Riot Grrrls, from devils to dinosaurs to Disney—the essays gathered here illuminate the vibrant intersection between children's literature and feminist criticism and spark new questions for scholarship.

P A R T I

History

Repudiating "Sleeping Beauty"

U. C. Knoepflmacher

I

As Karen Rowe noted long ago, the "literary versions" of Continental fairy tales disseminated in England throughout the eighteenth and nineteenth centuries "differed substantially for men and women" (69). Given their original emphasis on female empowerment, however, male retellings of stories such as "Cinderella" or "Aschenputtel" could be reclaimed by later women writers who adapted them for children's books or reworked them into adult romances. In contrast, texts that unequivocally embodied a male point of view, such as Charles Perrault's "La Belle au bois dormant," or "The Sleeping Beauty in the Wood," although also ending with the reinstatement of a dispossessed heroine, proved especially difficult for women writers to rehabilitate.

In his "Moralité," or epilogue, to "The Sleeping Beauty," Perrault betrays some discomfort when he jokingly calls attention to the unnaturalness of the princess's protracted waiting period for a mate. Although he holds that the hope for a rich, handsome, and gallant mate may be "naturelle" for all single women, the narrator contends that he knows of no husbandless damsel—or "femelle," as he calls her—willing or able to sleep so placidly ("si tranquillement") for an entire century (107). Perrault's mockery is extended by male translators of his *Contes:* "Many a girl has waited long / For a husband brave or strong; / But I'm sure I never met / Any sort of women yet / Who could wait a hundred years, / Far from fretting, free from fears" (A. Johnson 20–21). Presumably bothered by such male cynicism, Angela Carter gave a decided twist to this "Moral" in her own 1982 translation. Although she made no alterations in the story itself (having already reworked traditional fairy tales in her sub-versive *Bloody Chamber* [1979]), Carter rephrases Perrault's appended moral to call the narrative into question: "A brave, rich, handsome husband is a prize well worth waiting for; but no modern woman would think it was worth waiting for a hundred years" (20). The stance of a worldly male amused by the fretful ea-gerness of marriageable girls is here neatly turned into one that can be held by any mature "modern woman."

Yet more than Sleeping Beauty's excessive patience made this male fantasy a difficult one for women writers—or readers—to assimilate. Mid-Victorian adapters who reworked the story also tried to signify their distance from some of its contents. Thus, in *The Fairy Book: The Best Popular Fairy Stories Selected and Rendered Anew* (1863), Dinah Mulock Craik follows the example of the Grimm brothers' "Dornröschen" ("Little Briar-Rose") by simply excising the second half of Perrault's story, with its abrupt and seemingly incongruous shift to a new plot involving the mother-ogress who wants to kill her daughter-in-law and eat her own grandchildren. In *Fairy Tales for Grown Ups* (1867), Anne Thackeray gamely tries to convert the old tale into a social satire that ridicules the stereotypical "female passivity" so essential to the Victorian ideology of sep-arate spheres (see Auerbach and Knoepflmacher, "Refashioning" 15). Jean In-gelow's use of the story in her *Mopsa the Fairy* (1869) also remains ironic: al-though Jack's kiss is responsible for changing a chubby sleeper into a queen, this human boy is not allowed to become her consort once she grows beyond him in maturity and power. The same reeds that "he had penetrated" earlier soon grow into the "long spear-like leaves" that will keep him away from Mopsa's castle (311). Unlike the thicket traversed by the prince in "Sleeping Beauty" or in "Dornröschen," this barrier proves insurmountable: woman and boy are now incompatible, destined to remain apart.

In "The Prince's Progress" (1866), the title poem of Christina Rossetti's sec-ond volume of verses, an energetic and "strong" prince keeps straying from his avowed "progress" toward a princess who can be released only by his interven-tion. The poem's opening depicts the ostensible object of the young man's quest, an immured and drowsy bride: "The long hours go and come and go, / The bride she sleepeth, waketh, sleepeth, / Waiting for one whose coming is slow:—— / Hark! the bride weepeth" (1: 95, lines 3–6). The erotic prince evinces little interest in this languid and weepy inmate, preferring to be de-tained by the banter of a "wave-haired milkmaid, rosy and white," who meets him outdoors, seductively loitering by a stile (1: 96, line 58). When he finally ar-rives at his destination, the elixir of life he brings with him proves to be useless. Whereas, in "Goblin Market," the juices that Lizzie brings back to a "dwindling"

Laura remove this sister from "Death's door" (1: 18, lines 320–21), the male protagonist of the later fairy-tale poem cannot revive one who has fallen asleep forever: "Too late for love, too late for joy, / Too late, too late! You loitered on the road too long. / You trifled at the gate: / . . . / The enchanted princess in her tower / Slept, died, behind the grate" (1: 108, lines 481–88). Rossetti here not only subverts the masculinist emphasis of those who, like Perrault and the Grimms, had cast the prince as an animator of torpid female limbs but also goes beyond those male contemporaries who had a vested interest in the arrested femininity of aestheticized—and anesthetized—women.

By the start of the twentieth century, the repudiation of Perrault's text becomes even more pronounced. In E. Nesbit's *The Enchanted Castle* (1907), two boys and a girl enter a maze that lies beyond a rose garden—"out of a picture or a fairy tale"—bordered with "thick, close-cut yew edges" (17). In a clearing at the center of this enclosure, they find a recumbent female figure attired in a "rosy gold dress." Given the setting and the veiled figure's royal garb, the children agree that she can be none other than Sleeping Beauty herself. But Gerald, the oldest, refuses to bestow a princely kiss on the young stranger; when his sister Kathleen takes on that role, the sleeper fails to stir. As a result, it remains up to Jimmy, the youngest and most skeptical of the three trespassers, to plant "a loud, cheerful-sounding kiss on the Princess's pale cheek"; yawning and stretching her arms, the veiled young Beauty theatrically exclaims, "Then the hundred years are over? How the yew hedges have grown! Which of you is my Prince?" (23). Yet this dramatic awakening turns out to be a mere ruse, for the "Princess" is only a playacting impostor, Mabel, the housekeeper's niece. Magic will have to be found elsewhere in a story that Nesbit tries to free from all antecedent fairy-tale encrustations.

In *The Secret Garden* (1911), Frances Hodgson Burnett also rejects "The Sleeping Beauty in the Woods." She defies the earlier conventions by making a girl, rather than a young man, be the first to penetrate an overgrown, walled sanctuary and to animate that dormant female space. The garden at first reminds Mary Lennox of "some fairy place," but she quickly notes a fundamental unlikeness: "The few books she had read and liked had been fairy-story books, and she had read of secret gardens in some of the stories. Sometimes people went to sleep in them for a hundred years, which she had thought must be rather stupid. She had no intention of going to sleep, and, in fact, she was becoming wider awake every day which passed at Misselthwaite" (88). Mary clearly speaks for Burnett when she dismisses as "stupid" the notion of a hundred-year female coma. For the novelist wants to dissociate *The Secret Garden* from the male fantasy of "Sleeping Beauty." Mary is no passive sleeper awakened by a masculine rescuer; instead, she is about to lead a boy-collaborator into the garden she has already begun to revive. Her handiwork is quickly praised by Dickon: "'Tha' was right,' he said. 'A gardener couldn't have told thee better'" (104–5). As caretaker of the garden associated with her cousin Colin's mother, however, Mary will do more than tend plants. In a deliberate reversal of gender roles, it is she who awakens Colin from the paralysis caused by his mother's death and perpetuated by his father's neglect.

Why did "Sleeping Beauty" seem unacceptable to both Nesbit and a Burnett who had nonetheless worked the old tale into *A Little Princess* in 1905?[1] Traditional fairy tales certainly had become more difficult to accommodate by the end of the Victorian era. Forced, like Mary Lennox, to weed and prune overgrown thickets in order to make "a place" for new growths and give them "room to breathe," women writers had become increasingly aware of endless layers of deformation in the tales. The scholarly work of folklorists such as Marian Roalfe Cox, whose 1893 compilation of 345 variants of "Cinderella" was introduced by Andrew Lang and is still considered a classic today, made these writers far better schooled in identifying narrative antecedents and their permutations. Thus, Sir Richard Burton's posthumous 1893 translation of Giambattista Basile's *Pentamerone*, recognized as one of Perrault's major sources, may well have magnified the long-standing antipathy women writers felt for "La Belle au bois dormant." Aiming at adult readers, Burton had no compunction in fully reinstating the "coarseness" that John Edward Taylor, Basile's mid-Victorian translator, had partly expunged in an attempt to appeal to a dual audience of the young and old (Taylor xvi).[2]

Basile's story "Sun, Moon, and Talia" helps account for the strange unevenness that makes Perrault's "Sleeping Beauty" story so much less polished than his others. Indeed, as we shall eventually see, this blatant story of rape, adultery, and cannibalism proved so difficult to suppress that Perrault might have been better off had he simply tried to de-eroticize his text and removed its entire second half, as the Grimms did in their brief and innocuous "Dornröschen." His decision to disguise the source of the sexual rivalry between the fierce ogress and a passive Sleeping Beauty only made the contest between aggressive and passive female figures more amenable to misogynist readings.

II

In distinguishing Perrault's version of "Sleeping Beauty" from that of the Grimms, Lutz Röhrich stresses the Frenchman's ironic realism:

The German Sleeping Beauty is as old the day she wakes up as the day she fell asleep; it does not occur to the German narrator to calculate the effect of the magical hundred-year sleep. Perrault's Sleeping Beauty has hard skin because she is 120 years old; "one would be hard pressed to find an animal in the zoo with skin as hard as hers." The musical instruments which wake her play outdated music, and Sleeping Beauty is wearing an old-fashioned dress: "But the prince was careful not to tell her that she was dressed like his grandmother and was wearing a high-necked dress." On the wedding night the princess doesn't sleep much because she is already thoroughly rested. (164–65)

Röhrich might have added that, unlike the Grimms, who need a waking king and queen to approve their young child's impending marriage, Perrault removes his Sleeping Beauty's parents and condemns them to grow older and die.[3] Yet more than Perrault's time-conscious realism is involved in all these examples. Whereas the German Briar-Rose remains a virginal teenager who has yet to consummate her marriage by the end of the story, Perrault has his fun with the nuptials he places at the midpoint of his narrative. The idea that a hundred-year waiting period may have appreciably increased the libido of a bride old enough to be her inexperienced young groom's grandmother affords an opportunity for a sexual innuendo that Perrault simply cannot pass up.

One of the chief differences, then, between the French and German texts is their treatment of sexuality. The Grimms want their fifteen-year-old *Dornröschen* to remain innocent and childlike to the end. Her very name—"*little Briar-Rose*"—infantilizes her, as does the androgynous "it" ("*es*") used to refer to her in the German original. There is no prediction about the sleeping girl's redemption through a male kiss, as there is in Perrault's version. The prince, who merely happens to arrive on the very day when the spell is to be dissolved, is as de-eroticized as Briar-Rose. Unable to avert his eyes, he shyly gives her a buss, whereupon she awakens "and looked at him quite sweetly" (Grimm, *Complete* 241), or, as the German phrasing has it, "*ganz freundlich*"—"in quite friendly fashion" (Grimm, *Grimms Märchen* 1: 347). Like two obedient children, the pair soon report to her parents. Their behavior thus befits a *Kindermärchen* designed for the young offspring of a Biedermeyer bourgeoisie.

In contrast, Perrault's tale, intended for an older audience of teenagers and adults, seems far more prurient. His "trembling" young prince may also be somewhat immature, but the sexual excitement he exhibits as he kneels over the "radiant beauty" lying before him is unmistakable. And the waking princess, according to the narrator's gloss, "bestowed upon him a look more tender than a first glance might seem to warrant" (A. Johnson 13). Without the necessity of gaining approval from her parents, this princess and her eager lover can speedily consummate their desires: after eating and drinking in "an apartment hung with mirrors," they sleep "but little" on their wedding night (15, 16).

The parental authority that Perrault's Sleeping Beauty and her lover so easily evade in her castle comes to plague them as soon as the tale moves into its second half. The kingdom that was ruled by the princess's parents a century ago has "passed to another family" (9). Perrault's story also "passes" into a very different mode when the male offspring of this new "family" cannot bring himself to introduce his bride to his parents. For Sleeping Beauty's bold lover turns out to be a most timid son. To account for his escapade, the prince tells his father that he spent the night in the hut of a hospitable peasant who warmed and fed him. The "easygoing" king accepts this fiction, but the young man's more discerning mother is "not so easily hoodwinked" by the prince's "handy" excuses whenever "he slept two or three nights from home" (16).

When Perrault explains why this matriarch is to be feared far more than her complacent husband, he hardly exhibits the "French sense of reality" that Röhrich credits him with. The prince's periodic nighttime trips result in the production, first, of a daughter called Dawn and then of a boy named "'Day,' because he seemed even more beautiful than his sister" (16). One might expect the arrival of such a precious male heir to provide the prince with an olive branch to dangle before his parents; he has, after all, ensured the extension of the kingdom's ruling family. Yet the young man continues to conceal the existence of his wife and children. The reasons for concealment are made perfectly explicit in Basile's masculinist text, where, as we shall see in the next segment, the father of these children covers up more than a secret marriage. But in Perrault's story, the explanation for the prince's reluctance to trust his mother "with his secret" is handled in a manner so self-consciously extravagant that it undercuts the narrative's coherence.

For the prince knows that, far from melting a grandmother's heart, the beauty of his children will only stimulate in her carnal appetites quite different from his own: "Despite the affection which he bore her, he was afraid of his mother, for she came of a race of ogres, and the king had only married her for her wealth. It was whispered at the Court that she had ogrish instincts, and that when little children were near she had the greatest difficulty in the world to keep herself from pouncing on them." As if to call attention to the incongruity of this pseudoexplanation, the narrator cannot refrain from adding, tongue-in-cheek, "No wonder the prince was reluctant to say a word" (16). The prince's silence resembles the narrator's wordiness, for both greatly prefer female passivity to female aggression.

Upon the old king's death, the prince assumes that he can now safely bring home his long-concealed wife and children. Yet after deciding to make war "on his neighbor, the Emperor Cantalabutte" (sic!), the new king rashly appoints "the queen mother as regent in his absence" and foolishly entrusts his wife and children to her care. The mother is now free to indulge those ogrish appetites her son has inexplicably forgotten: she commands her steward to serve little Dawn with "piquant sauce" and, after enjoying the lamb the steward substitutes for the child, orders little Day and, eventually, Sleeping Beauty herself to be garnished in the same way. This last request poses a special problem for the well-meaning steward: "The young queen was twenty years old, without counting the hundred years she had been asleep. Her skin, though white and beautiful, had become a little tough, and what animal could he possibly find that would correspond to her?" (18). The narrator's gloss again borders on the burlesque. But his exaggerations do not, as Röhrich maintains, establish witty "connections to reality" (165). Instead, they are distractions designed to prevent the reader from demanding a more plausible explanation for the older woman's bizarre behavior. The narrator's humor discourages us from seriously speculating about the motivations that might make a matriarch want to devour her son's family.

The ogress who dominates the second half of "The Sleeping Beauty in the Wood" is clearly an analogue to the old, malevolent fairy who dominated the story's first half. The two powerful figures are linked in several ways. Both feel slighted by a patriarchal order: the fairy, by the king who failed to invite her to the christening party; the ogress, by the son who failed to acknowledge her primacy when he covertly married the young-but-old woman who promptly bore him two heirs. Though directed at male authority, each woman's enmity leads her to attack children and childlike adult women, since these innocents might perpetuate a royal succession. The fairy chooses to kill a girl who, having just passed puberty, is in a position to extend her father's lineage. Similarly, the ogress who acts as "regent" in the new king's absence decides to slaughter his offspring and wife because they threaten to undermine her dominance over her husband and son.

In this sense, the fairy who is denied a seat at the banquet and the ogress who is tricked into believing that she has devoured the prince's family are identical power-hungry, phallic women who are perceived as threats to a tenuous male rule. Both women also threaten the control over the narratives held by the two male storytellers, that is, the prince, Perrault's narrator, as well as Perrault himself as purveyor of tales he knows to have been authored by someone else. The spindle used by the old fairy as a weapon to kill Sleeping Beauty was associated, in real life as well as in folklore, with the powerful spinners of folktales whose authority Perrault acknowledges; yet there are more immediate female rivals, such as Marie-Catherine D'Aulnoy, whose recent adaptations of fairy tales Perrault seems far less willing to recognize.[4]

As a symbol of the very deflowering that the old fairy wants to prevent, however, the pricking spindle that draws blood from girls and makes them fall down in a "swoon" is clearly as masculine as its antidote, the prince's kiss that acts as a prelude to a true defloration. A similar gender reversal is at work when the ogress decides, after discovering that her victims are still alive, to throw them and the offending steward (and his wife) into a cauldron full of vipers, toads, and "snakes and serpents of every kind" (A. Johnson 20). Yet, in a feat rather difficult to execute, she ultimately chooses to be herself devoured by these "hideous creatures." No Perseus can slay the Medusalike ogress; instead, she overreaches even in her self-immolation by impaling herself on a bed of borrowed phalluses.

Perrault purports to side with the young and weak against such aberrant and overbearing female figures. Aware that she can hardly "undo all that my aged kinswoman has decreed," the young fairy who counters the spell can at best commute a death sentence into a century of "slumber" and place her hopes in the agency of a "king's son" (5). But the redeeming prince's own powers of protection seem far more curtailed than those of the young fairy or the kindhearted steward. Despite his brash military campaign against Emperor Cantalabutte, the young monarch seems almost as paralyzed and volitionless as Sleeping Beauty. And this Griselda figure takes female passivity to hyperbolic extremes when she asks the steward to slice her throat: "'Do it! Do it!' she cried baring her neck to him; 'carry out the order you have been given! Then once more I shall see my children, my poor children that I loved so much'" (19). (As Perrault's narrator quickly notes in accounting for Sleeping Beauty's death wish, "Nothing had been said to her when the children were stolen away, and she believed them to be dead." But why had the kindly steward not confided in her? Because this child-woman could not be entrusted with a dangerous secret?)

Sleeping Beauty's inability to defend her children, or to avenge them after supposing them to have been slaughtered, only helps to magnify the fierceness with which the old fairy and the ogress meet any challenge to their supremacy. Her lack of volition, however, parallels her husband's own reluctance to assert his and her interests. Perrault pretends that the young man's filial feelings prevent him from upholding his domestic rights against his devouring mother. Since matricide is something this dutiful son would never allow himself to consider, the ogress's suicide proves highly convenient. Perrault's ironic last sentence reinforces the young monarch's weakness by calling attention to his dubious grief: "The king could not but be sorry, for after all she was his mother; but it was not long before he found ample consolation in his beautiful wife and children" (20). There seems to be some consolation, too, as Perrault slyly hints, in the young king's certainty—and ours—that his tenuous control over her waking life will never be challenged by so utterly self-effacing and compliant a wife.

III

Both Perrault's ironic self-consciousness and the resistance to his text by later women writers are greatly clarified by a closer look at the major antecedent he tried to rework in "La Belle au bois dormant." For Perrault's tale must be read as a bloated version of "Sun, Moon, and Talia," the Fifth Diversion of the Fifth Day of *Lo Cunto Deli Cunti* (later known as the *Pentamerone*) that Giambattista Basile had published in Naples in 1636 for an adult readership. Retaining Basile's privileging of female passivity, Perrault embroiders a plot that Basile tells far more directly and compactly. Unlike Perrault, however, who feels compelled to protect a precarious male order from the threat of female usurpation, Basile unambiguously equates strength with masculine opportunism. Thus, whereas the gifts and curses of fairies determine Sleeping Beauty's fate at the outset of Perrault's story, Basile chooses to have the fate of his young sleeper foretold by divining male "seers": "These wise men, after many consultations, came to the conclusion that she would be exposed to great danger from a small splinter in some flax" (2: 129). Still, in a world ruled by chance, these soothsayers can offer no preventives or antidotes. The removal of all spindles by Perrault's king was a foolish attempt to forestall the irresistible mandates of matriarchal fate. But when undertaken by the "great lord" who tries to protect his motherless daughter in "Sun, Moon, and Talia," the same action can at least help to reduce the odds.

This ideological discrepancy accounts for each writer's almost antithetical handling of his narrative. Perrault's authorial uneasiness, conveyed by his diversionary wit and his reliance on excrescent detail, makes him as evasive as the young prince who finds it so difficult to tell a straightforward story. Basile, on the other hand, proceeds with the brash self-confidence shown by his own ruthless male protagonist. That hero turns out to be not a prince at all, but rather a lustful king who is already married before he stumbles upon a chance to rape and inseminate a sleeping beauty. Named Talia by her father (there is no mother who finds, as the queen finds in the opening of Perrault's tale, "that her wishes were fulfilled"), this young woman succumbs to the accident the wise men predicted. After being pricked in the manner of Sleeping Beauty and *Dornröschen*,[5] she falls into a seemingly irreversible coma. In Basile's erratic universe, there is no time limit of a hundred years or promise of future princely redemption. Bemoaning "this bucketful of sour wine," Talia's "stricken father" promptly deserts his inert child: "He locked the door and left for ever the house which had brought him such evil fortune, so that he might entirely obliterate the memory of his sorrow and suffering" (2: 130).[6]

Left unattended for "some time," this daughter of a luckless man is now ready to be repossessed by a more fortunate king, a hunter who accidentally follows his falcon into Talia's room. Like a falcon himself, he immediately pounces on his prey, carries her to a couch, and "having gathered the fruits of love, left her lying there" (2: 130). As uninterested in Talia's fate as her oblivion-seeking father, the rapist returns to his kingdom, "and for a long time entirely forgot the affair." One day, however, the king's memories of "the adventure of the fair sleeper" are somehow rekindled, and he decides to take "the opportunity of another hunting expedition" to press his luck a second time. To his surprise, he finds Talia awake and accompanied by "two prodigies of beauty," Sun and Moon, the twin children born during his yearlong absence. These heirs, a son and daughter (though twice called "sons" by the translator, Benedetto Croce), raise Talia's value in the king's estimation. He now remains in her company for "several days" and, upon returning to his palace, crassly brags about Talia, Sun, and Moon to his wife (2: 131).

As Perrault emphasized to his readers, his Sleeping Beauty was wide awake on her wedding night as well as during the renewed connubial intercourse that resulted in the successive births of Dawn and Day. Basile, however, keeps Talia asleep both during and after her defloration, for, like Thomas Hardy, whose Tess is also impregnated while asleep, he wants to stress the "purity" of his subject. She is still in a coma when her two children are born, having been kept alive by invisible fairies who act as friendly midwives and nursemaids rather than as powerful fates. Significantly, Talia's awakening is induced not by an erotic kiss but by the action of one of her own babes: unable to find her breast, the infant sucks her finger and "drew out the splinter" (2: 130). As a virgin mother, Talia is understandably puzzled about the possible origins of the "two splendid pearls" nestled beside her. She has no memory of a lover. As even the unsentimental king begins to grasp, this innocent is herself a pearl who may be more desirable than his legal, but childless, wife.

In his efforts to soften this crass tale of rape and adultery, Perrault converts Basile's determined king into a tremulous young prince and changes the revengeful actions of a wronged wife into the obsessions of a ravenous mother.

The ogress's appetite for children, however, remains far more contrived than the enmity Basile's queen understandably shows toward her husband's illegitimate children. This betrayed woman is not an insatiable flesh-eater, but rather someone who has good reason for wanting to destroy rival claimants to the throne. Luring Talia and her offspring to the court, she decides not to eat the children herself but rather to feed them to her philandering mate. When she urges him to take more helpings—"Eat away, you are eating what is your own"—her husband cruelly uses the occasion to remind her of her barrenness: "I know very well I am eating what is my own; you never brought anything into the house" (2: 131). Despite the king's obtuseness, however, the joke is on the queen. Thanks to a tender-hearted cook's maneuvering, the meats consumed are mere animal flesh.

Stung by her husband's "anger," the queen now vents her wrath on Talia, who, after all, may well bring more children into the king's "house." She has this rival hauled in and berates her in a manner more befitting a fishwife than a queen: "Welcome, Madame Troccola [Miss Busybody]! So you are the fine piece of goods, the fine flower my husband is enjoying! You are the cursed bitch that makes my head go round! . . . I will make you pay for all the harm you have done me!" (2: 131). The psychological realism that Röhrich attributes to Perrault is more evident here. There is no need to assign an ogress appetite to this enraged queen. Not only the reader, but Talia herself, fully understands the grounds for the queen's excesses. Talia even tries to "excuse herself, saying that it was not her fault and that the King had taken possession of her territory whilst she was sleeping" (2: 131). The queen understandably refuses to listen to any tall tale about a catalepsy induced by spindle splinters.

Whereas Perrault's ogress tries to eat her daughter-in-law, Basile's wronged wife wants to burn to death the woman who so enflamed her husband with passion and pride. At this point Basile reintroduces the story's earlier erotics. To delay her execution, Talia asks to be allowed to undress before being thrown on the bonfire. She engages in what amounts to a striptease bound to bring back the nearby king: "Talia began to undress, and for each garment that she took off she uttered a shriek. She had taken off her dress, her skirt and bodice, and was about to take off her petticoat, and to utter her last cry," when the king, undoubtedly stimulated by the little shrieks, comes bounding in "to learn what was happening" (2: 132). Upon being reproached by his wife "for his betrayal of her" and informed that she has fed him his children, he orders that she be thrown into the fire (2: 132). This monarch has none of the delicacy of Perrault's squeamish young king, who cannot bring himself to execute his mother. His will is paramount, curtailed only by the erratic turns of the wheel of fortune and not by any woman stronger than he. Yet, unlike Talia's father, this king turns out to be quite lucky, after all: his children are restored to him and his first wife has been conveniently supplanted by a fertile and pliable spouse. Rape can have its rewards, as Basile makes clear in the cynical couplet he deploys as the final "moral" for his amoral tale: "*Lucky people, so 'tis said, / Are blessed by Fortune whilst in bed*" (2: 132).

IV

A reading of Basile's uninhibited and nearly pornographic ur-text not only casts new light on "Sleeping Beauty" but also illuminates the resistance to Perrault's text by later women writers. Any interpretation of the texts by Craik, Thackeray, Ingelow, and other women writers whom I discussed at the beginning of this essay requires a double gender analysis, for in responding to Perrault these authors were also processing his own response to Basile. Instead of rejecting outright a text unsuited for his younger and largely female readers, the Frenchman preferred to dilute the amoral, aristocratic perspective of his Italian forerunner. His avoidance of rape, adultery, and wife murder notwithstanding, Perrault retained Basile's masculinist perspective. The uneasiness of his avuncular relation to the young women he coyly addresses at the end of each of his *Contes* is most evident in his handling of narrative detail in "La Belle au bois dormant."

Perrault's introduction of a passive sleeper erotically revived by a male kiss and his steady antagonism toward powerful older women expose a relation to the feminine that is considerably more complex, yet also far more equivocal, than Basile's overtly cynical sexism. Even his jokes about the prince's tough-skinned, centenarian bride betray discomfort. Perrault seems disturbed by the notion that the young *naives* he so jocularly patronizes might grow up into monstrous crones such as the cackling old fairy who tries to kill an innocent girl and the wronged wife he converts into a ravenous mother-ogress, killed by the deadly snakes she has unleashed.

There is little doubt that Perrault's fascination with virginal sleepers and furious female monarchs had an impact on later male fantasists. Lewis Carroll's drowsy dreamchild, after all, must, like Sleeping Beauty and Talia, confront the ire of those red-faced matriarchs who would cut off her head or spoil her own coronation. To be sure, a few male writers, such as George MacDonald, used "Sleeping Beauty" as a foil for their own constructions of femininity by comically exploiting the tale's many narrative incongruities.[7] But the repudiation of "Sleeping Beauty" was undertaken mostly by women writers. The authors whose work I briefly examine at the outset of this essay had reasons to be doubly offended. Perrault's surreptitious retention of so many elements of Basile's plot as well as his alterations and additions fueled their revisions, inversions, and subversions.

The erotic kiss central to Perrault's sexually charged version of the story becomes a focal point in the revisionist narratives by women writers. As soon as Ingelow's matured Queen Mopsa stoops down to kiss the little boy she has outgrown, the doors of her castle shut and Jack knows "that he should never enter them again" (311). Her action is maternal. Were he to stay with her forever after, Jack would be prevented from growing up. By returning the quasiparental kiss he gave her when she herself was still a tiny toddler, Queen Mopsa forecloses any possibilities of a sexual union. The boy kissed by his own mother before being sent to bed at the end of Ingelow's fantasy is still much too small to become a princely mate. The strawberries Jack has eaten replace his memories of an immured queen. He has no erotic dreams.

Nor can there be a sexual awakening or consummation in most of the other texts I introduced at the start of this essay. Even when the role of the kissing prince is not played by small boys such as Jack or Nesbit's Jimmy, fulfillment remains impossible: Rossetti's black-bearded prince is fully eroticized, but the bride he finally reaches has become a corpse. The very authenticity of the kiss can become questionable when a woman writer challenges the authority of male transmissions. Craik's retelling of "Sleeping Beauty," which dispenses with the story's second half, puts a very different spin on Perrault's boudoir scene: "Trembling, the prince approached and knelt beside her. Some say he kissed her, but as nobody saw it, and she never told, we cannot be quite sure of the fact" (6).

In a further attempt to do away with male domination, Craik allows her Sleeping Beauty to regain her own throne and to survive, as Queen Victoria would, the loss of her consort. Indeed, as her last sentence suggests, there may have been a gain in such a loss: "She lived a long and happy life, like any other ordinary woman, and died at length, beloved, regretted, but, the prince being already no more, perfectly contented" (7). Florence Bell's dramatic 1908 version of the story introduces yet another put-down of male authority, undermining not the prince, but his father. Defying Perrault by having Sleeping Beauty's parents survive, as in the German "Dornröschen," Bell deviates from her source even further by denying the old king the power of narrative closure. When the monarch proclaims that he "joyfully give[s] my consent to the union" of the young lovers, he is sharply put down by his wife, who claims to be a much better judge of their daughter's worth: "Nobody asked you for it. I joyfully give mine. My daughter, Prince, is a peculiarly gifted girl. The only thing she can't do better than anyone else in the world is to spin" (329).

It is Burnett's *The Secret Garden* that most radically subverts not only Perrault but also Basile. Burnett's consciousness of her predecessors, as I have already suggested, even colors her characterization of figures other than Mary, Colin, and Dickon. Thus it hardly seems coincidental that the first boy on whom Mary so fiercely turns after he has invaded her female sanctuary should be named Basil. Moreover, as husband of the dead Lilias, Archibald Craven reenacts the roles of both Talia's absenting father and a feminine sleeper in need of awakening. A maternal ghost must penetrate his defenses and lead him back to a son released from his own paralysis. Even the masculine ending of *The Secret Garden,* in which the embracing father and son repossess Misselthwaite Manor can, paradoxically, be read as a further distancing from Basile and Perrault. For the exclusion of Mary from this final tableau at least avoids the possibility that a strong "Mistress Mary" will turn into the submissive bride of the new "master" of garden and house. Whereas several film versions suggest that Colin and Mary will marry (and others suggest that she will become Connie Chatterley to Dickon's Mellors), Burnett avoids that inference. Like Ingelow and Nesbit, she prefers to de-eroticize her narrative.

Perhaps the most resounding subversion of "Sleeping Beauty," however, came in a text that was published much earlier and has been retold and adapted by a long succession of women writers: it is, after all, the kiss of a determined young woman that revives a torpid male in Marie LePrince de Beaumont's 1757 "Beauty and the Beast." Even the Disney version of this narrative seems to respect its long lineage of female antecedents. And it adds the figure of Gaston the hunter, a latter-day version of Basile's lustful hunter-king, only to undercut his male presumptions. But this, as the old story spinners liked to say, is another story to be told elsewhere and at another time.[8]

Child's Play as Woman's Peace Work

Maria Edgeworth's "The Cherry Orchard," Historical Rebellion Narratives, and Contemporary Cultural Studies

Mitzi Myers

I am going on in the old way, writing stories. I cannot be a captain of dragoons, and sitting with my hands before me would not make any of us one degree safer.

— Maria Edgeworth, *A Memoir* (20 June 1798, 1: 84)

Jane Austen's ironic dismissal of "history, real solemn history" in *Northanger Abbey* is often cited by feminist historians, who find the teenage protagonist's complaints much to their purpose: "The quarrels of popes and kings, with wars and pestilences, in every page; the men all so good for nothing, and hardly any women at all—it is very tiresome" (108; ch. 14). What they never seem to notice is that Catherine Morland speaks from a child's place. From the girl reader's point of view, history has no story to tell: she is not there. If there are "hardly any women," there are still fewer children; if feminist social historians and literary critics are now trying to count women in, they are still leaving children out. If "real solemn history" is being rewritten as something other than what Christina Crosby calls "man's truth" (1), an effacement of women and other marginalized groups from academic knowledge production, it is still a long way from counting children and their literature in.[1] Writing to, about, for, and as a child, being a cross-writer, as was the Anglo-Irish author Maria Edgeworth (1768–1849), remains a passport to canonical nowhere.

Yet what looks like private juvenile play, a story for very young children, can also be a woman's public peace work—in Edgeworth's case, a canny mode of political intervention that inserts children into the emergent discourses of citizenship during the French Revolutionary Wars of the 1790s, not as the objectified recipients of adult disciplinary regimes (as much post-Foucauldian analysis would have it), but as the speaking subjects and initiatory agents of a reformed community, as citizens from whom grown-ups, even politicians, might profitably learn. In identifying juvenile literary pastorals from the Irish combat zone as gendered 1798 Rebellion narratives, my aim is larger than the expansion of women's war stories or the reinscription of one writer in literary and cultural studies. In conjoining women's "little" local narratives with men's grand historical metanarratives (the masculinist "big" histories of public event as what counts in culture), I endeavor to rethink the polarized paradigm of private versus public spheres that still structures so much feminist theory, as well as to integrate the categories of the child and history. In accordance with much recent theory and practice, I am reading the histories in fiction and the fictions of history as complementary, suggesting that "history" and "literature," including the juvenile, merit equal narrative force within a cultural text. In contrast with most feminist cultural history and with most work in historical children's literary studies, I ask whether our customary paradigms—the conventional trope of the "spheres," the progressive teleology and romantic ideology of schemas such as "from instruction to delight" and "from rational to Romantic"—are just wrong. What if the critical narratives that constitute children's literary and cultural history were alternatively emplotted and contextualized? When Catherine Morland finds it "odd" that history "should be so dull, for a great deal of it must be invention," which, she says, "delights me in other books," she is as perceptive as she is naive. In implying that the written texts of history and literature construct the "real" to which they also respond, she adumbrates both the problems and the solution.[2]

Edgeworth's fiction is an ideal site for exploring the ambivalent relationships among modern feminist theory, revisionist literary history, and children's literature studies. Moreover, the blurring of genres, genders, generations, and nationalities in her literary production (as well as in her letters and memoirs, which interweave personal and political life) makes her work exemplary for revisioning children's literature within emergent cultural studies. Edgeworth was an extraordinarily prolific author for both adults and youngsters and a versatile cross-writer as well. Not only did she write for multiple audiences (child and adult, male and female, English, Anglo-Irish, and Irish), but her children's stories were often enjoyed by grown-ups and her adult works were read by a young audience, for almost all her tales feature pivotal parts for juvenile characters. She was extraordinarily popular, too—the best-selling British female novelist of the early nineteenth century. Her fame as a children's writer lasted even longer than her adult reputation: she was still being republished well into the twentieth century, and her work established models for "realistic" family fiction that still inform juvenile literature. Yet even though she was a protofeminist and a fervent advocate of female education, Edgeworth has not elicited much attention from feminist critics, because she often chooses to couch her most adventurous proposals for the reform of her native Ireland in the seemingly innocuous guise of the children's tale. Edgeworth is a very political writer, but her ambitious politics and her autobiographical reflexivity emerge only when her work is situated within its cultural context: she transforms the conventions of the juvenile tale by assimilating them to the "big" history of the French Revolutionary decades. As the product of a writer who was living through the tumultuous 1798 Irish Rebellion and its aftermath, "The Cherry Orchard" richly illustrates the convergence of juvenile genres and ambitious female reform.[3] In modeling a new community, Edgeworth demonstrates that child's play is indeed woman's art—and her politics, too.

One of Edgeworth's numerous stories for primary schoolers written during the years of Revolution abroad and Rebellion at home, "The Cherry Orchard" exemplifies and miniaturizes compelling public issues; moreover, the tale illustrates just how ideologically charged even the simplest fiction may be when we know its context. Literary history's stodgy readings of didactic moral tales distance them not only from more recent children's literature, but even from the noisy semiotics and cultural arguments that generated them. The stories' pointed lessons about how to live at a specific historical juncture get ironed out into timeless platitudes: good youngsters do not fight, they always obey their parents, and so on. Restoring children's texts to their political and literary matrix, however, both revives them as juvenile literature and shows how female authors used writing for the young to contest contemporary men's themes and forms and to generate their own literary answers to the cultural dilemmas posed by the French Revolutionary epoch. Literary Romanticism has been defined normatively in terms of male writers (and only six of those) and the contours of masculine desire. Children's literature and the criticism about it have been colored by what revisionist critics term the Romantic ideology; that is, our discourse about the period between the Revolution and reform and its literary production has been dominated by male Romantic authors' own mythology of the lyrical development of the solitary, untrammeled lad through his maturation amid—and privileged access to—ennobling nature.[4]

Because women's contemporaneous developmental stories and imagined communities do not glorify adversarial notions of selfhood and wild Nature, but value collaboration and the domestically cultured natural world, they have been situated within Romantic literary history as affectively insipid and politically conservative, watered-down Romanticism rather than as gendered responses to the French Revolution and Irish Rebellion. Yet realistic stories of everyday life may also function ideologically as reformist fantasies of how things should be: experiments in devirilizing bellicose patriarchalism; models of how men and women might collectively repudiate collective violence and work toward a more generous citizenship; reformulations of gender and national identities that eschew winners and losers, warriors and victims. "Big" history and men's literary scholarship still conceive of war as physical combat located in a space and time that excludes women and children, military events produced and resolved by masculine debate in a public sphere peopled only by adult men. Because women and children are supposedly absent from combat zones and diplomatic debate, they presumably have no war stories to tell and no entry into the formulation of belligerent or pacific national ideologies either. But civil warfare, like the Irish Rebellion of 1798, brings the combat zone home, uniting battlefield and domestic front and scrambling public and private. Nor can civil strife—whether termed wars, Revolutions, Rebellions, Risings, or mobs and riots—be delimited temporally. In Ireland especially (stereotypically marked as violent for centuries), local unrest was endemic, like a chronic disease, and since protest often took the form of rural guerrilla warfare, homes were fortified and armed.[5] As twentieth-century feminist thinkers from Virginia Woolf on have noted, wars, especially internecine struggles, destabilize binary oppositions and dissolve psychic as well as physical boundaries. When "the public world very notably invade[s] the private" (Woolf, *Diary* 5: 231), cultural constructions of gender come to the fore, either reified (the protected "feminine" who embodies the values fought for) or inverted (female figures, even little girls, who transgress established political ideologies by explicit critique or alternative Utopia).[6] Revisioning a story like "The Cherry Orchard" helps us begin to dismantle the plots that have determined misreadings of the crucial Revolutionary period's writing for the young and to rethink the Utopian discursive activism latent in much other children's literature as well.

This essay widens war stories from battle tales to representations of small-scale belligerence and its impact on personal relations and everyday life. Exploring the activism and agency embodied in women's writing and children's choices, it is especially concerned with slippages between child and adult worlds in "The Cherry Orchard," with the way the adult woman writer inhabits and enables the child protagonist, and with the way the expressive child instructor permits her textual mother implicit political commentary. Like many of Edgeworth's stories, "The Cherry Orchard" features a wise little girl as heroine and takes place in a highly emblematic rural setting, redolent of the author's personal passion for growing things and the garden's cultural associations with children, women, domesticated nature, pastoral, renewal, and rebirth. Because the story retains a timeless freshness, it is important to document its timely references to the politically troubled period. Here's Edgeworth writing to her cousin from Edgeworthstown, Ireland, on 20 June 1798 (contemporaries would have known that the date signals domestic insurrection and imminent French invasion):

Hitherto all has been quiet in our county [Longford], and we know nothing of the dreadful disturbances in other parts of the country but what we see in the newspapers. . . . Why cannot we be left in peace to enjoy our happiness? . . . We laugh and talk, and enjoy the good of every day. . . . How long this may last we cannot tell. I am going on in the old way, writing stories. I cannot be a captain of dragoons, and sitting with my hands before me would not make any of us one degree safer. . . . I have finished a volume of wee-wee stories. . . . My father has made our little rooms so nice. . . . Oh, rebels! Oh, French! spare them! We have never injured you, and all we wish is to see everybody as happy as ourselves. (*A Memoir* 1: 83–84)

The French march from the north concluded almost at Edgeworth's doorstep: the final battle of the scattered rebel Risings that punctuated the "Year of the French" was fought a few miles from Edgeworthstown at Ballinamuck. In early September 1798, the Edgeworths briefly fled a pike-armed rebel army through a corpse-littered countryside, returning home as soon as possible despite the danger. Ironically, although the "green" rebels devastated the village, the Edgeworths' home and belongings were twice spared in gratitude for the family's lack of sectarianism and their good relations with their tenantry shortly before Edgeworth's father and brother were brutally attacked by a Protestant loyalist "Orange" mob in nearby Longford town, where they had sought refuge. Richard Lovell Edgeworth narrowly escaped lynching for his Enlightened opinions and his supposed signals to the invading French. Ten days after the battle, father and daughter visited the battlefield (in a letter Edgeworth reduces the conquering heroes to blackberrying boys). On 2 December 1800, Edgeworth informs her cousin that the ten-part series containing "The Cherry Orchard" is forthcoming: "You are so near Johnson [Joseph Johnson, the radical bookseller who also published Mary Wollstonecraft and Anna Letitia Barbauld], that you must of course know more of Maria's sublime works than Maria knows of them herself. . . . The two first parts of 'Early Lessons' . . . two wee-wee volumes, have just come over to us." The rest "will, I suppose, come after with all convenient speed" (*A Memoir* 1: 104–5).

Edgeworth's deprecatory playfulness about the woman writer's reformist aims need not blind us to her story's contemporary relevance and ideological implications. Indeed, her reiterated "wee-wee" implies her juvenile fiction's status as instructive microcosm. Literally diminutive (like the "little rooms" refurbished for the family's new third stepmother), the narrative invokes a protected space (the rewarding orchard) that the juvenile protagonists must discover how to enter.[7] At the same time, the miniature community is itself a safe place from which Edgeworth can comment obliquely on "big" cultural affairs, an idealized version of Jürgen Habermas's rational bourgeois public sphere, with the kinks worked out and affectivity factored in.[8] As Edgeworth's title suggests, "The Cherry Orchard" is a rural idyll, an Enlightenment version of pastoral—or to be more accurate, of georgic—because half the story has to do with nonhierarchical group debate and communal work, rather than leisure. More specifically, as Edgeworth's letter implies in its juxtaposition of men's fighting and women's writing and in its heroic refusal to privilege imminent military destruction over the preservative "arts of peace . . . going on prosperously," the tale has a pacific agenda (*A Memoir* 1: 57). It is, among other things, a story about demilitarization that dramatizes how the combative habit of mind may be reformed. It is always tempting for women, who have not been their founders, to distrust societies as "conspiracies that sink the private brother . . . and inflate in his stead a monstrous male, loud of voice, hard of fist, childishly intent" on scoring boundaries that artificially separate groups and genders, and to universalize fighting as "the man's habit, not the woman's" (Woolf, *Three Guineas* 105, 6). "The Cherry Orchard," however, performatively embodies—and so helps summon into being—another social imaginary.

Conventionally, pastorals imagine Utopia; conventionally, too, they critique society.[9] Especially in its georgic mode, pastoral turns didactic. "Every utopia is a curriculum and vice versa," it has been said, and at this period a pedagogy also implies a politics (Lanham 4). Far from dissevering romance and vernacular realism, male and female modes of heroism, or the private play of children and the public sphere of adult political life, the story's characters and spatial movement embody their coalescence. In portraying a children's community, the threat to it, and the means by which that threat is overcome, Edgeworth by implication shows us how societies develop. The child's story is the story of a culture, of a possible community. Predicting a future, it seeks to construct that future within child readers, to give them prophetic visions to hope for and work toward. According to Edgeworthian educational theory, writing about development induces development. "The particular usefulness of childhood," Carolyn Steedman remarks, "is that it represents in itself an explanatory narrative; childhood is about the way we got to be the way we are" (27). More importantly, perhaps, it provides narrative arguments about how we can change the way we are and become what we would like to be. Offering progressive models of human relations, "The Cherry Orchard" answers the question it poses: what heroic qualities can lead us as a community to a better future? Its charming surface verisimilitude notwithstanding, it functions not merely as a naive representation of reality, but as a Utopian fantasy. Like many Enlightened sister writers for the young, Edgeworth images an alternative civic order from a woman's point of view. Her idyll of renewal celebrates neither the solitary, irresponsible child as artist (and vice versa) nor the unconstrained passion that male Romantic writers indulge.[10] Rather, renewal for her must blend Enlightened reason with affective feeling, an ethic of care and community taking precedence over individual self-assertion and masculine aggression.

Responding to the crisis of Enlightenment values posed by Revolutionary terror, Edgeworth appropriates the suborned language of rights, natural liberty, equality, and fraternity and rescripts it, so that the adult political discourse she kidnaps works to produce cultural relationships grounded in mutuality and respect. In a world disrupted by men's Romantic egotism and political tyrannies both Jacobin and reactionary, "The Cherry Orchard" significantly figures the heroic as a little girl at once childlike and caretaking, above all a peacemaker and harmonizer, yet very much the acknowledged and responsible leader of her little band of playmates, including the eldest boy, Cymon. Within the liminal space of the juvenile tale and the children's public sphere, Edgeworth can challenge rigid sexual polarization and represent her characters as cooperative citizens. If we want to construe the heroine as notional womanhood, incarnating virtue and the culturally "feminine," we must also notice that the story sidesteps gender boundaries. Eschewing passive girls and assaultive boys alike, the action images goodness as powerful and attractive, a negotiatory cultural force equally opposed to authoritative repression and unlimited license. "Remarkably good-tempered," Marianne is eight, an empathetic guide collaboratively selected rather than self-chosen.[11] Her cousin Owen, a year younger, acts out androcentric fantasies of individual autonomy; ill-tempered, violent, and physically combative, he embodies the hypermasculinity and warlike ways of thinking that Edgeworth deplores in the swaggering "party" spirit of green and Orange alike. Indeed, Owen derealizes the warrior—he cries, pouts, and threatens to tattle when he does not get his way—and deflates militarist politics in general, querying the British imperialist imagination as well as the ineffective rebel and the punitive loyalist. A passionate, overbearing bully who craves a larger, wilder world and determines to control everyone within reach, he comments on the Romantic will to power and possessive individualism. Edgeworth's miniaturization comically shrinks the "solitary walker" à la Rousseau, the rapist-hero of fiction, the traveler-adventurer, the military titanist, and a whole host of Romantic and Revolutionary masculinist ideologues. The story's play and work themes intertwine around the conflict between Marianne's and Owen's kinds of heroism and relating to others; the two represent alternative modes of power and hegemony which are economically presented in their contrasting attitudes toward communal play, work, and decision making.

Under Marianne's gentle and indirect tutelage, the eleven youngsters function harmoniously, except for Owen, who is always combative with everybody. No wonder his playfellows cannot love someone who is "continually quarrelling" and "would never . . . do what they wished; but he always tried to force them to yield to his will and his humour" (52–53). In the green summer world where the story takes place, the children naturally want to play along the flowery lane to dame school, but not Owen. He likes the dusty high road, with its adventurous carts, carriages, and horsemen. He will neither go alone nor abide by the group's doing things "our" way. Owen wants everything *his* way every time, and what he wants and his ways of going about getting it allude subtly and subversively to a whole set of contemporary masculinist postures and premises. The fractious little boy's binarism scores off what Paul Fussell and other students of the militarist mental set label the "*versus* habit."[12] He can only respond with rage and coercion when the children question, "what right has he always to make us do as he pleases?—He never will do any thing that we wish." Not only does Owen insist that "you *must* go my way," but he also demands that the whole group endorse his dominance unequivocally (56–57). He knows they are only going by the high road because of Marianne's mediation, so he proceeds to kick up clouds of dust to make them say they prefer his dirt to their flowers. But the ten other children band together at a turnstile and unite to shut out their tyrant until he promises civility: patriarchal power meets communal solidarity—and loses. Owen finds that kicking, pushing, struggling, and "roar[ing] as loud as he possibly could" do not work, for "now you are all of you joined together, you are stronger than I." Though he shoves "till his whole face was scarlet, and . . . his wrists ached" and screams until the turnpike man laughs at him, his playmates neither fight back nor give in (63–65). The core of war, Elaine Scarry observes, is "a contest . . . the activity of reciprocal injuring where the goal is to out-injure the opponent," a no-win situation wherein the victors cannot be differentiated from the losers without labels (63). Reworking adult Irish tragedy as reformative juvenile farce, "The Cherry Orchard" literally displaces the militarist, mocking his tough talk and ineffectual tactics and suggesting that the war game can be refused.

But Marianne's gesture of rapprochement negotiates another chance for the social outcast. When Edgeworth's heroine urges the glowering isolate— "'Come with *me*, and you shall *see*,' said Marianne, 'that is both rhyme and reason—Come with *me*, and you shall *see*'"—the little girl's verse playfully epitomizes the story's themes of inclusion and collaboration, revision and renewal (67–68). Yet despite Marianne's ability to wed the affective and the rational— and despite the lure of the cherry seller's eleven fine bunches tied along a long stick—Owen soon comes to grief again. He may "wish I was like" cousin Marianne, but only hard experience can teach him to give up his masculine myth of selfhood and embrace mutuality (68). More chilling than the turnstile scuffle, the second vignette of Owen's belligerence invokes for the informed reader Ireland's ongoing internecine struggle.[13] Who shall have the uppermost bunch of cherries, larger and riper than all the rest? Everybody wants it, of course, but the group's second thought is that Marianne is the most deserving. Dissatisfied with the fruit he draws and determined to impose his will again, Owen resorts to violence. Snatching the stick from Cymon and Marianne, he tramples every bunch to bits "in his fury, scarcely knowing what he did, or what he said" until the "ground [is] stained with the red juice of their cherries" (78–79). The combat scene, the phallic stick, the smashed fruit, and the gore-colored ground are primal enough to resonate in any context, but they especially reverberate within the context of 1798's hand-to-hand pike fighting and bloody atrocities.

The children, penceless and cherryless, retaliate by barring out the antisocial aberrant for his regressive indulgence in destruction; despite his cleverness, quarrelsome Owen is recurrently associated with impasse, stasis, and ineptitude. Holding himself aloof from communal rules, he imagines that even if he cannot dominate the natural and social world as he had intended, he does not need them anyway, but can live apart: "But he soon found that he was mistaken" (80). Without overt moralizing, the story economically images issues of self- and social control, contrasting separatist and integrationist ways of being in the world, competitive and collaborative modes of play and work that reduce the abstract issues of peace and war to manageable size. Notably, too, the children's communal activities fuse domestic with political economy and represent a dialectic of work and play which does not privilege one form of interaction over the other or one child's contribution over another's.[14] The girls and boys who embrace mutuality literally work to sustain it, for when they arrive at school their teacher greets them with a surprise—a way to restore the lost fruit and indeed to enter the earthly paradise of the cherry orchard itself. For six pence a ticket, the gate will open "on Thursday evening next." But no matter how "extremely" they wish to go or how "very happy" they picture themselves "sitting down under the trees, and eating fruit," they have spent all their pence on the cherries Owen trampled into crimson pulp "in the fury of his passion" (83–84). If they all work together plaiting straw for hats, however, perhaps they can repair Owen's ravages.

The ensuing scene of work vividly embodies the communal solidarity and relational sense of self the story sets against Owen's individualist values—and probably Adam Smith's as well, for it is a tongue-in-cheek reworking of the famous pin-making introduction to his *Wealth of Nations* (a work Edgeworth often cites). It is tempting to read the scene as a resolution to what philosophers still call the "Adam Smith Problem": how to reconcile the individual self-interest that animates society in Smith's later work with his earlier endorsement of the human sympathy that guarantees sociality.[15] Self-assertion, egomania, and irresponsibility are not attractive models of human interaction, the story shows, nor, Owen discovers, is moral instrumentalism effective: brute will does not work. The others break down the task efficiently, each doing what he or she does best and each assisting the others. But no one will work with Owen: "We are afraid that you should quarrel with us. . . . [T]herefore we will not work with you" (85–86). Arrogant Owen finds to his dismay that even though he can plait better and more quickly than anyone else, he cannot earn enough for the fête in time: "you have been obliged to do every thing for yourself. . . . If we had not helped one another, we should not have earned this money; and we should not be able to go to the cherry-orchard" (88, 99). Outcast from the circle of affective and rational interchange, the iconoclastic, socially uncouth boy learns that one has to give to get something and can thus be conditionally admitted to felicity. His trial by fire is to show that he has learned the culturally "feminine" qualities of cooperation and good temper, endorsed by Edgeworth for both sexes alike. It is a tough test, too; having lost the outing, he must lend the revelers a favorite basket and not lose his temper when Cymon disdainfully picks apart his crooked weaving. Only then will the other boys and girls set to work to help Owen so that he, too, can enter the reformed community and its reconciliatory emblem, the cherry orchard, a childsize earthly paradise: "whenever I feel inclined to be cross, I will think of your good-nature to me, and of

THE CHERRY ORCHARD" (106). Forgiveness, the action shows, breaks the cycle of sectarian violence. The benedictory social conclusion works aesthetically, rhetorically, affectively; this is not the utilitarian and strictly rational narrative to which literary histories reduce Enlightenment moral tales.

The story, then, is richer than its charming surface depiction of rural Georgian life, with walks along country lanes, dame school education, braiding straw hats for pence, and tasty treats of "red ripe cherries" (69). Like much juvenile literature, it speaks to a dual audience of child and adult, revealing that what is child's play is also woman's work—and art. A youngster can relate to the story's quotidian details and a depiction of child power and success in which adults, such as the cherry seller and the teacher, play only peripheral parts. For the maternal reader, the woman writer, and the feminist critic, the tale has a larger frame of reference, because its narrative conflicts also enact a dialogue between contending readings of literary and cultural history. As playful popular narrative rather than high Romantic poetry or Revolutionary rhetoric, "The Cherry Orchard" depicts social upheaval and its effect on personal relationships ironically, dialogically (the children's voices interacting), and spatially (emblematizing the communal in shared play and tasks), rather than through the individualistic assertion of a strong self that we habitually identify as Romantic art. The series title *Early Lessons* underscores the tale's status as a scene of instruction, but the story's didacticism is emplotted within its movements of exclusion and inclusion and enacted by its characters' progress from embattled enclosure—shutting out the aggressor—to enclosure liberated and renewed, the collaboratively earned opening of the magical place, the cherry orchard, to the whole little community: the villain reclaimed, paradise regained.

Sly, winsome, not at all preachy or sentimental, Edgeworth's representation of the dialectic between pugnacity and peace is not the clichéd contrast supposedly endemic to the feminine moral tale—good little girl redeems bad little boy. Rather, the story's feminist and communal principles are accorded both formal and philosophic significance. What the story teaches is organized spatially, so that narrative and social forms are cognate. Its method enacts its message about the relationship of combative and cooperative forms of playing, working, sharing, and knowing, for the plot literalizes new practices of cultural space through juxtaposed scenes indicating what happens when individualist aggression meets group amity and identifying the children's movements with agency, creativity, and social happiness. When Oskar Negt and Alexander Kluge observe that "it is an index of every cultural-revolutionary movement that children's public spheres come into being," the authors of what's probably the most theoretically provocative update of Habermas's much discussed formulation of the bourgeois public sphere do not cite the Utopian "experiment in the self-regulation and self-organization of children in their own specific forms" and spaces that informs much children's literature, although they are elsewhere concerned with reading and storying as positive collective pedagogy.[16] Ironically, the high German theorists make their ultimate political message relationality, a bringing together of the public and private, the political and psychic, as in the familiar feminist arguments developed by Carol Gilligan and Nancy Chodorow and elaborated by peace theorists like Sara Ruddick, who bridge the gap between public crisis and the affective realm with rational caring and "preservative love," maternal thinking versus "military destruction."[17]

For female authors as for male Romantics, children figure in renewal, rebirth, and reform, but, significantly, women's juvenile fiction does not celebrate what one historian of the masculine Romantic ideology of childhood terms "supra-social independence," nor does it equate innocence with the "refusal to admit the force of circumstances" (Plotz 72–73). Women's juvenile literature reads social bonds as affective ties, not bondage, as preconditions for self-realization rather than constraints upon it. It images the community as family, friends, and citizens and thinks in terms of collective rather than individual liberation, asking how we can play and work together more fulfillingly as a group, not how we can break free from the communal chains that bind. The little band of children look to Marianne as their leader because of her empathy and her collaborative skills which enable her to include everyone and make the group run smoothly. Marianne is not just an author's personal fantasy of being universally beloved and acknowledged within her domestic world, for she also exemplifies the connected "ways of knowing" and cooperative ways of managing that women have been culturally conditioned to adopt.[18] The child heroine likewise intimates that women's ways of fighting are based on women's ways of knowing and women's words.

Edgeworth's writing of and about the hostilities of the 1790s repeatedly images the private community's invasion by bellicose men; like other women who experience war at close quarters, she implies an economy of violences in which "the public and the private worlds are inseparably connected . . . [T]he tyrannies and servilities of the one are the tyrannies and servilities of the other" (Woolf, *Three Guineas* 142). But war's collapse of the public into the domestic realm works the other way around too. Marianne's success in achieving an integrated and harmonious community suggests a public application for these private juvenile lessons as well, a correction of men's historical master plots by women's micronarratives. The children's world is not cocooned outside dominant society's political and commercial relations; instead, it indicts adult malfeasance of rights and property. Edgeworth's story can be read as metarepresentation: like the children's collaborative activities in the story, the writing of the fiction images the cohesive work that women's words can perform in society. If, as Cecil Eby conjectures, grown-ups wage wars because of men's juvenile literature, it is important to notice that women write otherwise. Like Woolf's "tea-table" ideas that "think peace into existence," like the "Laboratories of Social Change" that Doris Lessing aligns with the writer's critical eye, juvenilia assume the agency of women's words as well as children's deeds.[19] The heart of Edgeworth's tale is a female Utopia long familiar to us now, an ideal community opposed to the alienation and individualism that have been hegemonic in Western capitalist societies for two centuries. Such conceptualizations of community, as one feminist critic argues, may well be only "an understandable dream, expressing a desire for selves that are transparent to one another, relationships of mutual identification, social closeness and comfort" and thus inadequate for transformative adult politics (Young, "The Ideal" 300).

Whatever their deficiencies as specific political agenda, however, "The Cherry Orchard" and like-minded fiction and poetry map for us the intersection between emergent feminist thought and Romantic cultural theory, which Cora Kaplan aptly characterizes as "separate but linked responses to the transforming events of the French Revolution." The dialectic between feminism and Romanticism and their "dynamic, and contradictory relationship to democratic politics" informs juvenile works as well as adult literary documents, as Edgeworth's narrative reminds us (150). With its participatory democratic communitarianism; its concern with care and mutuality; its focus on the small personalized task group; its refusal to seal off private life from public politics or to succumb to masculine ideologies of transcendence or regressive combat—and all the other ways it conjoins communal, feminist, and pacifist values to articulate a woman's response to Revolutionary trauma—"The Cherry Orchard" is an "early lesson" tailored for its time. When Francis Jeffrey commended Edgeworth, in an 1809 issue of the *Edinburgh Review,* for doing "more good than any other writer, male or female, of her generation," he had in mind not her dispensation of timeless moral verities, but her contribution to the well-being of a specific community at a specific moment in British history. It may be a truth universally acknowledged that "the great art is the art of living; and the chief science the science of being happy," but the particularities of that art and science vary by period and gender (Jeffrey 376).

Like Lewis Carroll's King of Hearts, conventional histories of children's literature bracket off the moral tale from the environing cultural and political argument in which, as I have just demonstrated, it participates. "If there's no meaning in it, that saves a world of trouble, you know, as we needn't try to find any." Like Carroll's testy Duchess, I have countered that "everything's got a moral, if only you can find it," and that "moral" is not so timelessly banal as to be meaningless (Carroll 159, 120). Because we have come to associate Romanticism almost exclusively with male writers and with poetic forms, "Revolution" with the masculine public sphere of civic debate and sanguinary guillotine, and "war" with men's combat experiences alone, we have had no place for women's variations on the Romantic developmental paradigm, for their Revolutionary educational aims, or for the noncanonical genres in which they typically express their reconciliatory communal agenda: marginal modes like letters, journals, instructional manuals, and children's literature, including stories like "The Cherry Orchard" which performatively enact the "arts of peace," as well as those Enlightenment tales that more overtly express the horrors of war, such as Barbauld's clever dialogue "Things By Their Right Names" (i.e., armies are murderers) in *Evenings at Home*.[20] Because Georgian women writers' representations of childhood have been read through interpretive conventions that are exclusionary and androcentric, their work has been simplistically dismissed as repressive rather than seen as the incisive commentary on the irresponsibilities of male Romanticism and men's Revolutionary wars that in large part it is. Even though formerly neglected adult female poets of the period between Revolution and Reform are currently undergoing something of a renaissance, masculinist Romantic depictions of childhood and its literature still remain unquestioned even by feminist critics who are busy rediscovering the beauties of the feminine "Romantics." When Charlotte Smith and Barbauld write adult poems, they're hot. As authors of works for the young, they're not— perhaps because public-spirited Enlightened juvenilia are notably free from the alluring sexuality that subtends Victorian representations of the child, as in Carroll's photographs and John Everett Millais's "Cherry Ripe."

Yet, only when feminist revisionists count children in too will we be able to see the cultural space staked out by "Romanticism" and "Revolution" as something other than male terrain with a few second-class female denizens. If we really mean to redefine literary history, if we seek more than an additive canon with female ghettos, we need child's play. To seal off women's juvenile tales from material lived in reality is to erase from culture both women's record *of* history and women's desire *in* history. This essay goes beyond a feminist analysis of one writer to seek a feminist interrogation of the ways we have been packaging history as well. Feminist *and* juvenile literary studies, I argue, can help us redefine the ways that we conceptualize and read literary and cultural history. As a historical feminist critic who takes the child's part, I have sought to replicate in my critical analysis the political intervention, the insertion of the child into public affairs, that Edgeworth enacted before me. Children's literature has been nobody's baby long enough. As every critical mode's child, it offers us an interdisciplinary multiplicity of ways to rethink our culture and to shape the emergent discipline of cultural studies—perhaps even as a liminal space unscarred by bellicose canons.

"These two irreconcilable things— art and young girls"
The Case of the Girls' School Story

Mavis Reimer

Late-nineteenth-century England saw the "apotheosis of [the] separate world of childhood," Peter Keating maintains in his social history of the novel (223). It also saw children's literature become a world separate from adult literature, although this separation was motivated as much by contempt as by awe. Felicity Hughes argues that children, who were part of the family audience to which the eighteenth- and nineteenth-century novel was directed, were excluded as potential readers of the "serious novel" by the terms of the debate in the 1880s between writers who maintained that fiction should be seen as art and writers who defended fiction as romance. By the turn of the century, such novelists as Henry James and George Moore made it clear that they "would no longer allow themselves to be held responsible for the moral welfare of the nation's youth" (Hughes 543). The "serious novel" addressed itself to the adult male reader; the "serious novel" was defined as "unsuitable for women and children . . . because it dealt with facts of life from which such people had to be 'protected,'" and "because it was too difficult, requiring not only maturity but discrimination beyond the reach of all but the highly educated" (Hughes 544).

The entrenchment of the assumption that serious fiction was fiction that was difficult to interpret, according to Allon White, allowed for the establishment of criticism as a high-status and intellectual enterprise.[1] It also promoted the equation of what Jane Tompkins calls the modernist ideals for fiction—

"stylistic intricacy, psychological subtlety, epistemological complexity"—with "universal standards of aesthetic judgment" ("Sentimental Power" 84, 82).

Given the formulation of these standards in definitions that explicitly exclude child and female readers, it is not surprising that Perry Nodelman finds that their application to children's literature fails to produce interesting readings of those texts. Nodelman's study leads him to two conclusions: first, that "children's fiction may be defined by a specific group of thematic concerns," and, second, that critics might need to "search for other means of interpretation" ("Interpretation" 20). In *The Pleasures of Children's Literature* (1992), Nodelman amplifies his first conclusion by developing a list of characteristics of children's literature as a genre. Central to this definition is his observation that children's literature is written from the viewpoint of innocence and tends to balance the idyllic and the didactic; that is, it both "celebrates the joys of the rural life, close to nature and in the company of friends" (83), and works "to counter the limitations of children" (86).[2]

In this essay, I pursue Nodelman's second suggestion and argue that it is crucial for critics of children's literature to search for "other means of interpretation," precisely because the current concentrated interest in generic mappings, canon formation, and methodological overview among scholars signals a movement to make the discipline of children's literature coherent and "serious." This attempt to establish foundations and to build systems should alert feminists and other readers of culture. What is being excluded by the definitions, listings, and historical narratives? The parallels to the campaign to institute fiction as art at the end of the last century are instructive.

Critics of children's literature have been successful in claiming "universal" appeal for only a handful of texts. Because children's literature as a whole is outside the "great tradition" of literature and because we read texts that, by definition, are not intended for us, critics of children's literature have never been able to ignore the presence, theoretical and actual, of readers situated in history or to pretend that texts are not apparatuses for the reproduction of ideology. It is, in fact, axiomatic for many critics of children's literature that, whereas they as adults read fiction for pleasure, children read, or should read, fiction to learn.[3] This duplicitous attitude has permitted professional readers of children's literature to retain Tompkins's aesthetic ideals—"stylistic intricacy, psychological subtlety, epistemological complexity"—and, at the same time, to practice, to some extent, cultural and contextual criticism.

The cultural criticism of children's literature, however, has too often amounted to little more than an evaluation of the proximation of the characters of particular children's books to a desired ideal. For example, in much of the criticism of the late-nineteenth-century school stories of L. T. Meade, the ideal girl implicitly is assumed to have no traits that might be considered stereotypically feminine and most of the conventionally masculine qualities and aspirations. Deborah Gorham reads Meade's first school story as clearly designed "to prepare girls for feminine domesticity, not for achievement in the public sphere" ("Ideology of Femininity" 54). Virginia Blain et al., in *The Feminist Companion to Literature in English,* concur: although Meade's books celebrate the "increased access for women to the education system," the stories "reproduce traditional stereotypes, tom-boyish girls invariably being transformed into young ladies" (729). Edith Honig discards in a single sentence those "[a]dventure stories and school stories written expressly for girls" as "insipid in comparison to those written for boys" (4). Even Kimberley Reynolds, who sets out to explicate the cultural reasons for the low status of girls' books within the children's system, ends by reinscribing that status: girls' books, she concludes, "justify passivity and self-regulation" (156), and girls' school stories, specifically those written by Meade, merely provide a setting for "new and greater opportunities for self-denial, service and adherence to the established principles of femininity" (135).

The assumption that there is a gender-neutral "ideal of universal humanity," as Iris Young and many other feminists have noted, "covertly slips masculinist standards into the definition of neutral humanity" (*Throwing Like a Girl* 6) and contributes to structures of domination. During the 1970s and 1980s, many feminists rejected this presumption of universality and turned their attention to retrieving women's experiences from the silences of history and affirming women's values. In literary theory this turn was labeled "gynocriticism" by Elaine Showalter. In "Feminist Criticism in the Wilderness," Showalter identifies the subjects of gynocriticism as "the history, styles, themes, genres, and structures of writing by women; the psychodynamics of female creativity; the trajectory of the individual or collective female career; and the evolution and laws of a female literary tradition" (248). All of these subjects, she argues, can be addressed most adequately by developing a theory "based on a model of woman's culture," for "a theory of culture incorporates ideas about women's body, language, and psyche but interprets them in relation to the social contexts in which they occur" (259).

On the face of it, the move to gynocriticism would seem to hold out much promise for theorizing about children's literature, because, as Anita Moss observes, women predominate in the field of children's literature as writers, teachers, librarians, and critics. Indeed, Nodelman suggests that "children's literature as a whole is actually a kind of women's writing" ("Children's Literature"

32), so that, presumably, the study of "the history, styles, themes, genres, and structures" of children's literature is itself gynocentric feminist work.

The recent history of children's literature criticism and theory belies such an easy equation. Theorists such as Jacqueline Rose, Zohar Shavit, and James Kincaid construct accounts of the genre by referring to a handful of texts authored by men; John Stephens asserts that the "positive" representation of "the individual striv[ing] for autonomous selfhood" is the "usual" pattern in children's literature (*Language* 57); and the *Touchstones* list of books "central to the traditions of children's literature," developed by the Children's Literature Association in 1985 to "allow us to better understand children's literature in general," includes twice as many books by men as by women. Far from being "naturally" woman centered, children's literature criticism has tended to write out the work of women in its account of styles, structures, and themes.

Paying attention to women's writing for children in relation to the social contexts in which ideas about the "body, language, and psyche" are produced would challenge our current understanding of the characteristics of children's literature, not so much by providing other characteristics to be added to the list as by challenging the limitations of a totalized theory and by tracing the dispersal of power in culture. Many recent theorists call on critics to produce careful, precise, local accounts of social subjects embedded in conflictual histories. For example, Isobel Armstrong remarks in her introduction to *New Feminist Discourses* that "[g]endered subjectivities constructed at particular historical moments in particular cultural circumstances through particular texts provide a starting-point for investigating the possibility of change and the conditions of change" (3). To demonstrate how such a focus on particularity might enable us to read children's literature differently, I want to return to this historical moment located by Hughes as marking the bifurcation of fiction into adult (i.e., realistic, difficult, artistic) fiction and children's (i.e., romantic) fiction.

Hughes suggests that it was the proponents of fiction as art who defined their work as unsuitable for women and children. The texts she cites indicate, more specifically, that women and children were often conceptualized as a single, composite figure—the young girl. "[N]ovels are not written exclusively for young ladies in their teens," Moore wrote in 1884 (37). In 1885, he pronounced that serious writers "must give up at once and forever asking that most silly of all silly questions, 'Can my daughter of eighteen read this book?'" and "renounce the effort to reconcile these two irreconcilable things—art and young girls" (21). But it was not only Moore and James who figured the girl as the antithesis of the literary reader; the practitioners of romance did so, as well. Robert Louis Stevenson's well-known dedication of *Treasure Island* (1883) is to a gendered reader, "boys of all ages." Stevenson's novel prompted H. Rider Haggard to define his novel, *King Solomon's Mines* (1885), as intended for "all the big and little boys who read," a readership he saw as distinguishing his work from that of "people who write books for little girls in the school-room" (qtd. in Showalter, *Sexual Anarchy* 79–80). In short, the oppositional terms in which this debate is framed imply comprehensiveness, but both terms exclude the young girl as reader.

During the same decade Hughes identifies as preoccupied by the realism-romance debate, however, books specifically for little girls in the schoolroom—in fact, books *about* little girls in the schoolroom—were being written. The girls' school story was popularized and many of its formulas set by the publication of Meade's *A World of Girls* in 1886. As Meade practiced it, the girls' school story was both realism and romance, a hybrid story that asked for the intense "sympathy and identification" of its readers—which Hughes sees as typical of romance—in its representation of the "real life" of girls (545), and that attempted to solve the real-life problems of girls in late-Victorian culture through its representation of them in romance quests.

A World of Girls, like Meade's other school stories, comprises two plots. In the main, comic line of narration, Hester, who feels herself pushed "out into a cold world" by her father (2) and determines to resist being "reduced to an everyday and pattern little girl" in the "first-class school" to which he sends her (3–4), is integrated into the school community. This euphoric plot is told in what Northrop Frye calls "the *low mimetic* mode" of realistic fiction: the story is filled with the daily details of class assignments, tea parties, friendships, and jealousies; the world of the novel operates according to the "canons of probability"; and the hero's "power of action" is consonant with her world. She appears to be "one of us" operating in a recognizable environment (33–34).

The "bright gipsy-looking" hero (8) of the second plot, Annie Forest, is identified closely with the "wild and unmanageable" qualities Hester is sent to school to be cured of (3). To a large extent, Annie takes over the role of rebel in the text, since Hester finds herself more "anxious and troubled" than rebellious when she encounters all the strange new ways of the school (6). This second plot, a series of secret events that occur between the public events of school life, is peopled with mysterious villains to be defeated and operates on a different level of postulates. In Frye's terms, the second plot of *A World of Girls* is romance, set "in a world in which the ordinary laws of nature are slightly suspended" (33).

Suzanne Keen describes such "alternate modes of storytelling" as "narrative annexes" (107). Although narrative annexes are characterized by the narrative shifting into "a different genre or mode, with its contrasting set of conventions," or moving "into a previously unrepresented space or location" (107–8), these alternate narratives do not subvert the main plot or sustaining narrative so much as attempt to complete it. According to Keen, a narrative annex "can reveal the ways in which worldmakers and made worlds struggle with their limitations in order to accomplish the very work that their sustaining fiction requires" (105).

The second plot of *A World of Girls* is a narrative annex in this sense. The sustaining fiction of Meade's story moves toward a celebration of the world of girls, a world only recently created through the reformed boarding schools that were one of the results of the educational campaigns of first-wave feminists.[4] Meade's ability to make this affirmation unambiguously is limited, however, by contradictions in late-Victorian ideologies of girlhood that the new girls' schools exposed.

The doctrine that women and men had their "separate spheres" of proper activity was hegemonic in Victorian England, a precept both "culturally mandated" and "internally policed" (DuPlessis 5). Some of the headmistresses of the reformed schools publicly represented their schools as extensions of the domestic sphere by emphasizing the close and maternal relationship they established with their students. Such a strategy made the schools more ideologically palatable to middle-class parents. In actuality, however, the organization of the schools was modeled on ideals of corporate life quite different from those of family life, as the writings of the reforming headmistresses and other feminist theorists and activists demonstrate. For example, in an article published in 1890 in *Atalanta,* a girls' magazine edited by Meade, headmistress Dorothea Beale spoke of the "good in a life which makes us feel strongly that we are members of one body," and emphasized that, at school, "the life of *each* is perfected only in proportion as the life of *all* is fuller, truer, nobler" ("Schools of To-day" 317). Moreover, the new curricula focused on the systematic training that would be required of women who sought remunerative employment, and the teachers themselves were examples of independent, single women.[5] In fact, schooling girls outside the home to take up service inside the home was a fundamental contradiction within the terms of Victorian culture, for school itself was part of the public, rather than private, sphere.

The nineteenth-century movement for reform in the education of girls and women was associated from the first with the movement to enlarge the sphere of women's work. When the Langham Place feminists, the vanguard of the women's movement, established the Society for Promoting the Employment of Women in 1859, one of its primary aims was "to awaken people to the necessity of better education for girls" (Holcombe 15). "The desire for education" among English women, observed Josephine Butler in *The Education and Employment of Women* (1868), springs "from the conviction that for many women to get knowledge is the only way to get bread" (72). Victorian society judged that the only paid work sufficiently genteel to be undertaken by middle-class women—and then only by destitute middle-class women—was that of governess or needlewoman. Both occupations were underpaid and overcrowded, "choke full," as Barbara Bodichon put it in *Women and Work* in 1857 (44).

The status of governesses and needlewomen as waged workers in itself threatened to expose the artificiality of the "free" occupations of the mother and homemaker. But, to the extent that governesses and needlewomen remained within the private sphere by providing domestic services, they could be read as extensions of or assistants to the wifely function. In contrast, if middle-class women chose to work in such public spaces as offices and hospitals, they not only would be competing with men on their own grounds, but also would be performing tasks dangerously like those of working-class women, thereby making visible the strenuous labor that was needed to underwrite the "natural" difference of the middle class. This "natural" difference was seen to reside in the finer moral sense of the bourgeoisie, as embodied, guarded, and taught by its women. In particular, the upper middle class, which occupied its economic position because of the work of its men and its class status in part because of the leisure of its women, was inherently unstable. "The basis of class stability," according to Mary Poovey, "was morality—specifically the morality of women and the integrity of the domestic sphere that that morality both depended on and reproduced" (60).

If a middle-class woman moved into the public sphere, as feminists recognized, she both challenged the underpinnings of domestic ideology and lost the caste status that provided her with some measure of respect, some moral safety. Given social codes in which women, moral virtue, leisure, and class are entangled, what identifies a woman in the public sphere as virtuous? Judith Walkowitz, discussing the movement of "respectable women" into the city after midcentury with the expansion of opportunities for shopping, philanthropy, and civic life (46), notes that confusions between "virtuous ladies" and prostitutes on the streets "were so frequent that they became the stuff of jokes" (50); in 1890, an article in *The Girl's Own Paper* advised its readers on how "to organize their gaze" to avoid being stared at "in any impertinent and abrasive way" (qtd. in Walkowitz 51). In fact, the threat of male lust was one of the main issues in feminist thought during the last half of the nineteenth century. Through their campaigns for the repeal of the Contagious Diseases Acts, feminists such as

Josephine Butler "highlighted a number of sexual and moral issues" (Maynard 232) that extended well beyond a specific analysis of prostitution to the more general representation of "women's bodies as under attack" from men (234).

Like working middle-class women, schoolgirls threatened the stability of domestic ideology when they moved into the public sphere of school; like women, girls were represented as "under attack." In 1886, when Meade wrote *A World of Girls,* there was a particular source for images of the girl's body under attack. Between 6 and 10 July 1885, the *Pall Mall Gazette* had published W. T. Stead's explosive series of articles on child prostitution in London under the title of "The Maiden Tribute of Modern Babylon." Stead first took up his investigation at the urging of a group of people, including Butler, who were dismayed at the lack of progress being made in the debate over the Criminal Law Amendment Bill in the House of Commons.[6] The best-known provision in the bill was the raising of the age of consent for girls from thirteen to sixteen. The bill had already been defeated twice by the House, in 1883 and 1884. With Parliament preparing to rise for its summer recess, the bill seemed in danger of defeat once again. It was in this context that Stead was asked to use his notorious "talents for journalistic agitation" for the cause (Schults 130).

The series "had an electrifying effect" (Walkowitz 81): W. H. Smith news agents at rail stations refused to carry the *Gazette* because they judged the material obscene; the pieces were debated in the House of Commons; windows in the newspaper's offices were broken as a mob of people tried to buy papers before they were sold out; and letters from prominent and common people alike, in exultant support of Stead's moral courage and in scathing indictment of him as a panderer of lewd material, poured in to the editor. The "massive outburst of public feeling" expressed itself in public demonstrations that continued through the summer in many English towns and cities (Gorham, "'Maiden Tribute'" 361), and the "popular indignation" resulted in the bill's being passed by the Commons in August (Walkowitz 103).

In her study of the "Maiden Tribute" series, Walkowitz suggests that one of the cultural consequences of Stead's narrative was the "opening" it provided for "women to discuss sexual matters in public" (132) and to articulate their sense of sexual vulnerability and sexual possibility. Walkowitz points, too, to the effect of Stead's work on some late-Victorian fiction, notably Stevenson's *The Strange Case of Dr. Jekyll and Mr. Hyde,* which the author wrote in the fall of 1885 after he had read "The Maiden Tribute." Male writers such as Stevenson responded to the ambivalence of Stead's representation of himself as *flâneur.* Meade, as a woman writing for girls, read another figure in Stead's narrative, that of the schoolgirl.

Schoolgirls appear frequently in the articles of the series. In the first "report of the Secret Commission," for example, Stead recounts the evidence of "an ex-brothel keeper" who recalled that she had once found "a likely girl" for her service by taking lodgings "close to the board school, where I could see the girls go backwards and forwards every day. I soon saw one that suited my fancy" (6 July: 4). Another procurer tells him that "[t]he easiest age to pick them up is four-teen or fifteen. At thirteen they are just out of school. . . . But at fourteen or fif-teen they begin to get more liberty without getting much more sense" (7 July: 5). In another installment of the "report," Stead depicts girls moving through the city to school as the prey of skilled hunters, who wait and watch "until the time has come for running them down" (8 July: 4). While most of these children are "daughters of the people," as Stead calls working-class children, he also tells of "respectable little girls of the middle class" being accosted in the street and re-lates the story of "the daughter of a city missionary" who was enticed into "the Babylonian maze" (8 July: 4). In fact, as a rhetorical figure, the schoolgirl allows Stead to blur class lines and to point to the congruity of the concerns of right-minded people in all stations of life. Telling the story of Lily, for example, Stead marks her as Other but clearly strives to elicit his middle-class readers' empa-thetic identification with this "daughter of the people." Lily is "an industrious, warm-hearted little thing, a hardy English child, slightly coarse in texture," who is, however, literate: "She had been at school, could read and write, and although her spelling was extraordinary, she was able to express herself with much force and decision." Stead even reproduces an affectionate poem Lily wrote for her mother (6 July: 4).

To use the schoolgirl as a rhetorical figure in the context of multiplying nar-ratives about actual attacks on schoolgirls is to identify schoolgirls as potential targets for attack. Thus, although Stead's narrative of monstrous male sexual-ity helped to effect progressive social legislation, it also functioned as a form of social control over girls and women; it had the effect of restricting where schoolgirls could go and what they could do and contributed to keeping them in their place, that is, inside rather than outside the home.[7]

In the main plot of the school stories, Meade negotiates the contradictions between the expectations of parents, particularly fathers, at home and the ideals of the reformed girls' schools in order to celebrate the achievement of the world of girls. Although Mr. Thornton, in *A World of Girls,* believes that Hester is be-ing molded by Lavender House into a compliant, domestic woman, she is, in fact, learning to accede to the communitarian ideals of corporate life espoused by headmistress Mrs. Willis. But the instability of meanings around schooling and girls, which allows Meade to carve out this imaginative space, is deployed by Stead in ways that threaten to unsettle her achievement. The celebration of the school as corps is undercut by the vulnerability of the body of the school-girl.[8]

As Keen's theory of the narrative annex predicts, Meade uses the second plot of her story as an "alternate workspace" (109) in which she attempts to resolve this "challenge to the trajectory" of her sustaining fiction (108). In *A World of Girls,* the complicating event of the romance plot is the midnight picnic that Annie, who loves "what she called a spice of danger" (92), organizes for her classmates. Keen observes that "[t]he clear border between the fictional world and its annex" and "the attention given to the means of crossing that border" are two of the "unmistakable" signs that the sustaining fiction has given way to the "alternate workspace" of the annex (109). In Meade's novel, the seven "young truants" pass through a turnstile that leads into the dense woods that ring the school (94). Their escapade is set in fairy-tale spaces and tinged with an ethereal quality, as Annie entertains the girls with "nonsense tales, all of a slightly eerie character" (96). On their way back through the wood to the school, their path is blocked by "a tall, dark figure" who seems to have sprung out of one of Annie's stories (96). Identifying herself as mother Rachel, "a gypsy-mother from the tents yonder" (97), she insists that the girls cross her hand "with a bit of silver" to secure her silence about their prank. Annie meets the gypsy again while on a walk with Hester's sister, Nan, and rebuffs her; as punishment, Mother Rachel lies in wait for little Nan in the undergrowth "at the end of the shady walk" (130) and snatches her from behind her nurse's back.

The vulnerability of girls' bodies poses a challenge to the trajectory of Meade's sustaining fiction about the world of girls. In working out this challenge in her narrative annex, Meade borrows the terms of Stead's "Maiden Tribute." The abductor in Meade's story is a woman who appears in the guise of mother and stranger; in Stead's narrative, the procurers and their decoys usually are female and a common disguise is that of nun or Salvation Army worker. In both narratives, too, the abduction is a violation of class boundaries and tied to economic transactions.

The motive for Nan's abduction, like the motives of the monstrous men of Stead's, is also sexual. Nan is hidden by the gypsies in "a long-disused underground Danish fort" (143), a subterranean prison that is like the underground rooms from which, Stead maintains, the cries of violated children cannot be heard (6 July: 5) and like the labyrinth of Daedalus in Greek mythology from which Stead takes the governing metaphor of his series. Nan's condition when Annie finds her on a bed of straw "moaning" in her sleep suggests that her abduction by the gypsies is a physical assault: "Nan's skin had been dyed with the walnut-juice, her pretty soft hair had been cut short, her dainty clothes had been changed for the most ragged gipsy garments" (146).

Stead, in fact, tells a similar story of the rescue of a young girl, who was drugged, raped, and given "a foul and loathsome disease" by her attacker: "My friend (who told me her story) found her literally rotting on some straw in an outhouse where the proprietor had left her to starve (8 July: 4–5). Over the course of the series, Stead tells few such stories of rescue and fewer still of escape. In his narratives, girls are hunted prey, lambs led to the slaughter, "dainty morsels" served up to "the passions of the rich" (6 July: 2). They seldom are invested with agency; they never are invested with their own desires. As Stead insists in this retelling of the Minotaur story, "those who were once caught in the coils could never retrace their steps, so 'inextricable' were the paths . . . of wrongdoing" (6 July: 2).

Meade borrows the motifs of Stead's narrative, but she reworks his conclusions by exploring the possibilities of the romance mode she has chosen. The low mimetic mode of her sustaining fiction invites readers to expect, in Frye's view, "the same canons of probability that we find in our own experience" (34). For Meade, the inescapable labyrinthine world reported by Stead was part of what determined the canons of probability, what could be coded as the real within a text. The hero of romance, however, "moves in a world in which the ordinary laws of nature are slightly suspended," and, while she is not more than human, in this world her actions can be "marvellous" (Frye 33).

In the world of the narrative annex, Annie performs the "marvellous" feat of rescuing Nan by undertaking a romantic quest. Like many other heroes of romance, Annie is marked for the quest by her special knowledge (of gypsies and their habits, since she was once in the care of a gypsy nurse); she must travel disguised in the costume of the low-born (as a gypsy girl); she endures physical hardship and privation (going without food and sleeping under a hedge); she defeats a powerful guardian at the threshold (a "ferocious-looking half-bred bull-dog" [142]); and she descends into the underground before she finds the object of her quest. Annie takes over the role of quester in which Stead figures himself in his narrative; unlike Stead, however, she succeeds, rescuing "the child whom [she] had come to save" (249). Within the symbolic logic of the romance plot, moreover, Nan represents an aspect of Annie herself, an identification intimated by the fact that their names—Nan and Ann—are anagrams.

Investigation of the particular cultural circumstances of Meade's story for girls has implications for the study of children's literature in general. First, the Victorian "apotheosis" of the separate world of childhood needs to be problematized as a construction of children, rather than accepted as a founding assumption of our discipline. Second, we need to ask questions about the extent to which current understandings of children's literature reproduce the gendered exclusions on which the separate genre of children's literature was predicated. The elision of girls' school stories such as Meade's in our definitions is especially ironic, since it is the girls' school story *The Governess; or, The Little Female Academy,* published by Sarah Fielding in 1749, that usually is identified as the first English children's novel (see, for example, Carpenter and Prichard 216).

What is being written out of the historical narrative by this oversight? "In anything fit to be called by the name of reading, the process itself should be absorbing and voluptuous; we should gloat over a book, be rapt clean out of ourselves" (220), Stevenson writes in "A Gossip on Romance" in 1882. But girls were marked by their connections to materiality, connections reiterated by cultural texts that emphasized their bodily vulnerability. Books such as Meade's school stories are not about being "rapt clean out of ourselves," but about working out ways to live in the actual, material world. At the same time, Meade does not "attempt to represent life" only so that a reader may assent to the veracity of "the picture of the child's experience," as James, in "The Art of Fiction" (1884), maintains novelists should do. Rather, she attempted to imagine new versions of the real for her audience of young girls. And for Meade, as for the girls in Meade's fictional schools, telling the story was itself part of this attempt. Annie's successful quest does not end with her rescue of Nan; her reintegration into the world of girls comes after she tells her story.

If we are to see past the categorical exclusion of young girls as an audience either for art or for romance, then we must understand girls' books as more than failed imitations of boys' books. To claim girls' books as part of children's literature, we must allow them to interrogate the theories of children's literature we are developing. For example, Annie's quest calls into question at least two characteristics proposed as typical of children's literature by recent theorists. The first is Nodelman's contention that children's literature is a form of pastoral idyll. *A World of Girls* does praise "the company of friends" (Nodelman, *Pleasures* [1992] 83), but far from celebrating a closeness to nature, Meade's narrative refuses the possibility of a nature that is unmediated by human desire and adult power: Annie's movement through the turnstile and into the forest immediately makes her vulnerable to the dangerous designs of Mother Rachel. Moreover, it is not her innocence that allows Annie to save Nan but rather her mimesis of the signs of Nan's violation.

Meade's story also challenges the value of autonomous selfhood, which Stephens claims is affirmed in children's literature (*Language* 57). In an elaboration of this argument, Stephens maintains that the "pervasive" quest narrative of children's literature "is characteristically built around a male career pattern" because there is an "absence in fiction" of a "paradigmatic female 'career' structure comparable to this male pattern" ("Gender, Genre" 19). The very notion of such a structure is strange enough, apparently, that it requires the markers of irony. Meade's school stories, however, are female quest narratives that suggest paradigms for reading children's literature. The initiating event of the romance plot in Meade's stories is one girl's attempt to retain for herself the exclusive affection of another girl in defiance of the ideals of corporate life. In *A World of Girls*, it is Annie's and Hester's quarrel over Nan's love that engenders the kidnapping plot, and it is their willingness to accede to the call of the community's well-being that brings about the happy ending. Annie's story, told in the broken sentences of delirium, can be completed only when Hester, too, tells what she knows.

Testing and contesting the boundaries of the definitions of children's literature is, perhaps, less glamorous work than erecting what Teresa de Lauretis calls "a fully constructed view from 'elsewhere'" (xi), but paying attention to the "alternate workspaces" of girls' books allows us to reconstitute our knowledge of the complex, conflicted ways in which adults have represented the world they share with children to those children. By uncovering forgotten or elided possibilities, this reconstitution of knowledge offers hope for changing the world we share with children and changing the world with children. Meade's schoolgirls, like the children Barrie Thorne finds represented in twentieth-century social theory, are both learners of and victims of adult culture. But they are also agents, resisting victimization, creating their own community, and telling their stories.

Romancing the Home
Gender, Empire, and the South Pacific

Claudia Marquis

I wonder if I shall fall right through the earth! How funny it'll seem to come out among the people that walk with their heads downwards! The antipathies, I think.
　　　　　　　　　　—Lewis Carroll, *Alice's Adventures in Wonderland*

In the course of exploring late-nineteenth-century British imperialism, Patrick Brantlinger comments sharply on the literature that most overtly supported it: "Britain turned youthful as it turned outward" ("Victorians" 209). He points here to the genre of adventure stories for boys ("the future rulers of the world") that rose with Frederick Marryat's nautical tales and flourished in the abundant romances of R. M. Ballantyne, W.H.G. Kingston, Gordon Stables, Rider Haggard, and G. A. Henty, written mostly between 1870 and 1900, precisely when British imperialism moved into its most aggressive phase.

　This imperial fiction is written by adult authors who are often widely traveled but who write at home, for youthful readers. What interests me here is the fiction that takes the South Pacific as its subject, and not just for the antipodean factor, but also for its tangle of opposed interests neatly fixed in Carroll's witty descriptive term, "antipathies": profit and delight, commerce and culture, but also boy and girl, adult and child, and, especially, margin and center. Mary Louise Pratt, discussing imperialist travel writing, identifies a dialectical relationship between Europe and the place to which Europeans travel: "While the imperial metropolis tends to understand itself as determining the periphery (in the emanating glow of the civilising mission or the cash flow of development, for example), it habitually blinds itself to the ways in which the periphery determines the metropolis—beginning, perhaps, with the latter's obsessive need to present and represent its peripheries and its others continually to itself." Pratt believes that not only travel writing but European literary history is "heavily organised in the service of that imperative" (*Imperial Eyes* 6). Nowhere in British fiction of the late nineteenth century is this imperative and this blindness more obvious than in the mass of imperial adventure tales: glamorous setting and action both draw the youthful reader on and leave him (mostly him) incapable of seeing the world "out there" as anything but the proper field, or face, of his desires and imaginings.

That the imperial romance is first and foremost a boy's story is abundantly clear. Typically, it removes the schoolboy-sized hero from his English world of privilege and subjects him to tests for which his upbringing has not strictly provided, except to the extent that it has imbued him with the qualities of resourcefulness, high courage, and perseverance—which prove, in fact, the necessary conditions of his survival. Because this testing tends to be carried out in combat, the innate strength of character and purpose of the hero is also that of his culture, so that when the unruly forces of savage society are ranged against the solitary British boy and that boy triumphs, the triumph of civilization is affirmed. Most modern discussion of this literature has concentrated, understandably enough, on the correspondence of textual ambitions and ideological goals centered on middle-class, masculine society, and the girl's part has received cursory attention at best.[1] Thus in this essay the first question I address is, How does the girl figure in this boys' fiction, this man's world? My second concern is the position of the indigenous Other of these stories, the one whose presence seems to require of the metropolitan writer the kind of representation that sustains the pre-eminence of his or her own culture. Mostly the antipodean romances I discuss deal with settler society after fifty or more years of vigorous colonization. Properly speaking, therefore, they do not come out of what Pratt usefully terms a "contact zone" (6), yet even at this stage of the Empire's development the negotiation between the colonizing and the colonized is viewed by the metropolitan writer as if it were a first encounter. Nevertheless, the crucial relationship in many of these antipodean imperial stories is not that between the boy and the savage but that constructed by a second axis between the savage and the figure of the girl.

The schoolboy hero whose typical adventures I follow first is Jack Stanley, in *Amongst the Maoris* (1874) by Emilia Marryat, Frederick's daughter. Both the hero and his adventurous story serve as exemplars. Marryat's authorship is itself not without interest, illustrating as it does that the general exclusion of the female character from active adventure in these imperial tales by no means excluded women from the business of writing them. The complicit enterprise of the late-Victorian woman writer at home and abroad is not my concern here, but it is worth noting. Charlotte Yonge was happy to recommend a number of her own novels along with works like *Robinson Crusoe* and *Masterman Ready* as examples of the kind of reading boys need: "Boys . . . should have heroism and nobleness kept before their eyes; and learn to despise all that is untruthful and cowardly, and to respect womanhood" (*What Books to Lend and What to Give*, qtd. in Richards, Introduction 4). *Amongst the Maoris*, the work of a woman writer, is just such a boy's story. Its moral underpinnings are quickly made clear with the arrival of its sixteen-year-old hero, Jack Stanley, who possesses "that noblest of qualities—unselfishness; noblest, because it is nearest to the godlike character" (7). Jack's adventure begins, conventionally enough, with a crisis, the accidental death of his father, which leaves him orphaned. Advised to find employment, he journeys instead to New Zealand, intent on tracking down the man responsible for the earlier loss of his family's fortune. His quest takes him from Wellington to Auckland, which suggests not so much a route as a vague but significant sense of direction—south to north!—always anticipating its final move, homeward. The privations he experiences in the bush and in encounters with the Maori affect his vengeful temper favorably, kindling compassion and charity to match his courage and earning him the spiritual and material capital for a final successful reentry into British society.

Imperial adventure, then, proves to be more than picaresque; it proves to be organized by the logic of quest romance. Central to this is the confrontation with evil, embodied here most extravagantly in a Maori *tohunga*, or priest, but also generally in the priest's tribal society, depicted as monstrously grotesque in appearance and in its unregenerate adherence to practices such as cannibalism and tattooing. If Marryat's story is justified by the meshing of adventure and moral point, it is also disturbingly infatuated with the gothicized figure of the Maori:

All the men were frightfully tattooed, their faces being seamed and scarred all over, so as to disfigure completely whatever of good looks they may originally have had: though beauty is very unusual amongst the Maories even without tattoo. . . . Their hair, with some, hung down their backs in elf-locks; with others, twined up on end, like hearth-brooms; and in either case it was thick with a sort of pomade of grease overlaid with dust.

There was an old man decorated with a pair of trousers. . . . He was a vicious-looking old person, and his dignity, or, perhaps it was his unpleasant temper, . . . induced him to stand on one side, looking at the proceedings, and scowling in a malevolent manner.

"Look, sir!" exclaimed Jack Stanley, impulsively and unthinkingly. "Look at that horrible old object! I dare say he thinks himself very attractive. What an old toad!" (110)

Colonel Bradshaw, Jack's surrogate father, checks the boy's ill manners but actually expands the underlying racism, even if he also seeks to make it more complicated. He supplies an informal ethnographical account of the kind to be found in missionary reports, in schoolbooks like Ballantyne's potted history of Captain James Cook's voyages, and in romances such as Jules Verne's influential *Voyage autour du monde* (1868).[2] His version of the life and times of the Maori includes notes on tapu, tattooing, diet, and head shape—so like the Caucasian's that he concludes the Maoris are "a very intelligent people, who do not at all come under the head of that very generic term, 'niggers'" (256). He can even argue that they are "an interesting people," whose fate it is to be submerged in and by the English, a "bullying race" whose dominance is nevertheless required by advancing civilization. He also describes, however, the Maori method of preserving heads: "A fire of hot stones is made in a hole in the earth, after the fashion of the natives; then, having scooped out the brains of the dead man, the nose, eyes, and mouth are sewn up, and the head placed over the fire so as to be thoroughly steamed. This has to be done until all the flesh is dried up" (180).

While this passes for scholarly information, clearly it is offered in response to Jack's demand for entertaining tales of antipodean savagery, in explanation of dim childhood recollections of fairground "horrors" such as "baked New Zealanders' heads." Colonel Bradshaw's account of Maori customs, then, is itself an instance of imperial exploitation, English "bullying"; it is locked into a circuit of ambiguous entertainment.

The same may be said of Marryat's story. Neither her appreciation of Maori intelligence, bravery, and loyalty nor her care to explain the differences between pagan and Christian disguises the conviction that the Maori is what he always horrifyingly, disgustingly was. The most sacred spot in the *pa* (the fortified settlement of the Maori) is described as nothing but a collection of rubbish: "rotten garments . . . human bones . . . a head with the flesh still partly on it" (126). The whole encampment is said to reek. Again, Jack's response is telling: "Feelings . . . I fancy they have about as much feeling as they have sense of smell" (121). At all points, the humanity of the Maori is brought into question. Supported by a Christian native informant, Colonel Bradshaw reports recent acts of cannibalism, a horror that here catches in innocence: "Children have been taken away from the schools . . . by their parents, in order that they might take part in feasts of flesh. Not many years ago, women were in the constant habit of murdering their infants, being apparently possessed of no natural affection" (192).

What I am emphasizing in all this is the Kristevan power of horror, the abjection, the fixation on abomination, filth, and threatening disorder. Marryat seems to join Bradshaw and Jack in their disgust. Jack's fastidiousness is treated with an exacting, ironic wit, it's true. A kind of poetic justice sees him kidnapped by the malevolent *tohunga* and reduced briefly to slavery in the latter's service, stripped of his European clothes, toiling in the priest's potato patch, burdened with the new name "Dirt," and almost turned into the object of the priest's skill at tattooing. He realizes what the priest has in mind for him "with a sensation which made him sick" (156). This is the closest the tale comes to figuring native resistance to the imperial power of the English, a resistance that obscurely warrants the later prophecy of eventual Maori revolt against English authority. Despite the fascinating inversions with which Marryat plays, however, we observe the familiar story of imperialist failure to acknowledge the Other, since Marryat's risky parody of imperial power finally demonstrates the frightening disorder that is identified in and by the savage.

The focal point for this pattern of fascinated disgust and horror is the cannibalism that seems never far from mind when the European observes the antipodean savage. Cannibalism is virtually a sine qua non of the imperial, romantic traveler's tale, and its description a prime exhibit in a cabinet of literary wonders. This is obviously the case where the imperial romance fuses, as it often does when it heads into the South Seas, with the Robinsonade, the tale modeled on Defoe's *Robinson Crusoe*. A useful example is Ballantyne's *The Island Queen* (1885), in which three children find themselves shipwrecked and cast on an unnamed Pacific coral island. Otto, the youngest, startles Dominick, his sensible, elder brother, by his delight at this disaster: "I've dreamed about being cast on a desolate island hundreds of times, and I've read about Robinson Crusoe, and all the other Crusoes, and I've longed to be cast on one, and now I *am* cast on one, so I don't want to escape. It'll be the greatest fun in the world. I only hope I won't wake up, as usual, to find that it's all a dream!" (23). Otto is greatly disappointed when they discover that the island is uninhabited: "What a pity. . . . It would be such fun to have a real Friday to be our servant" (31).

A Robinsonade like this one celebrates the spirit of youthful male adventurousness that led to British rule, sustaining and sustained by the dream of a fertile wilderness. Fertile, but of course unpeopled, as Charles Kingsley declares in an address to the Ladies' Sanitary Association in 1880 in which he recommends imperial expansion: "Four-fifths of the globe cannot be said as yet to be in any wise inhabited or cultivated, or in the state into which men could put it by a fair supply of population, and industry, and human intellect" (qtd. in Brantlinger, *Rule of Darkness* 44–45). Wildernesses uninhabited, then, except for those useful Fridays. No less than Kingsley, Ballantyne supports the colonialist mentality unreservedly: the boundaries of Empire are properly fixed nowhere, since the non-European other world merely awaits the imprint of England's culture, industry, and needs. Unquestionably inferior to the European settler, the indigenous peoples of England's colonized territories figure in the European mental equation as a natural laboring class to help realize the profits of investment and emigration. The late–nineteenth-century Crusoe names the savage, teaches him to call him "master," but in this textual act of nomination it is, of course, the white reader who is interpellated, called into a privileged subjectivity.

The management of England's colonies depends on what Edward Said calls an "ideology of difference"; this ideology justifies any action taken by the colonialist against indigenous peoples, including the writing of these culturally formative romances. What Ballantyne's history demonstrates is that within the safely pleasurable confines of the Robinsonade, the cannibal remains the most potent sign of this difference. Friday, Dominick warns his young brother, is more likely to "kill, cook and eat us if he could" than to serve; "all the best authorities," after all, record the fact that "South Sea islanders are given to this horrible practice" (31–32).[3] When Friday does show his face in Ballantyne's romance, it is indeed not the face of Defoe's biddable savage but a black, tattooed face signifying the unknowable and inimical. It shatters Otto's dream. On a sketching trip, he catches sight of a face peeping from the bushes; he "wheeled sharply round, and brought the heavy handle of an oar down with such a whack on the bridge of the savage's blue-spotted nose that he suddenly ceased to grin, and dropped his proboscis in the dust!" (190). A dramatic episode of capture by a "group of tattooed and armed savages" and rescue ensues; taming at the textual level follows, as Otto reduces this experience to the stuff of play by insisting thenceforth that the black natives be spoken of as "baboons" (200). The Pacific savage wears the same face as his African counterpart; he belongs as surely in the jungle, among its beasts; more to the point, he is subdued by the symbolic, by language and narrative.

Thus the islands of the South Pacific are beautiful, a new Eden, but they are inhabited by peoples whose evolutionary development differentiates them from the young English reader; tale after tale leads him to understand that these people need his mastery. How, then, does the girl figure in the British boys' story? First, the "respect for womanhood" that Yonge included among the desired goals of a boy's reading, however limiting it may be, does have more than incidental importance in many South Seas adventure stories. Even in a story such as *Amongst the Maoris,* in which women are virtually absent, the lesson that private will must be subordinated to the good of others, as the hero finally learns, is precisely the sort that justifies Claudia Nelson's argument for a feminine ethic in imperial fiction ostensibly written for boys (see esp. ch. 5, 117 ff). Second, the British boy's privilege of proving by his actions his right to manage imperial affairs in the antipodes is often underwritten by the presence of the woman—his orderly relationship with her finally must displace his hostile relationship with the savage.

This passive but ruling presence can take a variety of forms. In *The Island Queen,* for instance, there is little extended interest in the native inhabitants; they are not much more than a grotesque sideshow, useful for highlighting the contours of youthful romance and demonstrating the superiority of the militaristic British temper. The primary business of the tale is to show, through its three young heroes, the rightness of the British way of life, given added force by continued insistence that God's is the guiding hand. In these terms the savage is mostly active in the imagination—or the Imaginary. Otto, Dominick, and Pauline soon master all they survey. The society they lord over, however, is not indigenous, but produced by another shipwreck, which casts on the island's shores some three hundred emigrants en route to the new world. In effect, this group of Europeans constitutes a tiny colony that is yet large enough to justify familiar institutional forms of power—laws and a government. Most important, for our purposes, Ballantyne offers us the solemn coronation of the startlingly beautiful Pauline—blonde hair, blue eyes, and fair English complexion—as the island's queen. Although it is the men, large and little alike, who get the action, the story still wishes us to locate power in the woman. This may be bad faith, but Ballantyne allows his Pauline to prove a successful ruler: with grace, wit, and diplomacy, she establishes and maintains order within her empire, perhaps in imitation of a more distant queen.

Pauline's beauty is the sign of a charismatic power that derives its force in part from a secure British sense of social place and from devotion to the Law of the Father—the newly appointed queen, at her coronation, shows her fitness for rule by her disarming modesty as she holds up the Bible: "If I rule at all, I will do so by the blessed truths of this book" (167). Her beauty is the antipathetic opposite, then, to the monstrous image of the savage with his blue-spotted nose. Her beauty startles, but carnality is not admitted among her attractions; her beauty is the index not of bodily possibilities but of spiritual superiority. This spiritual authority, however, is in the service of an entirely practical vision, in Pauline's program of education. There is a schoolmaster for the children among the castaways, fortunately, but Pauline reserves for herself the more important task of educating the women, teaching them "their duties to their children and the community" (187). Otto responds to his sister's presumption by teasing her—"Being yourself such an old and experienced mother"—but Pauline's reply quells any criticism: "Silence sir! you ought to remember that we have a dear, darling mother at home, whose character is engraven on my memory, and whom I can hold up as a model" (187). When her adventure is over, Pauline is invited to forego returning to England: "We would take it kindly if you'd consent to . . . continue to be our queen, so as we may all stick together an' be rightly ruled on the lines o' lovin'-kindness" (247). She is the true bearer of bourgeois ideology, precisely by her assimilation to the figure of the mother.

We meet this figure—the mother—time and again in these South Seas family romances. H. A. Forde's *Across Two Seas* (1894), for instance, revolves around her. Even more than *The Island Queen,* this story is an exemplary romance of settlement, Robinson Crusoe displaced by the Swiss Family Robinson, but it is the mother who centers the story, since the crisis that precipitates the adventure of emigration is the death of the father. Henty's *Maori and Settler* (1890), for all its predictable militarism, similarly sees a family threatened, in this case by a father's incompetence: though his place is conveniently filled later in the story by the heroic Atherton, in the meantime his deficiencies must be made good by the mother, Mrs. Renshaw. In both these stories, the mother is not a recollected ideal but a material presence, ministering with sensitivity and tranquillity of spirit to the needs of her children. In *Across Two Seas,* Mrs. Vaughan is actually introduced through the eyes of her children: "'Mother's room!' Who has not pleasant associations with the name? And all these Vaughan boys and girls clearly loved a summons to the cosy, cheerful, upstairs apartment which belonged to 'the mother'" (2). The use of the definite article says it all— "the mother." Mrs. Vaughan anchors the narrative structure more by her presence than by her actions. She does have an active role in establishing culture in the New Zealand wilderness, although she properly gives over the important decisions to her eldest sons, her "prime minister." The story really belongs to the children, that is to say, the boy children, but its status as modern romance is ratified by her presence.

In a tale like this, where settlement is the adventure, motherhood and family easily suggest a larger cultural story—incidents and anxieties that are domestic in scale readily take on a different valence. Mrs. Vaughan is the still, affective center of her family's life and is instrumental in setting up devotional practices that make her home a spiritual center for her entire neighborhood. For family and neighborhood we properly read race and empire. Yet there is more than a set of parallels involved—the presence of the woman charges the daily tale of settlement with significance. To cultivate the land is to elaborate a structure of opposing conditions, a topographical complex of open spaces and closed, hidden places, pasture and wilderness. In these terms, the bush is a source of cultural anxiety rather than the place of romantic adventure. It needs to be tamed, felled, to open up on a different plane, as it were, becoming arboreal, a largely decorative image composing a familiar civilization in this antipodean world. No longer disturbing, it becomes the reassuring sign of the manorial domain; home proves, once again, the ultimate desire of the modern romance of a far-flung Empire. This status is won for settlement by the inexorable magic of romance plotting, yet up till the last moment both the sign and the place of wilderness are contested. The bush is the site of male activity; it is tamed by the Vaughan boys in *Across Two Seas* and by Wilfrid Renshaw in Henty's *Maori and Settler.* In the latter story, it is also brought to a different but related kind of order by the stout hero, Atherton, who is not merely a prodigious warrior but also a remarkable botanist; by his efforts, the New Zealand bush enters the catalogue of European scientific knowledge, becomes so many botanical specimens. Through these means—conquest, cultivation, and scientific cataloguing—the wilderness is made to give up its terror. Yet it retains terror insofar as it remains the natural habitat of the Maori.

In these antipodean romances of settlement, then, antipathies are articulated by binary terms: superior/inferior, order/disorder, clothed/unclothed, clean/dirty, wild/tame, buildings/bush, mother/Maori.[4] At any point the axis could tilt dangerously, and the adventurous tale lose its footing and plunge into tragedy. This possibility is actually built into *Maori and Settler,* which, as a romance, ends happily enough for us and its youthful hero with the British defeat of the Maori leader, Te Kooti. It is an elaborate story, but what is relevant to my purposes here is that the British military campaign is justified finally because of the outrages perpetrated by Te Kooti's followers upon settler families, who are slaughtered wholesale—man, woman, and child.[5] This is a romance, but tragedy is incorporated into the scene, if not directly into the action, and the tragedy is worked through in terms of mothers and Maoris.

Whereas the settler heroes of these stories live out their male adventures in exemplary relation to the family, the Maoris do not. Maoris have no mothers. There are women among them, and children, but there is no mother; there is a *pa,* but no talk of families. A cultural distinction is elaborated and constantly observed. In *Across Two Seas,* this odd complex comes most vividly into view when four-year-old Daisy, the baby of the Vaughan family, is abducted into the bush by a passing band of Maori—precisely the savage attack we learn to fear in Henty's New Zealand Wars. Daisy is found unharmed, but, equally threatening to the exemplary British family, she is almost unrecognizable, having been stripped of her European clothes and wearing instead a Maori mat. Danger tells in this, although decked in the teasing pleasure of incongruity; cultural cross-dressing figures the seductive horror of "going native."[6] In another episode Daisy, who has established easy, friendly relationships with the local Maori, briefly offers a future the book otherwise cannot envisage. Tatau, chief of the local tribe, goes so far as to offer a permanent alliance between himself and the British settlers, to be cemented by the union of Daisy and his eight-year-old nephew. Interracial marriage momentarily becomes a possibility, but the idea is dismissed instantly by Mrs. Vaughan. This Maori seems not to have heard of Said's ideology of difference; the story, on the other hand, raises the spectre of miscegenation, only to lay it smartly to rest. Once again, the subversive possibility tells in narrative jest. The joke betrays repressed anxiety; a tear in the fabric of the novel, it threatens cultural rupture. Perhaps for this reason it is emphatically set right: since the proposed marriage is also a parody of the romantic coupling that commonly brings such stories to their orderly conclusions, propriety is restored with the final European marriages between settler families, involving the eldest two of Mrs. Vaughan's children.

What I am suggesting is that although the violent, idealizing narrative action seems to offer the boy reader scope to identify with the hero, the girl is not excluded from the force field of the book's seductions. Freud's work on dreams and the unconscious suggests that the subject of fantasy finds him- or herself not simply in one figure, engaged definitively in one plot, but in an entire scene.[7] So it must be with the fantasy formed in the literary text. The women in these imperial adventure stories does figure, although she is seldom the character whose actions materially shape the destiny realized in the narrative. She guarantees the value of the actions performed in the book, and often her agency opens up the possibility of straightforward identification for the girl reader. In *Across Two Seas,* in something like an antipodean transposition of Alcott's *Little Women* (1868), Mrs. Vaughan's elder daughters represent options open to the girl—Joscelyn and Juliet form a Martha/Mary–like pair, the unruly out-of-doors predilections of the former being validated as the childish sign of an independent, practical spirit that supports colonial enterprise, rather than threatening it. Lissa Paul has noted the way girls in Victorian fiction interest the reader by their resistance to the settled social order of things, but also how this resistance must end ("Enigma Variations" 154). Likewise, although the colonial world may appreciate and even depend on female initiative, this power must eventually be checked in the imperial romance. In *Across Two Seas,* the rewards of romance—marriage and a lordly homestead, a domain—go not to the practical Joss but to her delicate sister, Juliet, who stands out in this new world precisely because of her potentially disabling ladylike qualities.

Female agency does count in those romances where practicality is wedded to idealism. European culture, even in the late nineteenth century, readily pits the girls directly against the savage to fulfill Europe's evangelizing mission. Here, too, we find an extended effort to appreciate a native subjectivity, although it is conversion that makes it interesting. Ballantyne's Pauline returns to England with her little Brown Eyes, having taught her domesticity and secured her devotion. In *Millicent Courtenay's Diary* (1873), Kingston's Australian settler heroine is likewise engaged in this sort of labor, teaching one "bright little fellow" to spell "sheep" (359) and instructing adult aborigines in appropriate Christian behavior: she notes they learn to "dress in shirts and jackets on Sundays as a mark of respect to the day, although they may very imperfectly comprehend even the simplest truths of Christianity" (443). Kingston's missionary romances, *Mary Liddiard; or The Missionary's Daughter* (1873) and *Waihoura* (1873)—subtitled *The New Zealand Girl,* where, in accordance with nineteenth-century usage, "New Zealand" means Maori—are still finer examples. Both show to a marked degree the common admixture of fear and fascination raised by the savage native, yet both celebrate the relationship between girls of different races in order to display in idealized form the gains to be won when evangelism is matched with colonial enterprise.[8]

Mary Liddiard's story is a simple one of faithful industry and patience. Left "orphaned" after her father fails to return from a missionary expedition to another Pacific island, Mary and her adopted sister, Maud, dutifully keep to a twofold missionary purpose: rescuing the body from savage custom as well as redeeming the soul. This shows in Mary's description of Lisele, daughter of one of the local chiefs and the site of Mary's most ardent reforming energies. Description of this redeemed spirit is worked out overwhelmingly in terms of the body, clothing her, it's true, but only so far: "She was about two years older than I was, and I think any one who had seen her dressed in her costume of native cloth of the finest texture, with a wreath of white flowers in her raven hair, would have thought her very pretty. She was as yet imperfectly instructed in Christian truth, and possessed of high spirits and an independent will—a mere child of nature. It was evidently necessary to treat her with the greatest caution to prevent her running away from us and rejoining her former heathen associates" (12).

Lisele is, perhaps, as close as we get to the noble savage in these South Seas stories, although nobility in savagery tends here toward confusion of categories rather then conceptual clarity. It marks Lisele as not only Mary's desired Other, but also different from her own people—intelligent, possessing an inquiring mind, and "very pretty." She is intelligent, one assumes, because she is malleable and willing to accept the European way. Like Waihoura, the Maori girl of Kingston's other romance of missionary adventure, who willingly takes on European definition of her people and culture, Lisele discards without regret the customs and manners of her tribe. Her desire for white knowledge is exemplary, prompting the narrator to exclaim, "What a happy thing it would be if boys and girls in Britain were so anxious to obtain spiritual knowledge as was the young savage in that Pacific island" (21). Nevertheless, she remains, in Mary's view, the daughter of chaos, "a mere child of nature" and, like some wild creature domesticated, always in danger of regressing to a life of "savage" instinct.

Kingston's liberal imperialism shows in sympathy for the native subject, but sympathy is ambivalent: on occasion referred to as Mary's dark sister, Lisele remains "the savage girl in that Pacific island." The concept of the savage who can be civilized is held in tension with the obvious desire to articulate and justify the moral authority of the colonizer—upon this careful tension depends what Pratt calls "innocent" conquest. Kingston's authorial cunning is revealed in his construing the imperial enterprise as Christian mission, dramatized first in this pure, sisterly relationship between two girls.[9] The allegorical romance of evangelism is secured by installing this relationship at the cost of the preceding bond between father and daughter; like Waihoura, Lisele is the "daughter of a heathen chief, who was very well disposed towards the Christians" but would not himself convert to their faith.

Mary, whose narrative this is after all, is manifestly superior by virtue of her race and her representation of Europe's imperial, Christian mission to the native girl who interests her. Yet, if this active superiority secures her agency as a character, that agency is also confined in due course. She endures many trials in the service of Jehovah, being forced into hiding in flight from heathen savages and enduring starvation at sea, but the narrative of her adventures concludes in true romantic fashion, when she is reunited with her lost father in time for his consent to her marriage to the English gentleman who has been her champion (and who, incidentally, she has reclaimed from a life of profligacy!). In *Waihoura*, Kingston takes the next step and awards both story title and the marriage that fitly concludes the evangelical romance to the Maori girl who has so desperately sought conversion to Christianity. She is the one given romantic presence. Once more Kingston engages in a fascinated play with difference, both identified and elided in the description of his heroine, who is immediately striking because of her European look: "Her complexion was much fairer than that of any of her companions, scarcely darker, indeed, than a Spanish or Italian brunette. No tattoo marks disfigured her lips or chin; her features were regular and wellformed, and her eyes large and clear" (18).

The stereotypically fixed differences between native and European are not so absolute in this case; marks of difference—tattooing—are erased, and blackness is subdued into the exotic, alluring, but also more familiar cast and coloring of Latin beauty. Kingston's exotic heroine is actually formed within the narrative by the sisterly but clearly superior Lucy, daughter of the settler Colonel Pemberton. The first of Waihoura's trials is the illness that brings her into Lucy's care, and that care is rooted in evangelism: "Oh! how sad it would be if she were to die in her present heathen state. . . . How thankful I should feel could I tell her of the love of Christ, and how he died for her sake" (28). Waihoura is Lucy's empire. Under her tutelage, Waihoura learns to wear European clothing and readily adopts both European religious faith and colonialism's material practices. In a passage designed to pluck at the colonialist's heartstrings, Waihoura, fearing a compelled apostasy, throws herself into Lucy's embrace and cries, "Till I came here I did not know what it was to love God, and to try and be good, and to live as you do, so happy and peaceable, and now I must go back and be again the wild Maori girl I was before I came to you, and follow the habits of my people" (69). She need not fear, since this is her romance: after a number of romantic-domestic vicissitudes she is granted marriage to Rahana, a Maori chief who knows something of virtue, and who is, besides, both handsome and untattooed! By this time, even Waihoura's language has turned white. In her person, at last, we find the promise of a "Maori" mother.

Waihoura, then, achieves something like Europeanness, even if her assimilation to the European ideal is always strained, approximate, never complete. We might take this as a flagrant instance of what Homi Bhabha calls "colonial mimicry." We might equally find in the way this Maori girl figures in a white girl's story a paradigm for the space the boyish imperial fantasy creates for the girl: it awards a certain agency, even if it instantly takes it away. Waihoura's exceptional story actually grants her the right to defy her own father, discounting his right to hold or to give away, but her defiance is legitimated by the fact that it brings her under the sway of the European universal Father. Evangelism invests this moment with more than romantic force in that Waihoura's new husband, chosen against her father's will, joins her in the new faith. This then proves an allegory of interpellation: when conversion works to construct subjecthood by instructing the girl in the Law of the Father, in a peculiarly scandalous way it also makes her neither more nor less than a *woman*. Her almost-white beauty has its tale to tell too: the very blankness of Waihoura's untattooed face, the guarantee of freedom from the bonds of savagery, now constitutes paradoxically the bodily sign of what Shulamith Firestone characterizes in *The Dialectic of Sex* as women's privileged slavery.

The truly interesting structural relationship in much imperial juvenile literature is that formed by the axis that runs between girl and savage. This is not a matter of connection or interchangeability. Rather, in the fate of one the other's fate comes to be implicated, with varying degrees of complexity. Broadly speaking, a limited but real space opens up for an active woman in late-Victorian fiction of Empire written for children, although the rule suggested by Carroll's term "antipathies" still obtains—the European female succeeds at the cost of the native. Yet this real space is also limited: one way or another, the best future a woman can know, even in relation to the fated savage, is the privilege in her "slavery."

Perhaps this is nowhere shown more clearly than in Henty's *Maori and Settler*. Atherton, something of a father figure to the young Renshaws, insists that not only should Wilfrid learn to shoot, train to kill, but the reluctant Marion should also do so, and eventually he provides *her* with justifications for killing the Maori, thereby making a true "man" of her: "Their intention is to slay man, woman and child without mercy, and I therefore regard them as human tigers, and no more deserving of pity. At the same time I can quite enter into your feeling, and think you are perfectly right not to take any active part in the affair unless we are pressed by the savages. Then, of course, you would be not only justified, but it would, I think, be your absolute duty to do your best to defend the place" (251).

Henty offers the woman active, imperial individuality, measured in the capacity to do violence. This individuality is not unmixed with paradigmatic maternalism, "lovin'-kindness," but it is still achieved in violence and directly against the "treacherous" savage. Nevertheless, even though she has secured this equivocal, problematic gain of imperialist individuality, finally all Marion can do is marry. The Maori wars come to an end and the land is made safe for European occupation, but, like so many of the settlers in these stories, Atherton returns to England, taking with him Marion as his bride. The late-nineteenth-century history of colonies such as Australia and New Zealand is one of continued advances toward self-determination by local governments; the continuing emphasis in imperialist romance is on the first encounter and finally the romantic return home. The final fruit of Marion's antipodean adventure is a wealthy, ever-so-English husband who is nearly old enough to be her father, but happy to be just "a child" in relation to her when it comes to love—privilege indeed.

In each of the examples of late-Victorian children's fiction of Empire I have discussed here, we properly register a complex play of antipathies from which the girl is by no means excluded—whether she would demur or not, she is called on "to defend the place." It is not so clear what "the place" is. Only in a few instances—notably Kingston's missionary romances—does the tale seem bound to any particular imperial policy, yet all seem to join in the work of the imperialist elder, drawing profit from their investment in the colonized, other world. There is a paradox in this, of course. The South Seas romance was a money spinner, a fine example of what Henry James protested against on behalf of the novel: "Great fortunes, if not great reputations, are made, we learn, by writing for schoolboys" (qtd. in Hughes 75). Money was made out of the alluring otherness of the "antipathies," exemplifying the "commodification" of the colonial subject analyzed by Abdul JanMohamed. It was this debased order of fiction, adolescent romance written with an eye to a more or less guaranteed market, generating and regenerating ever-novel scenes of fantasy that fixed cross currents of terror and desire, that proved the readiest instrument in the house of fiction for winning consent to the grand design of Empire.

Finally, let us make no mistake about what is going on here. These are not truly antipodean stories, after all; no antipodean voices can be heard in them. Edith Nesbit's marvelous parodic fantasy of these romances in *The Phoenix and the Carpet* (1904) makes my point, when the family's Irish cook chooses to stay on the South Seas island as queen and explains how she deals with the problem of communicating with her cannibal subjects: "Lor' love a duck. . . . I always thought I would be quick at languages. I've taught them to understand 'dinner' and 'I want a drink' and 'You leave me be' already" (79). The texts I have discussed make women—girls—full partners in a British, metropolitan, cultural project that gives no true audience to other worlds. The society from which these stories come, apparently, cannot deal with antipodean peoples except by annexing them for its imaginative pleasures or by enslaving them, after the fashion of Hegel's familiar dialectic, for the purpose of having them bear witness to its mastery. At this distance, it is sometimes difficult to forgive these British writers for making children's play—the South Seas story—do this unsavory adult work.

PART II

Theory

CHAPTER 5

The Liberal Bias in Feminist
Social Science Research on Children's Books

Roger Clark, Heidi Kulkin, and Liam Clancy

If literary critics sometimes fear that feminists have shown little concern for the care and feeding of children's culture, they overlook the efforts of at least one group: feminist social scientists. Unlike their sisters in other disciplines, who have tended to focus on isolated texts, feminist social scientists have directed their attention to whole genres and audiences. In doing so, they have helped transform both.

A case in point: in 1972, Lenore Weitzman and a group of colleagues (henceforth referred to as Weitzman), published a study in the *American Journal of Sociology,* one of sociology's two most widely circulated journals, that condemned the depiction of gender in American award-winning picture books for children. The article sparked great concern among social scientists: it has been cited well over a hundred times in professional journals and continues to be cited more than 25 years later. It also became a rallying point for feminist activism, energizing the Women's Action Alliance when it published *An Annotated Bibliography of Nonsexist Picture Books for Children* in 1973 and the Feminists on Children's Media when it printed *Little Miss Muffet Fights Back* in 1974. Through such lists and related efforts, Weitzman almost surely influenced publishing practices, from the founding of feminist publishing companies (Feminist Press and Lollypop Power) to the raising of consciousness among more conventional publishers, award committees, authors,[1] parents, and teachers.

Even sociologists may be a little uncomfortable with attributing all this change to one article written by sociologists a quarter century ago.[2] Yet by 1993, studies by Roger Clark, Rachel Lennon, and Leanna Morris and by Carole Kortenhaus and Jack Demarest showed that prize-winning books for children had become much more gender balanced by Weitzman's standards.

But what were those standards? Are they still the standards of feminist social scientists studying children's books? If feminist social scientists have effectively nurtured children's literature, have they nurtured it in accord with values that reflect recent versions of feminist thought?

A brief look at the Weitzman study suggests a fairly conventional liberal-feminist concern for egalitarian depictions of gender, without much reference to other variables such as race, class, and age. The group was appalled at the relative invisibility of female characters. They despised the fact that "girls are taught to have low aspirations because there are so few opportunities portrayed as available to them" (1146). They claimed that "perhaps our most significant finding was that *not one* woman in the Caldecott sample had a job or profession" (1141). Liberal feminism, with its emphasis on equal opportunity and individual achievement, was in the air in 1972 and Weitzman's work was redolent with it.

American feminist social theory then changed. Each new edition of Allison Jaggar and Paula Rothenberg's *Feminist Frameworks,* a standard women's studies collection, testifies to this change by enumerating new strands of feminist social thought. In 1978, Jaggar and Rothenberg Struhl juxtaposed the unequal opportunity decried by liberal feminists to the seemingly more impervious barriers of classism, sexism, and combinations of the two that concerned Marxist, radical, and socialist feminists, respectively. By 1984 they had added a fourth feminist contrast: something they called the feminism of "women of color," which they used to point to theories concerned with racism as well as classism and sexism.

Yet, as Donna Haraway would write a year later, "women of color" was "a name contested at its origins by those whom it would incorporate" (600). In their 1993 edition, therefore, Jaggar and Rothenberg called this feminism "multicultural feminism" not only to stress how "the issues raised by women of color have moved from the margin to the center of feminist concern" (123), but also to emphasize the differences (and we use this term intentionally) among its advocates. They also added a sixth kind of feminism, something they called "global feminism," to indicate an emerging concern with differences brought about by experiences of imperialism and postcolonialism.

This last addition may have been unnecessary, inasmuch as its object seems to have been an elaboration of the "multicultural feminist" critique of liberal feminism (and indeed of other modernist ideologies). Multicultural feminists argue that the world is made up of people experiencing different realities and that political effort should be directed to the "ongoing process of defining and living according to one's several affinities" (Lemert 499). Thus bell hooks's "feminist" and Patricia Hill Collins's "black feminist" share with Gloria Anzaldúa's "new mestiza" and Chandra Talpade Mohanty's "third world feminist" a desire to bespeak women's experience in particular details, rather than in universal diagnoses and palliatives. Mention of Anzaldúa, a poet, indeed of Haraway, a biologist, testifies to the increasingly interdisciplinary sources of multicultural feminist thought in the social sciences. Such thought advocates the openness to particular voices that is evident in this book in Lissa Paul's essay about Grace Nichols's poetry and Allen Douglas and Fedwa Malti-Douglas's analysis of Yûsuf al-Qaʿîd's story "Rabâb Gives Up Drawing" (chapters 6 and 15, respectively).

Changes in feminism over the last quarter century, then, make it difficult to argue that its central moral tenet is still that women should be equal with men—the preeminent value articulated in the Weitzman study. The movement, or its social science theoretical expression, has come to extol what liberal feminists might suspect as ambiguous values (e.g., listening closely to people for what they themselves value) or gender-normed female virtues. Such virtues as connectedness, caring, and personal accountability have been revalued by "cultural feminists" such as Carol Gilligan. Praised for their crucial role in the survival of multiply oppressed women, these virtues have been incorporated into certain versions of multicultural feminism (e.g., Collins, *Black Feminist Thought*).

The changing face of theoretical feminism has only recently been reflected in feminist social science investigations of children's books. The Weitzman study, perhaps partly because of its political success, established a liberal-feminist paradigm for social science investigations of children's books that has been virtually unchallenged, despite problematic findings and a significant shift in feminist thought. In what follows we document the grip of the liberal-feminist paradigm on feminist sociological and psychological studies of children's books and suggest, broadly, what a social science approach more in accord with recent shifts in theoretical feminism might look like. Our focus on sociology and psychology reflects our own situated positions and partial knowledges, though our sense is that something like the following story might be told of other social science disciplines as well.[3]

The Establishment of the Liberal-Feminist Paradigm

Weitzman's investigation may be considered the paradigmatic study in the field, in that it set out the "constellation of beliefs, values, techniques, and so on shared by members of a given community" (Kuhn 175). In the introductory paragraphs of their report, Weitzman and her colleagues claimed that through children's books "boys and girls are socialized to accept society's definition of the relative worth of each of the sexes and to assume the personality characteristics that are 'typical' of members of each sex"; that children "learn that boys are more highly valued than girls"; and, most important, that children's books are "a vehicle for the presentation of societal values to young children" (1125–26).

Beliefs and values aside, it may be the technique of content analysis that most clearly distinguished the Weitzman study. The study had a scientific precision: the researchers looked at a relatively well-defined sample of books, scrutinized the comparative visibilities of male and female characters, and fairly precisely showed how male and female characters were depicted. Although it examined children's etiquette books, Little Golden Books, Newbery Award winners, and earlier Caldecotts, the Weitzman study focused on Caldecott winners and runners-up of the previous five years (1967 to 1971): eighteen books in all. They found that female characters of any sort were practically invisible; in the Caldecott sample, pictures of males outnumbered pictures of females 261 to 23 (about 13 to 1). They also found that, when depicted, boys were much more likely to be active, to be rescuers, to be shown outdoors than were girls, who were more likely to be shown in service activities and dependent roles.

The Paradigm in Action: Supportive and Anomalous Findings

Even once one knows something about the values, beliefs, and techniques of a paradigm, Kuhn's definition implies a need to know something of its practitioners as well. Our investigation led us to see the community of feminist social scientists concerned with children's literature since the Weitzman study as composed of people whose probable class and racial backgrounds and whose professional training in positivist science made liberal feminism appealing. The two main types of research done by feminist social scientists since 1972 are embedded in the positivist tradition. On the one hand are the "experimenters," who have investigated the behavioral and psychological consequences of exposure to inegalitarian children's literature for boys and girls. On the other are the "content analyzers," who, replicating Weitzman in one way or another, have attempted to describe the portrayal of male and female characters in children's books with refined content-analytic techniques or different (sometimes more recent) samples. We have argued elsewhere (Clark and Kulkin) that the relatively clear-cut "equal opportunity" standard of liberal feminism facilitates quantitative or positivist methodology: this standard can, in a sense, be privileged over the concerns of real people (a general critique of positivist science made, variously, by Shulamit Reinharz, Dorothy Smith, and Judith Stacey). Without such a standard, experimenters and content analyzers would be like navigators without compasses.

Although these two groups follow the path of what Thomas Kuhn calls a "normal science" in investigating children's books, their commitment to liberal feminism has permitted them to overlook certain anomalies. Anomalies come in many stripes, including contradictory findings that are not adequately resolved by the paradigm and the perception that certain "facts" support the paradigm when in fact they do not. Elizabeth Segel points to two such factual distortions in Weitzman's illustrative materials: the claim that "Mrs. Noah, who had an important role in the biblical story of the flood, is completely omitted from" Barbara Emberley's *One Wide River to Cross,* when she is not, and the assertion that Lionni's *Frederick* is populated by a family of "brothers," when the gender of Frederick's family is at best ambiguous. Although factual distortions, as Kuhn points out, are rarely adequate reason to reject a paradigm, perhaps more than most anomalies they indicate how much the perceptions of a community of scientists can be controlled by the worldview implicit in their paradigm.

The Experimenters

The authors whose experimental studies we examined all seem to share the beliefs and values of the Weitzman paradigm, even while they necessarily use a different kind of positivist methodology.[4] All the experimenters start with the assumption that children's books provide inegalitarian depictions and assert with some enthusiasm their rejection of this depiction (e.g., Flerx et al. 998). Their research goals are to establish that reverse-stereotypical or nonstereotypical presentations would make a difference in children's behaviors, attitudes, or perceptions. (Although all such attempts are undoubtedly justified in terms of the light they may shine on the potency of stereotyped presentations, one sometimes gets a sense that experimenters investigating the power of reverse stereotypes are themselves promoting a stereotype, one that would idealize "feminine" boys and "masculine" girls.) In the typical experiment, a sample of children is divided into groups, some of which are exposed to stereotypical stories and others to reverse-stereotypical or nonstereotypical stories. The experimenter then measures attitudes, behaviors, or perceptions (or changes in one of these) to determine whether exposure to different kinds of stories has an effect.

The experimental procedure, deploying matched groups, sounds even more classically scientific than the content analysis performed by Weitzman, and its findings are frequently pretty interesting. Jerri Kropp and Charles Halverston, for example, find that preschool children actually dislike hearing stories in which characters of the opposite gender do gender-stereotyped things more than they dislike hearing stories in which characters of either gender do reverse-stereotyped things. Such a finding might have happy implications for the liberal-feminist cause, if one could be sure that pleasure translated into salient memories (and then perhaps appropriate self-images and behaviors). Unfortunately, the exploration of what children remember from stories read to them has generated some of the most puzzling contradictions in the experimental literature.

Depending on which researcher one reads, one could come away from the experimental literature believing that children remember best the stories in which characters do reverse-stereotyped things or the stories whose characters do stereotypical things.[5] Close investigation reveals a challenge to the liberal-feminist assumption that children of all races, classes, and ages are equally affected by stereotyped depictions. The most striking difference between Sally Jennings's study, which provides the strongest evidence that kids remember reverse-stereotyped characters best, and that of Sally Koblinsky et al., which offers the strongest evidence to the contrary, is the average age of the sample: about four for Jennings's group and about ten for Koblinsky's. Could it be that developmental differences (e.g., in memory or recognition of stereotypes) influence children's use of stereotypes as organizational frameworks? The liberal-feminist paradigm does not easily accommodate such a possibility. Perhaps no current feminist perspective does. But the evidence in this case does suggest that the perspective with the greatest sensitivity to a variety of socially significant variables, such as age, may do best at accommodating true variation in the social world.

One particularly curious finding makes this point with special force. In general, the experimenters attempt to minimize variation in their samples as much as possible, following standard operating procedure in the sciences. Middle- to upper-middle-class white children are studied in six of the seven investigations.

The one study (Jennings) that admits of class variation finds that class makes a difference. Jennings's findings that on average four-year-olds have better recall for stories with reverse-stereotyped characters hides a big difference, especially for boys: Whereas boys from a day-care (low-income) program remember, like girls of both groups, stories with reverse stereotyping better than those with stereotyping, boys from a nursery school (upper-income) program show distinctly better recall of stereotyped characters. Jennings acknowledges these differences, but she masks them in her concluding recommendation that "girls be depicted in more active and competent roles. Boys also need wider choices" (222). She mimics Weitzman's conclusions without acknowledging the class differences she accidentally discovered. No subsequent experimenter has picked up on them either. Surely multicultural feminists would not have been so diffident.

Jennings may be forgiven her indifference to a finding that washes out when one looks at overall averages. But one knows one is up against a potent paradigm when researchers ignore their central findings in order to sustain their belief in that paradigm, as Koblinsky et al. seem to have done. Their major finding was that ten-year-olds of both sexes remembered much "more of the masculine sex-types characteristics of male characters and more of the feminine sex-typed characteristics of female characters" (452) than they did of reverse-stereotyped characteristics. This led the researchers to admit that, "given that children exhibit selective memory for stereotypic content . . . , the predicted gains of curricular intervention may fall short of actualization" (457). In the end, however, they could not break with the liberal-feminist tradition. Their final sentence reminds one of the explorer who has peered into the abyss and found the view intolerable: "This discovery does not diminish the importance of utilizing nonsexist materials but does suggest the need to develop additional strategies for reducing the bias in children's memory for sex-role information" (457).

The great strength of the experimental method is that it permits the examination of causal connections (such as between hearing a story and subsequent behavior). Yet this strength is related to one of its weaknesses: the need to reduce variation in all conditions not directly related to the central concerns of the study. Thus, for instance, every study since Jennings's 1975 pathbreaking investigation has limited, as much as possible, the age, class, and race variation of the children examined. The studies likewise flatten out the complexities of the books themselves. Only when variation in these variables has slipped in by mistake or via interstudy sample differences have some of the most interesting relationships been revealed—and only then to attentive readers, rarely to the researchers themselves. Multicultural feminist experimenters, if such there ever are, would surely want to pursue the effects of age, class, race, and other variables besides gender on children's responses to children's books.

The Content Analyzers

The fourteen studies by content analyzers that we examined methodologically resemble Weitzman's paradigmatic study, despite occasional shifts in values and beliefs.[6] The research goals have usually been to determine whether more refined content analyses yield the same results obtained in the paradigmatic study or to see whether content analysis applied to other samples, frequently more recent ones, can detect differences in the depiction of gendered characters. However, using the same standards employed in the paradigmatic study—for example, whether females and males are equally visible or whether they are depicted with similar traits—has often produced results that the paradigm leaves the content analyzers at a loss to explain.

A painful example occurs in Piper Purcell and Lara Stewart's replication of the 1972 Women on Words study, which did for children's textbooks what Weitzman's study did for picture books in the same year. The question Purcell and Stewart addressed was whether textbooks had changed appropriately (by liberal-feminist standards) by 1989. A cursory glance at these researchers' tables would lead most readers, even liberal feminists, to an almost blissful sense of optimism. One learns, for instance, that in 1989 women and girls were depicted as often as their male counterparts (only 25% of adult and child characters had been female in 1972) and that school children were reading more biographies of women than of men (only 14% of biographies had been of females in 1972). Moreover, tables presenting characters' behaviors show that in 1989 female characters were depicted as being just as clever, industrious, helpful, skill acquiring, and rewarded as male characters, whereas in 1972 they had lagged far behind on all these behavioral dimensions.

What do Purcell and Stewart make of these results? They do not discuss the content of the table on behavior at all. They simply state, "Although we did analyze story content by themes, we were not comfortable with this method of analysis. Several articles in our literature review criticized this types of analysis as being too subjective. . . . As our intercoder reliability was only 70%"—not bad by content-analytic standards—"we do not feel we can draw any firm conclusions about the measures. Our results are included, but should be read with the above considerations in mind" (183). This self-flagellation, almost unheard of in the social sciences, prevents the researchers from making explicit mention of the happy changes they uncovered. They seem to feel that any mention of glad tidings would be a betrayal, perhaps not so much of the values as of the tenor of the liberal-feminist paradigm. Or perhaps they are groping for an interpretive framework that their techniques, so enmeshed in that paradigm, do not accommodate. In any case, having shown that in 1989 women characters were much more likely to be depicted in a broad range of occupations than their 1972 counterparts had been, Purcell and Stewart seem to miss the donut for the hole: "While women were shown in what were once primarily male fields, only men were shown in the more adventurous areas. A woman doctor was now common, but women explorers and big-game hunters were still few and far between" (182). Okay, but the portrayal of so many women doctors is a good thing, right?

A certain timidity characterizes the rest of the content analyzers as well. Albert Davis defines more precise ways of studying behavioral traits than Weitzman did and applies them to Weitzman's sample. What does he find? That Weitzman's sample contained much less behavioral stereotyping, by his measures, than previously supposed. What does he say? That maybe he was not looking at the right traits (13). Elizabeth Grauerholz and Bernice Pescosolido performed a content analysis of the *Children's Catalog* description of 2,216 "Easy Books" published since 1900 and found, interestingly enough, that female characters were relatively visible early in the century, lost visibility until the early 1950s, and have gained visibility since. They did not examine *how* females have been portrayed, but, apparently thinking they couldn't end on too upbeat a note about visibility, they conclude their report with a downbeat note about something they did not study: "Stories about women, however, still do not portray them in the variety of extrafamilial roles that characterize the actual social situation of women in contemporary American society" (124).

Two final studies, seemingly on the brink of a paradigmatic breakthrough, are those by Clark, Lennon, and Morris and by Kate Peirce and Emily Edwards. Having participated in the project by Clark et al., one of us—Roger—can vouch for a conscious effort to bridge liberal- and multicultural-feminist approaches to picture books. My coauthors and I reexamined the Caldecott winners and runners-up studied by Weitzman, looked at Caldecotts twenty years later (1987–91), and examined recent Coretta Scott King winners (1987–91) to gauge differences in books illustrated by whites and blacks. We found that female characters receive considerably more attention in recent Caldecotts than in older ones and that male and female characters are depicted with more similar behavioral traits than they were in the sample investigated by Weitzman. We then turned our attention to recent Kings, finding that, using liberal-feminist standards of female visibility and behavior, these books looked good, even compared to recent Caldecotts. Applying a short list of what we decided were multicultural-feminist standards to the books, we found the Kings more likely than the other award winners to depict female–female relationships and co-operative and nurturant females. Nonetheless, I realize in retrospect, what we undertook was not a fully multicultural approach. We were still too much a part of Weitzman's paradigm to embrace the fundamental differences between liberal and multicultural feminism, implying still that the standards and methods of the latter might entail mere elaboration, rather than fundamental revision, of the former.

Peirce and Edwards, rather than performing content analysis on literature for children, analyzed the stories written by 266 children, all about eleven years old. They then determined whether girls and boys used distinctive styles of conflict resolution in their stories. Their major finding was that boys used more violent resolutions (for example, fighting and shooting) than did girls, who showed their characters using reasoning and analysis to settle conflicts. Given the changes in feminist thought that had occurred by 1988, one might expect Peirce and Edwards to have interpreted their results in terms of differences in the ways girls and boys are socialized, perhaps in the mode of Gilligan, or even to have applauded the less violent approach of their preadolescent female authors, as bell hooks might have done. The authors settled instead for a conventional liberal-feminist interpretation: "Results suggest that . . . schoolchildren have internalized society's expectations for them. A girl child is expected to be passive and cooperative, while a boy child is expected to be aggressive and competitive. The children did not think of defying cultural norms—not even in their wildest dreams" (402).

Conclusions and Possible Future Directions

Children's dreams, of course, are not the only human creations affected by cultural norms. Our reading of two strands of sociological and psychological analysis of children's books suggests that feminist social scientists have been limited by the liberal-feminist standards set a quarter of a century ago. We have offered three reasons for the pervasiveness of these standards: (1) the political effectiveness of the paradigmatic study made it seem particularly worthy of emulation; (2) the backgrounds and training of feminists studying children's literature may have left them particularly open to liberal-feminist, rather than other feminist, thought; and (3) the methodological inclinations of experimenters and content analyzers led them to adopt frameworks whose basic values (for example, men and women should have equal opportunities) can be taken as obvious and unproblematic.

What would a more multicultural-feminist and less liberal-feminist social scientist look for in children's books and their audiences? The paradigmatic studies have yet to be conducted in sociology and psychology,[7] so we can only speculate.

Certain guesses seem pretty likely, however. We doubt, on the one hand, that multicultural-feminist social scientists would abandon all of the liberal-feminist agenda. They would probably retain, for instance, a concern with the comparative visibility of female characters in children's books and the presumed impact of such books on girls and boys.

On the other hand, it is not clear that multiculturalists would continue to use the techniques that characterize liberal-feminist analyses of children's literature. Clark and Kulkin, for instance, performed a qualitative analysis of recent adolescent fiction featuring main characters who are not white, American, or heterosexual and found themselves "listening" to themes of oppression and resistance, and to nuances of expression, rather than "looking for" evidence to support one hypothesis or another. This analysis was more similar to reader-response literary criticism—and not unlike William Moebius's essay in this book about his research with a variety of picture books (chapter 8)—than were any by the experimenters or content analyzers described earlier. It may be that as feminist social scientists rethink their commitment to liberal feminism, they will also rethink the commitment to positivist science that has so far typified feminist social scientific approaches to children's books.

Multicultural feminists may continue to conduct content analyses and experimentation, but, if they do, we would not expect them to put as high a premium as their liberal-feminist sisters have on female role models pursuing personal interests in the capitalist marketplace. We would expect them to cast more appreciative glances at books in which female, and male, characters exhibit the kind of nurturance and mutual support that have grated on liberal feminists. Moreover, we would expect them to be more appreciative of stories that imply approval of various kinds of nonbiological parenting (by, say, adoptive, including gay, parents, distant relatives, community members, and so forth). Certainly they would seek a children's literature that depicts and values the expression of non-Western culture. Multicultural experimenters, if such there were, would probably show concern with the effects of children's stories on a broader spectrum of the child population than has been previously looked at. Race, class, ethnicity, and age, to name a few characteristics, would assume greater salience. Multicultural feminists would likely validate more than one "correct" response to a story, acknowledging that different readers read differently. They might design experiments that test not just salient memories and patterns of liking but changes in such attitudes as respect and tolerance. Moreover, we would expect them to appreciate a wider range of story contents than has heretofore interested liberal-feminist experimenters. Stories about achievement-oriented children might be replaced by stories about environmentally sensitive or caring children (see, for example, Adler and Foster).

Whether feminist social scientists will, in fact, start studying children's books in different ways remains an open question and may not be of great social importance after all. We began this essay with the assertion that feminist social scientists have had an impact on what children get to read, but the assertion is admittedly speculative. Others may claim that the connection we have drawn between Weitzman's study and publishing changes in the past twenty-five years is a spurious one and that each, for instance, can be traced to the liberal-feminist movement of the 1960s without reference to the other. In any case, the recent proliferation of published narratives about nontraditional families, Chicano and other cultures, and slave experiences suggests that the input of feminist social science researchers may not be crucial to the establishment of a children's literature that multicultural feminists might approve of. Still, feminist social scientists have played a role, and they are not alone; the essays in this book (and, more important, the presence of a community that reads them) lead us to suspect a misleading modesty on the part of certain children's literary critics.

Coming "to sing their being"
The Poetry of Grace Nichols

Lissa Paul

The piece proposed by Lissa Paul seems to be more about advocacy than anything else; flak for a writer [Grace Nichols] she thinks we should care about, rather than analysis of one that we already do. As a result, it's hard to see its relevance in the current context: if this writer does represent something of importance, why isn't she more widely known?
—Anonymous reviewer of the abstract of this essay

In *The Genesis of Secrecy,* Frank Kermode explains, at length, his reasons for writing about a novel that is not "of such value that every effort of exegesis is justified without argument." Kermode reassures readers, in his comforting way, that a "confession that one had not read *Party Going* [by noncanonical author Henry Green] would not be humiliating (a rule-of-thumb of canonicity)" (5). Kermode is a famous critic. It is unlikely that anyone would dare to question his right to write about anything he pleases anyway. Not even Harold Bloom. Bloom's tome, *The Western Canon: The Books and School of the Ages* (1994), hit the market in the waning years of the millennium, just in time to arbitrate on canonicity. When I checked with Bloom, it came as a bit of surprise to find that he immortalizes (that might be too strong a term) both Henry Green and *Party Going* in his compendium of canonical books. Perhaps Bloom missed Kermode's apologia. Or maybe something divine happened in the fifteen years between *The Genesis of Secrecy* and *The Western Canon* to render Green canonical. If so, I didn't know about it. If Bloom knew about it, he didn't think it worth a comment.

Unlike Henry Green, Grace Nichols doesn't make it into Bloom's canon. That may not prove to be much of a shortcoming, especially as knowledge of Bloom's canon of classics does not necessarily define an educated or cultured person. In fact, it might be well to remember, as Peter Stallybrass and Allon White do at the beginning of *The Politics and Poetics of Transgression*, that our idea of "classic" texts and authors "originally derived from ancient taxation categories": the rich "*classici*" at the top, and the poor "*proletarius*" at the bottom (1). Furthermore, the equation of knowledge of classic books with a good education was not established in American educational institutions until late in the nineteenth century, as Gerald Graff points out in *Professing Literature* (100). Even then, neither the books nor the definition of what was worth knowing about them was particularly clear.

At the end of the twentieth century, it looks as if the value placed on classical or canonical books is waning. Canonical books are now tainted with the suspicion that their greatness is determined by their implicit ideological concerns, that is, the ways in which they inscribe the power of Western, white male adults. As different voices and different ideologies rise, the old ones lose their authority.

Nichols speaks very much in the voice of the new millennium. A woman of Caribbean origin living in England, she is well schooled in the tradition of standard English literature, as well as in feminist literature and theory and in colonial history and politics. She writes out of maternal traditions, Caribbean traditions, and English traditions, and she writes for both children and adults. She is one of a cluster of poets—James Berry, Jackie Kay, and John Agard among others—revitalizing English poetry with another "english." Lowercase "english" is, incidentally, the preferred term of Bill Ashcroft, Gareth Griffiths, and Helen Tiffin, who use it in *The Empire Writes Back* (a book about postcolonial discourse) to distinguish hybrids from the standard English exported to the colonies. That English has been recreated as a range of "englishes" now revitalizing standard English.

My initial encounter with Nichols was, I'm happy to say, in the nursery—not the university. Her first children's collection, *Come on into My Tropical Garden*, was among the books recommended for the 1988 *Signal* poetry award. The collection did not win that year, but I bought it and began reciting some of the poems to my first child, my infant son. Ten years later, the title poem remains a favorite for bedtime recitation, although there are now two boys to whom I say it.

Through the late 1980s and early 1990s, my critical interests grew to encompass changing forms of feminist and postcolonial theory: Gayatri Spivak taught me to recognize the subaltern position of colonial subjects; and bell hooks taught me how to read representations of blackness in a white Western world. In that context, I found and read Nichols's adult poetry collections—*i is a long memoried woman* (1983), *The Fat Black Woman's Poems* (1984), and *Lazy Thoughts of a Lazy Woman* (1986)—and her novel, *Whole of a Morning Sky* (1986).

Through the mid-1990s, I was also working on a maternal literacies project, funded by the Social Sciences and Humanities Research Council of Canada. The project began as an account of the literacies children bring to school from home. The plural "literacies"—common in educational contexts these days— is meant to include media literacy and visual literacy. In our project, we saw mothers bringing what used to be called, condescendingly, "domestic" arts (quilting, cooking, and gardening in particular) into schools. Male and female teachers welcomed the domestic. I also found records of seventeenth- and eighteenth-century pedagogical practices that included domestic arts in the curriculum.[1] Both the historical research and the field research reminded me that knowledge need not be of the muscular Christian boys' school kind. It could be equated with affection, community, and a thriving domestic economy.

Gradually, connections between the politics of the nursery and the politics of colonial subjects became clear. Nichols addresses both in her poetry. She writes out of her history, but is never silenced by it, even though she writes from positions conventionally seen as marginal: as a woman, a black woman, and a poet for children. None of those identifying tags explains why Nichols is worth reading and writing about.

I have two reasons for writing about Nichols: one has to do with language, the other with ideology. Nichols handles expertly a wide range of images and subjects, and demonstrates a virtuoso linguistic flexibility with rhythms and figurative language. And she reinvents her ideological position as a colonial subject. She is able "to decenter the communal and fraternal modes of understanding that have organized discussion of nationalism and subnationalisms," as Mary Louise Pratt says ("Criticism" 87). What I like so much about Nichols is her ability to "decenter" the colonial order with regard to both canon and pedagogical practice.

Through the colonial period, school became a major instrument for transmitting European culture to the colonies. There was a corresponding devaluation of the literature and material practices associated with women, children, and colonial subjects. Nursery verse, for example, is still regarded as inferior to the verse of canonical poets such as Yeats or Eliot. Nichols disturbs those assumptions.

Increasingly, I came to think of Nichols as a "contact zone" poet, demonstrating what Pratt calls "transculturation," a term she appropriates from ethnography, where it is used to describe how "subordinated or marginal groups select and invent from materials transmitted to them by a dominant or metropolitan culture." Pratt augments the term to include "ways in which the periphery determines the metropolis" (*Imperial Eyes* 6). At this point all the reasons for my focus on Nichols came together.

Though Nichols is not yet canonical, her writing offers an extensive look at transculturation in action. In her work, the garden, the domestic, food, and the nursery all appear as authoritative poetic subjects. The language in which she writes, her english, is one that informs the language and culture of a postcolonial world. Nichols sometimes writes in Creole, sometimes in standard English, and sometimes she mixes the two, but there is never any doubt about her own authority to choose.

She resolves the problems of poetic language experienced by colonial poets, European emigrants who tried to make their old words describe their new worlds. As Ashcroft, Griffiths, and Tiffin explain in *The Empire Writes Back,* the "vocabulary, categories and codes [were] felt to be inadequate or inappropriate to describe the fauna, the physical and geographical conditions, or the cultural practices" of the new territory (10).

If Nichols is a postcolonial poet, her colonial "opposite number" is Robert Louis Stevenson, a poet writing at the height of England's empire. *A Child's Garden of Verses* was published in 1885, a time when imperialism was regarded as a good thing. *Come on into My Tropical Garden,* published just over one hundred years later, marks the distance from a colonial to a postcolonial world.

Although much of Stevenson's *A Child's Garden of Verses* remains canonical (my own children still like "Windy Nights"), at least one poem makes late-twentieth-century librarians and teachers squirm: "Foreign Children." Racism is not the problem with the poem. The problem is that it demonstrates the inadequacies of colonial language and codes in dealing with "foreign" environments. Here are some of what are now considered the most damning lines:

> Little Indian, Sioux or Crow,
> Little frosty Eskimo,
> Little Turk or Japanee,
> O! don't you wish that you were me?

You have seen the scarlet trees
And the lions over seas;
You have eaten ostrich eggs,
And turned the turtles off their legs.

.   .   .   .

You have curious things to eat,
I am fed on proper meat;
You must dwell beyond the foam,
But I am safe and live at home.   (41)

The narrator—by setting himself in opposition to anyone not English—constructs a value system that names what is normal and what is not: "You have eaten ostrich eggs, / And turned the turtles off their legs." The assumption is that foreign children are cruel to animals, a very un-English, uncivilized way to behave. Without a trace of irony, Stevenson asserts the privilege of carnivorous English children to eat proper meat and designates "other" food as foreign.

The constitution of a "proper" dinner offers a broad clue to how much English culture has changed, even through the waning years of the twentieth century. Meat has become especially problematic. The Sunday "joint," as it is still affectionately known in England, is increasingly suspect. "Proper" meat is now linked to fat, cholesterol, possible antibiotics, artificial hormones, and other vestiges of an unhealthy life, including the specter of "mad cow" disease. Caribbean food, with its emphasis on high carbohydrates, low fat, and low protein, looks like the healthier option. In an example of transculturation, the food from the periphery has become the fashion food of the metropolis.

In "Wha Me Mudder Do," Nichols celebrates both the food of the Other and the maker of the food: "Me mudder pound plantain mek fufu / Me mudder catch crab mek calaloo stew" (*Come on into My Tropical Garden* 14). She acknowledges the whole process of food preparation, the work of making dinner. The "mudder" pounds the plantain and catches the crab before she makes the fufu and the calaloo stew. The stress is on organic connections in the production of dinner, not on the categorical differences between fishing as an "outside" job and cooking as an "inside," domestic job.

It was while puzzling away at the problems of defining borders between the metropolis and the periphery that my mind began to dwell on the perennial borders in English gardens, and then on *A Child's Garden of Verses*. I mused for a while on the distance in time, space, culture, and language between Stevenson's English country gardens and the tropical gardens of Grace Nichols. Stevenson's gardens are formal pleasure gardens, tended by others. I think of "The Gardener," whom Stevenson describes as "Old and serious, brown and big" (104). For the fair English at the turn of the nineteenth century, to be brown was to be either foreign or a laborer. In either case to be brown was to be of a lower order. In "My Gran Visits England," from *Give Yourself a Hug* (1994), Nichols twists the scene and the language in a physical act of transculturation. The poem begins in the iambics of standard English verse:

> My Gran was a Caribbean lady
> As Caribbean as could be
> She came across to visit us
> In Shoreham by the sea.

Once Gran arrives, she goes on a "digging spree" and finds "That the weeds were as weedy / That the seeds were as seedy" as the ones she left "back home." She demolishes the distance between Guyana and England. And in a playful inversion of the trope of the colonizers "planting" the flag of the old country in the "new" one to stake a claim, Nichols positions the Gran:

> Then she stood by a rose
> As a slug passed her toes
> And she called to my Dad
> As she struck pose after pose,
>
> "Boy, come and take my photo—the place cold,
> But wherever there's God's Earth, I'm at home."   (16–17)

In constructing "home" as something made of "God's earth" (Guyanese or English earth), Nichols strikes a postcolonial claim that mimics the colonial claim for king and country—reverses the colonial imposition of "home" explored by Claudia Marquis elsewhere in this volume. As Nobel laureate Derek Walcott says, we "earn home." In "Home: Our Famous Island Race" (one of the Reith lectures for BBC radio) author/critic Marina Warner glosses the idea of "earn[ing] home" to mean "using memory, imagination, language, to question, to remember and to repair, to wish things well without sentimentality, without rancour, always resisting the sweet seduction of despair" (94). That is what Nichols does—in both subject and language. The poem turns at the end, as Nichols lengthens the tidy iambic lines of English verse and roots the strong jazz stresses of Creole into the English landscape. She transforms English into an english. She "writes back" to the Empire and stakes a claim. The poem exemplifies transculturation: Nichols selects a trope from the dominant culture (planting the flag to stake a claim on a Caribbean beach) and transplants it (a photograph of a Caribbean granny presiding over an English rose in an English garden).

I switched back to "The Gardener," who makes the child narrator of Stevenson's poem "keep to the gravel walk." The child is in a garden for looking at rather than playing in. I realized why the garden of "Come on into My Tropical Garden" (the title poem of the collection) is the more desirable one for my own children. Nichols invites readers in to play:

> And yes you can stand up in my hammock
> and breeze out in my trees
> you can pick my hibiscus
> and kiss my chimpanzees
>
> O you can roll up in the grass
> and if you pick up a flea
> I'll take you down for a quick dip-wash
> in the sea   (3)

The reader is invited to "roll up in the grass," not something encouraged in the Stevenson gardens, which are for looking at through a window, as in "Night and Day," or through the parlor blinds, as in "Summer Sun."

I soon found other examples of transculturation. Stevenson's poems are often about boys' toys and possession: "My Ship and I," "My Kingdom," and "My Treasures." In contrast, Nichols speaks of the lives of girls, women, and the community in which they live: "They Were My People," "Granny Granny Please Comb My Hair," and "Wha Me Mudder Do." She imbues her subjects, combing a child's hair or cooking dinner, with the same poetic authority that Stevenson accords to subjects who own property.

Even the encomium Stevenson writes to his nanny (as a dedication) positions her only in relation to his ownership of her: "My second mother, my first wife" (I'll skip the Freudian commentary). Nichols, on the other hand, praises the mother of "Wha Me Mudder Do" for her domestic prowess inside and outside the house. On the domestic front, the "Mudder" fishes, catches crab, and cooks it into "calaloo stew." She also builds furniture: "Me mudder beat hammer / Me mudder turn screw." And paints it "red," then "blue." She fights unruly domestic animals: "Me mudder chase bad-cow / with one 'Shoo.'" But she also leaves the domestic site and has her own adventures: "she paddle down river / in she own canoe." Property and treasure do not enter into the picture. The "Wha Me Mudder Do" mother is very differently constructed from the Hallmark card version of Mother's Day–type mothers; or from Stevenson's invocation to his mother to read his verses so she can "hear once more / The little feet along the floor."

Even though I have set Nichols up in opposition to Stevenson, I want to acknowledge that Stevenson writes about women (besides his mother, he writes about his nanny and his aunt) and Nichols writes about men ("Moody Mister Sometimish" and "Old Man's Weary Thoughts"). I'm not trying to set feminism against colonialism. It would be churlish to devalue Stevenson solely on ideological grounds. *A Child's Garden of Verses* remains a classic for good reason (Bloom bestows canonicity on Stevenson's works, but not on *A Child's Garden of Verses*). Many of the poems continue to speak to the subjects of early childhood. "Bed in Summer," "Windy Nights," "My Shadow," and "The Swing" are poems to which my children return. They do so, I think, because the poems continue to speak to the strangeness of ordinary events, such as the way a shadow changes size depending on the time of day. As an adult, I know that the strangeness will soon wear away into the commonplace of life. But I suspect that the economy of Stevenson's verse will stay with my children long after the verse of trendier poets (Jack Prelutsky, for example) fades.

Aidan Chambers, in a letter, reminded me that it was Stevenson who gave a "different" voice to children's poetry, "claiming . . . something they had been denied too in the adult colonization of them that had gone on and still does." Chambers acknowledges that Stevenson's voice "may be cracked now and out of tune, certainly out of fashion, but the notes of it are retuned in Nichols." After I read the letter, I remembered that Chambers had been one of the judges for the *Signal* Poetry Award (Jan Mark was the other). It was his review of Nichols that had initially prompted me to buy *Come on into My Tropical Garden*. Still, I find it difficult to acknowledge the ideological shift from Nichols to Stevenson without diminishing Stevenson's work. I do not want to give the impression that Nichols is a better poet because of some accident of progress. Value is not measured like that. But it does help to remember that there have been massive cross-cultural movements in populations over the last hundred years, and those have determined shifts in value systems. As Caribbean poet and critic David Dabydeen points out, in the 1970s and 1980s, Britain became "the largest West Indian island after Jamaica and Trinidad" (12). With that ironic comment Dabydeen turns Britain into an outpost of Caribbean culture and the relation between margins and centers reverses itself. So does the colonial order.

The New Poetry, an important British anthology of poets who were born after 1940 and came into prominence after 1982, includes Nichols. In triangulating her position on the cultural map, the editors, Michael Hulse, David Kennedy, and David Morley, locate her not only with poets writing about their Caribbean heritage, but with poets exploring their Scots, Irish, and Welsh roots. The editors remark on similarities in "strategies and tone" between Nichols and, for example, the Anglo-French author Michèle Roberts. The prevalence of poets of diverse origins, they say, tends to undermine, in contemporary poetry, a notion of culture "based on isolated achievement and originality" (18). Thus what distinguishes the poets of *The New Poetry* is not their originality, but their pluralism, their ability to operate in the contact zone of culture. The editors do not speak, however, about the way much of the poetry of Grace Nichols has a "crossover" appeal for both children and adults—which just goes to show that even in the state-of-the-art cultural context of a noncanonical press like Blood-axe, poetry written for children remains in the colonial domain.

Nichols, it seems to me, embodies the spirit of the contact zone, which Pratt explains as "an attempt to invoke the spatial and temporal copresence of subjects previously separated by geographic and historical disjunctures, and whose trajectories now intersect" (*Imperial Eyes* 7). Nichols writes for adults and children. She writes in standard English and Creole. She mixes the two and writes in english. And in poems like "My Gran Visits England," the colonized redefine relations with the colonizer. Nichols foregrounds (to use Pratt's terms) "the interactive, improvisational dimensions of colonial encounters" (7) to destabilize the borders between adult and child, male and female, black and white, colonizer and colonized. In the foreword to *Poetry Jump-Up: A Collection of Black Poetry*, Nichols writes, "Some would argue that poetry has no colour and that one wouldn't dream of putting together an anthology of 'white poetry'. One might well say as a parallel to this, that the fact that one wouldn't need to describe an anthology of poems by men as 'men's poetry' as opposed to 'women's poetry' points to certain real issues of omission and neglect by the literary establishment and to the whole question of power" (7).

The poems in *Poetry Jump-Up* include those Nichols understands as being within the hearing of children, though some (such as one by David Dabydeen) are drawn from collections intended for adults. Like other poets who write across age-defined border lines (Charles Causley and Ted Hughes, for example), Nichols places some of her poems into both her books for adults and her books for children. Only the reader of all her work would be the wiser. "Sea Timeless" and "Mango" cross the adult/child divide, appearing in *The Fat Black Woman's Poems* (intended for adults) as well as *Come on into My Tropical Garden*. "My Black Triangle," discussed below, crosses the other way. It originally appeared in *Lazy Thoughts of a Lazy Woman* (for adults) and is included in a collection of poetry intended for adolescents, *Culture Shock*, edited by Michael Rosen.

In the contact zone, the authority of a stable, canonical text is diminished, partly because of what Pratt describes as "the unprecedented acceleration of two global-scale phenomena: immigration and communication—flows of people, flows of messages, flows of money" ("Criticism" 85). In Stevenson's world, communication was slower, and the border lines more clearly defined between adults and children, rich and poor, and servants and masters. Children (rich European and American ones, anyway) lived in nurseries, which were physically separate from the rest of the house and from adults (except for nannies). In Nichols's world, in our world, there is a constant flow between adults and children. Nothing much can be hidden from children who have access to television and the Internet. As we revise our collective understandings of what children are like, we also redescribe our memories of what children were like.

The landscape of memory is fickle. It changes, as Simon Schama monumentally documents in *Landscape and Memory*. Schama takes "moments of recognition" and excavates layers, so that, as he "scratches away" at what appear to be surface commonplaces, he discovers "bits and pieces of cultural design" (16). In "My Black Triangle," Nichols also discovers a "cultural design" by scratching away the surfaces of historical commonplaces. She appropriates the "master's voice" by writing in standard English and reclaims a fertile, female vision of the land:

> My black triangle
> sandwiched
> between the geography
> of my thighs
>
> is a bermuda
> of tiny atoms
> forever seizing
> and releasing
> the world
>
> My black triangle
> is so rich
> that it flows over
> on to the dry crotch
> of the world
>
> My black triangle
> is black light
> sitting on the threshold of the world
> overlooking my deep-pink
> probabilities
>
> and though
> it spares a thought
> for history

my black triangle
has spread beyond history
beyond the dry fears of parch-ri-archy

spreading and growing
trusting and flowing
my black triangle
carries the seal of approval
of my deepest self   (74–75)

The central political/topographical/anatomical conceit of the poem revisions colonial history. Nichols constructs what Pratt would call an "autoethnographic" text, one that enables the colonized subject to represent herself in a way that engages with the colonizer's own terms (7).

Because *Culture Shock,* which includes this poem, is intended for adolescents, the poem also revisions conventional ideas of what is "suitable" for adolescents. When I first taught "My Black Triangle" to students (most in their midtwenties) training to be teachers, there was a tense debate in class about whether the poem's sexual explicitness was appropriate for the raging hormones of adolescents.

In "My Black Triangle," Nichols rewrites the male, imperialist thrust of colonial empires spoiling the Caribbean island (she "spares a thought/for history"). She changes the direction of the colonial takeover, supplanting the colonial flag with her female, watery, black, fecund island: it flows over onto the "dry crotch of the world." The black triangle waters the dry "parch-ri-archy" that had sought to strip the Caribbean island of its natural assets. It also repositions the Bermuda triangle from a dangerous place to a fertile place. I also cannot help reading "pink probabilities" (from the version of the poem printed in *Culture Shock*), simultaneously, as pink genitalia, pink beaches, and English skin—perhaps made pink by the Caribbean sun.

The "black triangle" alludes not only to the Bermuda triangle but also to the fertile Nile overflowing its banks and becoming the source of the wealth of the land—and the source of civilization. As female pudenda, the black triangle also carries the idea of "the female body as the *fons et origo* of verdant life," as Schama says (273). I don't know whether Nichols was thinking of Gustave Courbet's famous 1866 painting of female pudenda, *The Origin of the World,* a picture of a black triangle, but I thought of it when I read the poem. Schama, citing Michael Fried's *Courbet's Realism,* makes the connection between Courbet's erotic black triangle painting and his landscape paintings of water-caves. Both return us, says Schama, to "Renaissance river grottoes, . . . where the secret of creation was promised in a fusion of wisdom and love" (374). However, unlike Nichols, who celebrates her subjectivity, Courbet reads women as objects of desire, in much the same colonial spirit as Charles Baudelaire, who, after a trip to Mauritius, wrote "Exotic Perfume," which includes the lines "I breathe the warm scent of your breast, I see / Inviting shorelines spreading out for me" (49).

One of Nichols's great gifts is that she changes the view of erotic landscapes. Unlike Baudelaire or Courbet looking in, she writes as an insider looking out. She turns us away from the colonial story of Caribbean islands harboring dangers to civilized men—from exotic women or from cannibals. The word *cannibal,* as Marina Warner reminds us in *Managing Monsters,* "was adopted from the people of 'Carib,' in whom Columbus confidently recognized the famed anthropophagi, or maneaters, of myth" (72). Nichols reconstructs Caribbean islands as fertile, redemptive places now repopulating and recultivating what used to be known as the Western world.

She also destabilizes the school version of colonial history, the one that valorizes the explorers and renders the natives in need of correction and protection. Nichols sees the possibility for restructuring history. In a poem titled "of course when they ask for poems about the 'realities' of black women," she writes,

> Maybe this poem is to say
> that I like to see
> we black women
> full-of-we-selves walking
>
> Crushing out
> with each dancing step
> the twisted self-negating
> history
> we've inherited .
> Crushing out
> with each dancing step   (*Lazy Thoughts of a Lazy Woman* 54)

In this passage, Nichols invokes a telling mix of standard English and Creole through her handling of the first person, both singular and plural. When Nichols uses "full-of-we-selves" she speaks standard Creole: an english in which the objects of a sentence are seen as "always dominated" or "governed" by the subject, in the way in which white Europeans governed the slaves, though Rastafarians have tried to reconfigure that usage by using "I" as both subject and object (Ashcroft et al. 49). Nichols takes a different linguistic approach. She begins this passage in standard English, with the narrator as subject: "I like to see." Then she recalls her history: "we black women," "full-of-we-selves." Even that is a pun as it contains pride, a sense of being "full of ourselves," and being small, "wee." Nichols finishes with the corrective, with the black women "crushing out" the "self-negating" history (standard English). The (self) recognition scene is rendered in grammatically correct standard English: "we've inherited." And in the recognition of the inherited origin is the possibility of earning—as Warner suggests—an alternative "home."

Nichols resists the victim mentality. In "The Battle with Language," she acknowledges the danger of "wallowing in 'Look what they've done to us.'" Instead, she writes about "black women with a surmounting spirit and with their own particular quirkiness and sense of humour" (284). These are the women who inhabit Nichols's poetry—the "fat black woman" of *The Fat Black Woman's Poems,* the "long memoried" woman of *i is a long memoried woman,* "Gran" of "My Gran Visits England." All these women "earn home," as does Nichols herself.

That home is the tropical garden of "Come on into My Tropical Garden." It is an inviting place: a place to eat ("my sugar cake"), drink ("my pine drink"), and be merry ("pick my hibiscus" and "kiss my chimpanzees"). It is a place where the imperialist imperatives of cleanliness, order, and obedience have lost their high value. You can "roll up in the grass," and if you "pick up a flea" (or otherwise get dirty) you can have a "quick dip-wash in the sea." My own children continue to love the licensed space of the tropical garden Nichols constructs. So do other children, as well as adults, across Canada and the United States with whom I share her poetry. Nichols speaks, in the idiom of a gifted poet, to the cultural sensibilities of those who have watched the dismantling of the old colonial world and are participating in a rearranged postcolonial society.

Nichols sees herself as one of the people in the contact zone of contemporary culture who are "creating and reshaping" myths for the new millennium. In "The Battle with Language," Nichols writes about that new mythology. "We have to offer our children," she says, "something more than gazing at *Superman 1, Superman 2, Superman 3* and possibly *Superman 4,* so that when they look out on the world they can also see brown and black necks arching toward the sun so they can see themselves represented in the miraculous and come to sing their being" (289). Coming "to sing their being." The line resonates with the embodiment of *jouissance,* to use the French feminist term (popular in the 1970s and 1980s) to designate pleasure: female, multiple pleasure. As Nichols is a poet who "come[s] to sing their being," it pleases me to be one of the people who comes to sing her being.

I hope I've addressed the anonymous reviewer's concerns (cited in the epigraph) as to why I've written about Grace Nichols. If not, I can offer a little story that speaks to my ability to pick "winners," poets likely to be famous enough so that s/he knows them.

At the oral examination for my Ph.D. (1984), one of the members of my examining committee asked me how I knew Ted Hughes, on whom I'd written my dissertation, was a famous poet. At the time, I thought it was obvious (though I answered politely). A few months later Hughes was made poet laureate.

C H A P T E R

Fictions of Difference
Contemporary Indian Stories for Children

Rajeswari Sunder Rajan

Recent intellectual historians have persuaded us that childhood and children's literature are concepts and categories with specific histories and cultures, and not "natural" entities inhabiting some timeless realm. This realization has altered both the critical attention directed at writing for children and, more radically, literary theories themselves. Reception studies, histories of women's writing, cultural studies, semiotics, psychoanalysis, linguistics, folklore, and anthropological studies have investigated childhood as well as its culture and in turn have altered, or further developed, their theoretical positions. It is within the broad parameters of feminist cultural studies that I explore, with deliberate ambiguity, the fictions of difference in writing for children in India.

I focus my analysis on two contemporary stories for children written by Indian authors and published in India. Indi Rana's book-length *Devil in the Dustbin* and Sigrun Srivatsava's short story "Trapped!", both written in English,[1] explore the concept and reality of differences of race, religious community, nationality, caste, gender, age, and species. Such exploration of difference is both fraught with contradiction and of the utmost significance for children's fiction produced in contemporary India. Therefore I begin this essay with consideration of the question of difference in relation to children. I then describe the scene of writing for children in India today. In my discussion of the two stories, I focus on questions of ideology and the postcolonial framing of the "national" and the "transnational" within the problematic of difference in children's texts in India today.

I

Writers who attempt the exploration of difference must first decide whether to represent difference as natural or constructed, real or imagined. The implications of these choices are theoretical as well as political. In this debate—central to feminist, antiracist, anti-imperialist, gay/lesbian, and nationalist theories—the "constructionist" position has generally been viewed as having liberatory potential. It argues that differences are "imagined," that is, culturally constructed as ideology and subject to historical change, thus challenging the "naturalist" position, which deterministically claims significant and unalterable differences among people of different races, sexes, genders. In disputing difference, constructionists do not deny the real effects of difference but identify the possibilities of resistance to and overthrow of the hierarchies that structure it.

One reason for the difficulty of representing difference as ideology to children is to be found in the contradictory ways children themselves are viewed "in ideology": as both singularly "free" of ideology, that is, of received ways of knowing, conditioned beliefs, taught wisdom; and particularly vulnerable to it, as a function of their dependence on adult guidance of their minds. Romanticism first popularized the now-prevalent view of childhood as the "innocent" condition of ignorance of difference. But if children's acknowledgment of difference is a "fall," it is also a necessary aspect of their socialization and identity formation. In the Lacanian sense, the relationship of difference to identity—that is, the recognition of the self (only) in distinction from the other—structures the world of children by constituting their entry into the symbolic. But difference typically appears in binary structures that also signal hierarchized values—and become the ground of social conflict.

The adult as parent or mentor functions as the agent of the child's initiation into difference. What role does the "progressive" children's book play in this process? The paradigmatic figure of the author of such books is the mother in Blake's poem "Little Black Boy." The child says,

> . . . I am black, but O! my soul is white;
> White as an angel is the English child,
> But I am black, as if bereav'd of light.
>
> My mother taught me underneath a tree,
>
> . . . .
>
> ". . . these black bodies and this sunburnt face
> Is but a cloud, and like a shady grove."
>
> . . . .

> And thus I say to little English boy:
> When I from black and he from white cloud free,
> And round the tent of God like lambs we joy,
>
> I'll shade him from the heat . . .
> .   .   .   .
> And be like him, and he will then love me.   (28–29)

Like the mother, the author of children's books must reconcile being adult, and hence complicit in leading the child reader toward recognition of difference, with being progressive, and hence committed to keeping intact his or her cognitive ignorance of it within the moral universe of "innocence." The author has recourse to two major strategies. One is the simultaneous teaching and unlearning of difference, the introduction of the child to the "reality" of difference followed by returning him or her to an "original" state of ignorance—which must now overlook or transcend it: a double teaching, both difficult and contradictory. An alternative strategy interprets "difference" in two different ways, one meaning dissimilarity, nonidentity, variety, or heterogeneity, and calling for acknowledgment, even celebration, as an aspect of the created world; and the other meaning inequality, opposition, and conflict, and requiring disavowal, as an aspect of human distortion of relationships. A complex distinction, it moves from the cognitive framing of reality to the diagnosis of social attitudes and the ordering of values. These difficult strategies create ambivalent effects in children's fiction.

The ambivalence is most visible in the negotiations the text must perform between hard truth and reassuring falseness, especially in the resolution to the situations of difference-and-conflict that the narrative constructs. Yet, formally, without such conflict there would be no narrative. Children's writing built on the Romantic view of the "fall" cannot withstand the claim that children-in-the-world always already "know" conflict grounded in difference and therefore that their imaginative world in fiction, if it is not to be bland, palliative, or simply false, must turn this often inchoate "knowing" into recognizable shapes as a preliminary to tackling the problems it poses. Rana's and Srivatsava's stories seek to reconcile the difficult alternatives available by framing a universe of cultural relativism and espousing liberal values of tolerance, sympathy, cosmopolitanism, and the recognition of universal human rights within the "fiction" of difference. Rana's *Devil in the Dustbin* promotes the relativistic outlook by showing that a devil too is human; Srivatsava's "Trapped!" reasserts the values of humanity after the young hero's difficult discovery that human beings can turn into devils, insensate, furious, and murderous. But neither story is free of contradiction or compromise in its exemplary representation of differences or of the values it promotes toward harmony or in the resolution it fashions for the narrative of conflict.

Constructionist theories of difference, Lacanian narratives of the symbolic, Romantic versions of childhood, liberal ideologies of multiculturalism, and the "plot" of conflict—these are the explanatory frames within which the problematic of children in difference may be viewed in contemporary Indian children's fiction.

II

Contemporary writings for children in India that reveal sensitivity to issues of difference are recent and self-conscious attempts to counter the common biases found in almost all institutions and practices. Differences of class, community, caste, religion, and language in this vast multicultural nation-state create social tension and recurrent conflicts. Equally tenacious as a social problem is discrimination against girls. Therefore sensitivity in the representation of difference assumes political significance. Testifying to the urgency that attends reform and innovation in writing for children, official bodies such as the National Council for Educational Research and Training and National Book Trust monitor textbooks, sponsor supplementary readers, study "local" knowledges, and translate and disseminate written material.

The majority of works written for children in India are educational in purpose (for example, textbooks, literacy and numeracy primers, postliteracy material, informative posters and magazines, and health and civic manuals) and are produced in Indian languages. Arguably, the most innovative and challenging new writing for children is found in the materials produced by the nonformal education centers run by voluntary organizations that engage with the problems of difference as an aspect of development activities,[2] and the most reactionary and stereotyped ways of seeing are reproduced in the larger proportion of formal teaching material.

Imaginative literature intended specifically for children is not part of Indian literary tradition. Adults do of course tell their children stories drawn from a vast repertoire of folk narratives, religious myth and legend, and local and regional histories, but these are not exclusively children's stories. Filled with rich fantasy and marked by narrative intricacy—as in the ancient *Panchatantra*[3]— they amply fulfill the imaginative requirements of stories for children, but the didactic function of children's literature is blurred. Printed texts targeting child readers are few and recent. Story texts in English represent an even smaller proportion of children's literature in India.[4]

It is not only numerically that these texts are insignificant. The emphasis on school texts marginalizes leisure reading for children—so much so that storybooks must appear under the guise of supplementary readers with specific "educational" inputs, in order to appeal to teachers and parents as acceptable reading for children. In addition, the recent explosion in entertainment television through the arrival of foreign cable networks—even though programming specifically for children is sparse—has meant that reading is no longer a significant leisure activity among children. This marginalization, not to say neglect, of imaginative children's writing is reflected in the low sales of children's books (whether to libraries or individuals). All the same, there are trends in this kind of fiction worth noting because they signal change, or the desire for change, in the situation of and attitudes toward children.

The child who reads English-language books is a product of the "English-medium" public school (that is, the private school where the medium of instruction is English), supported by the Indian middle class. Until recently, the only imaginative literature available was imported from Britain or the United States, so that books popular in the Anglo-American West provided the staple of the Indian child's leisure reading as well. The scene today shows an increase in the number of Indian writers writing about India for children and in the number of commercial publishers (in addition to state-sponsored bodies) publishing their work. This development reflects the situation of Indian fiction in English in general in the 1980s and 1990s after the appearance of Salman Rushdie's landmark *Midnight's Children* (1981). Though the majority of children's books in India are adaptations, retellings, and even comic-strip renderings of Hindu myths, classics, and folklore or are Indianized versions of children's genres popular in the West (school stories and adventure and detective stories, for example), a small number are now specifically written from within a realistic, contemporary Indian context. It is this category to which *Devil in the Dustbin* and "Trapped!" belong.

Thus, on one hand, children's literature in English in India must be viewed as an aspect of the current surge in imaginative writing in English, even though as writing for children it suffers from devaluation as a marginalized leisure activity. On the other hand, it must also be viewed in conjunction with the fresh attention to universal primary education and adult literacy in the Indian state's developmental agenda. The two extremely divergent literary products—expensive English-language storybooks for upper-class children in public school, and nonformal educational materials for rural or urban working children who are not in school—may share a progressive purpose and ideology and even authorship. Rana exemplifies this conjuncture, being both a consultant in a rural communication project and an established children's writer in English.

The majority of Indian writers of children's fiction are women, for reasons that undoubtedly have to do with their putative understanding of the child "sensibility" and the marginalization of such writing as literature. Still, the gendered division of authorship, like the divide between writers for adults and writers for children, is not as extreme in the English-language children's fiction in India as it is in the West. For example, Rushdie has himself written a delightful children's book, *Haroun and the Sea of Stories*, a profoundly allegorical fable about censorship and imaginative literature; Vikram Seth, another major contemporary Indian novelist and poet in English, has produced a lighthearted collection of verse for children called *Beastly Tales from Here and There*. The novelist Ruskin Bond is one of the most enduring and prolific of children's fiction writers. Prominent women novelists—Anita Desai and Shashi Deshpande, among others—also write fiction for children. The English-educated middle-class Indian woman today is a significant consideration also as the major buyer of children's books, and her liberal political preferences are reflected in the carefully progressive gender and secular positions adopted by both Rana and Srivatsava, who are fairly representative of the class of women for and by whom English fiction for children in India is written.

As fiction in English, these texts signal—beyond their class elitism—a class-derived secularism that is a function of the role of English as a national language (see Dhareshwar). As one of the two official languages of postindependence India, English functions as a link language in a federation of multilinguistic states. Therefore fiction in English has implicitly come to represent a literature that is "Indian" as opposed to "regional." Srivatsava's "Trapped!" draws on this assumption of a secular "Indian identity" among middle-class (educated, English-speaking) citizens to counter the phenomenon of religious animosity between sectarian groups that provokes pogroms and riots. (She is careful to show, however, that this secularism is not antireligious, or even agnostic.) English is also the language of the cosmopolitan postcolonial intelligentsia, in particular those who travel to the West to study or work. A significant portion of the Indian immigrant community in the West is made up of upwardly mobile aspirants to the professional and material rewards of the "affluent society." Rana's *Devil in the Dustbin* (like her second book for young adults, *The Roller Birds of Rampur*) is written explicitly for this Indian immigrant community, who must cope with the experience of racism and come to terms with the problems of deracination, such as knowing only English. Thus, in postcolonial fiction, English implicitly addresses the problems of conflict among groups within the nation and between racial/national identities by encoding a nationalist secularism and an internationalist cosmopolitanism.

III

Rana's *Devil in the Dustbin,* written for ten- to twelve-year-olds, is a fable of transnational travel and exile originally published in Britain and clearly intended for children of immigrant Indians. The eponymous devil in the dustbin is Chellappa, a small, green-skinned, red-eyed, black-fanged spirit visible only to sympathetic (usually young) human beings. Chellappa is a *puliamchedi brahmarakshasha,* or tamarind tree–dwelling spirit. Transported by accident from his tamarind tree home in Madras and deposited in a dustbin in Wimbledon, England, he is forced to adapt and adopt an elm tree in order to survive. Despite his new elm tree dwelling and his friendships with other nature spirits and the little human girl, Ranjana, who takes care of him, his extreme homesickness leads him to accompany Ranjana back to India on her next trip home. Once in India, Chellappa realizes that his old safe affiliations—with his caste, his friends and family, his neighborhood, even his old tamarind tree—have vanished. Now irrevocably "cosmopolitan," a "citizen of the world," he returns to England—to his elm tree and neighborhood spirit friends—with Ranjana and her family, who have come to the same realization. Henceforth he will be a traveler between two worlds.

In this story, Rana invokes the proliferation of differences entailed by the cross-cultural interchange as the traveler encounters new climates, flora and fauna, languages, customs, dress, and food that challenge received ways of knowing and living. In exploring the migrant condition, Rana poses questions of different allegiances and loyalties. In addition, she explores other oppositions—those between human and supernatural beings, adults and children, boys and girls, country and city, as well as different castes—and identifies the various ways in which human (and spirit) beings negotiate these differences. Less programmatic in the story than my paraphrase suggests, Rana's touch is light, humorous, tactful, and moderate.

The central issue of the story, the problems of the immigrant living in a foreign land, is represented by the tree spirit Chellappa (the accidental tourist) and his human counterpart Ajoy, Ranjana's older brother. In contrast to these two, Ranjana is well adjusted and happy in England, having been born and raised there. She is the Blakean child, a being who has faith in the supernatural and is thus the only human privileged to see Chellappa and to mediate between him and the world; she possesses the wisdom to understand and solve the problems of adjustment experienced by Ajoy and Chellappa. Ranjana's behavior is identified as characteristically female by her brother, who dismisses her as a "silly girl!" Yet Rana gives the same kind of wisdom to the fairy Miss Pennyworth, the "direct descendant of King Oberon," as well as to the central narrator.

Typically, the psychology of male adolescence impels Ajoy's distrust and competitiveness toward his English peers; similarly, it is the life of hard struggle with trees and rivalry with his fellow tree spirits that Chellappa misses most in England. (The English elm tree, in contrast to the fierce young tamarind trees in India, is characterized as "peaceful and graceful.") If adjustment is the product of the female child's intuitive wisdom, and negative immigrant attitudes are specifically gendered male and linked with adolescent aggression, then the working out of hostility—its virtual exorcism, as the dream experience of the English boy Alec makes clear—and submission to and acceptance of difference entail the twin processes of feminization and the unlearning of adult values.

Two problems pervade the immigrant experience that Ajoy and Chellappa experience: a painful longing for the home country, accompanied by dismay at the strangeness of the new country, and subjection to racial prejudice. Rana deals with the first as a process that requires time and changes in the immigrant's attitudes in order to be overcome. Eventually Ajoy and Chellappa discover, in the course of their longed-for visit to India, that they wish to return to England after all: "It was strange coming back to this cold, damp, grey country . . . because it suddenly felt like home. And that really confused me" (107), says Chellappa of his second, voluntary, passage to England.

Alongside this personal revelation, *Devil in the Dustbin* proposes that it is a moral necessity to escape parochialism and develop broad-mindedness through travel and residence abroad. "He [Ajoy] thinks that if he stays here [i.e., in India] now he'll become somehow smaller." Chellappa agrees: "There will be a time when our hearts will become bigger and we'll have a whole new world" (106).

The strength of this narrative resolution to exile is undercut by the force and conviction with which Rana represents the condition of homesickness as a poignant and actual physical sickness. Chellappa describes it thus: "I began to feel ill. . . . I dreamed of the young tamarind tree in Madras, and how hard it had fought, and how its bark felt to my touch. And I woke just aching to be back home" (48). A painful realization accompanies the protagonist's later acceptance of the new country, the price at which it is achieved: the loss of his original affiliations and the safety, comfort, and emotional satisfactions they provided and, worse, the rejection by his community (for Chellappa, his fellow spirits; for Ajoy, his cousins), which is felt as defeat. To belong everywhere is, in a sense, to belong nowhere. The satisfactions of the new life achieve only the thin resonance of sour grapes rather than a full and inherent meaningfulness.

Nevertheless, we might describe such a resolution as a compromise rather than a contradiction and find it acceptable at the level of verisimilitude. The other major problem of immigrant life, racism, is more intractable in children's fiction. Rana faces the familiar problem in representing racial difference: she must reproduce stereotypes even while repudiating them as a negative and reductive way of knowing the Other. When writing about the international community of nature spirits, for example, she resorts to easily recognizable linguistic inflections of English as the easiest way to designate different nationalities—Indian, Caribbean, East European, and Chinese, for example— though, like much stereotyping, this is done with benign and humorous intent and effects.

Representations of racial conflict informed by liberal sympathies work well in certain respects in fiction for children. Rana's painstaking explanation of how negative racial stereotypes gain currency would undoubtedly help the immigrant child refuse and even contest them, while the child of racist parents is helped to understand, from the other side, how ill founded they are. As an instance of the latter, Alec, the son of the Bannerjees' English neighbors, believes that "Asians are dirty" on the basis of "what he sees," but what he sees is conditioned by what he expects to see, a sophisticated point. Alec, like Chellappa and Ajoy, eventually learns to see without preconceptions. This resolution of conflict through personal conversions or changes in relationships leaves the structural problem of racism intact, however. Rana recognizes that the proximity created by common schools, play areas, and workplaces causes competition, fear, anxiety, prejudice, and hostility between resident and alien communities. She confronts this reality by invoking, first, globalism—that is, the argument that "our world is becoming smaller and problems in one place affect everyone, everywhere" (69)—and second, universalism—that is, the belief that "under our differences we are all the same" (106). Geographical smallness versus vastness, proximity versus distance, and neighborhoods versus nations—these options are translated into the opposed political, moral, and visionary categories of prejudice, discrimination, and hostility versus tolerance, true knowledge, and universalism.

If harmonious coexistence in multicultural societies depends on liberal values for implementation, then the philosophical frame that will hold them is cultural relativism. By making Chellappa belong to an order of being altogether different from the human, Rana is able to illustrate how narrow our (human) judgment of measures and values may be. About his age, for instance, Chellappa says, casually, "After all, I was only 1758 years old. Young, for a brahmarakshasha" (45). Recognizing that skin color is the most visible, indeed flagrant, sign of racial difference, Rana uses Chellappa's colorful appearance as a way of deconstructing the black-white opposition. Even as Chellappa preens over his green skin and black fangs, he concedes that he may not be a human ideal: "I'm green, which I know you think isn't the most attractive colour to be, but it suits us creatures who live in trees. I've got, I think, a dashing smile, but unfortunately, humans who see me seem not to think so. . . . when I smile they usually faint dead away with a piercing shriek. . . . All in all, from the human point of view I'm not a lovely sight. But among brahmarakshashas I'm known as a handsome devil" (15–16).[5]

The limits and contradictions of liberalism in the context of multicultural societies have been widely discussed in recent philosophical debates (see Taylor et al.). My point is that these values carry conviction in the story written for children. There is strategic effectiveness in the way Rana draws the limits of her fictional world, within which the world of adult human beings is bracketed doubly—as both exclusion and frame. By figuring children and spirits as protagonists open to these values, she suggests their difference from—and superiority to—adult human beings, with their hegemonic constructions of difference (which the gnome Zielinski describes as "that stupid 'us-them' business humans get into!" [77]).

In addition to the psychological verisimilitude and the ethical force with which Rana negotiates the problems of immigration, racism, and multicultural coexistence for the child reader, she raises the question of the historical understanding of these issues. Rana uses the broad category of "difference" as a heuristic device to draw parallels between racism in Britain and casteism in India. (The book was reprinted in India under Penguin India's Puffin Books imprint, in all likelihood because of its perceived expanded relevance to readers in India.) Further, by juxtaposing casteism in Indian society with its irrelevance in the Indian diaspora, Rana productively distinguishes between affiliations that we may term primordial and voluntary commitments to new forms of community and political struggle made in response to historical pressures. Individuals' "original" affiliation to a caste, a linguistic community, a race, or a nation locates them within a setting that "naturally," and hence painlessly, shapes their identity and commands their loyalties. While fixed loyalties and identities may be jeopardized as the Third World diaspora creates new definitions of location—home, neighborhood, workplace, ghettos, margins, centers—in Rana's story openness accrues value and carries historical significance.

But by addressing the problems of traditional Indian social organization in the context of modernity, that is, postcolonial migrancy, Rana also connects the two: through Chellappa's example, she argues the belief that the outmoded social practice of caste will go away when Indian people are subjected to the historical changes of modernity, such as globalism. As migrants cope with the new problems of cultural adjustment, it is believed, they will leave behind the old problems of their "national" histories. But what we have seen instead is the revival of religious, linguistic, and cultural orthodoxies among "Third World" immigrant communities in the West: a fundamentalism that is the beleaguered nativistic response to a First World hegemonistic modernity defined by industrial capitalism. In positing the migrant's change of identity from an "original" caste/community/nation to a new cosmopolitanism, Rana neglects the actual historical realities of Asian immigrant communities in Britain, which contradict the belief in such an easy conversion. Postcolonialism and transnationalism cannot be read in the uncomplicated light of historical progress.

Cultural relativism has similar problematic theoretical implications when we look beyond its underpinning of liberal communitarianism, in that it feeds into postmodern celebrations of migrancy as freedom from history, as the choice rather than historical necessity of residence/citizenship, and as the privileged perspective of the cosmopolitan exile. Aijaz Ahmad condemns Rushdie's novels for precisely this quality of postmodern historical irresponsibility (127–32). Rana moves into the postmodern frame via several moves. First, she makes a virtue of the immigrant's necessity for "adjustment" in the new country. (The historical compulsions of immigration, such as jobs and political exile, are not touched on, since the protagonists are children, who have simply accompanied their parents to Britain, and spirits, whose travels are fantastical.) Next, the negative aspects of uprooting—homesickness, alienation, and the like—are "overcome," and a progressive, "modern," secular, and cosmopolitan outlook replaces the immigrant's earlier parochialism. Finally, as a definition of the diasporic condition itself comes the assertion that migrants do not have to choose between their two countries, but can become perpetual travelers between them and thereby gain the best of both worlds—or what Ahmad describes as an "excess of belonging" (130). For the intended child readers of this posthistorical narrative, the denial of historical identity serves as a consolatory fiction.

IV

Srivatsava's "Trapped!", which appeared in a children's literature supplement of the *Book Review,* is one of a collection of adventure stories entitled *Danger in the Mountains.* Based on the riots in Delhi in 1984 that followed the assassination of Prime Minister Indira Gandhi, in which the Sikh community was attacked by Hindu mobs and more than two thousand male Sikhs were killed, the story narrates the events of one fearful night of communal violence as seen through the eyes of Ranjit, a young Sikh boy. Ranjit and his family—his mother, brother, and grandmother—are hiding in their house from the rampaging mobs. When the attackers enter the house, it seems they are led by a young Hindu neighbor and friend, Surinder Sharma, whom Ranjit had always liked and admired. Ranjit's anger at Surinder's betrayal is quickly replaced by gratitude as he realizes that Surinder is only pretending to be part of the vengeful mob in order secretly to help Ranjit and his family escape to his own house. The story ends with Surinder's restoration of the family's Sikh holy book, the revered *Adi Granth,* to Ranjit's mother and his sorrowful announcement that he was unable to save the old grandmother.

Friendship, neighborliness, and the innate goodness of human nature reassuringly resist the hatred and violence generated by communal conflict; violence is attributed to mob feelings, insensate fury, the drunkenness of the rioting men, or their instigation by others.[6] Thus the terms of the irrational are used to explain the sudden disruption of normality. Srivatsava endorses these beliefs by exemplifying goodness in the Hindu neighbor, Surinder, and his family, and by making Ranjit's mother the sympathetic diagnostician of this situation, saying, "It is neither the neighbours nor our friends who seek revenge. It's a group of misled fanatics, driven by personal grievances against society. They stir the mob, they poison their minds and spark off these fires of violence" (17). Like the mother in Blake's "Little Black Boy," she mediates between the child and the hostility of the real world and performs the authorial surrogate function of providing reassurance and renewal of faith to the child (protagonist/reader). By interposing the shield of adult explanation in gendered, maternal terms, between the male child and his exposure to collective adult male aggression, Srivatsava spares the child from a traumatic entry into male adulthood, or at least delays it.

This resolution is reassuringly humanistic, but it is not necessarily false for that reason, or, at any rate, it is not false when measured against the facts of the situation. On the contrary, stories of neighborhood solidarities and sacrifice by Hindus on behalf of Sikhs were widely reported during the rioting as a way of asserting the decency of the common people even in times of communal conflict. And many commentators tended to view communal riots as either irrational or instigated, denying any real agency to the rioters (see Taylor et al.'s collection of essays). I want instead to ask other questions, locate other contradictions in the story.

There is, first, the passage in the text that narrates Ranjit's longing for his father's presence and protection at the height of his terror: "He wished his father were here. . . . Oh, how he wished his father were here, if only for a while, for a few minutes, till everything was over" (18). Nothing could be more psychologically realistic than this longing, given the traditional gender ascription of the role of protector of the family to its male head. However, there is a particular reason why Srivatsava created an absent father in this text: in the riots of 1984, male Sikhs were systematically hunted out from their houses and killed. Had Ranjit's father been present in the house, not only would he have been in great danger, but he undoubtedly would have endangered his sons' lives rather than saved them. (But we note that because the heroic Surinder substitutes for Ranjit's absent father as savior in the narrative of danger, the traditional connections among masculinity, heroism, and homosocial bonding are not entirely disavowed in the unique construction of the case.) Srivatsava implicitly invites the reader's knowledge of an *hors texte* to lend an almost unbearable irony to the passage; this unspoken knowledge acts in the way a censored passage in a text often does when one knows of the censorship, as a gesture toward the unmentionable. The ironic knowledge therefore undercuts the reassurance that is the message of the story.

But there is a scapegoat offered up to the "realistic" requirements of the story, the victim who must die in the interests of narrative credibility: the old grandmother. Of course, a Darwinian logic justifies this dispensation: unable to escape, expendable because of her age, gender, and lack of sentimental function, the grandmother is no great loss for the family or the narrative in which she figures so briefly. (In the narrative of violence, women have at best a fragile presence: as Srivatsava recognizes, even the mother's presence and her pedagogic authority do not adequately substitute for the absent father's protection in the child's time of need.)

But though the grandmother dies, the holy book is saved. This substitution is interesting because of the priorities it indicates within the secular ideology that Srivatsava promotes. In India, secularism is the desired and official antidote to sectarian conflict arising from regional, religious, linguistic, caste, and other differences. Typically, it is understood as tolerance of all communities, regardless of one's own affiliations. Surinder's rescue of a different religious community's holy book, and Srivatsava's highlighting of this as the story's climactic resolution, must be understood in this light. The author could not have treated religion as irrelevant in this context without being accused of another, negative kind of secularism, one equated with irreligion, skepticism, and bad aspects of modernity.[7] Thus the grandmother's death, however gratuitous in actual terms, substitutes within the narrative for the death of the father and the destruction of the holy book, both of which are thereby averted.

The happy ending of "Trapped!", which is indicated by a Hindu boy's rescue of his Sikh neighbors and their holy book, may also be read as a formal requirement of the children's adventure story, a genre that typically conducts the (child) protagonist through a variety of dangers and narrow escapes into safety. The protagonist of such stories is often relatively passive, as in this instance, serving only as a reflecting and suffering consciousness, while the actual heroism and initiative may be given to an older, or adult, hero (Robert Louis Stevenson's *Treasure Island* is a case in point). The adventure story cannot, of course, be expected to plumb the depths of emotional disturbance that the child is likely to experience after his adventures. Recent research in India reveals that child survivors of communal riots are profoundly traumatized and may harbor deep feelings of hatred for, and fantasies of revenge against, their attackers. Srivatsava lies only by omission when she opts for a narrative conclusion that stops at the boy's immediate escape into safety and does not hint at the aftermath of the night's happenings. Clearly, the narrative modes available to writers of children's fiction, such as adventure or fantasy (as in *Devil in the Dustbin*), negotiate representations of difference in ways other than that of stark realism. These alternatives are invoked both as cognitive structures accessible to children within familiar textual frames of reference and as formal alibis for the mitigated representation of the full consequences of conflict. My point in discussing the tensions in "Trapped!" is to indicate how another knowledge—which the contemporary child reader in India who has recently lived through these experiences may be expected to possess—would impinge on the narrative's formal and ideological thrust. This reader may be responsive to the excitement of the adventure narrative, as well as its message of faith in human goodness, or he or she may read it as a darker, ironically sentimental "fiction" of difference. A postcolonial nationalism that expresses itself in the desire for a unitary nation, as opposed to sectarian conflict and division, harbors contradictions at its core that are reflected in the fictions it fashions for children.

The two texts I have discussed here as representative of contemporary children's stories in English in India exemplify these difficulties in spite of the great sensitivity to the issues of race and communalism they display. They risk reducing difference to a problem of human behavior and attitude, resolvable fictionally in ethical and psychological terms. But difference is not a "problem" that can be tackled head on, as it were, by representing situations requiring problem-solving strategies of fictional resolution. It is less judgments of political correctness that one seeks to arrive at in responding to questions of difference in writing for children, than acknowledgment of the difficulties of the project.

Making the Front Page
Views of Women/Women's Views in the Picture Book

William Moebius

Where images resist the totalitarian word; where the semiotic *chora*,[1] or the space of unlimited possibilities for the significance of the image, as these are attached to feminine subjects or feminine agency, takes precedence over the logos, dances before it, and subverts it; where female characters emerge as complex agents of change and renewal; where female authors and author-illustrators challenge their male counterparts and invite new interpretations of feelings and notions of authority—these are the front lines of my inquiry. I inquire as well into the stances that picture books, of both male and female authorship, take toward girls and women, engendering a body and a way of thinking about gender.

Women's contributions to the images of the picture book, not to mention to its text, may be greater than histories of children's and adults' literature have acknowledged.[2] As Trina Robbins chronicles in her fascinating and richly documented *A Century of Women Cartoonists,* in the United States women were, from the early 1900s on, actively producing cartoon art that featured child characters. From Rosie O'Neill's Kewpies to Grace Weiderseim/Drayton's Toodles and Dimples to Marge Henderson's Little Lulu, the world of children was portrayed in a cartoon art that was the resistant woman's take on the gendered conventions of her times. It was a sentimental art, but so was Walter Crane's and Kate Greenaway's; it favored light humor, a gentle nudge and occasional punch at the man's world that had the upper hand at the bank. It was not yet quite in picture book format. I turn to the picture book, then, as a site where women struggled for authority in a world in which men largely controlled the means of production, the presses, the paper, the banks, the bookstores: only in schools and bookstores might some women find leverage.

As Leonard Marcus demonstrates, two important leaders in picture book innovation emerged from the Bank Street Writers Laboratory in New York City: in the 1920s, Lucy Sprague Mitchell (1878–1967), who had been the first dean of women and first instructor in English at the University of California at Berkeley, and, in the 1930s, Margaret Wise Brown (1910–1952), Mitchell's student. Mitchell's theory of child language development found its signal demonstration in Brown's writings. Both authors challenged the "male-order"[3] narrative tradition of the storyteller, first with Mitchell's groundbreaking *Here and Now Story Book* and later with Brown's nonnarrative Noisy Books and the famous *Goodnight Moon*. In its repetitions, Brown's work bears tribute to Gertrude Stein. (Brown recommended to her senior editor and publisher that he solicit a manuscript from Stein, who sent a version of *The World Is Round*.) It is a tribute, too, to the broken borders and collapse of narrative structure Brown must have admired in the middle chapter of one of her favorite author's books, *To the Lighthouse*. For Brown, the picture book was a place to put the "wildest and best words into literature" (Marcus 99). While a critic as acute as Jacqueline Rose is troubled by the deceptions inflicted on children by male modernists (42–65), Marcus highlights the favorable influences of Stein and Virginia Woolf: "The modernist aesthetic of recreating in art the immediacy of sensory impressions seemed to coincide with young children's natural reliance on their senses as the primary means of both experiencing and expressing themselves about the world" (86).

Going it alone, creating both text and illustration themselves, Esphyr Slobodkina (1908–ㅤ) and Wanda Gág (1893–1946) put their Eastern European narrative folk art in the service of the American picture book. In Sweden, Elsa Beskow (1874–1953) gave impetus to the remarkable progress of the Scandinavian picture book, inaugurated by such distinguished contemporaries as Ottilia Adelborg and Jenny Nyström, as vividly reported by Kristin Hallberg and Boel Westin.

Although it is certainly worth celebrating the virtuosity of women producing their own picture book texts and illustration, it may be instructive to focus momentarily on the books women jointly produced with male illustrators. A number of female picture book authors produced scenarios, concepts, and written texts but did not illustrate their own work. The man's role (for Leonard Weisgard, Charles Shaw, Garth Williams, or the likes of Clement Hurd, a former student of Fernand Léger) was to second, to augment with illustrations the force of the woman's text.[4] In keeping with the primacy of text, the author's name remains the key to the library's classification of the book, regardless of the illustrator's pervasive or invasive treatment. A picture book written by Charlotte Zolotow and illustrated by Maurice Sendak, William Pène du Bois, or Eric Blegvad would be *by* Charlotte Zolotow, perhaps not only because, like Brown, she was a talented editor but because her words constituted the stamp of her authority. In such instances, it could be said the woman was spinning the story, talking to the reader, while the man peered over her shoulder, looking into, or even through, the text, interrupting it, coining it with his values, and putting a face on it, a visual return. What took Brown a morning or perhaps a week to produce, in between her editorial chores and her many excursions to Europe, would take Clement Hurd months to illustrate (Marcus 184, 189, 190).

Perry Nodelman goes so far as to argue that Sendak's pictures for Zolotow's *Mr. Rabbit and the Lovely Present* (1962) redeem a text he finds "a mechanical juggernaut that repeats and repeats itself—repeats itself so constantly and regularly that it comes to sound as if it is being told by a computer with a loose screw." For Nodelman, "the mood of Sendak's light-filled picture implies a calm peace that takes over and controls any of the possibly negative implications of the text" (*Words* 89, 90). In the list of books he cites, Nodelman puts the illustrators' names first. This has an impact, no doubt unintentional, on the visibility of the women authors of a number of the picture books he cites.

The partnership between the female writer and the male illustrator (or vice-versa) could be difficult or blissful, mutually compensatory or mutually challenging. Perhaps most illuminating are the difficult cases of a few picture book couples, spouses in life and art, in which the woman's role seems remarkably decisive. In this essay, I look at the collaborations of three such couples and one less divided, before taking a closer look at a one-woman show and a sampling of representations of the feminine by male authors and illustrators.

L I S S A   P A U L singles out the trickster as a figure feminists can reckon with as they look for the hidden cause, the woman or the child, in the cracks of folklore and literature ("Enigma Variations" 153, 154). Hans A. Rey (1898–1977) has long been celebrated for his invention of one of the most endearing and intriguing tricksters (or almost)[5] of the twentieth century, Curious George. Rey's name alone appears on all but two books in the series. Ten years after his death, his widow Margret (1904–1996) participated in festivities celebrating the fiftieth anniversary of Curious George's first appearance. At age 81, Margret was ready to disclose to interviewer Deane Lord that it was she who served as the model for George: "All my life I spent standing behind Hans at his drawing board. . . . I made all of the movements George makes" (42). But Margret animated more than the monkey. "She says she literally pulled each book out of him. 'Hans was the artist, a genius and a dreamer,' Rey says. 'He loved animals. We both did. When I say "pull," I mean he had them all inside. I'd write the text, supervise the drawings—you might say I was the midwife or the art director'" (42). That he was not particularly disciplined or committed to this work helps to explain the somewhat bicameral effects of the Curious George books: what Margret the writer would legislate (George is too curious, George is naughty), Hans the picture boy would, with his model's collaboration, set aside in the name of a higher freedom (George looks happy only when he is high. . .).[6] Margret initiated, cajoled, composed, posed, performed, conducted; Hans subverted. Margret's textual universe is, at least in the early books, neatly divided between the vulnerability of the little-too-curious monkey and the authority of the man with the yellow hat seconded by his fellow law-abiding citizens. Hans's visual world is one of a frequently smiling monkey amid hundreds of admiring spectators, including law enforcement officers: George is, after all, one might say in the Reys' native German, *ein Fräulein* dressed up like a monkey, and the issue here is not law and order but the rule of instinct. Remarkably, the unnamed Margret would enable the named Hans to perform his acts of liberation by undoing her words, stripping them of their stark authority as she modeled for George. In their relationship, as Margret makes clear in the Lord interview, it was she who was the shaker and mover, Hans the shaken and moved, the spectator to her spectacle.

The relationship was inverted for a second picture book couple, Russell (1925–   ) and Lillian (1925–1998) Hoban, who wrote and illustrated, respectively, the well-loved "Frances" books. In these stories, Frances is often at odds with other girls, her sister Gloria or her friend Thelma. At one moment Frances is the very spirit of lyricism, and the next she is the most troublesome spoiler. One hesitates to read the text as a critique of women, but one cannot help noticing the animus in lines such as these from Thelma in *A Bargain for Frances* (1970):

> She never got the tea set.
> That is what happens.
> A lot of girls
> never do get tea sets.
> So maybe you won't get one.   (25)

Read aloud without reference to Lillian's pictures, Russell's sophisticated text can be taken as mean, even cynical. Nothing in the text reveals the species of the speakers; only feminine gender and moral error are conveyed. The speakers have the traits of feisty survivors and might convincingly have been represented as snapping turtles or as cagey devils like those in *The Far Side*. As if to confirm that the author might be a difficult man for a woman to live with, Selma Lanes reports that after a fight with Lillian, Russell left to live with Maurice Sendak for a month (29–32). The Hobans later divorced.

And how do Lillian's pictures "live with" Russell's text? Her furry creatures with big eyes dull the edge of Russell's fury. The quiet aloofness of her badgers turns moral error into innocent confusion, well meaning and harmless. One is reminded of Woolf's account (echoing her mother) of Mrs. Ramsay's reign of calm in the face of Mr. Ramsay's reign of terror. The cover picture of the Hobans' *A Bargain For Frances* shows a smiling badger in black and white between an upper field of pink and a lower field of blue, holding at her waist a tray or basket with pink vertical stripes on its rim and with the blue scallop shades of a tea set on top. The female Frances appears to be mediating the difference between the lower, blue domain and the upper, pink one: the male and female. But the story, in black and white with blue wash as a highlight, features four female characters whose language consistently undermines its own reliability. Frances's mother warns her about Thelma: "because when you play with Thelma you always get the worst of it" (12). Gloria denies the value of Frances's purchase of a plastic tea set: "That is a very ugly tea set" (34). Thelma cons Frances into believing that real china tea sets are no longer available: "I don't think they make them anymore. . . . I know another girl who saved up for that tea set. Her mother went to every store and could not find one" (24). Frances cons Thelma into believing that Thelma had sold her a plastic tea set with a lot of money in the sugar bowl: "I don't have to say how much money is in the sugar bowl" (47). Russell's text stresses the untrustworthiness of feminine discourse.[7] Even the mother's "Be careful" to Frances at the beginning is undermined by Frances's challenge to Thelma at the end: "Do you want to be careful or do you want to be friends?" (55).

Is masculinity represented in the text? Something almost unsaid to balance the negative evidence of womanly wiles? Perhaps. Frances takes her dolls to Thelma's house. "She took her alligator doll and her elephant doll. She took her snake doll and her teddy bear too" (14). It is one thing to qualify the words "alligator" and "snake" with the word "doll." It is another thing to portray them on a page in which "I want" leads the way in the text and, in the accompanying picture, a snake's tail lies in the jaws of an alligator. It is Lillian who puts the snake and alligator that lurk behind Thelma and Frances (19) and below Frances (24) in the service of a traditional symbolism of greed, envy, and temptation. On

The snake whispers.

page 19, the snake appears to be whispering in Frances's right ear; on page 31, it whispers in the alligator's ear. Frances's tea party, which they attend, reminds us of *Alice's Adventures in Wonderland;* Alice celebrates "the little crocodile" and is said by the Pigeon to be a serpent. These companions of Frances, although not specifically gendered in the text, match in number (four) the number of gendered female characters. In the absence of textual gender markings, but given the visual reference to the figure of the tempter on pages 19 and 31, it may make sense to connect Frances's inner circle of "party animals" with a band of associates from the once male-controlled world of ownership and exchange. The storekeeper (37–38) might just be the only male badger in the book, and it is he who, as a broker, helps Thelma betray Frances. Russell's text may specifically brand the speakers as female and unreliable, but Lillian's pictures recast that feminine fall within the framework of a masculine seduction and deceit and a male-controlled system of exchange. The tricksters in the text are female: first Thelma, then Frances. The most elusive trickster of all may be Lillian Hoban herself.

When two people work together on a picture book, each is, in effect, claiming a space on the page (unless, like Ingri and Edgar d'Aulaire, to whom I return later, they refuse to take credit separately).[8] Even the point size in which each collaborator's name is printed on the cover may tell a story, as does, for example, the smaller line "Words by Arnold Lobel" hovering over the larger line "Pictures by Anita Lobel" on a windowsill over which a large red rose peeks, on the front of *The Rose in My Garden* (1984). This somewhat odd book, dedicated to William Gray and James Marshall, balances an increasing number of words in the frame on the left-hand page with an increasing variety of foliage in the frame on the right, from "This is the rose in my garden" to

> This is the fieldmouse shaking in fear
> That hides by the sunflowers tallest of all,
>
> . . . .
>
> That stand by the hollyhocks high above ground,
> That give shade to the bee
> That sleeps on the rose in my garden.

Throughout this little folio, the pages slowly fill with their time-honored art forms: Arnold Lobel (1933–1987) mimics the cumulative nursery rhyme, while Anita Lobel (1934–   ) offers us reminiscences of eighteenth- and nineteenth-century colorized botanical drawings. The format is old and predictable, presenting first his side, then hers.[9] Instead of the memorable figures of angst we encounter in his picture book series on Frog and Toad, Arnold here plays only the somewhat stiff formal rhymester, and Anita is given room for a series of lush still lifes, joined by little insect and rodent accessories. Four openings from the end, however, his text starts over ("This is the cat with the tattered ear, / That chases the fieldmouse shaking in fear"), and in two ensuing double page spreads, one image straddles both pages while the text in the lowest level of both facing pages undoes the still lifes of preceding pages (e.g., "That shatters the bluebells with petals like lace, / That scatters the daisies as white as the snow"). The feminine itself is under attack, with broken lace and sullied daisies. The text attributes the destruction of the many facets of the feminine *nature morte* to the impulse of a single cat, whose broad body stretches like a lion rampant across the broken flower bed in one opening and like the Roman emperor Heliogabalus himself, recumbent, in a second. Heliogabalus is celebrated for having snuffed out his own life and that of his female slaves in a bed of rose petals, an event depicted in a famous nineteenth-century painting. Thus Anita's gallery of the rose and its companions (one is reminded of a "Roman de la Rose") becomes a moral tale of corruption and punishment, as the rose, apart from her damaged peers, emerges unblemished, while the cat (in a small inset on the text side) bears a Band-Aid on its nose, stung by the bee that slept on the rose. If Arnold's text instigates a "cat"-astrophe, Anita's images, through the agency of the bee, uphold the continuities of the rose. Between them, the Lobels seem to tell us more about masculine power misplaced and the female victims and survivors of that power than we might care to know.

Representations of masculine and feminine power within the boundaries of the text may not, like waves, be blown by the winds of authorship, but rather, like the tide, be drawn by a kind of reflecting moon of cultural consensus. When the d'Aulaires (Ingri: 1904–80; Edgar: 1898–1986) attempted, after World War II, a *Pocahontas* (1946) that might model the spirit of America as it had been and would be once again, we cannot discern which d'Aulaire was responsible for telling us that the squaws "worked from morning till night and their girls had to help them. But the mighty Powhatan's dearest daughter was allowed to skip and dance. / He gave her the name Pocahontas, which means the one who plays mostly" (12). Did one d'Aulaire make much of the medicine and lore of Pocahontas's grandmother ("But there was no end to all that she knew" [16]), while the other inserted the medicine man, "who knew still more about spirits and magic than Grandmother" (17)? Why invent two medicine characters, call the male one stronger, and then show his utter ineffectiveness? Why tell a story about a girl who could "run and play with the boys," help set a white male prisoner free, provide corn for white men, entertain the white men by "leaping and yelling" in a dance around the fire, and marry John Rolfe, only to have her appear thus before the queen in the grand finale: "The Queen showed her much honor and everybody admired the beautiful Virginia [sic] princess" (44)? The authorship question dims; we cannot establish the priorities of one d'Aulaire over those of the other.

The issue of feminine power does take hold, however. In the early pages of this picture book, the d'Aulaires show Pocahontas bare-chested, a child of sun and water, diving naked into the cold water (14–15). Before the queen, who embodies the highest female power of the day, Pocahontas kneels in submission, fully appareled, in a tableau of remarkable stiffness and make-believe. The narrator undresses her: "Perhaps, if they had seen her running about in the woods, barefoot and dressed only in a skin, they would not have thought her so much of a princess" (44). For the European d'Aulaires, the figure of Pocahontas interrogates the signs of power or nobility. Like Curious George, Pocahontas has tremendous drawing power; she makes people want to see her and write about her: "Artists painted her portrait. Poets wrote songs in her honor" (42). The figure of Pocahontas has earned the right to be the apple not only of her father's eye but of every spectator's eye as well. Would she be taken seriously if people knew her as the little savage she once was and might still be? Would her agile body, the very core of her power (as rescuer, dancer, and mate) at home, still serve as her secret weapon for anyone other than the admiring readers of this picture book? As the d'Aulaires reach the end of their tale, they reverse perspective. In the final tableau at court, the king stands between Pocahontas, kneeling, and the queen, "who showed her much honor." He enters the text as an afterthought: "And as for Pocahontas, when she bowed before the King and saw the skinny legs that could hardly carry the fat body of the King of England, she thought of her stately father. He needed neither a crown on his head nor a scepter in his hand to show that he was a ruler" (45). Pocahontas's nobility must be mediated through her father, even her father's telling body, and finally through her son:

> And when Pocahontas' son was a
> grown man, he sailed to his mother's
> country. There he became the
> father of a great, big family
> which lives on to
> this very
> day.   (45)

FIFTY YEARS before the Lobels, Marjorie Flack (1897–1958),[10] best known as the scriptwriter for *The Story about Ping,* had discovered a way to spa-

Pocahontas dives into the cold water.

tialize the male and female domains on the picture book page. In her remarkable *Angus and the Cat* (1931), Flack shows in just one book how the story of female power can be told on both vertical and horizontal axes.[11] Anticipating by more than thirty years the cover layout of Sendak's *Where the Wild Things Are*, Flack puts her title in the subtitle position, below the wide screen of her players (Sendak puts his above), and then sets Angus the dog just above his name and the Cat just above her "name," as Sendak has the words *Wild Things* over the bull-like sleeper on his cover. Angus occupies the left zone, and the Cat, the right side, the "here-we-go-off-into-adventure" side. On the title page, Angus stands below left, partly out of the framed title and credits, and the cat sits on the credit frame on the top right. Already the female Cat dominates the top and the right of the page, leaving the male Scottie to hold the ground.

As the narrative begins, we see the narrator at play with her dog. "Now as Angus grew older and longer he learned MANY THINGS. He learned it is best to stay in one's own yard and / [page break] FROGS can jump but / [page turn]." Flack also anticipates Sendak's broken syntax in *Where the Wild Things Are:* "One day when Max put on his wolf suit and / [page turn] made mischief of one kind / [page turn] and another / [page turn]." Whereas Sendak's narrator offers few clues to the inflections of the spoken word, Flack makes use of capital letters both to signify vocal register and to poke fun at her hero. Whereas Sendak's narrator invokes the complexities of meaning inherent in any definition of "mischief," Flack's narrator clearly articulates the boundaries of correct behavior: "Angus also learned NOT to lie on the soft and NOT to take SOMEBODY ELSE's food and things like that."

Having introduced Angus as a well-tutored male dog, Flack proceeds to offer him up to the temptation of her wild things, CATS, which are "SOMETHING outdoors." Unlike Max, Angus can never gain control of these wild things, although his experiences in the book constitute opportunities for research concerning the "SOMETHING outdoors Angus was very curious about but had NEVER learned about." While Angus is at the end of his leash on the left-hand page, five cats romp in the bottom right corner of the right-hand page, and one of them, out of the circle, faces across the page to Angus on the left. Flack participates in a tradition as old as the *Odyssey* by portraying one male encountering the many females, just as the Lobels would in *The Rose in My Garden,* as if the man were singular and the woman diverse, split into many, according to some diabolical law of diminishing returns.[12]

The many cats are quickly reduced to one in the following opening. The cat lies on the sofa. She jumps onto the arm of the sofa. Everywhere she goes, Angus is either forbidden or unable to go: "Up jumped the CAT onto the sofa back, up to the mantel—and Angus was not high enough to reach her!" The cat can steal Angus's food: she is a trickster, elusive and agile. From his somewhat dull vantage point on the left-hand page, Angus sees her sitting in his space, "WASHING HER FACE," until she leaps up into a window. Finally, Angus chases her "UP-THE-STAIRS" into a bedroom, where, as if by magic, "THAT CAT" disappears.

The difference between feline vision and canine confusion.

That he had not been "UP-THE-STAIRS" before suggests that this territory is strictly feline and that he, a fellow meant for the downstairs world, may be intruding. In the four-color double-page spread that follows, Angus peers out of a dormer window onto the lawns and trees of neighboring yards. The spread affords a panoramic aerial view from a vantage point not in the house itself, but above and beside it. Once again Flack has seized a visual opportunity somewhat ahead of her time, one the Reys in 1939 will capture for George during his escape from jail via telephone wires and during his balloon adventure. Her cat enjoys the view from the roof above and beside the dormer window through which Angus peers. Nowhere is the difference between feline vision and canine confusion made more plain. She knows where he is, what he sees, and that she is out of his sight, but "Angus looked out of the window / [page turn] into his yard, into the next yard—no CAT could he see ANYWHERE." Angus's anguish tumbles out in the verbal narration; everywhere he looks, upstairs and downstairs, "no CAT" is there. Finally, anticipating the rhythm of a famous line in Brown's *Goodnight Moon,* the narrator intones, "Angus looked on the table and / [page turn] on the window sills—no CAT was indoors ANYWHERE." When the cat announces herself downstairs at last with a "P U R R R R R" coming across the right-hand page toward Angus, who looks up from his food bowl on the left-hand page, we see the "learning" that Angus has now acquired beside the "knowing" the cat has had all along: "And Angus knew and the CAT knew that Angus knew that—" as they sup together from the same bowl.

IN ADDITION to Flack, there are many other extraordinary female practitioners of both the arts of the picture book, from Beatrix Potter to the many stars of today, such as Molly Bang, Nancy Burkert, and Elzbieta. By way of rounding out a discussion of gendering in the picture book, I now venture

down the rock-strewn paths of women and authority as they are mapped in recent picture books by men.

When picture book makers are men, women who have achieved some level
of autonomy do not always fare as well as Flack's cat does in her friendly management of Angus. Harry Allard and James Marshall's *Miss Nelson Is Missing*
(1977) highlights the vicissitudes of the woman at the head of the class. One
could say that the teacher role, whether played by a man or a woman, is fraught
with all the tragicomic consequences of any assumption of power. But in this
picture book, the framing of the "weaker sex" seems less than benign.

Miss Nelson has both a "sweet voice" (4) that carries no weight with her students and, in her subaltern form as Viola Swamp, an "unpleasant voice" (8). She
can be seen wearing a pink dress or an "ugly black dress" (10), leading her students to "see that Miss Swamp was a real witch" (12).[13] Miss Nelson has a somewhat plump face with a round chin and blonde hair; her alter ego has a nar-
rower face with a pointy chin and black hair. The woman in authority splits into
two personae, the witchy one that gets results and the nice one that does not.
Miss Nelson's witchy persona is a trick she is playing, of course, but the price of
that trick is the momentary sacrifice of her robustness as a woman. In the
penultimate opening, Miss Nelson is in her bed, beside a mirror and makeup.
Behind her on a shelf in the closet is a box marked "WIG," beneath which hangs
the black dress. Miss Nelson puts one hand to her lips, the other on an open
book in her lap: "When it was time for bed she sang a little song. 'I'll never tell,'
she said to herself with a smile" (30). Thus her power lies not in her "authentic
being" but in her painted lies and frauds. Detective McSmogg, the only adult
male in this picture book, will never figure her out.

Tomie de Paola's (1934–   ) *Strega Nona's Magic Lessons* (1982) and Anthony Browne's (1946–   ) *Piggybook* (1986) are more conscious treatments of
women's plight and power. Both of these male author-illustrators attempt to
come to terms with women's need and desire to be seen as equal partners, owners of their own space, and thinkers and initiators who deserve as much credit
(including equal pay) as their male counterparts.

Sturdy Bambolona, the baker's daughter in *Strega Nona's Magic Lessons*,
would be an unlikely candidate for the kind of royal treatment afforded Pocahontas. In her diminutive stature and black hair, we may recognize a Calabrian
type, but in the context of North America, we may also read Bambolona as
working class. In the miniaturizing of this powerhouse, a folklore trope equates
smallness (e.g., Tom Thumb or the African rabbit up against the baboon) with
agility and cunning. Geometrically, she is a pyramid, and Big Anthony (also Antoinette), her counterpart, is a tower. As in the case of Curious George, her lack

of complicated body parts emphasizes that she is an emblem for a thought process, rather than a representation of a body. Her mentor, the kindly Strega Nona, knows everything and need not suffer comparison, as Pocahontas's grandmother does, to a male "better."

When the story begins, Bambolona, shown in four "shots" on the same page, sends out angry vibrations in three of them, which show her in phases of her bakery work. One shot is particularly striking: feet planted squarely on the ground, her angry countenance directed at the reader, loaves of brown bread stacked on her head, her two braids sticking out on either side like quivering antennae—Bambolona is *oppressed*. We look for an oppressor: the baker. By the second opening, his mustached obesity has given his hard-working employee more directions, she complains, and as he departs for the piazza, he asserts, "That's the way things are." In the scene across the page from this law of the father, he is seated in the sunny piazza beside two compadres, his eyes closed, while one gesticulates toward him, making, no doubt, an important point, while Bambolona, now apronless, moves firmly off the page to the right: "I'm going to change the way things are," she states.

Although the shift from the baker's workplace to Strega Nona's house still keeps Bambolona indoors, reinforcing the notion that her work is centered in an interior space, in Strega Nona's space the man who walks in enters as a guest or an employee, and is obliged to follow the strega's (witch's) rules. He has no authority or power to make changes in her world. A promising conversation between Strega Nona and Bambolona is interrupted by Big Anthony's entering (after first standing in the doorway, as the baker had stood in the bakery entrance) and bursting out, "Strega Nona, teach me your magic, me too."

What is big about Big Anthony is not only his height; he owns a large share of feelings of entitlement, enabling him to eavesdrop and procrastinate when he is supposed to be working, a factor that leads to his dismissal at the baker's after he first leaves the employ of Strega Nona. There's something else: he is a big blond, a bimbo to Bambolona. The potential in this setting for reading his whiteness/blondness as emptiness should not go unmentioned. De Paola makes remarkably successful use of this trait in later creating the cross-dressed Anthony, now Antoinette, as he once again stands in the threshold (this time, being a woman, waiting to be invited in), wearing a pink kerchief over his blond locks and a long yellow gown. Most fetching is the heavy application of pink lipstick in a heart shape on his plain lips. Strega Nona takes in this new pupil, who is in effect a rival to Bambolona. His cross-dressing may or may not have deceived the canny Nona, but even in his female guise Big Anthony is no match for Bambolona. Strega's book does not make him wise. Big Anthony's inappropriate behaviors as he tries to learn magic are funny; whether he makes Strega Nona disappear or she does so on her own to unmask him, he cannot but come out looking ridiculous because he cannot rise to the challenge of being a woman. Bambolona can make him a man by recognizing who he is in the first place.

De Paola's uncanny visual sense allows him to create a powerful instance of female solidarity by pairing Strega Nona and Bambolona, equal in proportions, cunning, and spirit, to confront the tall intruding male on their own terms and make him talk. When Big Anthony makes his confession to Strega Nona, he stands between her and Bambolona, in profile, his borrowed yellow gown swept back on the ground as he kneels. For all we know, Big Anthony's gown makes him a priest. This impression is confirmed in the book's second and final double-page spread, when Anthony stands with his hands folded together, looking hapless, imploring a now huge Strega Nona to take him back into her service. Strega Nona stands facing away from the failed magician, the priest who went astray, and literally unfrocks him: "Don't forget you're wearing Signora Rosa's most beautiful dress." In the house of Strega Nona, Bambolona and her mentor have merged into one woman who wordlessly gazes through the door at Big Anthony with the John the Baptist forefinger pointing not to the sky, but to his mouth.

Like *Strega Nona's Magic Lessons*, Browne's *Piggybook* reverses an insidious pattern coursing through several of the books I have examined here, from the Hobans' *A Bargain for Frances* to *Miss Nelson Is Missing*, and that is the splitting of the female figure. Even the front cover of *Piggybook* proclaims the new division, with not one but three males riding piggyback on a single female. Like Bambolona, the lone female enters the tale weighed down, saddled with husband and sons, whose pink cheeks radiate a health missing from hers. The title page features a single pink, winged pig in a field of whiteness. On the dedication page that follows, the number of pink pigs in that field has doubled. It is not long before even the wallpaper (yellowing in one early spread) that forms a backdrop for the ensuing action is teeming with images of pink pigs. First we encounter the grinning Mr. Piggott and his two grinning sons, Simon and Patrick, who greet us from the expanse of a "nice" front garden to a "nice" suburban house with a "nice" red car in its "nice" garage. There is a brief pause, the beginning of a new paragraph, an adjustment of focus from the car in the garage to what is "inside the house": "his wife." The momentum of the list of the "nice" attributes of Mr. Piggott carries over to the mention of the invisible supplement, the wife supplement, that extra something "inside the house."

Even this somewhat shocking introduction does not quite set in motion the wheels of attitude change. Browne torments his readers with more of the masculine reflex, showing the father calling for breakfast from "dear," and the sons calling "Mom," each ready to fuel up before going to the "important job" or the "important school." The father's behavior is made more egregious by his throwing up the newspaper to hide his face from the very readers he grinned at on the previous page. The sons' O-shaped mouths clamoring for breakfast at either end of the table repeat not only the father's demand but that of many identical mouths pictured in the newspaper qua scripture that conceals the face of the father (Gott, after all, is in his name). The culture of the mouth, of speaking and consuming, clearly dominates the male-centered universe at the table.

Where the man's world reveals many empty mouths, the woman's world of Mrs. Piggott betrays many repetitive tasks, especially at home. Mrs. Piggott washes up after breakfast, makes "all" the beds, vacuums "all" the carpets, and goes to work. In none of the four pictures that offer initial insight into her domain do we get more than a hint of what she might look like: her self-effacement as a woman is complete. Where the male domain is full of color and difference, Mrs. Piggott's world appears through a yellow filter, with the gaze aimed low, cutting off the pictures on the wall and the sign above her head at the bus stop. Apart from the breakfast plates and the bedsheets, she is the only rounded form in the space she occupies, in which horizontal lines (a railing, a baseboard, multiple courses of brick in a brick wall) mark boundaries everywhere. Her space is defined: walls and wallpaper, even bricks, hardly a window to look out of. She is in the perfect place for a wallflower.

Browne continues to drive home the male obsession with eating and hollering, providing an almost Gulliverian close-up of Mr. Piggott that shows only his mouth, chin, and jerkined torso, a table knife in one fist, a fork in the other, and a large pork sausage impaled on the fork above a plateful of french fries and other sausages. After dinner, the narrator enumerates Mrs. Piggott's round of wifely chores, shown through the same yellow filter. A somewhat similarly yellow-hued, double-page bleed (without words) of father and sons sharing two sofas with their eyes on the TV and their mouths closed summarizes the pattern of masculine dependency and prepares us for change with the appearance of a pink porcelain piggy bank. (A piggy bank is, after all, for change.) While the father lies sprawled beneath a rough facsimile of Frans Hals's familiar painting "The Laughing Cavalier," the father's cavalier attitudes are in jeopardy. We cannot help but realize we are looking up his suddenly rather porcine nostrils. Exit the faces of father and sons; enter three hapless pigheads!

Mom, like Bambolona and Miss Nelson, has gone away, leaving the men to fend for themselves. She has left a note, which Mr. Piggott holds with his pig-

Mr. Piggott.

toes/fingers (against pig-flowered wallpaper) to read: "You are pigs." This is as close to a feminine discourse as we will find in *Piggybook*. Now the fireplace is cold, and everywhere, from doorknobs to wall switches, the pig motif holds sway. Even the Delft tiles register pigs upon pigs. Browne seems to delight in challenging the reader both to find the pigs in every corner and to see what is *not* in the picture, even the one over the mantel. In the absence of a feminine principle of order and respect for others, meals become messes: "The house was like a pigsty." Under the moon in the evening, a wolf's head appears in the window of these three little pigs. With the living room in almost complete shadow, and the Laughing Cavalier now also a dashing pig, the pigs are reduced to their hands and knees, their rumps prominently displayed: "'We'll just have to root around and find some scraps,' snorted Mr. Piggott."

The "turning of the other cheeks" does not lend dignity or power to these bent-over male figures. The hitherto faceless and enigmatic Mrs. Piggott returns, towering over her swinish mate and brood. She stands before us, giving us clear glimpses of her face for the first time. Now it is she who is wearing red under her drab business suit; until the pig phase, her sons could be seen in red blazers, but she was, as it were, colorless. With her return, the males resume their human shape and decide to distribute her many tasks among them. Her redemption is almost complete on the closing page where, in a white space without a wall or background, she is seen in coveralls and red shirt smilingly leaning under the hood of the red car: "She fixed the car." That "she" can fix a car may mean more than that Mrs. Piggott has mechanical skills; she can get things moving, she can be a prime mover, beside the car, a *dea ex machina*; the male Piggotts are, in effect, moved over, off the page entirely. Not only does Mrs. Piggott get the car started, but through her new presence she has the last page all to herself. And all without ever having to say a word, not even the personal pronoun "I."

THROUGH THE MAZE of authorships and artistic responsibilities to the contested spaces in textual and visual universes, picture books enable us to see gender not only as a construct governed by the interests of the most powerful, and not only as a biological datum, but also as an impetus for creativity on pages that face each other, cover each other up, and open each other to a world beyond gender. Engendering is never finished; the gender clashes over privilege and power do not end when the picture book shuts its doors.[14] The conventions surrounding gender will have as long a shelf life as the books that take them for granted. But to some who cannot keep silent on these matters, the picture book, like the story of Eve, offers the opportunity to reveal the "timeless" as timebound, the eternal yellow wallpaper and ever-present piggy bank as messages addressed to the masculine occupants of the moment. Bambolona can change things as they are. So can Mrs. Piggott and Miss Nelson. These picture books not only reveal cultural assumptions about gender but open up a space for the tensions between text and image, as between male and female, that release creative force.

Discourses of Femininity and the Intertextual Construction of Feminist Reading Positions

John Stephens and Robyn McCallum

A significant effect of feminism has been the production of adolescent fiction that constructs an implied reader who occupies a feminist reading position. Such a reader is often constructed intertextually, out of a dialogue between the current narrative and particular pre-texts or more general plots implicit in the genres that the narrative uses or evokes. With these dialogic strategies, writers challenge the ideological gendering both of genres and of social practices directed at young people, exposing the processes whereby femininity is constructed and naturalized in texts and enabling more autonomous forms of female subjectivity to be expressed. Readers are thus able to interrogate the texts and genres of the past (what might be loosely called the tradition of children's literature). For example, the discourses of femininity that inform the fairy story, romance, and school story are made visible as socially constructed discourses. Dialogic strategies also have metafictional possibilities: by drawing attention to a text's fictiveness, they encourage readers to think about the processes through which narrative fictions are constructed, read, and interpreted (see Waugh; G. Moss; McCallum). Thus writers can foreground the molding of characters' expectations and behavior by the femininities represented in fairy tales, romance fiction, films, and other cultural discourses. In this chapter, we illustrate how adolescent novels can expose the gendering of the discourses of femininity in a wide range of texts, and offer readers alternative feminist subject positions, by examining Zibby Oneal's *In Summer Light* and Adèle Geras's *The Tower Room* (the first volume of her "Egerton Hall" trilogy).

These two novels self-consciously explore how a discourse of femininity is related to culturally privileged texts and, through their narrative processes and outcomes, construct an implied reader position that may be called feminist, informed by what may be broadly described as a pragmatic liberal-humanist feminism. We take the concept of a "discourse of femininity" from Dorothy E. Smith, though in applying it to fictional representations we narrow its reference. Smith views femininity as "a social organization of relations among women and between women and men which is mediated by texts, that is, by the materially fixed forms of printed writing and images" ("Femininity as Discourse" 39). The discourse of femininity has no particular local source and is not embodied or produced by individuals, but individuals "orient themselves to the order of the discourse in talk, writing, creating images (whether in texts or on their bodies), produced and determined by the ongoing order, which is their concerted accomplishment and arises in the concerting" (40). The process Smith describes coincides with Althusser's "interpellation," or the summoning of individuals into a place within a structure and an identity in which they seem to recognize themselves (Morris 28–29, 197). Thus femininity is not simply an effect of patriarchal oppression, though in *The Tower Room* and *In Summer Light* patriarchal practices and assumptions play major roles in orienting female subjectivities toward a "feminine" discourse centered on submission to authority (the voice of the father), conformity to codes for appearance and behavior that define the self as feminine, complicity with restricted career choices determined by others, and subordination of the self in romantic love relationships.

In Smith's framing of it, the discourse of femininity is always already intertextual because it is a complex of textual relations among magazines, television, advertisements, shop and fashion displays, and (to a lesser extent) books (41). Within the novels we examine here this intertextual effect is produced by the relations among (fictive) individual experiences, some of the cultural texts cited by Smith, and more or less specific literary pre-texts. The novels (and others like them) explore how gendered behaviors are inscribed and can be resisted during the transition from childhood to adulthood and thus lay bare the ways in which "conservative" gendered discourses are inscribed within social and narrative discourses. The negotiation of intertextual space enables resistant reading positions that challenge patriarchal discourses. Each text constructs a narrative in which the focalizing female character comes to recognize the ways in which she has been interpellated and seeks a more personally empowered subject position. Along the way, she experiences misperceptions and misdirections, but each text's dialogic strategies enable readers to recognize these. Read-

ers' alignment with the point of view of the focalizing characters and evaluation of that point of view construct a reading position from which the narrative outcomes are affirmed as coherent and socially satisfactory. Insofar as the
outcomes conform with a feminist agenda—for example, "to understand the
social and psychic mechanisms that construct and perpetuate gender inequality and then to change them" (Morris 1)—the implied reading position constitutes a feminist reading position (see also Cranny-Francis 25).

Of the two novels, *In Summer Light* is a little less self-conscious about addressing these processes. It constructs an interrogative feminist reading position by means of its intertextual relationships with Shakespeare's *The Tempest*
and John Fowles's *The Ebony Tower* and its dialogue with dominant cultural
constructions of the artist figure.[1] The interrogative reading position is implicitly aligned with Kate, the only focalizing character in the novel. Throughout the novel, she attempts to write a school essay about *The Tempest* and uses
her struggle with the character and functions of Prospero to reassess her sense
of her artist father, Marcus Brewer. Insofar as Brewer conforms to the romantic cultural construction of the artist as an alienated, socially rebellious, and
self-absorbed figure, Kate's assessment of him and of her relationship with him
enables a questioning of the masculinist cultural assumptions underpinning
romantic and modernist constructions of the artist. This interrogation exposes
the patriarchal assumptions embodied in the romantic figure of the "great
artist," around which revolve official, high-culture discourses; modernist constructions of the artist as alienated subject; and, beyond this, the humanistic
construction of the individual in quest of identity and self-expression. As a paradigmatic way of being, this individual quest can be seen as inimical toward, or
even destructive of, alternative paradigms, especially cooperation and community. Kate is also a painter, but two years before the novel opens, she stopped
painting, partly because of her father's patronizing attitude toward her work.
Thus her refusal to paint is tied up with her rejection of him—she rejects him
by rejecting that activity within which his position and subjectivity are defined.
She also stops painting because she is unable to construct a position for herself
within an essentially patriarchal cultural discourse that valorizes individuality
over community.

The Tower Room constructs a more self-conscious interrogative, feminist
reading position by means of its structure, intertextual relationships, and use
of the girls' boarding school setting. The novel is structured as two alternating
narratives, both of which begin on the opening page. The first narrates the story
of seventeen-year-old Megan's life in the Tower Room at her boarding school
(Egerton Hall) and her falling in love with Simon, a temporary teacher several

years her senior. Allusions throughout the novel indicate that this first narrative reworks the Grimm fairy story "Rapunzel," but it also intersects with other genres: the school story, popular (teen) romance, and Gothic fiction. It ends with Megan and Simon leaving Egerton Hall together. The second, later narrative begins on Megan's eighteenth birthday and comprises a series of journal entries addressed to Simon. In this journal, Megan charts over twenty-four days her decision to leave Simon and return to school. The contrapuntal narrations construct a reading position that constantly challenges the gendered romance/ fairy story. The mixing of genres is in itself dialogic, as the genres blend and clash with one another. Further, that these are masculinist discourses is established by such elements as classroom lessons that inculcate sublimated desire within a social context that suppresses female sensuality.

A primary purpose of each novel is to affirm the individuality of its main female character and her right to self-determination free from social and textual discourses of femininity. In each case, the main character finds a sense of agency that transforms her everyday world, and she finally returns to school with a stronger, more focused sense of self. As with most adolescent fiction, the subjectivity represented as a desirable outcome is formulated in terms of contemporary humanist ideology. This being so, we have found Pauline Johnson's *Feminism as Radical Humanism* particularly helpful for examining how a novel constructs a feminist reading position in relationship to contemporary humanism. Johnson argues that modern, or "radical," humanism is grounded in "the ideas of a self-conscious life, of authentic self-realization and autonomy," expressed through "a commitment to the cause of radically democratic processes of communication and interaction between subjects" (8), and recognizes that its ideals are historically contingent, rather than universal. This formulation, Johnson argues, coincides with the project of modern feminism. *In Summer Light* and *The Tower Room* engage feminism through narrative rather than theorize about it, but both articulate a position similar to Johnson's: they construct feminist narratives within patriarchal contexts that inhibit democratic interaction for women.

Kate develops an awareness of her subjected state, but Megan develops only partial awareness, so that insight is deduced by readers from the novel's interplay of genres. The growth of awareness is more obvious in *In Summer Light*, because Kate struggles to define a self against her father's assumptions about family and creativity, and she develops a voice of her own through this struggle. Her sense of self is at first defined oppositionally—countering the assumptions about femininity, society, and artistic creativity that underlie her father's position as artist and male. She attempts to define a sense of self by constructing herself as different from her father—hence her decision not to paint—and by undermining the mythology that grounds her father's position. She eventually realizes that the social alienation that informs the image of "the great painter" is solipsistic. She begins to formulate this view by the middle of the novel: "My father has to have the foreground all to himself. He has to be the center of attention. It took me longer than it should have to understand that. I thought that the way to please him was to become a better and better painter" (68). In using the discourse of art criticism to reflect on how she has been interpellated, she draws attention to how such a discourse operates and hence enables readers to contest that interpellating discourse.

Patriarchal authority in *The Tower Room* is more dispersed and indirect. It permeates an education program that, although administered and delivered by women, uses texts by male authors and requires students to please external examiners whom they think of as male. In addition, Megan becomes only vaguely aware that her role in her relationship with Simon has all along been determined by a particular discourse of femininity. That is, as the female in the tower, she is simultaneously constructed as the ethereal Other, a (temporarily) inaccessible object of desire, and as the virginal female naif who waits in the tower to be initiated into sexuality by a male guide. When, upon being kissed for the first time, Megan feels sexual arousal, the experience is described in the language of romance cliché, and the generic affiliations are underscored first by Megan's own contrast with the expectations she has formed by "reading all the right books with particular emphasis on 'the good bits'" and then by the exchange that concludes it:

"I think," I gasped when Simon stopped for a moment, "I must have died and gone to Heaven."

"It gets better," he answered. "This is only the beginning . . . oh, I shall show you such things . . ."

That means, I thought to myself, that he wants to see me again. (85–86)

The discordant effect of Megan's misinterpretation (and generic shift) of what Simon says reveals her unawareness of the implications of the discourse into which she is interpellated. Geras uses register shifts to foreground the text's mixing of genres and hence to draw attention to discourse itself to imply a feminist reading position. In fact, we argue that the ruptures and discordances make sense only from the perspective of a feminist reading position.

Generic mixing and metafiction thus offer readers stances from which to interrogate patriarchal discourses that present female experience as inferior and subordinate. As might be expected in books directed at adolescent female readers, the most pertinent discourses bear on the experience of being a daughter, a student, a lover, and a young adult in a state of becoming. In *The Tower Room* and *In Summer Light*, such discourses are focused in three main fields and represented thematically as both intratextual and intertextual elements. First, Megan and Kate are in some way physically isolated, and this isolation functions as a metonym for female vulnerability and subjection; second, both are reaching for autonomy from patriarchal assumptions; and third, both must assess and resist the available familial, social, and textual patterns for becoming a woman.

For Kate these things happen within a hiatus created by the physical isolation of the island setting and by the emotional effect of illness (she is in the last stages of recovery from mononucleosis). The island setting and the arrival of Ian, a graduate student who is working for her father, loosely replicate the situation of *The Tempest* (and of *The Ebony Tower*). Direct and indirect allusions to *The Tempest* compound the connections among the three texts. Kate's father is constructed as a Prospero figure, and Ian's arrival evokes *The Tempest* when he is described as "wet as the survivor of a shipwreck" (9). Kate, however, refuses to play Miranda to her father's Prospero, and although she does attempt to reproduce the role of Miranda in relation to Ian/Ferdinand, the romantic involvement remains only a possibility—as it does in Fowles's text too. This becomes a key example of how intertextuality constructs a reading position. In the Shakespearean romance, first love transfers Miranda from her father's possession to her husband's. In contrast, the relationship between Kate and Ian does not develop romantically because, ironically, not Kate but Ian refuses the scripting of *The Tempest*. Significantly, in focalizing her own feelings Kate discloses a semi-awareness that "love" may be just attraction to the new or a crush, a suspicion confirmed when, during her last conversation with Ian, she thinks of the moment in which Miranda first saw men other than her father. Although it is Ian who offers the axiom that "here and now aren't all that there will ever be for you" (130), Kate subsequently appropriates this insight. The intertextual moment thus deconstructs the authority of narratives that valorize romantic outcomes for first love encounters and thereby imply that a young woman achieves the high point of her life before she even reaches maturity. Readers are hereby positioned to affirm the novel's close, in which Kate resumes her painting and returns to school, with a sense of empowerment gained from having negotiated these complex relationships.

In *The Tower Room*, a different conjuncture of social factors and discourses inimical to female autonomy impinges on Megan. She has been an orphan since the age of eleven and, still a minor, has no access to the money she has inherited from her parents. As a student at Egerton Hall, a girls' boarding school, Megan is subject to a particular process of feminine fashioning and in fact is locked more firmly into it than others because her guardian is a live-in teacher, making the school her home. For many, chiefly male, heroes of children's fiction and folktale, these circumstances might be the prelude to an adventure culminating in agency and freedom, but Geras forecloses that possibility here by mapping the female version of that plot onto the Grimms' version of "Rapunzel," in which the heroine is denied comparable autonomy.

The dominant psychological reading of the Rapunzel story is that it portrays "essential processes in life. Testing, threatening danger, destruction and salvation, development, and maturation" (Lüthi 113). Geras rejects this "slow incubation of selfhood" explanation and suggests, rather, that Megan/Rapunzel has been denied a proper process of maturation. Because she is isolated from wider society—"stuck away in Egerton Hall with three hundred girls and an almost completely female staff" (16)—her concept of male-female relationships has been formed only by popular fiction and classroom texts, and this renders her susceptible to dreams of romantic love and seduction by the first man who desires her.

The nature of Megan/Rapunzel's susceptibility is most overtly established in two carefully juxtaposed episodes on pages 66–70. In the first episode, which presents Megan's second conversation with Simon, Simon identifies her as "The damsel in the Tower. The one with the golden hair falling over the windowsill" (66). The exchange establishes Megan as an object of male gaze, as well as restating the parallels with Rapunzel. From here Megan goes straight to a conventional English lesson about Keats's "The Eve of St. Agnes," specifically, about "Keats's appeal to the senses: sight, sound, touch and so on" (68). The girls do not take it entirely seriously, and their private observations—such as Bella's "Is it right to feed such sexy stuff to impressionable girls?" (69)—indicate the disparity between the sensual materials they study and the austerity of their everyday lives. They do not, however, apprehend the constructedness of their experience, though this should be evident to readers: as a parody of pedagogy, the lesson discloses how the cultivation of "sensibility" in the English classroom is divorced from practical or ethical insight or outcomes. The point becomes clearer when the two episodes are considered together: "Rapunzel" and "The Eve of St. Agnes" are versions of the same story. Megan's reverie during the reading of the poem—"a dream of myself as Madeline, running along the tapestried halls with my lover" (69)—underscores the connection. Rapunzel, Madeline, and Megan are all passive objects of desire, to be seduced and taken away. Once again Geras mixes discourses—fairy tale, everyday conversation, Keats, pedagogy, schoolgirl flippancy—to offer her readers an interrogative position that points toward a feminist analysis of Megan's experience.

The parallel between "Rapunzel" and "The Eve of St. Agnes" is introduced again at the climax of the inner story, when Megan recalls the final stanza of the poem as she and Simon leave Egerton Hall together (141). Readers grasp the hollowness of this romantic ending because they have simultaneously been reading about the aridity of Megan's subsequent life through the journal entries. The double-stranded narration allows Geras to juxtapose the romantic ending, when the lovers flee into the night, with the close of Megan's farewell letter to Simon, in which she announces that she is choosing autonomy and self-determination over the dream of romantic love. Although she does not repudiate her love for Simon, Megan has discovered that she wants more than what romantic "love" presages. She wants to finish school, go to university, spend time with her friends, travel, and "above all, be able to go back to Egerton Hall" (141). In short, she wants individual agency, to be free to negotiate her own way in the world and become something other than somebody's partner, and she sees that to do this she first needs to regain the sense of community offered by the school that she lost by entering into heterosexual romantic love. Geras adds an extra nuance to Megan's self-realization by choosing to set this 1990 book in 1962 and so, in effect, to write a historical novel in which the experiences of a young woman anticipate some of the developments of the modern women's movement. As Sara Maitland, among others, points out, social changes in the 1960s enabled the women's movement of the 1970s. *The Tower Room* evokes a moment at which a paradigm shift was taking place and exemplifies the "analysis and hard work" (Maitland 3) women needed to sustain that shift and assist another generation of young women to become aware of how textual and social discourses keep inscribing disadvantageous versions of femininity.

In Summer Light depicts a particular social structuring of male-female relationships through the roles and relationships of Kate's family members. Kate's mother, also a painter, has not painted for fifteen years. Because she subscribes to a common romantic and modernist conception of the artist, she has spent her life in servitude to her husband's art. Brewer's position as artist essentially defines the identity of Kate's mother, whose fragmented life reflects its construction around him and whose artistic activities take the form of conventional female creativity (arranging flowers and caring for and teaching children). Kate may be undervaluing her mother's life, and only belatedly sees how positively it has shaped her own, but its focus does confirm the masculinist definition of the artist figure. In doing so it articulates the problem of self-definition Kate is struggling with, a problem Germaine Greer has identified as central for a female artist: "For all artists the problem is one of finding one's own authenticity, of speaking in a language or imagery that is essentially one's own, but if one's self-image is dictated by one's relation to others and all one's activities are other directed, it is simply not possible to find one's own voice" (325).

Another aspect of the cultural construction of the artist implicit in the characterization of Brewer and hostile to feminine creativity is the connection between creativity and masculinity as an expression of a power hierarchy. As a Prospero figure, Brewer is the locus of authority and creativity by which the female members of the household are defined. Although as a child Kate painted alongside her father, aspiring to an apprentice role, the person who is actually willing to pass on knowledge and skill is her mother. Masculinism is implicit in the equation of sex and creativity in Brewer's monologues about painting being "like making love" and criticism being "dead from the waist down" (there are echoes here of Henry Breasley, the aging artist in *The Ebony Tower*). Kate's use of her whole body as a brush while painting a rock with clay toward the close of the novel might be read ironically back on these comments.

Against these patriarchal images of the artist Kate attempts to define a sense of herself, as a female, as a painter, and as a self who is also her father's daughter. To develop as an artist, to find her own voice and style, she must reject the master-apprentice relationship. Initially, to reject the role of apprentice means that she will no longer paint. However, through her thinking about painting and struggling with her essay on *The Tempest,* she reassesses her father as an artist and her own relationship to him and is enabled to negotiate her own sense of herself as painter.

The image of the artist remains a central problem for the novel: the image is critiqued but not dismantled, just as Kate ultimately cannot reach a conclusion about Prospero and includes two endings in her essay. She first decides, "It is wrong . . . morally, politically, humanely wrong for a ruler to ignore the needs of his people. To use others for his own purposes with no concern for the cost to them is unforgivable." She then adds, in a move that "messed up her conclusion, her neat case," this rider: "And yet at the end of the play . . . Prospero has become an old man. His magic powers are nearly gone, and then they are gone entirely. In the Epilogue he asks us to set him free. I think Shakespeare means for us to forgive him. I think he means that if we refuse, we will be trapped like Prospero was, on his island" (143). This comes just after Brewer has explained to Kate the significance of a retrospective (the assumption that a painter's best work is in the past) and she realizes that her father has become an old man. Hence Kate is able to recognize her father's talent when it is a thing of the past, but the implication that she should also forgive him for being self-centered is problematic. Nevertheless, it seems symptomatic of her developed maturity that she must forgive him in order to get on with her own life. To continue seeing him in opposition to herself would deny her a position from which to paint. She must recognize his talent in order to "leave the island," to become free of domination by the Other, but in forgiving him she fails to dismantle the cultural construction of the artist.

Kate's effacement in relation to her father is metaphorically figured in repeated references to one of his paintings, *The Studio: Morning.* Although Kate sat for this painting as a child, references to it make it clear that the work is not her portrait but a study of light and color: the objects represented in the painting are of interest only insofar as the play of light and color on their surfaces gives them interest. The descriptions of this painting are crucial, because they encapsulate some central concerns in the novel, but there is a double analogy between the painting and Kate's subjectivity. First, to the extent that Kate is not the subject of the painting but merely a vehicle, the painting depicts her objectification and effacement by her father. The painting denies her a subjectivity in the same way that her perception of her father denies her a subject position. Second, the idea that the painting is not a portrait might be read as an analogy for the formation of subjectivity. Just as the objects represented in the painting (Kate, the cat) are given form and meaning via the play of light and color on their surfaces, Kate's sense of her own selfhood is constructed via her relationships with others.

Kate's reconstruction of her selfhood involves putting herself back in the picture, transforming her body into a metonym for agency when she and Ian paint the rocks by the ocean with red clay. This is something that Kate did as a child, and it becomes a moment of catharsis and freedom in the novel. She paints the whole of a large rock, climbing up the rock as she does so, and then jumps from the top when she is finished. The descriptions of Kate emphasize technique, the physical process of painting. She critically surveys the rocks, looking for the right surface, before she begins, and as she paints she imitates other patterns she has seen, consciously playing with form and space. These features of the narrative discourse construct her as a painter, implying the discipline and critical thinking behind the process. They also suggest that her painting is the expression of suppressed desire. This is implicit in references to her "half-remembering"—half-remembering a childhood experience and previous painting—and her use of her body as a brush. References to "cave painters" and her self-absorption, focus, and sense of being driven—"carried by the momentum of the curving shapes she was painting" (90)—imply that her desire to paint is innate. Finally, her leap from the rock when she is finished expresses freedom and affirms creative agency.

Whereas Kate is able to define herself against the domestic female role model represented by her mother, Megan, stuck away with "three hundred girls and an almost completely female staff," is depicted as lacking models for growth. Her femininity is defined in relation to images from fairy tales: Rapunzel; Dorothy, the witch-guardian, who is incapable of showing Megan any affection; in a minor way, Bella's young stepmother, Marjorie, who is obsessed with her own physical beauty; and Miss van der Leyden, a kind of folktale wise woman reminiscent of wise grandmother figures in George MacDonald's fiction, who offers unconditional love to the girls in her care. Geras's modification of the witch-guardian role adds a piquant nuance to the Rapunzel story: it is Dorothy who brings Simon to Egerton Hall, because she desires him herself. By focalizing her unreciprocated desire through the perspective of seventeen-year-olds, Geras presents Dorothy as ridiculous and pathetic, "a laughing-stock," as one of the girls puts it (125). Representing generational conflict is apt to be a problem for any re-version of "Rapunzel," and Geras resorts to a rather unkind stereotype, the sexually unfulfilled career woman. Strategically, however, the contrast between the witch and Rapunzel particularizes a contrast the schoolgirls perceive between the lives of their teachers and the sensuous possibilities of the world promised in texts.

As a mother substitute, Dorothy is complicit with the objectives of patriarchy, exposing her ward to socialization into a discourse of femininity within which professional women sacrifice emotional growth for intellectual. Her plans for Megan are not expressed beyond a notion of "my responsibility to see that [Megan] fulfils herself. Lives up to her potential" (124). Yet like the witch in most retellings of "Rapunzel," Dorothy is a childless woman who desires a form of self-replication but loses what she desires because the attempt to suppress the social and sexual impulses of youth is counterproductive. Rapunzel is kept in total isolation until the prince chances upon the tower, learns how to enter by climbing Rapunzel's hair, and seduces her almost immediately. It is paradoxical that when Rapunzel inadvertently discloses that the prince has been visiting her, the witch exclaims, "Wicked child . . . I thought I had shut you away from the world, but you've deceived me" (Grimm, *Grimms' Tales* 48), since deception must be predicated on knowledge. The same then applies when Dorothy confronts the lovers in Megan's room and replicates the words, and narcissisms, of the witch, describing Megan and Simon as "deceitful and underhand and wicked" (137) and demanding, "How dare you betray *me?* After all these years . . . all I've done for you" (138).

The most powerful model by which Megan's femininity is defined is not Dorothy but Rapunzel, especially given the metonymic association between her long blonde hair and sexuality. Geras plays with this link overtly, and the strongly visual descriptions of Megan's hair evoke innumerable, if unspecified, illustrated versions of the Rapunzel story. Megan's hair is a potent symbol throughout the novel, and by the end she can self-consciously analyze its significance for herself (and for readers, of course) and have it cut off to free herself from its twofold constraining significances. When her hair is braided, it ties her to Dorothy and childhood; when it is loose, "almost as though it were separate from me" (143), it constructs her as an object of sexual desire. In some versions of "Rapunzel," it is the witch who cuts off Rapunzel's hair to punish her for her sexual awakening; in *The Tower Room*, it is Megan's decision, taken to shatter the duplicitous discourses of femininity and of sexuality that forever threaten to deprive her of agency. The novel closes with Megan writing, "I will return to Egerton Hall with hair as short as any boy's. Bella will think me fashionable at last, but I will know that what I am is free" (143). From the 1990s moment of writing and reading, this is a culturally historic as well as a personal turning point, since Megan is going back to negotiate a selfhood that is different from either of the discourses of femininity she has previously been exposed to. In the closing section of the novel, her analysis of her situation has finally come together with the feminist reading position prompted throughout by the interrogation of the informing pre-texts.

In their critiques of the patriarchal formations that aspire to shape and define the lives of young women, these two novels presuppose critical feminist reading positions. Their engagement with and disruption of canonical texts and genres, from Shakespeare through fairy tale to the modern school story, together with their historical perspectives, offer the present generation of young female readers reading positions and strategies with which to question textual and social discourses apt to disempower women. Through their different uses of intertextuality, genre mixing, and narrative focalization, they demonstrate that a reader's subject position can be double, and hence interrogative, so that conventional formations such as romance are transformed into possibilities, rather than scripts, for living. Thus although the novels do not offer neat formulations for being female, or even feminine, they do offer strong positions from which to interrogate what that might mean.

Taking Over the Doll House
Domestic Desire and Nostalgia in Toy Narratives

Lois R. Kuznets

The personal is political. This axiom is as true of the doll house as it is of the real home, I have learned since I began examining images of the doll house in toy narratives such as those of Rumer Godden and Russell Hoban. I see these narratives by the light of feminist theories about literary representations of domestic structures and domesticity. These increasingly complex theories, which acknowledge cultural shaping as well as personal intensity of reader response, have encouraged me to examine my own experiences and feelings about houses and domesticity in my daily life and my reading. My critical responses to literary representations have also become more complex since I first discovered myself to be a feminist.

So fraught with feeling is the topic of domestic space for me that, before assuming the stance of scholar/critic, I am compelled to make a personal confession: practically any house, large, small, or miniature, real or imaginary, can seduce me into wanting it—until I see the next one. I am the Dona Juana of domestic and imaginative real estate.

There is more. I hate housework; I have counseled survivors of domestic violence; and I am appalled by the oppressiveness of patriarchal family values. I nevertheless find myself, in exploring imaginative depictions of domestic space, avoiding negative accounts and touching only lightly on children's books that, like the Gothic novel, show the dangerous side of the domestic for women, children, and certain vulnerable men. Freud, whose ideas have certainly influenced my thinking in other matters, uses the word *unheimlich* (literally "unhomelike," but translated as "uncanny") to label such strange and terrifying experiences and feelings that paradoxically arise within the familiar domestic.[1]

Yes, rather than examine the negative, I have indulged my appetite for felicitous domestic representation, salivating over doll houses of all varieties, but particularly elaborate reconstructions of Victorian houses: structures that open to reveal all the rooms and, sometimes, their tiny inhabitants. At one end of the continuum from imagination to reality regarding these domestic interiors lies my fascination with not only nineteenth-century domestic novels for adults or children but also toy narratives that take place within doll houses elaborately described. At the "real life" end lies my barely controlled obsession with buying and decorating houses, a fervor frequently reignited by early evening walks that provide me the opportunity to glance into lighted but not yet shuttered windows and witness the scenes unfolding within.

This personal obsession may account for the influence that a work of phenomenological criticism, Gaston Bachelard's evocative exploration of images of "felicitous space," had on some of my earliest criticism of children's books. And certainly, like any other party who suspects that her obsession stems from pathological sources, I have been delighted to find fellow addicts of doll houses who reveal this same voyeuristic longing in their writing, giving it a respectable, imaginative tinge, subject to deeper analysis. One such is Vivien Greene, who calls the doll house "the home, the evoked dream . . . the old human dream of *being small enough*, Thumbelina on the lily leaf, Alice outside the passage leading into the garden" (23). Greene made me suspect in myself a wish to return to the womb. Katherine Mansfield may use the image of the doll house more originally in "The Doll's House": "There you were, gazing at one and the same moment into the drawing-room and dining room, the kitchen and two bedrooms. That is the way for a house to open! . . . Perhaps it is the way God opens houses at the dead of night when he is taking a quiet turn with an angel" (181). Mansfield, as Genevieve Sanchis Morgan suggests, may be defending her godlike position as author to depict life whole and from many points of view rather than as just a "realistic" slice.

With these authors' works I have tried to erect intellectual and aesthetic defenses of my domestic desires. However, through ongoing self-exploration, especially after reading feminist texts, I have come to find these desires suspect and necessary to analyze in increasingly complex ways. I have come to consider my virtually ineradicable longing a self-limiting and untrustworthy "homesickness," associated with a generalized nostalgia for an idyllic past, by definition unrealized and unrealizable. On the one hand, I consider this nostalgia a

product of my individual psyche developing within the confines of my particular family romance. On the other hand, society and literature have molded
and shaped both my class and gender expectations in ways that have helped to
construct my concept of domestic space.

A point of real confrontation with the troublesome aspects of my longing
came with reading Susan Stewart's *On Longing*. Stewart's poststructuralist,
neo-Marxist, semiotic analysis of the doll house destroyed my comforting il-
lusions about the charm of miniatures in general—especially the elaborately
furnished "dwellings" that I admire, which were never really intended for childhood play but were constructed for adult contemplation and collection. These
items of conspicuous consumption did not make it into a nursery, unless it was
the nursery of a princess, and are now displayed in museums such as the
Chicago Art Institute.[2] Stewart finds the doll house the "most consummate of
miniatures," with "two dominant motifs: wealth and nostalgia" (61). She suggests that the realm of the miniature in general and of the lavishly furnished
doll house in particular reveals a bourgeois adult attempt to claim an objective
interiority in order to replace a subjective emptiness. For Stewart, this fictitious
fulfillment has the deleterious effect of denying this voracious emotional
hunger a history in time, space, or sociopolitical reality.[3]

Sociopolitical realities of domesticity and family values are treated at length
by Stephanie Coontz in *The Way We Never Were*. Coontz not only sensitively
recognizes the sources of our unease in the troubled present but also examines
critically the myths about the past integrity and independence of the American family that support our nostalgia. She reminds us, as the Surgeon General
noted in 1991 when speaking about domestic violence, that "the home is actually a more dangerous place for American women than the city streets" (3).[4]

I discovered a similar distrust of nostalgia, defined as a longing for "*nostos*,
the return home," in Janice Doane and Devon Hodges's *Nostalgia and Sexual
Difference*. They introduce their study of American literary figures with these
words: "As feminists, we argue that nostalgic writers construct their visions of
a golden past to authenticate women's traditional place and to challenge the
outspoken feminist criticisms of it." They see nostalgia as not just a sentiment
but also "a rhetorical practice" designed to persuade, "to authenticate women's
traditional place" (3)—that is, the home. This view of nostalgia, like Stewart's
and Coontz's views, is worth considering with regard to the doll house.

Doane and Hodges echo earlier feminist critics of "the image of woman"
in literature who influenced me in the first flush of my feminist critique of my
own life and reading. I had never heard of Coventry Patmore and his four-vol-
ume paean to the "Angel in the House" (1854–62), in which he gave a name to

the figure of wife and mother that fitted popular Victorian ideals, a name that outlasted his poetry. I was certainly aware, however, of the Angel's presence even if I could not brag, as does Virginia Woolf, that "at last I killed her." Nevertheless, some time in the 1970s, I could characterize her as could Woolf in her day: "She was intensely sympathetic. She was immensely charming. She was utterly unselfish. She excelled in the difficult arts of family life" ("Professions for Women" 285). Not only could I see how my own life was still lived in her shadow, but I could easily discern her in the nineteenth-century novels I loved. I would, therefore, chime in with the feminists who disapprove of this familiar "Angel." I considered this stance one that appropriately raised consciousness about the dangers of romanticizing women's place in the home, emulating Ibsen's *A Doll's House* (1879), in which Nora's slamming of the house door seemed to symbolize her new freedom to find herself away from domestic concerns and belittling condescension. I still believe in that raised consciousness, but I hope my thinking about "woman's place" has become less simplistic.

My review of earlier feminist literary criticism as well as recent feminist theories helped me to grasp the nature of my own troubled longings and anxieties as well as socially constructed middle-class expectations about domestic space and the literature that exalts it. As I turn here to specific exemplary toy narratives, I will try to convey an increased complexity with regard to analysis of domestic space that has not only appeared in the criticism but also gradually seeped into my thinking. Both class and age become factors to add to my gender analysis.[5] I now have a greater understanding of my fascination with domestic space, acknowledging its sheltering aspects for both children and adults but critiquing an essentialist view of the familial roles that are played out within it and what they may signify for women, children, and unprivileged men within a patriarchal world.

In some toy narratives, the sound of Nora slamming the door of her "doll's house" seems still to resound. Take, for instance, Beatrix Potter's *The Tale of Two Bad Mice* (1904), written ostensibly to honor a little girl's new doll house, described on the first page as "very beautiful": "red brick with white windows, and . . . real muslin curtains and a front door and a chimney" (9). Real as its curtains may be, the two live mice that invade the beautiful house find it to be inhabited by two lifeless female dolls—locked into social roles as owner and cook—but to provide no nurturance or sustenance, offering "extremely beautiful" fake food items that "would not come off the plates" (13). These items become a source of frustration and eventual rage to the mice, Tom Thumb and his wife, Hunca Munca, who wreck and scavenge the house to benefit themselves and their children. Despite the conventionality of their family life as well as their eventual remorse and efforts to make some amends, the mice subvert this clear representation of the bourgeois home in which Potter herself was imprisoned from childhood to early adulthood. The subversion is most fully conveyed in Potter's illustrations: one picture shows Hunca Munca proudly displaying an offspring to a lifeless doll dressed up as a policeman to guard the house; another depicts the undaunted mouse couple discussing a mousetrap with their interested but unfrightened children.[6]

In the same vein, one of Rumer Godden's many doll stories, now often cited for its supposedly uncharacteristic 1950s feminism, features the adventurous Impunity Jane: she eventually escapes her doll house for a life of adventure in and out of the pocket of Gideon, who finds through her his own entry into a gang of adventurous boys. Like *The Two Bad Mice, Impunity Jane* (1954) in its own way—but not without ambiguity—suggests that the feminist reader may find in the rejection of the doll house a key to a liberated view of woman, dispensing with the "Angel in the House" role.

More recently, feminist analyses of women's "traditional" place in the home and in British domestic fiction have viewed domesticity and domestic spaces from another perspective, considering what power Nora had to lose as well as gain in slamming that doll house door. In particular, Nancy Armstrong's *Desire and Domestic Fiction* and Elizabeth Langland's "Nobody's Angels: Domestic Ideology and Middle-Class Women in the Victorian Novel" both affirm and criticize the power that lay in the middle-class role of "Angel in the House." They differ in their analysis of that power. Armstrong claims it is a trade-off between mistress and master to exert power in completely separate spheres, a trade-off celebrated in the novel but one that eventually resulted in depoliticized households that downgraded public concerns. Langland, more class conscious, claims that middle-class women in their use of this power aided and abetted middle-class men, not only in spending money and accumulating capital, but also in oppressing the working classes, especially those in domestic service, and thus exerting influence on public as well as private life. Like nineteenth-century domestic conduct books, nineteenth-century fiction, according to both critics, celebrated this gendered power as attainable and desirable without recognizing its dichotomizing and lasting dangers.[7]

It seems to me now that we must add class as well as gender to any analysis of the doll house, since a servant—woman or man—exerts less power than the appointed "Angel" in the domestic workplace. Class issues may appear alongside gender issues in even the simplest narratives. Take, for instance, Faith Jacques's picture book *Tilly's House* (1979), which begins with a topos that stereotypically mimics the assignment of spaces within the home: "Upstairs in the dolls' house there lived a family of wooden dolls. Father worked in his study all day, while Mother did her mending in the parlor. The two children played in the nursery on the floor above. Downstairs in the kitchen, Cook prepared the meals, and gave orders to Tilly." Shortly thereafter, Tilly, the kitchen maid, and hence obviously at the bottom of the power hierarchy, thinks to herself, "I'll be washing and scrubbing all of my life if I stay here. I've got to find a place where I can be free and decide things myself."

Like Nora, Tilly runs away. She is aided in her search for a new home by Edward, an equally animated teddy bear whom she finds downstairs in the big house that shelters the doll house. Tilly sets up housekeeping in an abandoned and therefore cost-free greenhouse. There we last see Edward in "the best chair" and Tilly doing some knitting. This cozy scene has some "Angel in the House" flavor for me. Nevertheless, I must perhaps reconsider my initial reaction on class lines and remember that the power exerted by the "Angel in the House" mending in the upstairs parlor is perhaps more apparent to, and even more desired by, the woman who serves downstairs.[8]

Taking into consideration the representation of both class and gender in the traditional doll house (whose inhabitants are usually manipulated by children in training to become middle- or upper-class adults), I would like to discuss in somewhat more detail Godden's *The Dolls' House* (1947). Here Godden depicts the doll house as a more empowering yet more endangered space than it appears in her *Impunity Jane*.

Godden's Plantaganets, a family created artificially, like all doll families, have been crowded together in two shoeboxes until their present owners, Emily and Charlotte Dane, inherit a doll house from their great aunt. The doll house—shabby at first but renovated by the children—seems the answer to the dolls' dreams and wishes, to which the reader is directly privy but which their child owners are required to intuit. Depicted as conscious and desiring in all of Godden's toy stories, dolls are also shown to be totally dependent on sympathetic human owners for the fulfillment of their wishes. Their existential position is well to keep in mind: perhaps analogous to that of children to adults or allegorical of humans' relationships to an all-powerful God or gods, it can also be compared to that of the poor, the declassed, and those made homeless for whatever reason (including the London blitz of such recent memory in 1947). Godden reminds us of this deprivation: "The Plantaganets were as uncomfortable as anyone in London; they had to live crowded together in two shoeboxes that were cramped and cold" (19).

Margaret and Michael Rustin interpret the fantasy conflicts that ensue among the dolls as psychological projections of the "real," developmental conflict between their sibling owners. The Rustins see the attempts of the older Emily to overpower the less aggressive Charlotte, who eventually learns to fight back, as merely echoed in doll conflict over the ownership of the doll house. This conflict ensues when the motley crew of Plantaganets are displaced by the elegant, antique Marchpane—a doll of china and kid clad in a wedding gown. I find the conflict to be important in its own right, agreeing with Frank Eyre, who describes *The Dolls' House* as succeeding "brilliantly . . . in depicting *adult* situations and conflicts" (qtd. in Carpenter and Prichard 209, emphasis mine).

Significant for my analysis are the peculiarities of the Plantaganet family, which, despite the echoes of royalty in its surname, is hardly of high pedigree or traditionally patriarchal. The father is a china doll who has suffered past abuse and is "still easily made afraid"; his wife, Birdie, is a cheap celluloid doll who came out of a Christmas favor and has something loose rattling in her head; the only candidate for "Angel in the House" is the small wooden Tottie, assigned the role of older sister to a mischievous boy doll, Apple, made of pink-brown plush. Arriving after the doll house and also a gift from the girls' great aunt, the doll Marchpane, supported by Emily, is clearly a doll of a higher class, whose wedding dress might also make traditional claims on the doll house. She is in conflict not only with the sturdy Tottie, whose woodenness, if plebeian, is equally antique and who is also a family heirloom, but more interestingly with the flighty Birdie, whom Emily downgrades to cook once Marchpane arrives. Birdie is immolated while saving Apple from the flame of the birthday candle that lights the doll house lamp. Her heroism contrasts with Marchpane's self-absorption and opportunistic use of Apple, whom Emily has just decreed Marchpane's child. After Birdie's disaster Charlotte, finally emboldened to fight her older sibling, sees that Marchpane does not take Birdie's place: in the restoration of security and order, the cold, haughty, and egotistical doll—who may represent the powerful Angel turned bad as well as the higher-class woman lording it over the lower—goes to a museum.

This doll household has its traditional aspects, yet its establishment shows that Godden recognized both the artificiality and the precariousness of familial relationships. The doll house itself has seen better days and is passed down from one generation of human females to another—to maintain or disdain.[9] Through these permutations, the doll house offers its inhabitants shelter and fits them, however disparate and odd they may be, into conventional social roles, fulfilling a need for connection through familylike activities. Moreover, the Plantaganet parental figures, in particular, have a vulnerability and marginality that call attention to the protective aspects of domesticity for adults as well as children. Meanwhile, the power- and space-hungry Marchpane reminds us of some of the dangers of familial domesticity.

Although, unlike the Rustins, I have chosen to emphasize the adult conflicts in *The Dolls' House,* undeniably questions of age as well as class add a complicating factor to feminist analysis. Indeed, in the narrative theory of children's literature, the handling of the concept of "home" has become, arguably, a marker of works for children rather than adults. In contrasting *The Wind in the Willows* with *The Adventures of Huckleberry Finn,* Christopher Clausen concludes that "when home is a privileged place, exempt from the most serious problems of life and civilization—when home is where we ought, on the whole, to stay—we are probably dealing with a story for children. When home is the chief place from which we must escape, either to grow up or (as in Huck's case) to remain innocent, then we are involved in a story for adolescents or adults" (145). In an analysis of attitudes toward home in five children's novels, Virginia L. Wolf observes a range in tone from mythic to ironic but likewise writes, "We might expect many books for the very young to focus on place as home, often a mythic house. Then, in books for increasingly older children, we might expect the focus to shift to the need to protect, make, find or recover a home. The next shift might be to a character's internalization of the meaning of home, and finally perhaps to the ironies of homelessness" (56). Although Wolf regards the myth of home as a nourishing one, fostering a sense of "being at one with the world," she worries that the embodiment of such a myth "requires freedom from pain and suffering—our own and others'—and obviates the desire for change and growth" (66). I share her broader socioeconomic worries: an idealization of home may endanger the powerless within it even as it answers the apparent and perhaps variant needs of men as well as women and children.[10]

Russell Hoban's *The Mouse and His Child* (1967) addresses masculinist needs at several levels. In this book, the doll house becomes a central object of a traditional quest narrative, going through metamorphoses that seem to echo those of the characters. With forays into existential philosophy, Hoban's novel about tin toys and animals inhabiting a dump at the edge of a human town seems "far out" at first. Yet Hoban seems to echo Clausen and Wolf in distinguishing between children's and adults' literature when he answers recurrent questions about the status of *The Mouse and His Child* as a work for children: "I believed that the winning of a dolls' house was truly a victory and I believed that victory might be a permanent thing. That's why the book is a children's book" (*Books for Your Children* 3).

The Mouse and His Child is of concern here because of the primacy of the doll house, itself, which at every stage is described in loving, if often satiric, detail. Also, of special note from a feminist viewpoint are the central male protagonists: the toy mice, designated father and son, are attached at their hands and, at first when wound, dance in a circle. Their emergent desires show us just what domesticity might have to offer to the male adult and child and also perhaps what Hoban thinks the child, at least, requires of the female to meet these needs. This novel complicates the signification of the doll house even further in terms of age. Its multilevel representation of male desire makes tough demands on feminist theories.

For the mouse child, the elegant doll house, which he glimpses in the toy shop at midnight when he and his father first come to consciousness, signifies a focus of his longing for a family in which "female" toys—an officious elephant and a graceful seal—glimpsed near the doll house will be transformed into a mother and sister. His longing for this arbitrarily constructed family seems so primal that when first denied this "splendid doll house . . . a full three stories high, and a marvel of its kind" (2), he is heartbroken and begins to weep. However, since they belong, as the elephant insists, to the "transient element" (8), the dancing mice are soon sold.

The mouse child represses his longing for the doll house and family through five more Christmases, during which he and his father are taken down from the attic to dance for human children. The appearance of a less elegant doll house as a gift for these children finally makes him cry again, attracting the attention of the cat, who knocks the pair off the table and breaks them. This mishap leads to their arrival at the dump, where they quickly gain the attention of a powerful oppressor, the mechanically brilliant dump boss, Manny Rat, who turns tin toys into worker-slaves to his capitalistic desires.[11] Ironically, they become his nemesis, as well, but not until the father and son go through much developmental pain and suffering.

During this period, the elephant, seal, and doll house all arrive at the dump as well. The doll house is now a "charred ruin of a doll house with its mansard roof smashed, its lookout missing, its ladies and gentlemen long gone" (51). The elephant there undergoes a virtual rape by Manny Rat, who enslaves her as his personal servant. Her humbling appears connected also to false female assumptions about the doll house: "She had thought herself a lady of property, secure in her high place, she had been sold like any common toy. . . The house itself, *her* house, as she had always believed, had been cut off abruptly from her sight" (29). She must be rescued, in traditional fashion, by her future husband (and son) and acquire the house through marriage. The other female, the seal, has more interesting adventures and ends up in less stringent servitude to a kingfisher, who, nevertheless, uses her as bait. The females' later roles within the restored doll house are questionable to me.

Meanwhile, after leaving the dump, the father and son make friends and acquaintances who become allies in their fight against Manny and are called "Uncles," another expression of the child's need for family. The father discovers how to express his own masculinist desire for place, defined at first as "territory" by a warring male shrew almost immediately killed in battle: "It's what you fought for, or what your father fought for, and you feel all safe and strong there. It's the place where, when you fight, you win" (45). After many adventures, they end up back in Manny's home territory, where the rats first turned the doll house into a house of ill repute and then Manny took it over as a symbol of his upwardly mobile status, giving still another masculinist insight into the nature of domesticity for the adult.

Under cover of Manny's "housewarming," however, the mice and their allies are able to complete their winning of territory/home through a pitched battle that unmans Manny by knocking his teeth out and frees the elephant. Victory is achieved with the help of the Uncles, who now include the kingfisher attended by the seal. Thus, the child's desire for family and the father's for territory can focus on the doll house, and the father can now ask the elephant, so humbled is she, to be his wife. The seal, like everyone else, is won over by the enthusiasm of the mouse child and agrees to become a sister.

The house, in turn, is renovated but not restored to its traditional splendor or exclusiveness. Its many transformations have left their mark; yet, "phoenix-like, the place seemed reborn of itself. . . The house assumed a look of wild confidence and reckless bravado" (157). Attractively, this reconstruction leads to no elitism. Won by pitched battle, the doll house does not become the traditional masculine inheritance regained, like Toad Hall cleansed of its invaders. Nor does it remain a "private" domain as one might expect from the child's insistence on family and the father's wish for territory. Unlike Godden's *The Dolls' House* house, this house won back becomes an inn, open to transients and site of edifying gatherings for all the friendly dump inhabitants. More violent, satiric, and ironic than Godden in his depiction of victory and more generally masculinist in his vision of the needs fulfilled by the doll house, Hoban seems, nevertheless, reluctant to include only the winners or the nice characters in his reconciliation. Eventually, even Manny becomes an Uncle, although he is barely foiled in one more cunning yet disastrous attempt to regain his ascendence. Inclusively and communally, the characters may all live happily ever after in this doll house become inn.

To make a clear feminist statement with regard to these two narratives is surprisingly difficult. Godden's work is hardly an iconoclastic depiction of domesticity and domestic space. Still, her image of the doll house in this immediately post–World War II novel can be read not as partaking of a nostalgia for a "home sweet home" of the past but as embodying shelter for a variegated crew of beings of good will but very different pasts and ages, who can join under one roof and construct a family for their mutual protection against a traditional, yet ill-willed, claimant. And Godden makes fewer stereotypical gender distinctions than does Hoban, who, for all his inclusiveness, engenders both elephant and seal in stereotypical ways. Their suffering and struggles before the recovery of the doll house produce no such aspirations as those of the mouse and his child to become self-winding. After the inn is set up, the females lead only "The Fashion Forum and Homemaker's Clinic" (177) among the inn's seminars. Traditional female roles are reinforced rather than reexamined in Hoban's revisioning of the doll house.

In 1967, when Hoban published *The Mouse and His Child,* Betty Friedan's *The Feminine Mystique* (1963) had not yet had wide impact. Friedan's testament and then Kate Millett's resounding *Sexual Politics* (1969), with its "images of woman" approach to literature, had profound consciousness-raising effects on me, however. They form part of my suspicion of the doll house. In addition, as I work through these images of doll houses, I begin to think that still more basic questions should be asked, even if they cannot be answered here. These questions strike at the heart of the association between domestic security and family. They problematize the ways in which Godden and Hoban construct their motley and/or extended families. They require a deconstruction of what Godden, Hoban, and even I, at another stage of life, might have considered only "natural" for humans. Why need any one of these fantasy beings ensconced in their doll houses take on any particular traditional role—husband, wife, father, son, mother, daughter, uncle—all of which appear arbitrary? Indeed, a glimpse of the arbitrariness of gender and other roles is one liminal element that toy narratives can offer. Yet, the inflexibility with which Godden and Hoban alike deal with the issue of roles suggests the difficulty of avoiding an essentialist view or at least the assumption that child readers cannot do without assumed fixed roles any more than they can do without the secure shelter that is part of each book's happy ending.

In this age of increased homelessness, no feminist could deny the desire for safe shelter, but perhaps we should consider the longing for fixed familial roles a product of self-limiting nostalgia. In literature and in life, need we assume that children's (or adults') emotional and material needs can be met only by both traditional domestic space and inflexible roles played by all? After all, in literature, doll houses offer unorthodox possibilities for human life by sheltering motley groups of toys and animals; theoretically, we could break with assigned family roles in real life as well. These roles unfortunately tend not only to reestablish patriarchal hierarchies but also to foster impossible expectations of emotional satisfaction for all inhabitants within an unchangeable "felicitous space" called home.[12]

Comforts No More

The Underside of Quilts in Children's Literature

Cheryl B. Torsney

Quilts, called "the symbol of American identity at the *fin de siècle*" (Showalter, *Sister's Choice* 147) and the "Great American Art" (Mainardi), serve not just as a vehicle of political propaganda intended to evoke warm feelings of family and national unity, but also as the form in which we memorialize our loved ones taken by AIDS, the worst plague of the modern age.[1] Perhaps it is not surprising that the quilt has been adopted by the political left as a representation of multiculturalism and by the political right as an embodiment of family values. Like the doll houses inspected by Lois Kuznets, the gardens explored by Lissa Paul, or even the dinosaurs exhumed by Susan Willis elsewhere in this book, quilts are multivalent. Unlike any other contemporary image or material artifact in our end-of-the-century culture, quilts connote warmth, security, and comfort and trope ideas of family, community, and national harmony.

At least that is how we read the pieced quilt top, which has emerged in the American consciousness not only as decorating motif and national symbol but also as the focus for narratives designed for juvenile and adult audiences. As narrative subjects, quilts are further troped, for they are intensely textual as well as textural. Literal as well as figurative fabrications, assembled of a pieced (or appliquéd) top, a middle (usually batting but sometimes another quilt or blanket), and a back, they are fairly Aristotelian in construction. Although the general public's vision of the quilt is largely limited to the Amish abstract tradition or patched scrapwork bedcover, quilts have long functioned as representational accounts. Some quilts, like those stitched to promote presidential candidates and the temperance cause, have functioned as political speech acts in fabric. Others, like Harriet Powers's famous Bible quilts and the NAMES Project AIDS quilt, tell complex intertextual tales about other narratives.[2] As bonafide narratives, story quilts have invited the critical examinations to which we subject other representations; however, even the abstract, appliqué, and presentation quilts tell stories about their makers', givers', receivers', and cultures' engagement with them.

At their most basic level, all quilts, as layered structures that are, by convention, knotted or quilted to secure the three strata of fabric and to fix the shifting middle layer, offer models of text in a Barthesian sense. Thus, much as our culture wants to read quilts as straightforward statements of solidarity, I suggest, rather, that they are models and metaphors of textuality. As such, readings of quilts are only provisional, dependent upon the audience, potentially subversive. The gaps between the layers and in the stitching cannot be ignored. Neither can the underside of the cover, where the quilting is itself more readily visible and speaks in a different register than the pieced top.

Unlike most other texts, however, quilts are culturally positioned within the women's sphere. Traditionally, a girl learned to piece and quilt at a very young age, storing up quilts as part of her dowry. During her lifetime, fabric was exchanged, quilts were presented as gifts for departing friends, and quilting bees were anticipated occasions for companionship.[3] In the rush to reclaim and revalue women's history in the 1970s and 1980s, quilts were adopted as the image par excellence of women's creativity in the face of hardship, as speaking for women in the political arena. Only recently have we moved beyond that unexamined sentimentality to recognize that quilts—and narratives focusing on quilts and quiltmaking—are not as innocent as they seem. Because of their textual construction and their association with women's sphere, we can use feminist theories (particularly literary and anthropological theories) to illuminate how quilts and quiltmaking, particularly as they are represented in children's literature, subvert the status quo. Feminist theories can help us to dismantle the pathos connected with quilts and show us how quilts offer models not necessarily of domestic happiness or of a thriftiness that reinforces patriarchal culture, but of a potentially aggressive refusal to accept hierarchies of race, class, and gender.

One of the earliest texts in American culture to use quilts figuratively is a short essay titled "The Patchwork Quilt" (1845), written by a pseudonymous "Annette" for the *Lowell Offering*, a literary magazine for young women employed in the fabric mills in Lowell, Massachusetts. Although Annette was not literally a child—child labor was rare in the Lowell mills, and most of the female employees had completed common school—she was writing for a "female and grassroots" audience that would have included poorer rural women and their urban middle-class sisters *and* their children, especially, undoubtedly, their daughters (Eisler 16).[4] On the surface, Annette's article takes the patchwork quilt as the talismanic device that recovers her autobiographical narrative: "how many passages of my life seem to be epitomized in this patchwork quilt" (152). Annette calls her quilt a "bound volume of hieroglyphics" and then, in one of the first instances in American literature of a character reading her quilt, recalls the provenance of each block of fabric:

Here is a piece of the first dress I ever saw, cut with what were called "mutton-leg" sleeves . . . and here is a fragment of the first gown that was ever cut for me with a bodice waist. . . . Down in this corner a piece of that in which I first felt myself a woman—that is, when I first discarded pantalettes. . . . Here is a piece of the first dress which was ever earned by my own exertions! What a feeling of exultation, of self-dependence, of *self-reliance*, was created by this effort. (152–53)

This moment of communion when the patched top is read becomes conventionalized in narratives to follow Annette's, providing a climax of almost religious proportions, a sense highlighted by the description of the quilt as "a bound volume of hieroglyphics."[5]

This curious double metaphor of quilt as text and patch as hieroglyph is significant, for the first half of the nineteenth century brought a revolutionary shift in the West's understanding of ancient Egyptian script. From the beginning of the sixteenth century, with the publication of Marcilio Ficiono's *Hieroglyphics*, the script was understood as allegorical religious writing that revealed the presence of one god in the pre-Christian world (Senner 20). In 1822, however, Jean François Champollion's reading of the Rosetta Stone marked hieroglyphics as a composite writing, consisting of some figurative and symbolic signs but primarily of phonetic characters (Irwin 6).[6] I suggest that Annette's hieroglyphs can be read in two ways. Read romantically and platonically, the quilt becomes quite nearly a religious artifact, with each patch functioning symbolically as a relic. Read using a "phonetic," that is a context-dependent, or even abstract, rather than religious/symbolic or allegorical, code, this quilt uncovers sounds of a quite different register, which are revealed on its metaphoric underside.

Whereas Annette's surface reading of her quilt top is a warm, symbolic scene of a life progressing from childhood to adult independence, the underside of her narrative is stitched with a progressive restriction of freedom.[7] Among the first patches Annette cites is "a piece of that radiant cotton gingham dress . . .

to wear to the dancing school." This reference to girlish attire and broadly physical activity is followed by her signifying the patch of her first dress with a bodice and then the patch from the dress she wore when she "discarded pantalettes," that is, when her clothing began to be tailored to a developing feminine silhouette and the pantalettes, which permitted a childhood freedom from adult modesty, had to be discarded in favor of conventional women's undergarments. The patches of clothing, then, represent the increasing surveillance and regulation to which Annette and her sister are subjected as they move into womanhood. Annette gives the quilt to her sister upon her marriage, which all too frequently was a prelude to death in childbirth. Annette's sister does die, in fact, though not while delivering a baby but from what we assume is tuberculosis, the "white death," the scourge of the mills, given the "knell-like cough" Annette describes: an illness Annette might have feared for herself (154). At her sister's passing, the patchwork, which now represents death, reverts to Annette.

This short essay was excerpted in *Hearts and Hands,* a rosy, nostalgic documentary film about quilts in American women's history, which was funded, in part, by the Reagan-era National Endowment for the Humanities as part of the Bicentennial effort. Not surprisingly, the film features formal oval portraits of pink-cheeked mill girls accompanied by cheerful voice-overs about how the girls arise at 4:30 a.m. and work until 6:00 p.m., with only a short lunch break, amid the danger and noise of the machinery. In the past, readers have focused on how Annette's quilt figures the family as an integrated unit and constructs its history as a meaningful narrative of independence. Such a reading, however, reinscribes the patriarchal power of the American bourgeoisie, which put its marginalized young women—those without men to protect them—to work at dangerous jobs without adequate pay and benefits.

A subversive reading recognizes that the patriarchal economy of the country put these girls at risk and that Annette's quilt, instead of presenting the family as an integrated unit, performs quite the contrary operation. It is a "bound volume of hieroglyphics," which narrates Annette's family saga using patchwork symbols and also serves as a critique of the more abstract mill system. The quilt is double-voiced, for Annette was, finally, disempowered, "bound" in quite another way. She may have thought she was presenting a narrative of self-reliance in the service of family. We must remember, however, that Emersonian self-reliance was limited to men and that Annette lived at the mill dormitories and sent her money home: she worked as a near slave in poor conditions, both at her overcrowded, poorly ventilated boardinghouse and in the factory.

A generation after "The Patchwork Quilt," Louisa May Alcott's short story "Patty's Patchwork," from *Aunt Jo's Scrap-Bag* (1872), also contains seeds to subvert the male dream of domesticity and submissive, sewing women. This tale presents ten-year-old Patty, whose maiden Aunt Pen has decided to teach her to piece quilts while her mother is having a baby. Here, too, the bed quilt is presented as a text to be read. However, the focus is not on the provenance of the patches but on the grammar, that is, the stitching, which faithfully reflects Patty's moral state when she is piecing. Patty is intrigued by Aunt Pen's skill in reading the text of the patchwork: "This pretty pink and white one so neatly sewed is a good day; this funny mixture of red, blue, and yellow with the big stitches is a merry day; that one with spots on it is one that got cried over; this with the gay flowers is a day full of good little plans and resolutions; and that one made of dainty bits, all stars and dots and tiny leaves, is the one you made when you were thinking about the dear new baby there at home" (195). After the baby dies, having lived only a week, Patty produces symbolic "puckered bits and grimy stitches" (208), which reveal her sorrow. But the more complete narrative of Patty's moral progress is provided by the couplets Aunt Pen embroiders on the four corner squares. These rhymes relate Patty's stealing a bun between meals, tweaking the tail feathers from her pet canary, giving a flower to a poor neighbor child, and weeping over her dead baby sister: of her improvement from a greedy, prank-playing child to a charitable, sensitive girl soon to be a woman.

Just as one reading of Annette's "Patchwork Quilt" has it shoring up the status quo, sentimentally reading the oppression of labor as the engendering of independence, one reading of "Patty's Patchwork" has it patriarchally endorsing the rehabilitation of a rebellious girl into a docile comforter. The story opens with Patty decrying piecing: "I perfectly hate it! and something dreadful ought to be done to the woman who invented it. . . . Well, it *is* tiresome, isn't it, Aunt Pen?" (193). In refusing to piece—taking aggressive action against cultural expectation—Patty "send[s] a shower of gay pieces flying over the carpet as if a small whirlwind and a rainbow had got into a quarrel" (193), putting into action the very forces of nature. This response is more active, more satisfying, perhaps even more "creative" than doing what is expected; such behavior is, however, unacceptable for a girl in high Victorian culture. Once Patty is converted by Aunt Pen to the cultural norm and begins to piece cheerfully, abandoning the aggressive creativity represented by two grand and sweeping natural phenomena—the whirlwind and the rainbow—she becomes, like Aunt Pen, a fairy—a diminutive creature attendant upon something more powerful, perpetually childlike. Patty next learns that by asserting her class prerogative and helping Lizzie, a poor, crippled child, she feels "sort of warm and comfortable" in her heart (205). The lesson in the story can be read as follows: the goal of all little girls is to grow up to become comforters, negotiators, and help-meets, that is, to maintain the status quo rather than pucker the warp and woof of class and gender.

An alternative reading is stitched into the underside of Patty's quilt, how-ever, a reading that focuses not on Patty but rather on Aunt Pen. Although it is true that, as represented in "Patty's Patchwork," a woman's lot involves endless, repetitive handwork, self-sacrifice, and the death of children, we learn that there is strength—and salvation—in work. Here the stitching of patchwork, which Alcott calls "the task which we all find rather tiresome and hard" (197), serves as a synecdoche of women's work, which, interestingly, includes the writ-ing Aunt Pen embroiders on the corner patches.

Elaine Hedges points out in "'The Needle or the Pen'" that feminist literary theorists' recent reading of quilting and other needlework by women as metaphors for female creativity and thus as empowering tropes is not only overrated but historically inaccurate. Hedges claims that many nineteenth-century American women writers viewed sewing "as a powerful symbolic marker of their cultural condition, their restricted domestic role," and thus re-fused to take up the needle (340). Women who wrote did not sew. "Patty's Patch-work," however, deconstructs the opposition Hedges establishes. Here, both needle and Pen perform the moral work of life.

To Patty's opening lament "Well, it *is* tiresome, isn't it?" Aunt Pen answers, "Sometimes; but we all have to make patchwork, my dear, and do the best we can with the pieces given us" (193). Her response may seem simperingly sen-tentious when in fact it can be read as boldly existential, a model of textuality: women must stitch their own selves, create a personal bricolage, if you will, through labor of all sorts. Metaphorically speaking, "making patchwork" is an identity-creating salvation, much like writing. In fact, in Alcott's world, sewing, teaching, and writing were equivalent enterprises through which women could earn a living (Brodhead 76). Aunt Pen performs all three activities, demon-strating an enviable versatility and control over her situation both within a do-mestic economy and, as an unmarried woman, on the margins, which is where she places her couplets on Patty's quilt.

This marginal position is not without power and authority. As Aunt Pen ex-plains, "Every task, no matter how small or homely, that gets well and cheer-fully done, is a fine thing; and the sooner we learn to use up the dark and bright bits (the pleasures and pains, the cares and duties) into a cheerful, useful life, the sooner we become real comforters, and every one likes to cuddle about us" (196–97). This is the authority of nineteenth-century domestic ideology, through which a culture was "literally disciplined through love, made other-directed and self-denying by the force of their mother's love for them" (Brodhead 71).

Aunt Pen is a writer, as we know from her inked verses, but she is also a reader. (We are told she is nearsighted—perhaps from too much reading?) We see her reading and writing, but we never see her piecing. She is the Pen, the very instrument of writing and self-creation. A Penelope, a woman without a man, here a spinster, she is further positioned outside the bosom of the nuclear family: "I see what is going on, and I have queer plays in my mind just as you little folks do" (195).[8] In seizing the power of the pen (and the pin), she has chosen another option for happiness. She is clearly a member of the class of women Alcott describes in her occasional piece "Happy Women": "superior women who, from various causes, remain single, and devote themselves to some earnest work; espousing philanthropy, art, literature, music, medicine, or whatever task taste, necessity, or chance suggests, and remaining as faithful to and as happy in their choice as married women with husbands and homes" (203). Her piecing—her work—is writing and, through it, teaching Patty "something better even than the good old-fashioned accomplishment of needlework" (196). Patty's patchwork becomes an album quilt, responding intertextually to the narratives of Patty's "sins" by presenting comforting lessons about ethical behavior as written by contemporary domestic ideology. The quilt, stitched by Patty but constructed by Aunt Pen, becomes a sort of book, a cultural agent of what Richard Brodhead calls disciplinary intimacy. The narrative of book and quilt—and its collaborators—becomes a comforter. The power of the pen and the pin—the power of narrative—becomes the power of comfort, a valued commodity indeed in Alcott's world.

Three recent picture books imagine quilts not as warm domestic comforts that support a hegemonic economy but rather as fabric narratives that upset the culturally dominant worlds of power and privilege. Patricia Polacco's award-winning *The Keeping Quilt* features several generations of a Russian immigrant Jewish family cherishing a quilt as an inalienable possession. In Deborah Hopkinson's *Sweet Clara and the Freedom Quilt,* Sweet Clara, a pre–Civil War slave, upends the masculinist notion of a singular artist/genius creating art in the absence of community. Faith Ringgold's well-known *Tar Beach* presents panels from one of her famous story quilts, which narrate the heroine's escape from obstacles associated with race, class, and gender.

Beautifully illustrated in sepia tones, except for the brightly colored family quilt and the originary babushka, *The Keeping Quilt* is about the quilt's power to narrate not only women's history but also family history. Women's lives are represented by Polacco's substantial female figures as vibrant, bustling, creative. Whereas "Annette" lived without female models of independent action and yearned for self-reliance, Polacco's Great-Gramma Anna, even as a girl, is a figure to be reckoned with, the independent matriarch-to-be. It is on the boat to America that we first see her, wearing "the same thick overcoat and big boots she had worn for farm work." Like Alcott's Aunt Pen, she wears glasses, suggesting not so much impaired as improved vision. Like most children, she is a natural linguist, learning English quickly. And like the youthful Annette, she loves to dance. When she outgrows her clothes, her mother organizes a quilting bee, and the neighborhood ladies appliqué animals fashioned from the old fabric onto a quilt bordered by Anna's babushka.

The quilt becomes a significant (and signifying) object in the domestic life of the household, linking the family, through its text of memory, to the community of the Old Country and its customs. The family uses the quilt for all manner of religious and secular purposes: the Sabbath tablecloth, a picnic blanket, the wedding *huppa,* a baby blanket, a lap blanket, and a shroud. In its multipurposiveness, Polacco's quilt resembles other literary quilts. It is different, however, in the author's positioning herself as an oral storyteller, who is merely, according to the flyleaf, "the present caretaker" of the quilt. Throughout the years this quilt has come to encode family history, but whereas family Bibles (another venue for writing family narrative) normally descend patrilineally, these quilts descend matrilineally.

The last page of the book depicts Polacco and her husband cradling their infant daughter in the quilt: "Twenty years ago I held Traci Denise in the quilt for the first time. Someday she, too, will leave home and she will take the quilt with her." The quilt will serve as a rite-of-passage gift signaling adulthood for Traci Denise, who will carry on the matriarchal traditions of the family begun by her great grandmother.

The narrative offered by Polacco's quilt ranges more broadly across time and space than that told by either Annette's or Patty's patchwork, for we hear the Keeping Quilt speak to four generations in two countries. Whereas the patchwork quilts imply the generational transfer of power through the vehicle of the familial text(ile), the handing down of authority is the very subject of *The Keeping Quilt*. In this narrative even more clearly than in "The Patchwork Quilt" or "Patty's Patchwork," the quilt functions as what the revisionary anthropologist Annette B. Weiner calls an inalienable possession, which, by definition, empowers its owner.

Weiner argues that anthropological gift theory has been biased toward masculinized Western constructions of the gift economy. Older theories, such as those of Marcel Mauss and Bronislaw Malinowski, have assumed male power in the economic sphere and discounted women's contributions. In many cultures, however, women control textile possessions, which then form "a currency of sorts made from 'cloth'":

Intricate symbolic meanings semantically encode sexuality, biological reproduction, and nurturance so that such possessions, as they are exchanged between people, act as the material agents in the reproduction of social relations. Most important, cloth possessions may also act as transcendent treasures, historical documents that authenticate and confirm for the living the legacies and powers associated with a group's or an individual's connections to ancestors and gods. Historically, women's control over these arenas has accorded them powers associated with magical potency, sacred prerogatives, political legitimacy, and life-giving and life-taking social controls. (3)

Possessions, Weiner concludes, are "given, yet not given. Some are kept within the same family for generations with retention not movement, bestowing value" (4). Women gain power through protecting these possessions, which "provide authentication of historical, ancestral linkages" (152). Even if these possessions are symbolically and not literally kept, they are nonetheless inalienable, illustrating the paradox of keeping while giving. Weiner concludes: "Cloth may be the most apt metaphor to visualize the paradox of keeping-while-giving as societies in all parts of the world associate weaving with acts of tying and unraveling, sacred threads and dangerous dyes, woven warps and unworked woofs, expressions of longed for unity juxtaposed against the realities of death, destruction, and change" (153–54). Quilts function perhaps as the inalienable possessions par excellence of the Western world.

Polacco's Keeping Quilt, for example, is given (passed on matrilineally) and yet kept (within the family) at the same time. Like all inalienable possessions, the quilt functions as an agent against change. A tie to the family's Russian past, it "authenticates cosmological origins, kinship, and political histories," militating against change and loss (Weiner 9). At the same time, paradoxically, it is the symbol of change—the object used to celebrate passages into birth, marriage, death. Further, an inalienable possession like Polacco's quilt "authenticates the authority of its owner." Thus the quilt, that gift of Great-Gramma Anna that was never, in fact, given away, empowers Polacco to speak and will confer that authority on Traci Denise when she reaches her majority. As Weiner explains, "Inalienable possessions are the representation of how social identities are reconstituted through time. The reproduction of kinship is legitimated in each generation through the transmission of inalienable possessions, be they land rights, material objects, or mythic knowledge" (11). In *The Keeping Quilt,* authority is legitimated, social identity is constituted, and mythic knowledge is transmitted through the vehicle of Great-Gramma Anna's quilt.

Authority, identity, and knowledge are formulated and communicated with a substantial difference in Deborah Hopkinson's *Sweet Clara and the Freedom Quilt*. Here the quilt is a collaboratively constructed artifact, whose purpose is to produce the redefinition of the very group that originated the artifact. This is a tale of one young girl's selfless strategy of escape from slavery, that peculiar institution that entailed, among other cruelties, the separation of family members to eliminate loyalties and thus the potential power in them.

Twelve-year-old Sweet Clara has been brought from North Farm to Home Plantation to pick cotton. At her new home, her guardian, Aunt Rachel, reasons that for her charge to survive, she must learn to be an expert seamstress; otherwise, the hard work of the fields will kill her. Aunt Rachel accomplishes her goal, and Sweet Clara joins the household staff. In her sewing room off the kitchen, Clara overhears a discussion among other household staff about the Underground Railroad. No one knows how to locate the way stations, although one man asserts softly, "It be easy if you could get a map . . ."

Sweet Clara's project becomes sewing a map to freedom into a quilt, "a picture that wouldn't wash away." She listens to visitors describe the landscape beyond the plantation and then appliqués her patches accordingly: "Sometimes I had to wait to get the right kind of cloth—I had blue calico and flowered blue silk for creeks and rivers, and greens and blue-greens for the fields, and white sheeting for roads." In the end, of course, Sweet Clara follows her own map to freedom, leaving the Freedom Quilt behind with Aunt Rachel, now old and frail: "People go to look at it, even folks from neighboring farms. I know because some of them come and tell me how they used it to get free." Pieced communally, this map is used to deconstruct the community that constructed it in slavery and to reconstruct it in the context of freedom.

In de Certeauvian terms, Sweet Clara's strategy is "tactical" in its exercise of subversive power by one who is socially and politically powerless. According to Michel de Certeau, a tactic is a catch-as-catch-can—or, in this case, patch-as-patch-can—opportunity, which the powerless must use to create their own advantage. Our lives are composed of everyday practices that are by nature tactical: shopping, tricks, shortcuts, conversation, food preparation (xix). Quilts in general are tactical, and Sweet Clara's Freedom Quilt is especially so.

Normally, we think of maps as being strategic, which de Certeau defines as the opposite of tactical. "Strategies . . . conceal beneath objective calculations their connection with the power that sustains them from within the stronghold of its own 'proper' place or institution" (xx). While strategy belongs to the language of the general, tactic belongs to the language of the subaltern. In texts about quilts, maps are most frequently associated with male adventurers (see, for instance, Joyce Carol Oates's poem "Celestial Timepiece," in which women sew quilts while men create maps), but here the map sewn by Sweet Clara is a tactical maneuver undertaken by a female slave, which strikes a blow to the peculiar institution created by the white patriarchy. In fact, her artistry is the final product of a kind of feminist collaboration, since the male slaves who give Clara the information she needs to craft her quilt are feminized and disempowered. She does not position herself as the romanticized male version of the solitary artist/genius;[9] rather, she sees herself as a member of a community and perceives her duty as contributing to communal happiness by removing her collaborators to freedom. Finally, Sweet Clara stitches a quilt whose importance lies not in its everyday use but rather in its use for a series of specific days during which the memorized text would guide escaping slaves to freedom. Just as Alice Walker's "Everyday Use," a short story for an adult audience, presents quiltmaking as "*the* signal mode of confronting chaos through a skillful blending of patches" (Baker and Pierce-Baker 720), *Sweet Clara and the Freedom Quilt* offers Clara's quilt as an exemplary map, an ordering of community experience in an effort to revolutionize that community.

Serving as a comfort (and literally a comforter) to Aunt Rachel, who remains behind, the quilt is likewise a comfort to the book's audience, for whom the experience of slavery is, shall we say, "whitewashed." Readers are left to believe that the inner strength and creativity of a disempowered little girl defeats, locally at least, the horrific institution of chattel slavery. The message confuses, however. James Ransome's illustrations create a sun-dappled Home Plantation, presented on the title page as a neat and orderly landscape filled with cotton-picking slaves, an overseer, and the mistress sitting in a carriage, observing the progress of the workday. The illustration that faces the first page of the text features another sunny sky and Sweet Clara and Young Jack in conversation while they pick cotton. Jack is smiling broadly. The slave cabin is warm and nurturing, if sparsely furnished, and Clara's natural world is sunny, bright, and flower filled. When Jack is returned to the plantation after having run away, we are told only that "he didn't smile the way he used to." Slave life is so sanitized in this tale that one might well wonder why Clara felt the need to run away—perhaps in the service of telling a comforting story about a special quilt. A subversive reading might question how that motive serves children and history.

Faith Ringgold's "Tar Beach" quilt, the first in her series *Woman on a Bridge*, provides the premise for her picture book *Tar Beach*. After seeing a poster of the "Tar Beach" quilt, Andrea Cascardi, an editor at Crown Books for Young Readers, imagined it as a successful children's book and approached Ringgold, who enthusiastically transformed a piece of art for an adult audience into a picture book for children. Ringgold sees the narrative as universal: "Kids all over the world love *Tar Beach*, even in places where they have no tar roofs. They still have dreams, don't they?" (Krull 62).

These dreams find their articulation in quilts. Like Sweet Clara's Freedom Quilt, Ringgold's text provides a tactical map to be used in a campaign for self-empowerment. Like Polacco's Keeping Quilt, the way to power is through family history, even if, in the case of the book *Tar Beach*, that history is somewhat fictionalized. Like Polacco's bedcover, Ringgold's "Tar Beach" is an appliqué quilt, and, like Patty's Patchwork, it features a verbal narrative inscribed at the margins. Retextualized as a picture book with a reproduction of the quilt included at the end, *Tar Beach*, like "Patty's Patchwork," deconstructs the apparent binary between pen and pin, pulling the marginalized narrative into the center. As in Alcott's story, the quilt *is* the text, though even more richly so.

The story is narrated in the first person by Cassie, who, like Sweet Clara, is an African-American girl in braids whose dreams of ownership and possession are recorded in the quilt. Whereas Sweet Clara dreams of owning herself in a land that promises her freedom, Cassie, in the late 1930s, is technically free, but because of her race, she and her family still face enormous obstacles. Like Sweet Clara, Cassie dreams of proprietorship and the power that possession confers on the owner. We learn that she was born in 1931 on the day the George Washington Bridge opened and that ever since she has wanted the bridge to be hers as an inalienable possession, if not a capitalistic one.

Evoking both the liberated slave in the African-American folktale and Dedalus, Cassie flies over the bridge in her dreams and claims it as her own.[10] Because she can fly, that is, disappear into freedom and create art in this new space, "that means I am free to go wherever I want for the rest of my life." Her father is not so lucky. Of mixed race, he cannot join the construction union and is thus deprived of work, even though he helped to build the George Washington Bridge and thus is a type of artist himself. Cassie decides that she will claim the building that houses the union hall for her father. For her brother, she will fly over the ice cream factory. As she tells Be Be, whose name suggests an imperative to create oneself, "All you need is somewhere to go that you can't get to any other way. The next thing you know, you're flying among the stars." Through her artistry, through her flight, the fictional Cassie (like Ringgold herself) is able to escape the obstacles erected by race, class, and gender privilege and seize the power to create her narrative of self.

This power has been seized by other important African-American artists, such as bell hooks, who credits Ringgold's artistry with her own enfranchisement as a writer: "Seeing Faith Ringgold's elaborate story quilts, which insist on naming, on documentation, on black women telling our story, I found words" (*Yearning* 115). hooks recognizes the relationship through artistry between herself, who chose writing as her medium, and someone like Ringgold: "Since my creative work is writing, I proudly point to ink stains on this quilt which mark my struggle to emerge as a disciplined writer" (121). As in "Patty's Patchwork," quilts and writing are again linked through the notion of discipline. Ringgold's story quilts, especially perhaps "Tar Beach," a narrative of creative possession and the possibilities for self-identity through artistry, become for hooks an icon of the power of African-American womanhood: the proud product of the needle and the pen.[11]

As texts in themselves, quilts are more than simply entertaining; they are magical and often miraculous life-giving forces. hooks cites Ringgold's explanation of the quilt as "art and artifice, resid[ing] in that space where art and life come together": "'It covers people. It has the possibility of being a part of someone forever'" (hooks, *Yearning* 121). As represented in children's literature since the nineteenth century, quilts are among the texts that do indeed create and illuminate the quiltmaker's and quilt owner's identities. But they do not always shore up the status quo. They are not always comforts. Rather, they are complex, double-tongued, tactical, textual metaphors, inalienable possessions that, like all works of great artistry, confer power by their possession. Thanks to the Rosetta Stone provided by feminist theories, we can understand that if children's books representing quilts are "bound volumes of hieroglyphics," they are more intelligible—and more complexly layered—than we ever thought before.

PART III

Culture

A Bad Hair Day for G.I. Joe

Karen Klugman

In the aisle marked "Action Figures" at Toys "R" Us, I held in my hands a five-inch plastic doll named Throttle and tried to imagine him as the 6′ 2″, 200-lb. hulk described on the package with his "Nuke nuk gloves, vape gun, laser gun and arm-mounted sprocket launcher [that] hurls deadly motorcycle sprockets." My home was populated with more than a hundred Playmobil guys and countless Lego body parts, but until I arrived home with Throttle, my nine-year-old son had not owned a bona fide action figure, not even G.I. Joe, "a real American hero." Days earlier, however, I had had to face the fact that I had lost the battle against the violent impulses of boys: I had found in Seth's room a gruesome diorama of Lego people—one burning at the stake, another hung by his neck, a third beheaded, and all, including the fallen head and the executioner, wearing that placid Lego expression. Still more to my surprise, Seth was able to tell me all about the Biker Mice from Mars—how the mice (Modo, Vinnie, and Throttle) were the good guys battling the evil Plutarkians (Evil Eye Weevil, Greasepit, Lectromag, Dr. Karbundle, and Lawrence Limburger). How did a kid who lives in a house with neither a television nor action figures in it come to know so much about Biker Mice?

"I saw them on TV one day at a friend's house," he explained. "And we talk about them in school."

"It is a middle class delusion—though one often propagated by child experts—that children can be shielded from consumption, that proper parenting will nip children's interest in toys and television in the bud," writes telecommunications professor Ellen Seiter (3). Once they reach school age, children share a culture, if not through the media, then through an informal "show and tell." Parents often interpret a child's begging to buy a particular toy solely as an expression of greed, when it may convey a longing to be part of a community (Willis, *A Primer* 32–33). As Seiter has found for television and Willis for toys, however, despite its communal aspects, children's culture is segregated into a boys' culture and a girls' culture. In my informal surveys of elementary and middle school children, I found that although a kid's familiarity with Biker Mice correlates little with his parents' socioeconomic, educational, or philosophic background, it correlates almost perfectly with his gender. For some parents, such as the mother I passed in Caldor's whose son was reaching out from the seat of the shopping cart for a Pocahontas lunch box, gender-specific marketing may determine the gamut of their children's possessions. "No!" she said as she pushed the cart faster, "I told you Pocahontas is for girls." But even parents who make a concerted effort to change gender attitudes encounter opposition in the form of media pressure, peer pressure on the child, and possibly innate gender preferences.

This pressure to segregate children by gender begins at birth with strict rules about color coding. Parents find that baby clothes and paraphernalia still come in pastel pink for girls, pastel blue for boys, and white or yellow for babies who have yet to be born and whose sex is unknown or babies whose parents do not mind that a stranger might mistake their gender. Later, parents will adapt to market standards for older kids: pastels have a place in the female palette for life, but the color scheme for boys toddler age and older excludes these shades. Pink is so taboo for boys that one of the most subversive acts a parent can perform is to dress a boy in a hot pink shirt.

The upscale Playmobil building/fantasy toys that come in a variety of primary colors for older toddlers and elementary school kids used to be considered unisex. Although the toys are weighted toward males in their historical and adventurous themes and by the small percentage of female figures included among them, their doll-like design and easily assembled environments encourage role playing as well as construction. Playmobil also has a recent line of toys called Playhouse, which is packaged in pink and lavender and includes lots of girl figures, pictured in traditionally female activities, such as food preparation, child care, and horseback riding. In the Playhouse, the male figures get married, push the baby carriage, and read newspapers, whereas the guys in the primary-color Playmobil line ride motorcycles, fight fires, and pilot spaceships. The introduction of color segregation in Playmobil toys subtly but clearly affirms traditional gender roles. If the domestic lifestyle advertised in pink was taboo for boys, then what about the girls who had been playing with more adventurous figures featuring primary colors? Had the girls been practicing a form of gender bending?

In spite of contemporary commentary that plays down differences between the genders, dolls—our earliest symbolic role models—continue to be manufactured, marketed, and purchased along gender lines. A glance at the pastel color coding for baby dolls confirms that they are marketed exclusively for girls. On most packages, furthermore, there is a photograph of a girl cuddling, feeding, grooming, or simply smiling at the doll. Although some baby dolls are male, no packaging that I have seen depicts boy owners. Parents who buy baby dolls for their sons defy the gender roles circumscribed by the toy market. When I mentioned to a colleague that I was doing research on gender divisions in toys, she told me proudly that her four-year-old son loves to play with Barbie and that he brought one into nursery school for "Barbie Day." Barbie is no baby, but implicit in the mother's statement is Barbie's identification as a girls' doll and this career mother's belief that her son's playing with dolls is not only to be condoned but to be encouraged. This mother's point of view reflects current media emphasis on the importance of fathering: in stories and images, men are increasingly depicted as sharing in child care. In fashion advertising, men carry toddlers on their shoulders and hold naked babies against their chests. Yet in spite of this new dad fad, dolls that require care and teaching are not marketed to boys: the insidious message to children and adults alike remains that nurturing is something that boys do not do.

In contrast, there are plenty of dolls for boys that encourage behaviors that could in no way be called nurturing. Children ages three and older are eligible to play with dolls that "contain small parts which may present a choking hazard": for boys, this means they enter the world of action figures. John Berger's observation about gender manifestation in visual arts, that "men act and women appear" (45), applies to children's dolls as well. With guns, swords, nunchakus, and sticks of dynamite, action figures for boys reinforce Berger's claim that, traditionally, "a man's presence is dependent upon the promise of power which he embodies" (47). Jointed at the elbow as well as the shoulder and at the knees in addition to the hips, the dolls are capable of actually operating their weapons. They come with instructions on how to place the weapon in the hands and pull back and release the arm so that the spring thrusts it toward an enemy. Variations on this procedure abound, such as raising Ninja Shadow's right arm, then squeezing his knees together so that he will perform a "Rapid Striking Chopping Action." Sometimes a part of the body itself might double as a weapon, as is the case with Robot Wolverine, who has "robotic arm

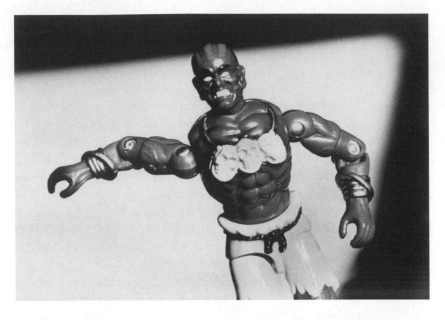

weapons." "Squeeze Robot Wolverine's legs together and his arms fly off!" But The Tick (otherwise known as Human Bullets™) takes the cake for sacrificial body part: "Push the button on Human Bullets™ to see him shoot off his head!"

Meanwhile, over in the pink and lavender girls' section, the comparable three- to ten-inch dolls reaffirm Berger's observation that "a woman's presence expresses her own attitude to herself, and defines what can and cannot be done to her" (46). Equipped with self-directed accessories, such as combs, mirrors, nail polish, and hair dryers, the dolls serve as objects to be acted upon. Even if their hands were designed to hold the comb (which they seldom are), most girls' dolls are jointed only at the shoulder and the hip and thus are incapable of reaching their own hair. Some girls' dolls are dwarfed by their accessories, such as a comb the size of the torso, which are obviously meant to be used by their caretakers rather than by the dolls themselves. In the Liddle Kiddle collection, the dolls, who each hold a tiny hairbrush, are themselves accessories encased in a plastic bubble on a string to be worn as a necklace. The statuesque Perfume Secret Beauty serves double duty as doll and perfume bottle: squeeze her wings, and she sprays perfume from the top of her head. Likewise, Lipstick Secret Beauty, when spun *en pointe* on a plastic base, reveals her body to be the container for the bubble-gum–scented lipstick that emerges from her tiara. (Maybe Victoria's Secret is that she, too, can double as an accessory.)

Whereas collecting the figures in a boys' series can mean learning the names, nationalities, individual histories, allegiances, and attack moves of a dozen wildly different creatures, girls' sets typically have such subtle defining characteristics that, like Barbie, they appear to be one doll in different outfits. The Princess of the Flowers series by YES! Entertainment Corporation, for example, consists of eight members that differ only by the colors of the edges of their dresses, by their names, and by their accessories. A new adventure edition for girls, Sailor Moon, depicts eight young female scouts lined up in a row in the same frontal stance, distinguished only by the colors of their outfits and their hair colors and styles. Their bio cards (a "clip & collect" feature used like sports cards for almost all boys' sets and a recent marketing crossover for girls' collections) read like kindergarten surveys, in which children must define themselves in terms of Favorite Food, Favorite Color, Favorite Animal, and Favorite Subject. This series introduced the radical idea of a bad doll in a girls' collection, but the narrative is simplistic, requiring only that Sailor Moon and her friends—Sailor Venus, Sailor Mercury, Sailor Jupiter, and Sailor Mars—"use their special powers to save the world from evil Queen Beryl!" Unlike the boys' stories, which situate the action in exotic territory, the script abruptly takes a turn into domestic space by inviting the doll's owner to take care of the doll: "Each doll has a poseable body, removable outfit, and beautiful hair you can

style." For all that some members of society advance notions of empowering women and making responsible caregivers of men, girls' collections of dolls reinforce the traditional female preoccupation with physical appearance and homemaking, while the boys' collections embody conflict and superhuman power.

More than twenty years ago, Berger suggested a simple but powerful exercise to anyone who wanted to learn about the gender differences that we take for granted in the visual arts—to imagine men in familiar paintings and photographs of nude women. In the same way, imagine a collection of girls' dolls that differ in their body shapes—some are fat like Goro or Boss Man, some are short, and all are incredibly muscular. Their jointing permits multiple actions, they operate their own accessories, and they can transform into multiple personalities. Then imagine a collection of immobile boys' figures that differ only by the colors of their outfits, their alliterative names (Football Frank, Sleepover Sam, Beach Party Bob), and their hair, which is stranded and styleable. Dolls similar to these crossover fantasies actually exist, but they are marketed for the opposite gender. With delineated muscles, large breasts, and green plastic hair, She-Hulk, a creation of Toy Biz, is capable of firing her gamma crossbow, but under the name of Jennifer Walters she "still maintains her law practice and has even served as the Assistant District Attorney for New York City!" Meanwhile, in the Barbie Shop, barefooted Butterfly Art Ken and his African-American counterpart, Butterfly Art Steve, relax in identical mesh shirts, cutoffs, and woven necklaces. Their accessories include a pair of sunglasses and a set of "cool, washable decorations."

The way that dolls are packaged and advertised further stereotypes gender roles. Many packages for girls' dolls feature photographs of girls holding, grooming, or otherwise caring for a doll or sometimes just gazing at the doll in the plastic wrapping. These images of girls, like the layering of accessories from doll to owner, create a link between fantasy play and real life that you will not find in the marketing of boys' dolls. A young female consumer is expected to identify with the model in the photograph as much as, if not more than, with the doll. Although they have distinctive racial traits (the ethnicity of the model must match that of the doll), the models, posed and smiling, reveal no individual personality. The girls on the packages differ only in the same subtle ways the dolls do—in clothing and hair style. Selecting which doll to purchase within a set means simply choosing among accessories or hairdos.

The packaging of action figures rarely makes use of photography, let alone photographs of boys. Instead, the doll visible through the plastic wrapping is usually surrounded by colorful, elaborate illustrations that depict the figure as more expressive and lifelike than it actually is. The overall package design for the boys' figures—the lettering, the facial expressions, and the activity of the illustrated figures—is more complex and of higher print and color resolution than that for girls' dolls. If there are a dozen figures in a boys' set, each will have a unique illustration that competes with the others for dynamic design.

Since most figures are depicted in midthrust toward the viewer, with expressions that seem to shout "I kill!", it is usually impossible to tell an action figure's morality from its appearance. But somewhere embedded in the text on the package is the answer to the first thing a boy wants to know about an action figure: Is it a good guy or a bad guy? Though Big Boss Man's expression looks scary, he wears a police uniform, pledges a "strong allegiance for the land" and reveals in his favorite quote—"You're gonna serve hard time, punk!"—that he is on the side of law-abiding citizens. Similarly, a boy might be fooled into thinking that the dark-skinned Dhalsim, who has spent his life unifying his body and soul through the discipline of yoga, is a peace-loving Gandhi type, but a close reading of his bio card discloses that he "will meditate then destroy you."

For years, female dolls—representing both good and evil and capable of fighting with the same strength as the males—have been a part of boys' collections. When the makers of Mighty Morphin Power Rangers made two of its five "good guys" female and designated Rita Repulsa to lead the villains, they gave female action figures the highest profile within a series to date. Nevertheless, as in some of the girls' collections, the Power Rangers in their supernatural mode look identical, except for the colors of their outfits and the shapes of their masks. Likewise, they are packaged in a sleek, minimalist design with little accompanying text. Whereas older boys immerse themselves in the facts and figures of complex personalities with exotic names like Liu Kang and Sub Zero, younger boys and girls beg for Tommy or Kimberly or, more simply, the "white rangers" or "pink rangers." Power Rangers also cross gender boundaries by locating the action both in earthly space, when they are average teenagers, and in extraterrestrial space, when the teens transform into Rangers. Perhaps some of these gender-bending strategies accounted for Power Rangers' reaching the top of the charts in sales of action figures.

Although girls and boys alike might be interested in the Power Ranger dolls, the Zord system accessories are shelved with other extraterrestrial systems in the boys' aisle. Unlike girls' accessories that collapse the play into the real world, Zords build on one another in an outward direction, offering endless possibilities for add-on marketing. Consider that each member of the Mighty Morphin Power Rangers' Thunderzord Assault Team can combine with the White Tiger-zord to become a Megazord or with the Red Dragon to provide a Thunder Megazord. Just as Thunderzords can morph and interlock with one another to create even more powerful combinations, culminating in Thunder Ultrazord, so a Ninja Megazord or Shogun Megazord combines with Falconzord and Titanus, to form the "awesomely powerful" Ninja Ultrazord or Shogun Ultrazord. I sympathized with the French woman in the checkout line at Toys "R" Us who was holding two large boxes, or about $70 worth, of Zords and was worried that her selection might not be compatible with the Zords her nephew already owned. As she and the store manager struggled to make sense of the Zord system, I stood mesmerized by the sound of the Power Ranger vocabulary pronounced with a French accent. The drama ended when a ten-year-old boy from another checkout line came to their rescue.

"Once, there was a clear connection between the official American story taught in the classroom and the versions acted out at recess, on floors, and in backyards," writes Tom Engelhardt, but today, "to step beyond the classroom into the world of toys is to enter a space disconnected from history." Making no distinction between boys' and girls' toys, however, he fails to note that girls' play has always been disconnected from history. Yet girls' figures, based on self-projection and relationship play, cannot escape taking on contemporary issues. In the racially diverse Family Corners collection by Mattel, female dolls come with a wedding dress and a house, while the males come with tuxedos, an add-on nursery, and a baby. The text on the package suggests the possibility of mixed marraiges—"Any combination makes a family!"—while the photographs show racially matched bride and groom dolls. Next to the infant doll, which is hidden inside a stork's bag, Mattel offers another message about family values: "INSIDE! A BABY FOR YOU after saying 'I do!'" Engelhardt pessimistically forecasts that "tomorrow's floorscape will provide solace for neither multiculturalists nor their opponents." Surprisingly, in fact, many action figures have down-to-earth nationalities (Russian, Chinese, or Thai, for example) and, like many American soldiers, do not represent their country of origin in battles but rather are multiethnic members of extraterrestrial gangs.

Though the physics may be bogus in the boys' supernatural worlds, the level of the technical language carries the force of the Zord's "50,000 megavolts" in predisposing boys to technical activities and giving them a sense of power. Nowhere in the girls' stories will one find vocabulary as sophisticated as "doppelganger" and "cybernetic," numbers of astronomical magnitude, any assumption of a knowledge of the natural sciences, or facts for the sake of facts. In lighting the way for a technical career, Astronaut Barbie doesn't hold a candle to Biker Mouse Lectromag, who is "energized with electromagnetic power and radiates magnetic beams." Even if the beauty products in girls' collections were described like Infantry Squad Leader Grunt's weapons as "a clandestine assortment of attack gear" for their "covert missions," there would still be an important difference between the texts of the girls' social dramas and those of the boys' high-tech conflicts. Aside from scientific-bent and SAT-boosting language, the stories differ predictably in the characters' abilities to direct their own fates. Even the female figures in the boys' collections possess innate power to control their destinies. "Fighting alongside her fellow Avengers" from the Toy Biz series for boys, Scarlet Witch "affects probability fields with her hex powers." "A witch by name only," she has actually helped save the world several times over. Too often the heroes of the girls' collections rely on luck, magic, or natural beauty, and their stories read like variations of the Cinderella theme. For Swans Crossing socialite Mila, "the big question of the evening [is] which lucky teen beauty [will] spend the evening dancing in the arms of super-hunk, Garrett Booth?" Dawn, swimsuit model in the Starr Model Agency collection, is popular in high school "not only for her looks, but for her amazing athletic talents." She has even won an athletic scholarship to college. But it was not for her athletic achievement that she was chosen to be a supermodel. Rather, an agent who spotted her at a swim meet was "overwhelmed with Dawn's natural beauty and offered her a contract."

The downside of the technical language and implied power of the boys' characters is that most of it sanctions warfare and crime, sometimes even in ways that subtly appease pacifist parents. Whenever I see my son's pudgy fingers flying nimbly over the keyboard in a video game fight and it is time for him to practice the piano, I think of Hasbro's clever advertising strategy in writing the G.I. Joe bio cards: "HEAVY DUTY sees little difference between playing Bach's 'Two Part Invention in D Minor' and operating his Man-Portable Heavy Weapons System. They both require right and left hand independence, exceptional hand-eye coordination and the ability to concentrate simultaneously on two or more complex operations." Mattel sums up the ambivalence that society feels about toys and violence on the package of Last Action Hero: next to Dynamite Jack Slater's warning that "in real life, guns and violence are a BIG MISTAKE! Play it smart . . . never play with real guns!", an illustration demonstrates how to secure dynamite or bricks in the doll's hand and hurl the weapon forward.

Television programs, commercials, and video games, unlike the associated action figures, have been closely monitored by citizens who are disturbed about the possible relationship between depicted violence and children's behavior. If marketing executives had their way, television commercials for boys' toys

would follow the same rule of excluding real people as the packaging of action figures does. In response to parents' concerns that young children might not be able to tell the difference between the TV programs and the ads or between the ads and real life, television toy commercials must now contain some concessions to reality, if only to show arms holding the toys. Yet, as Seiter observes, television commercials still differ blatantly in their presentation of action figures for boys and dolls for girls. In commercials aimed at boys, "close-ups of the toys in action are the rule, rather than shots of children playing with them. . . . The boys on screen do not look at one another or speak to one another, except 'in character'" (130–32). Even such minimal use of actors in toy commercials is regarded by boys as an unwelcome incursion: as my friend's son said of a television advertisement that showed a boy playing with a toy military station, "They spoiled it by showing that it's not real." On the other hand, "girls' commercials use facial close-ups of the girls or the dolls": they are shown close to one another, talking about their dolls in bedrooms, livingrooms, and kitchens, while in boys' ads, "usually it is impossible to discern *where* the boys are playing" (128–31).

Whether these marketing strategies are based on innate gender preferences or have partly created the preferences, they complement a host of other factors that affect not only which toys children buy, but also children's relationships with one another. From my seat-of-the-pants research gathered during sixteen years as a carpool mother, I know that little girls talk with friends about relationships and personal experience, whereas boys—like the boys whom Susan Willis describes in Chapter 13 as spouting the weights and measurements of dinosaurs—relate to one another through systems of information external to their own lives. During one forty-minute commute in which two boys in the back seat were meeting for the first time, the conversation began shyly with the question: "Do you know Dave Justice?" The reply: "Yeah. He played for the Braves. He's cool. I also like Roger Clemens. He pitched for the Red Sox. He's nicknamed the Rocket." For a solid twenty minutes, they volleyed names and statistics from every sport they could think of and then proceeded to quote lines from movies. For boys, this sharing of systems of cultural knowledge is not only sufficient to forge a friendship but is often the extent of the friendship. When boys invite other boys to sleep over, there is no prerequisite secret that they intend to share. They are content to whisper quotes from Calvin and Hobbes comics into the wee hours of the night.

Are these gender differences innate or learned through culture? Certainly there is a lot of anecdotal evidence that "boys will be boys." I remember the idyllic summer day when my neighbor handed out a snack of carrots with leafy green tops to her toddler-age children and their friends. The boys raced around the yard, pointing them at one another and making shooting noises. We have all heard of home experiments in gender reversals, such as the boy who, when

given a doll, proceeded to push it around the floor, making vroom-vroom noises, and of the girl who cradled and "made nice" to her new fire truck. Girls and boys within a family may play together, but the play often involves compromise—"I'll play house, if you'll help me build a fort." Parents who encourage playing with unisex toys report that their boys and girls play with them in predictably different ways. At a local nursery school, there is a two-story structure where girls put their dolls to bed on the upstairs mattress and boys plan attacks from the lookout tower.

A friend of mine was astonished when her eighteen-month-old son repeatedly threw the doll he had been given across the room. So she bought him a football. "You know," she said, "sometimes we just have to recognize we're different—males and females. We're different when we're older too. For instance, it just never would have occurred to me, not in a million years, to throw my six-month[-old] baby into the air like his dad did." She did not offer, however, that in tossing the doll across the room, the son might have been mimicking his father's behavior with him. Most observations that parents make about a son's behavior with dolls seem to confirm that it is simply not the nature of males to nurture. But what if nurturing were defined more broadly to include those activities that most fathers do with their children? Maybe there should be dolls packaged with pictures of boys tumbling with baby dolls or teaching toddler-age dolls with Velcro hands to play catch. How about dolls that make guttural (and even gastrointestinal) noises—the kind fathers like to share with their infants?

As science continues to discover biological explanations for behaviors previously regarded as environmentally determined—for example, a gene that controls obesity and a physiological difference in the hypothalamus of gay males—perhaps toys that encourage Stone Age tendencies of women to prepare food and men to hunt and gather will prove to be justified by our genes. But in our modern world of fast-food drive-thru and hormone-injected cattle, the toy market has responded to revolutionary changes in our occupational options by adding pink microwaves to the girls' Small Appliance section of Toys "R" Us and by giving boys herds of grotesque creatures to shoot at. While schools work to overcome girls' tendency to hate math and science, the toy market that embellishes the plots of action figures with scientific vocabulary and meganumbers gives Barbie a Dream Workstation with a monitor and fish tank but no CPU (Willmott) or lets her spout, "Math class is tough." Society is crying out for men to take their fathering role more seriously, yet the marketing of baby and toddler-age dolls exclusively to girls proscribes boys' playing daddy. It *is* acceptable, however, for boys to collect the G.I. Joe Streetfighters in order

"to create [their] own street fightin' battle action . . . today!" These social contradictions most profoundly affect the working class, who shop at K-Mart, Bradlees, Toys "R" Us, and the like, while higher-income families browse through catalogs that show boys and girls playing together in little kitchens. Still, even highly educated families who try to protect their children from culturally imposed gender distinctions conduct their experiments in the uncontrolled laboratory of a media-wired society. It is mind-boggling to consider the widespread cultural influences that have led to my son's desire to know—regarding the Superbowl, the Persian Gulf War, and the presidential elections— which are the good guys and which are the bad. As a parent of two girls and a boy, I have witnessed more traditional gender behavior than I ever anticipated. Yet, as long as the media continue to separate children by gender, we can never know to what extent cultural influences such as the toy market have influenced a child's behavior.

Or, for that matter, an adult's behavior. When they grow up, the boys who were in the back seat will move up to the driver's seat and will still be talking about sports, cars, and computers. The girls who shared secrets will be discussing their relationships, their bodies, and their hair. Proud that they have advanced in their occupations beyond the traditional roles of their parents' generation, the women may be executives and the men may share in child care. But, like distant relatives whose postures, expressions, and stories remind us of our inescapable connection to them, our childhood dolls accompany us through life. They attend our weddings, not only as barely recognizable kin, bearing traditional gifts from our pasts, but as unfamiliar in-laws whose habits we may someday wish we had studied more closely. Until death do us part we coexist, not only in marriage but in all of our social relations, as people whose childhood experience with fantasy play remains forever segregated into bride side and groom side.

Imagining Dinosaurs

Susan Willis

Extinct long before human time, dinosaurs left us their footprints; fossilized bones, eggs, and spore; and various incomplete strands of DNA. These are the shards with which science and culture collaborate to produce dinosaurs. I became interested in dinosaurs and simultaneously recognized that they are cultural constructs when I realized that the accounts my children were bringing home from school did not jibe with the sorts of dinosaurs I remember from my own childhood. If you had asked me as a child in the 1950s to describe dinosaurs, I would have painted a picture quite different from the ones kids today give me. I would have told you about the ponderous Brontosaurus standing belly-deep in the swamp and the horrible, bloodthirsty Tyrannosaurus rex (T. rex). Now kids tell me the Brontosaurus was wrongly named. It is really an Apatosaurus, and it probably grazed on land rather than while half submerged in water. As for predators, T. rex was nowhere near as mean as today's dinosaur of disrepute: the Velociraptor.

My Stone Age perception of dinosaurs was shaped by two media products that seem truly antiquated by today's media and scientific standards: Walt Disney's *Fantasia* (released in 1939 but still being reissued for theater play in my youth) and a huge book published by Time, Inc., and produced by the editors of *Life* magazine: *The World We Live In.* In *Fantasia,* Stravinsky's "The Rite of Spring" evokes a brutal world where drought and death prevail. Its conclusion, permanently etched in my memory, features a fight to the finish between a Stego-saurus and a T. rex. Thunder clashes, the dinosaurs pound and rip each other, the world around is in the throes of an earthquake. Less dramatic but equally memorable was *The World We Live In,* a sort of precursor to the multi-

textual CD ROM, featuring foldout pages that opened up to reveal vast dinosaur panoramas replete with volcanos, swamps, and lush vegetation. The editors balanced the wondrousness of the rich illustrations with concern for readers' scientific pedagogy, as each image was meticulously labeled.

As I now see them, the dinosaurs of my youth were as much a product of Cold War ideology, with its penchant for depicting the world polarized between dramatically opposed forces, as they were a celebration of patriarchy, with its devotion to heavily masculinized authority figures. Since then two factors have dramatically transformed the way we represent ourselves culturally. First, the Cold War was thawed by the quantum leap to global corporate capitalism and the demise of simplistic us-versus-them thinking, and second, patriarchy was challenged by the women's movement and the development of feminist theory, whose critique of patriarchy was so strongly felt as to be now the object of an antifeminist backlash.

As a result, many patriarchal and Cold War–imbued cultural icons (such as the T. rex of my youth) have been replaced by newer constructions more in keeping with today's political and social climate. As Stephen Jay Gould points out in "Dinomania," his review of the movie *Jurassic Park*, today's dinosaurs are "team players" appropriate for a world no longer polarized between superpowers and instead dominated by global corporate networks. The icon of the

corporate state is not the domineering aggressor, T. rex, but the cunning and
techno-efficient Velociraptor, who in the movie is expressly coded as female
(more so than any other of the park's dinosaur species, who have all been biologically engineered as female; laboratory, rather than natural, reproduction is
intended to ensure human control over the dinosaurs). "Clever girl!" are Muldoon's dying words. As the park's great white hunter, Muldoon embodies masculinity, outsmarted and vanquished by the superior female. Extending the
logic of Gould's evaluation to include patriarchy as well as the Cold War, the
Velociraptor clearly represents a reversal of the masculine orientation of previous definitions of predatory dinosaurs. Because she doesn't play by the rules,
but is instead absolutely ruthless and treacherous, she also expresses the recu-
peration of masculinity rooted in vehement antifeminism. Compared with
other popular culture representations of antifeminist backlash, such as Sigour-
ney Weaver's portrayal of the corporate bitch in *Working Girl*, the Velociraptor
is so artful, cunning, and vicious that she makes all human versions appear in-
ept. In this context it is significant that Steven Spielberg's *Jurassic Park* concludes with the reassertion of T. rex's dominance. In a scene reminiscent of
Fantasia, T. rex subdues the faster, more intelligent raptors with sheer brute
strength. This puts T. rex squarely in the adventure-hero tradition of
Schwarzenegger and Stallone and it solidifies the link Spielberg wants to artic-

ulate between himself and the Disney tradition. But in a larger sense, the con-
secration of T. rex as hero and savior gives allegorical expression to the ambivalence and fear felt by a society that imagines itself cut adrift from male authority figures and fantasizes itself beset by usurper female bitch brigades. At
least T. rex fights face to face, like a man.

Dinosaurs have offered themselves to socially generated gender meanings
and conflicts for as long as they have existed in the popular imagination. The
overwhelmingly masculine dinosaurs of my youth appealed largely to little
boys, who took every opportunity to draw them or to show off by spouting their
weights and measurements with uncontested authority. I don't recall any girls
having dinosaur envy or attempting to muscle in on dinosaur territory with a
tomboyish display of equality. Girls who wanted to affirm strength and independence drew horses, primarily stallions. (At least they did in the West, where
I grew up.) Even though today's toy and media industries have attempted to
open dinosaur markets for young girls, my research in public schools indicates
that boys still surpass young girls in their interest in dinosaurs. In their enthusiasm, they resemble the adult male paleontologists who delightedly carry out
their fieldwork in the pedagogical videos aired on public television, used in
schools, and available at public libraries. These typically feature the paleontologist, clad in jeans or khakis and flannel shirt, and perhaps sporting a beard,
clambering over a fossil find in a Western landscape or posing alongside a giant femur or jaw as a means of showing scale. I mention these videos because I
recently had occasion to see a lot of them in an undergraduate course I taught
on the cultural meanings of dinosaurs. Although the students avidly critiqued
the videos whenever they recognized outdated science, they never remarked
the absence of women in the field, even though half the students were women.

It doesn't take a degree in child psychology to recognize that dinosaurs readily lend themselves to a young boy's oedipal tensions and anxieties. In this regard, my own son's drawings from twenty years ago are typical of many that I
see today in elementary schools. My son's particular trauma was having to ad-
just to a new "Dad," which he evoked in countless dinosaur drawings that depicted a hugely menacing predator besieged about the ankles by a diminutive
dino who used its horn or teeth to attack the giant, sometimes leaping up to jab
it in the belly. Because this was the Vietnam era, my son's oedipal drawings often included a historical dimension. Sometimes the giant predator was attacked by tiny missile-launching or bomb-dropping airplanes. All together, my
son's dinosaur drawings embrace a blend of pop culture iconography as old as
King Kong, updated to Vietnam, and used to express his personal fears and
wishes. What is most important about a child's dinosaur drawings is the way

extinction has turned dinosaurs into vessels for all sorts of encoded meanings. Because they are produced by the imagination (more so than any other pop culture hero such as Batman or Power Rangers, who come freighted with narrative baggage, as Karen Klugman shows in Chapter 12, or any living creature, such as a lion or a whale, whose species characteristics restrict the imagination), dinosaurs can be molded and shaped to embody a huge variety of cultural meanings and serve a range of personal needs.

The oedipal dimensions of a young boy's fascination with dinosaurs need not be graphically drawn to represent a challenge to patriarchal authority. I have encountered many young boys (and a few girls) who use their knowledge of dinosaur facts and figures as a means of demonstrating mastery in a particular subject equal to the sorts of masteries they see their fathers (and possibly mothers) brandishing, but in a field not likely to impinge on parental expertise (unless, of course, the parent is a paleontologist or the sort who competes for knowledge no matter what). This is an important consideration, especially in professional families in which the acquisition of knowledge is valued as a stepping-stone to a good education and a secure future. It is also often a point of contention. This is because knowledge has become a form of capital, and rivalry over ownership, control, and use of knowledge extends into professional family life, where it takes on an oedipal dimension. Knowledge about dinosaurs, particularly statistical information, enables children to brandish expertise without directly challenging parental authority.

No one knows what our understanding of dinosaurs might be today had their fossils first been exhumed and interpreted by women, discovered in a society in which knowledge was not a basis for institutional power, or interpreted by a society that valued gender equality. None of this being the case, we are the recipients of a particularly skewed notion of dinosaurs. As I cast about for gender meanings in my 1950s version of dinosaurs, I suppose the Brontosaurus's cowish docility and helplessness suggested femininity. These traits were inferiorized by the masculine orientation of reptilian life generally and the brute force of the carnivores particularly. Indeed, one of the results of the current debate over the possibility of warm-blooded dinosaurs is the slight but perceptible approximation of dinosaurs to more feminized life forms, such as birds and mammals, which care for their young. In contrast, during the time when dinosaurs were indisputably reptilian, I recall not being able to conceive of dinosaur procreation. Because they all seemed to be males, I simply assumed each one lived for hundreds of years with little need for mothers and babies. My childish imaginings were no less influenced by the prevailing aura of male authority than were those of many scientists. The most amusing example of masculine bias in paleontology is the example of a nineteenth-century Oxford University chemistry professor who unearthed a giant dinosaur thighbone and thought he had found "the scrotum of a giant" (Lessem 36).

Coincident with the women's movement and the era of feminism is the 1978 discovery of a "new" dinosaur: Maiasaura, whose name means "good mother lizard." Actually the history of "new" discoveries in paleontology is itself a study in gender. Clearly, the fossil remains of Maiasaura, as well as a host of smaller mammalian and premammalian remains, have been lying about in the Badlands as long as the fossils of T. rex have. These fossils, however, were not noticed or not considered important during the institutionally driven rush to acquire dinosaur bones in the 1920s and early 1930s. In excavations spurred by the intense rivalry between Othniel Charles Marsh and Edward Drinker Cope, the Badlands were ransacked, trainloads of bones were sent east, and careers and museums (namely, Yale's Peabody Museum and Pittsburgh's Carnegie Museum) were made. The smaller species were simply not as impressive as the big ones. They were not noticed, not exhumed, and not sent east on the trains. Anything that smacked of femininity simply had no clout.

Given paleontology's masculine orientation, the advent of the Maiasaura represents a dramatic reversal in the gendering of dinosaurs. Everything about Maiasaura is feminized to the point that it is difficult to imagine a male one. They all seem to be "mommies." They are said to have developed a survival strategy based on sheer numbers. This sounds like a prehistoric version of the rabbit syndrome women are accused of having when their fertility results in pregnancy (of course, only women are fertile). Compared with the host of masculinized dinosaurs, from Triceratops to T. rex, Maiasaura are characterized as pathologically sweet tempered. They nested in colonies, where they did double duty tending to hatchlings and year-old juveniles. Finally, they exhibited the true coffin nail of mommyish behavior: food sharing.

The discovery of Maiasaura has paved the way for other startling discoveries that have expanded our notions of dinosaur gender. For instance, the Oviraptor was for decades stigmatized as an egg-stealing culprit simply because its bones are typically found in or near nests, with an egg occasionally gripped in its teeth. The revised feminist reading of the same fossil evidence has recast the Oviraptor as a protective, birdlike parent, who tended its nest and used its mouth to rotate the eggs. Capping recent feminist influence on the way dinosaurs are perceived is the case of a dinosaur named Sue, whose remains are the object of intense litigation involving Native Americans, the government, private fossil collectors, and nonprofit institutions. Most significantly, Sue is not a Maiasaura or some other feminized dinosaur species, but the "best Tyrannosaurus-rex skeleton ever excavated" (M. Browne C1). Journalists have capitalized on Sue's transgressive status with a host of headlines that ape Johnny Cash's ballad "A Boy Named Sue."

Just as changes in our culture made possible a variety of feminized accounts of dinosaurs, so too have recent scientific constructions affected our culture to generate a commercial boom in domesticated dinosaurs. Significant among these is the first of Stephen Spielberg's dinosaur movies, *The Land before Time*. This animated saga begins with the tearful death of a soft-spoken, sweet-natured mommy dinosaur reminiscent of Bambi's mother. It plots the epic journey undertaken by her orphaned child, Little Foot, who must cross a landscape torn asunder by drought, earthquake, fire, and predators to reach a land of plenty. As does much of contemporary children's media programming, the movie doles out a pedagogical dose of environmental pessimism. On the journey, Little Foot encounters a number of similarly orphaned or abandoned baby dinosaurs, and they join forces to evade the stock dinosaur nemesis: T. rex, here named Old Sharp Tooth. Each of the toddler dinosaurs speaks in a childish voice, which lends itself (along with their pudgy bodies and awkward movements) to a generally infantilized version of dinosaur life. The movie manifests Spielberg's characteristically maudlin sense of social utopia, here manifested as noncombative interspecies relationships among the youngsters, whose colloquial names for one another suggest the sort of distinctions inherent in racialized epithets: Long Necks, Fliers, Swimmers, and Spike Tails. Indeed, the little dinosaurs have to learn to recognize the stigmatizing aspect of othering by beginning to appreciate each other's species differences. While their primary fear of Old Sharp Tooth marshals a formulaic oedipal conflict, the divisiveness of their ethnic bickering offers an apt allegory for a world more balkanized than polarized. The movie also typifies the capitalist logic of diversified profit making. Characteristic of all prearranged media hits, *The Land before Time* spawned a number of merchandising spin-offs, most notably the rubber "Petries," "Little Foots," and "Duckies" that kids received "free" with the purchase of a McDonalds Happy Meal. Indeed, McDonalds led the way in introducing infantilized dinosaurs with an earlier Happy Meals dividend: an audiotape series depicting the exploits of Baby "Bones" and his pals.

By far the most whimsical infantile dinosaurs crop up in children's picture books. Public libraries stock a rich assortment of these in their prereader sections. Many children's picture books anthropomorphize their dinosaur protagonists by shaping their reptilian faces into human expressivity. Picture book dinosaurs do everything people do. They play soccer, lounge on the couch, drive cars, and talk on the phone. They can play Santa or dress up for Hal-

loween. They are big but nonthreatening, like Danny the Dinosaur, who gives kids rides on his back and plays hide and seek behind a pole. They are kids in dinosaur bodies, goofy and awkward, but capable of evoking someone more powerful than any adult.

The most remarkable repercussion of the advent of domesticated and feminized constructions of dinosaurs in the scientific discourse is the flood of consumable dinosaurs available in malls and supermarkets. There are dinosaur macaroni, cereals, bubble baths, backpacks and lunch boxes, T-shirts and underwear, as well as dinosaur cookies and fruit bites. There is even a T-shirt on which a glow-in-the-dark dinosaur transforms from flesh to skeleton. Science becomes a marketing gimmick. In a curious blend of scientific accuracy and hucksterism, the Salerno dinosaur cookie box assures consumers that the cookies illustrated are the "actual size" of the cookies in the box.

Science is itself consumable. Besides museums and museum shops, there are now a host of trendy, upscale, environmentally correct, and pedagogically oriented toy stores that feature wooden (not plastic) models of dinosaur bones and kits that enable children to discover facsimiles of dinosaur footprints in prepressed molds. As an experiment in consumer research, I brought an assortment of these toys to my students. They reported the fun of turning their dorm rooms into scientific play areas. Embarrassed but amused, they thought the packaged dino projects were all "fun" but wondered why all were touted as "authentic" replicas when everything was precut and prefabricated. As an antidote to postmodern authenticity, one of the students brought in a number of shoe boxes containing his childhood fossil collection. The specimens were jumbled, some had no name tags, but all produced awe as we passed them around and realized we were touching the past.

The development of commodified versions of dinosaurs points to a coincidence between feminized accounts of dinosaurs and traditional constructions of women as shoppers and consumers (see, for example, Bowlby). Before the discovery of Maiasaura, representations of dinosaurs generally subscribed to a masculinized form of large-scale, frightening spectacle, rather than the diminutive and trivial feminized consumerist model. Spectacular renditions date from the nineteenth-century Crystal Palace sculptures of the Iguanodons (all of them anatomically wrong by today's standards) and attained their most potent embodiment in the dinosaur dioramas built by Walt Disney for the World's Fair in Montreal and later moved to Disneyland, where I saw them as a child. Although the dinosaur exhibit has since been dismantled (some of the species were also anatomically incorrect), I suspect one of the dinosaurs is alive and well in the Exxon exhibit at Disney World's EPCOT Center. As amusements, spectacular renditions of dinosaurs are also commodities, but, unlike breakfast cereals and bubble baths, they have not been tamed by the domesticating influence of characteristically female nurturing activities, such as shopping, preparing food, and drawing a child's bath. I suggest the opposition between masculinized spectacle and feminized consumerism as a general rule of thumb, although I am fully aware that the culture never wholly conforms with such models. A good example of nonconformity is Sinclair Oil's Gertie the Dinosaur, the reptilian equivalent of Borden's Bossie the Cow, who represented a feminized appropriation of dinosaur iconography long before the Maiasaura-induced revisions in the scientific discourse.

Movies are the most prevalent site for spectacular dinosaurs, notwithstanding the crossover film *Baby,* which featured an orphaned Maiasaura and her paleontological benefactors. Otherwise, the majority of dinosaur flicks have been of the action/adventure, sci-fi genre. These usually feature a dinosaur dredged up from the deep and miraculously brought back to life. Another formula features a band of marooned sailors or explorers lost in the pre–Ice Age paradise that has been inexplicably cut off from evolution and is inhabited primarily by dinosaur predators. Precursor of the 1950s and 1960s B movies is the 1925 version of *The Lost World,* whose mobile dinosaurs, their jaws gnashing and tails thrashing, facilitate the movie's desired aim of bringing together the sole marooned female with her proper romantic suitor. Even *Juras-

sic Park with its more technologically advanced dinosaur models, capable of sneezing and spitting, fulfills the needs of romantic story resolution, this time evoking not only romantic pairing but leaping ahead to the anticipated family, with the movie's two children rounding out the relationship between paleo-botanist and paleontologist. In this way, opposition between the spectacle and the domestic collapses. The masculine hero model enacted by human and di-nosaur actors serves the interests of the happy home.

Coincident with the trend toward feminizing dinosaurs is the reversal of di-nosaur ontogeny. Gould remarks a similar backwards development in Mickey Mouse, who began his career with a thin, adult, ratlike body characterized by sharp features and developed backwards to attain the current infantilized pro-portions of big, round baby face and ears ("Biological Homage"). Writing from a biologist's perspective, Gould explains that infantile features trigger an in-stinctual caring and adoring syndrome in adults. Whether the Disney car-toonists understood this or not, they tapped a reservoir of sympathy when they began to draw Mickey with progressively more childish features. Of course Mickey could no longer act like a rat, either; hence, he became the emcee of his own fossilized celebrity, appearing as a big head at Disney World but suspended as a cartoon star, until his recent revival in the cartoon short "Runaway Brain."

There has been a similar trend in dinosaur iconography from the rapa-ciously adult rendering of T. rex that I remember from my childhood to the in-fantilized, big-bellied, round-headed, and purple Barney now appearing on TV and on children's clothing. Barney may look like a baby, but he's no dope when it comes to making money. As I recall from radio news program summaries of the 1993 Fortune 500, Barney ranked as the third biggest moneymaker, just be-hind Spielberg and Oprah Winfrey. Does this mean Barney has a bank account and an investment analyst? Does the person inside the big head reap any of the rewards? I recall a talk given by Alexander Wilson, one of the great utopian thinkers of all time, who argued that anthropomorphisms have the potential for challenging the human domination of the planet by offering a sense of the interconnectedness of all life. Wilson pointed to examples in art including drawings by Native Americans and the Canadian artist Stephen Andrews. He even saw redemptive possibilities in Disney's anthropomorphized portrayals of bears in the nature feature *Bear Valley*. However, unlike Disney's "Father Bear," a real wild bear in a wilderness setting who is assimilated to human so-cial relationships by the film's voice-over and editing techniques, Barney is 100 percent pop culture commodity. (He trades on the connotation of dinosaur but fails to generate the utopian energies that might otherwise arise from the dis-junctive association between animal and human life.) Moreover, as a TV personality, Barney unites spectacle and domesticity, since the TV screen offers a smaller, safer image than a movie or diorama does and one that can be consumed in the comfortable familiarity of the home.

The profusion of consumable dinosaurs in supermarkets and toy stores does achieve one remarkable end: it produces the cohabitation of humans and dinosaurs. This is the much-sought-after goal of the creationist paleontologists, who attempt to bend dinosaurs to divine purpose. Only proof of cohabitation will substantiate the short time of the world's existence tabulated in the Bible and refute the billions of years recorded by geologic time and corroborated by carbon-dating techniques. Today we may not be Paleolithic hunters, but we do live with dinosaurs. They are all around us: in the movies, on TV, and in theme parks, supermarkets, toy stores, schools, and museums. While creationist paleontologists search for the footprints of human hunters alongside the tracks of dinosaurs, we pack our children's school lunches with dinosaur-shaped cookies and fruit snacks. The aim of pop culture is not to substantiate divine creation, but to make profit out of our sense of wonder and loss. It is sad to have missed the dinosaurs, particularly since we live in a culture that seems to offer everything. It is also quite safe to invent dinosaurs as commodities rather than really clone them and actually live in Jurassic Park—although a number of scientist/adventurer entrepreneurs think otherwise, at least according to recent newspaper accounts of attempts to secure entire strands of dinosaur DNA. (My kids ask, "What's wrong with them? Didn't they see the movie?") There is a lot of fear associated with dinosaurs. This is particularly evident when I ask parents why they think their young children are so fascinated by dinosaurs. In the words of one father, whose son passionately collected dinosaur replicas and displayed them at the town fair, where he won a blue ribbon, "They're big, scary, and safely extinct." I think the fear—or thrill—of coming face to face with a live dinosaur is the real reason why the movie *Jurassic Park* received negative notices from child psychologists. Missing the point, they condemned the movie for its violence. What about the mayhem in movies deemed acceptable for children, such as *Home Alone?*

I have a hunch, too, that some of the fascination with dinosaurs is bound up with complicated attitudes toward extinction. How often have you heard the warning that we might "go the way of the dinosaurs"? In our media-generated eco-conscious culture, extinction includes a fair amount of First World guilt for all the annihilations and species endangerments our wanton lifestyle has wrought. These attitudes permeate public school pedagogies, producing an odd mix of wonder and anxiety among, for example, the North Carolina second graders I visited during their state-mandated unit on dinosaurs. Many

were not sure who disappeared first, the cave men or the dinosaurs. In the context of the rise and development of industrial production, most have no way of apprehending extinction. It is not out of the ordinary to hear a child express some sort of self-blame for the plight of endangered and lost animals. In children's minds, media accounts of the spotted owl tend to merge with the portrayal of dinosaur extinction that they glean from the school library. Today's endangered-species list includes 954 animal species (*World Almanac 1995* 189), all of them put at risk by humans' infringements on their habitats. At least in the case of the dinosaurs we aren't directly to blame, even though we are the beneficiaries of their death. The great dying created a huge space and a lot of ecological niches for mammalian evolution and, eventually, us. It's a good trick to let culture reinvent the dinosaurs now that all the economically dominant niches have been filled by humans.

It's clear that dinosaurs can be just about anything. They can be your worst oedipal nightmare or an insipid, infantilized TV host. They can be masculinized or feminized. They can be used to prove divine creation or Darwinian evolution. They can be cold-blooded, warm-blooded, or something in between. They can be scientifically classified as reptiles, in which case they gave rise to crocodiles, or they can be classified as the nonreptilian precursors of birds. Museums have displayed them with their heads wrongly mounted at their tail ends. Curators have mismatched skulls and bodies and misidentified them on instructional placards. Because dinosaurs can be almost anything, both in science and in culture, they lend themselves to the child's imagination, which shuffles and re-sorts all the available bits of knowledge to construct a version of dinosaurs. This may replicate dominant ideologies and depict prevailing attitudes toward gender and the larger political configuration of the world, or it may just as easily transform these meanings to give utopian content to dinosaur play and drawings.

Grrrls and Dolls

Feminism and Female Youth Culture

Lynne Vallone

Riot Grrrl is about not being the girlfriend of the band and not being the daughter of the feminist, and all that stuff, and being whatever it is that you *are*, and not being the addition.

—Emma, "What Riot Grrrl Means to Me"

Many adult feminists would be taken aback by Emma's statement. What's wrong with being the "daughter of the feminist"? Isn't feminism about "mothering" daughters—whether literal or figurative—in a Chodorovian reproduction that will ensure feminism's survival? My questions betray my own orientation as an adult and a mother, assuming too much about the relationship between adult and child, older and younger feminist. Emma's declaration of independence from boys *and* adult feminists foregrounds the theoretical issues that underpin any adult discussion of youth culture: in these discussions, the child/young adult is automatically subordinated and othered because of age. Some of the difficulty in theorizing or understanding difference due to age is exacerbated by the inherent mutability of the child/adolescent: everyone grows older. Whereas the differences and dissonances created by divisions of class, race, and gender are customarily invoked in cultural and literary studies, age has been less carefully attended to.[1] It is also difficult to ascertain when one becomes an "adult" feminist. Is physical age the only criterion, or does one need to pass certain tests, show gender-battle scars, or self-consciously declare oneself to be a feminist to become "adult"?

Age matters. The British cultural critic Angela McRobbie confides her "acute anxiety at the thought of writing about youth. It is at once too close and too far away" ("Shut Up" 406). This anxiety is not misplaced, it seems to me. I want my young daughter to grow up to be a feminist—just like me. If she does not learn feminism from me, from whom will she learn it? Certainly not from mainstream American culture. And if feminists are made—not born—how might older feminists continue to make them while at the same time remaining sensitive to the younger generation's need for autonomy? It has become clear to me that while feminism *needs* girls and girls need feminism, adult feminists cannot engender the next generation simply in their own image. In considering feminism and generations, the generation of feminism, and femininity, we must query the means by which we culturally transmit the beliefs and values of feminism to subsequent generations.

Arguably, it is in adolescence that girls need feminism most. The research of Carol Gilligan and the Harvard Project on the Psychology of Women and the Development of Girls, as well as that of the American Association of University Women, has shown that at about age eleven or twelve girls are in danger of "losing their voices" and "hitting the wall" (Gilligan et al. 25, 19), falling from the positions of strength, freedom, and self-confidence they had in childhood into "traditional patterns of low self-image, self-doubt, and self-censorship of their creative and intellectual potential" (Orenstein xvi).[2] Since girls need help negotiating psychological, sexual, and cultural barriers, and adult feminists have had some experience in these maneuvers, it would seem natural that they would instruct the younger generation in its ways and delights. Yet Emma's comment seems to suggest that sometimes female adolescents do not want this help.

The problems and misunderstandings between generations of women need identification. Reports of feminism's "middle age" or "menopause" have abounded since the mid-1980s (Amiel 24). This metaphor—based on the inaccurate assumption that menopause means the loss of female potency—is due not only to the advancing age of the movement's founders, but also to the fact that many of the legal, social, and political gains made in the 1960s and 1970s—such as employment opportunities, reproductive rights, and legal protection —are today accepted as givens by teenagers who have not had to fight for them (Ferree and Martin 6).[3] Paula Kamen agrees in her *Feminist Fatale: Voices from the "Twentysomething" Generation* and discusses at length the apparent stigma attached to the "f-word": she cites a recent poll by a magazine for female college students, according to which only 16 percent of those polled considered themselves feminists (31). One can imagine that the percentage of younger women—girls—who would claim to be feminists might be even lower. If feminism has an image problem, how can it be improved in order to bridge this generation gap?

To be fair, the misperceptions between generations are not only one-sided. Older women must take some responsibility for their reluctance to understand adolescents and young women. The journalist Anne Taylor Fleming comments that many older feminists have behaved or felt "uncharitably" toward younger women because of the latter's political apathy and ignorance of feminism's importance to their lives (16). Yet Kamen notes that while many of the issues of feminism, such as reproductive rights and parental consent laws, affect *only* young women, young feminists are kept to the outskirts of the current feminist movement (2–3). Who is failing whom? As Christine Doza plaintively writes in her personal essay "bloodlove," "I feel like we're all dying of anorexia and heartbreak, and everyone—you—you just turn the other way. I read *Ms.*, looking for anything but what's there. I don't have a career, I don't have a husband, I don't need to know how to raise my son. I need to know what to do when I stop wanting to be an astronaut and start wanting to be Bobby's Girlfriend" (40).

It seems that feminism alienates girls, the very group older feminists want most to impress. To impress not because of some matriarchal pride of lineage, the desire to see our daughters with our "name," but because as feminists we are attempting to create a world hospitable to and supportive of girls (*and* boys). These are the reasons that feminists are working so hard to fight sexism, harassment, and violence and to gain legal and social equality. Behind the sparring of prominent feminists in the media, the youngest of whom are, after all, in their twenties, stand the girls who need feminism. The stakes are very high. Furthermore, the apparent scarcity of feminisms in the younger generation may partially result from the older generation's inability to accept newer (younger) forms of feminism that seem less "personal as political" and just more personal, that is, individual and anti-institutional. Older feminists look at the younger generation and find little they recognize as feminist. And that, I think, is ultimately the point. Some feminist tenets do not change with the age of the individual feminist: thus feminist networks have been formed—such as SOS (Students Organizing Students), created in response to the 1989 Supreme Court *Webster v. Reproductive Health Services* decision, or FURY (Feminists United to Represent Youth)—and NOW (National Organization for Women) sponsored the first Young Feminist Conference in 1991.[4] However, by and large, the younger, rebellious generation of feminists mimics the older generation about as much as youths in general mimic adults. That is, not often. In a 1993 *Newsweek* commentary, Susan Faludi contends that far from defining women as victims out of touch with their sexuality, "real-life" feminism has been recreated in young women's lives in newly formed groups such as Riot Grrrl, Guerilla Girls, WHAM, YELL, and Random Pissed Off Women (61).[5]

In *Mother-Daughter Revolution,* Elizabeth DeBold, Marie Wilson, and Idelisse Reading pose a crucial question: "What if girls were to keep their psychological strength, courage and voice? What would the world be like if women said what they knew and said it with authority?" (xv). I think that I have had a glimpse of that unconventional world and it might be Emma's girl-style revolution promoted by Riot Grrrl. Social critic Kim France intones—tongue in cheek—"They're called riot grrrls, and they've come for your daughters" (23).

In the rest of this essay I will explore Riot Grrrl as an example of contemporary youth feminism and a "bona fide subculture" (Gottlieb and Wald 263). This punk-inspired network of girls ages fourteen to twenty-five includes angry, "pro-sex," pro-choice music devotees (particularly of girl bands like Bikini Kill and Bratmobile) who hold their own convention, without the sponsorship of an established feminist group, and produce their own "zines."[6] The zines "reflect the style of the Riot Grrrls themselves, who mix baby-doll dresses and bright red lipstick with combat boots and tattoos" ("GRRRL Talk" 134). Most important, Riot Grrrl zines "foster girls' public self-expression, often understood as the ability to tell private stories (secrets) which are otherwise prohibited or repressed by the dominant culture" (Gottlieb and Wald 264). In exploring Riot Grrrl, I examine their representation in the media, as well as in their song lyrics and zines, and compare them to younger girl feminists, as represented by the readers of *New Moon* magazine. I argue that Riot Grrrl is an active, powerful feminist youth movement that older feminists cannot afford to ignore, even though interactions with these women must be minimal, out of respect for their autonomy as "girl-style revolutionaries."

A loosely organized, grassroots group of girls nationwide (and in England), who sprang up from the punk scene in Olympia, Washington, in the early 1990s, Riot Grrrl does not have a recognizable leader; part of the group's ideology is to eschew patriarchal hierarchies of control and give power to each individual voice who would speak.[7] Hence the popularity of writing and publishing one's own zine. This form of life-writing is, of course, intensely personal. The Riot Grrrl zine exists to broadcast—to as many or as few people as want to read it—the deeply felt, often crudely written, and obscene, humorous, or serious opinions on anything the writer has felt or experienced. Zines have been criticized for their self-absorption and their opacity, but I think adult critics often miss the point of the zine enterprise.[8] Although, as I am doing, older critics may study these materials as cultural artifacts, texts of youth subculture, the materials cannot fairly be judged against some kind of universal literary standards. They are not literature; the zine is a conversation that the girl engages in with herself and like-minded sisters. By the fact of their age (and/or gender), most commentators are naturally voyeurs, and it is a privilege for them to read this writing so reminiscent of diaries or letters. This privilege carries the responsibility to reflect with sensitivity on the material. Gottlieb and Wald warn against the "exploitation, trivialization, and tourism" (270) that can exist in any outsider's (including an academic's) attempt to describe the Riot Grrrl movement; I do not take this responsibility lightly.

If one is outside the movement, reading Riot Grrrl zines can be arduous. I have found it difficult to explore Riot Grrrl culture—to track down the undated and often anonymous photocopied zines and their authors.[9] Some of this slipperiness is by design: many in the Riot Grrrl movement do not want to be dissected and scrutinized by the mainstream in order to become a "sound bite from the underground or a heartwarming hopeful story about the youth of America" (E. White 18). In their collaborative "Six reasons why riot grrrl press is important right now, bi Marika," May and Erika make it clear that the Riot Grrrl message needs to repudiate traditional methods of publication, promotion, and production, which are, they believe, dangerous to the movement's autonomy and beliefs.

We need to make ourselves visible without using mainstream media as a tool. Under the guise of helping us spread the word, corporate media has co-opted & trivialized a movement of angry girls that could be truly threatening & revolutionary. & even besides that it has distorted our views of each other & created hostility, tension, & jealousy in a movement supposedly about girl support & girl love. In a time when Riot Grrrl has become the next big trend, we need to take back control & find our own voices again.[10]

The Riot Grrrls are willing and eager to take responsibility for the success of their own movement. For example, the Riot Grrrl Press tries to distribute zines to girls who cannot afford to buy them and promotes zines that are not well known. It also facilitates communication between Riot Grrrl chapters through its central clearinghouse.

Riot Grrrl authors are confident, powerful writers. Their "pointed prose" can be sarcastic, harsh, and biting, yet also sensitive, funny, and savvy. For example, *Secret Weapon* derides the possessiveness and damaging exclusivity of young relationships by mocking the boyfriend's "voice": "i love you. you are my girlfriend. mine. mine. mine. all mine. you are just cute and sexy, you are just for me. i am a part of everything you do. there is only ONE KIND OF LOVE. . . . mine. mine" (10). In *Riot Grrrl NYC #1*, Kake's "Who Is Choking and Dying?" takes umbrage at *Sassy*'s use of ultrathin models in their fashion pages and the magazine's other insulting features, such as the "cute band alert" that highlights cute guys in guy bands. She concludes, "But that's why Riot Grrrl exists—so all that our grandmothers, mothers, sisters, aunts, friends and selves have fought and suffered through will not be compacted into easily digested bullshit bits of information."

The catalogue of the Riot Grrrl Press lists zine titles and prices (usually between $.20 and $2.00 each) and briefly describes the contents of each zine featured. The descriptions for the "early 1994" catalogue range from "The Adventures of Big Grrrl" ("We can't run a revolution and starve ourselves at the same time! Beating our bodies into submission takes valuable time and physical and emotional energy away from doing the things we really want, and need, to do") to "Youth Revolution" ("Feminism . . . Youth . . . Revolution . . . Words for Thought . . . grrrl love . . . empowered Women . . . powerful fiction and harsh reality . . . anger, fear, hope, love . . . all in one zine"). The zines address body image, gay pride, "wimmin's rights," racism, sexual abuse; they include selections from diaries, poetry, stories, cartoons, music reviews, and political analysis. The zine writers hope to provoke comments and letters from girl readers. It is clear that the zine phenomenon can counteract the isolation that many girls feel in high school and after; in this way, the Riot Grrrl culture may be seen as a healthy alternative to the depression, fear, and silence of adolescent girls reported by researchers such as Gilligan and Orenstein.

It is impossible to quantify the impact the Riot Grrrl culture has had on mainstream teens of the 1990s: there are reports of a few hundred members in 1992 (Chideya 86) and fifteen hundred members in 1993 (Buchsbaum 23). Counting the numbers of girls involved is short-sighted, however, because the Riot Grrrl influence may be greater than mere numbers. *Sassy* has been crucial in "translating" Riot Grrrl ideology to the average young teenage girl (Gottlieb and Wald 266), and yet many Riot Grrrl members dismiss its importance. I posit that exposure to the "revolution girl-style now" could help teenage and even preteen girls to overcome the struggles of adolescence through a delight in the positive and powerful aspects of girlhood. In *Reviving Ophelia,* Mary Pipher calls contemporary America a "girl-destroying place" (44) Through their revolution, the Riot Grrrls hope to change this depressing reality and to repair the selves and souls of girls who are at risk in adolescence.

One method of rescue is music—joining or creating a band, or at least listening to girl bands, buying records, and attending concerts. One really cannot understand the Riot Grrrl phenomenon and its values without listening to the music the members idolize and reading their lyrics.[11] The examples I give here include albums under the Kill Rock Stars label (of Olympia, Washington) by the bands Bikini Kill (*Yeah, Yeah, Yeah, Yeah*), Bratmobile (*The Real Janelle*), and Heavens to Betsy (*Calculated*), in 1992 and 1993. (These bands also record under other labels, such as K and Candy Ass.) The liner notes and lyrics pages are highly stylized in the "made by hand" zine manner; slangy ("wanna," "cuz"); loosely punctuated; and riddled with expletives, as is much contemporary music.

Like the zines, the songs cover a variety of topics, but a few themes stand out: exultation over girl power and control, anger over masculine oppression, and girls' love for each other. There is an aggressive "I'm not going to take it anymore" attitude in many songs. In Heavens to Betsy's song "Terrorist," the narrator begins by expressing anger over sexual harassment and ends by turning the tables on the harasser:

> you follow me on the fuckin street
> you make me feel like a piece of meat
> you think i don't know what war means
> now i'm the terrorist see how it feels.

In "Brat Girl," Bratmobile transforms the pejorative "brat" into a word denoting female power in opposition to the male superhero fantasy or any patriarchal co-opting force (such as the media):

> We're gonna kill spur posse boys, it's the
> surest way to yr heart lil' boy
> ain't gonna be yr press darlings
> i'd rather be fucked and throwin things.

Bikini Kill's "Rebel Girl" celebrates the girl-style "revolutionary" who is sexy, assertive, and self-possessed:

> That girl thinks she's the queen of the neighborhood
> She's got the hottest trike in town
> That girl she holds her head up so high
> I think i wanna be her bestfriend

Not every song contemplates or protests gender relationships. "White Girl," by Heavens to Betsy, is a self-reflexive song about the racism that well-meaning whites practice unconsciously:

> white girl
> i want to change the world

but i won't change anything
unless i change my racist self

The turn toward self-awareness in this song is indicative of some of the more sophisticated feminist tenets that the Riot Grrrl members and musical groups espouse. In the liner notes to *Calculated,* Corin Tucker and Tracy Sawyer write, "i [it is not clear which singer is speaking here] wrote the song 'white girl' because i wanted to address the audience for this record—mainly white people— about racism in the punk/alternative community, in myself, in riot grrrl. . . . So many punk songs by white people address racism as something 'other' and not at all a part of the white people who are singing. . . . You can write me a letter about this song and this subject if you want but i can't answer every letter."[12] For further reading "on racism and sexism," they suggest books including *This Bridge Called My Back: Writings by Radical Women of Color,* edited by Cherríe Moraga and Gloria Anzaldúa, and works by bell hooks, Toni Morrison, Audre Lorde, and Alice Walker as well as punk fanzines such as *Gunk.* This amalgamation of the scholarly with the popular, the serious with the shy admonition that every letter cannot be answered, characterizes Riot Grrrl feminism and serves as a segue to my discussion of "capital-f" feminism and youth culture.

Their sometimes shocking anger might seem to differentiate Riot Grrrls from feminists who have learned to play boardroom games, become institutionalized, and compromise, yet the Riot Grrrl movement is as idealistic, energetic, and committed to girls'/women's rights as the grassroots women's liberation movement was in the 1960s and 1970s. Riot Grrrl even echoes the consciousness-raising groups and rap sessions so important to the feminist movement then. One reason the Riot Grrrl strain of feminism has not become mainstream, or "mannered," is that as an "adolescent" youth movement, its members will usually merge with the dominant culture once they grow up— literally in the case of the younger girls or figuratively for older members who are technically "grown" but who repudiate some middle-class "adult" obsessions, such as the suburban lifestyle. However, after reading Riot Grrrl publications, I anticipate that the Riot Grrrl of today who listens to Bikini Kill and publishes her own zine will become the feminist of tomorrow, volunteering at a battered woman's shelter, writing her congressman/woman, raising feminist children, if she is not doing some of these things already. In fact, part of the energy of the Riot Grrrl movement comes from the desire to *act* rather than theorize, fight rather than compromise.

It may be argued that feminism has always embraced acting out, but Riot Grrrls take it so far as to call for a new "revolution girl-style now!"[13] They well understand the feminist adage that the personal is political, and their revolution focuses on the social issues that beset young, middle-class women (rather than economic issues that may have less currency in their lives), such as harassment and rape, reproductive rights, eating disorders, incest, and abuse (Chideya 84). The "revolution" itself is protean: self-proclaimed "fatgrrrl" Nomy Lamm writes, "For now the revolution takes place when I stay up all night talking with my best friends about feminism and marginalization and privilege and oppression and power and sex and money and real-life rebellion. For now the revolution takes place when I watch a girl stand up in front of a crowd of people and talk about her sexual abuse. For now the revolution takes place when I get a letter from a girl I've never met who says that the zine I wrote changed her life" (86). *Riot Grrrl NYC #2* reveals one reason for the networking existence of Riot Grrrl when a writer states, "Every time we pick up a pen, or an instrument, or get anything done, we are creating the revolution. We ARE the revolution" ("Riot Grrrl Is . . .").

Riot Grrrls are often misunderstood, which accounts for some of the reticence they may have about the media; feeling like the "flavor of the month," they are wary of misplaced attention. Erin Smith of Bratmobile relates that Sally Jessy Raphael called her to inquire about doing a show on "rioting daughters." Smith says, "So far, I haven't read a single thing [about Riot Grrrl] that's true" (Kim 55).[14] Even within activist circles, the Riot Grrrls can be unconventional and sometimes annoying to others. According to a Los Angeles reporter, the Riot Grrrl participants in the 1992 pro-choice march on Washington "'refused to participate in the conventional chants.' Instead, they beat on pots and pans with sticks and 'screamed at the top of their lungs, drowning out everyone around them'" (Antrobus 18). Do we love these girls? Can we learn to live with them? We might ask, with Sally Jessy, who are these "rioting daughters"?

Because of their brash tactics, anger, distrust of the conventional, and independence, I must admit here to my own ambivalence about the Riot Grrrl movement, an ambivalence that has been brought into focus by another example of contemporary youth feminism: *New Moon* magazine for girls ages eight to fourteen. *New Moon: The Magazine for Girls and Their Dreams* was begun in 1993 by Nancy Gruver and Joe Kelly of Duluth, Minnesota, after they read Gilligan and other writers, looked for resources for their eleven-year-old twin girls, and found none. The bimonthly, advertising-free magazine has a twenty-three–member Girls Editorial Board that works hand-in-hand with adults to produce a magazine largely written by girl contributors. Their mission statement reads, in part, "*New Moon* celebrates girls, explores the passage from girl to woman, and builds healthy resistance to gender inequities." Some features of the magazine include a girl-to-girl advice column ("Ask a Girl"),

"How Aggravating!" (a forum for reporting unfairness to girls and women), accounts of science experiments, interviews with girls who achieve distinction, ("Herstory"), and fiction. The magazine is earnest, upbeat, and well written. It is also a media darling (not unlike the Riot Grrrls but for different reasons), winning, among other awards, the Feminist Majority Foundation's 1993 Feminists of the Year Award and a 1995 Gold Award from the Parents' Choice Foundation. The magazine has a paid circulation of twenty-three thousand in more than thirty countries.

From my perspective as a feminist adult, there is nothing not to like about *New Moon*. Do I want my daughter to be a *New Moon* girl? Yes. I want her to be, as I commented earlier, just like me. *New Moon* seems comfortable and comforting because its readers share the goals we older feminists have for them: equality, confidence in the world, global understanding, historical awareness, and health. It is easy to dichotomize these two groups of young feminists into "good" girls and "bad" girls: *New Moon* readers are progressive and accessible, whereas Riot Grrrls are radical and remote. *New Moon* reaches out to all girls (there is a distinct multicultural feel), whereas Riot Grrrls have a narrow constituency. The younger *New Moon* girls are gung-ho and charming, reflecting liberal feminist ideals—as is made evident by the Girls Editorial Board's introduction in the July/August 1995 issue: "Here are some things that are in this AWESOME issue of New Moon: How to make a New Moon cover, a winning dream essay, an interview with activist Angela Davis, an article about girl athletes and eating disorders (it's with Cathy Rigby who was an Olympic gymnast!!)" (2). Riot Grrrls, on the other hand, can be alienating with their "antisocial" attitudes and loud music. *New Moon* is a magazine, above all, for self-expression. As one thirteen-year-old reader wrote in 1994, "I'm pleased to know that there is a magazine for feminists my age. It's wonderful to see strong, determined young women expressing their creativity and opinions" (Noble 5). Girls' opinions are solicited on every topic conceivable, and each month numerous pages (in a forty-eight–page format) are devoted to girls' letters.

Of course, the desire to communicate with a supportive audience and inspire others is at the core of the zine phenomenon as well. *Function #6* asserts (in a drawing of the woman symbol): "Take power and stand up for your rights. Know you exist as your own person. You don't need someone else to make you feel real" (D. Williams 3). *Riot Grrrl NYC #2* includes a "Heroine of the Zine" feature (Caroline Maria de Jesus, novelist), much like *New Moon*'s "Herstory" articles. Taking a stand that *New Moon* would vigorously support, *Hangnail* complains about the censorship girls face: "Freedom of expression, thought, and demonstration is being looked down upon. . . . NO, NO, NO, NO. You're not

New Moon: a multicultural, gender-neutral cover.

being oppressed, you're not being abused, you're not being taken, you're not silenced, you're not being ignored, you're not being overlooked, and YOU'RE NOT
BEING TAKEN SERIOUSLY!!!! Censorship sucks" (Lee Ann 14).

Although Riot Grrrl can sound abrasive and hostile, challenging liberal feminism with a movement older feminists cannot join or direct, I have come to
believe that the affinities between *New Moon* readers and Riot Grrrls are much
greater than their differences. Both can be understood as part of a "girls' move-

ment" that reclaims girlhood as a moment or symbol of power and activism. "Girls can do anything" is more than just a slogan to both groups: girls are encouraged to create, write, talk to one another, reject limitations, and look within. By supporting girls' voices, *New Moon* has made an important step toward bridging that difficult gap between girls and adults. It cannot, however, take the girl all the way to adulthood.[15] Perhaps this is where the older "adolescent" Riot Grrrl is needed.

A quick analysis of Riot Grrrl clip art and *New Moon* cover art captures key differences between the two youth groups. The July/August 1995 *New Moon* cover (by an adult artist) delivers a utopian vision of multicultural, creative, and fun-loving girlhood by way of primary colors, blue sky with shining sun, a pet, and gender-neutral clothing. The cover is attractive and drips with symbolism: the arch of the beautiful celestial rainbow frames the figures in light and color and confidence. In contrast, Riot Grrrls often use retro images juxtaposed with ironic commentary—1950s-style housewives mouthing Riot Grrrl mottos—or sentimental and "girly" images such as hearts, stars, or playing children to decorate their zines. As one might expect, Riot Grrrl illustrations can also be more disturbing—for example, a reproduced photo of a woman who had died from a self-induced abortion; the picture of a praying nun framed by the words "Ownership May be Habit Forming"; or a drawing of a female torso as a mutilated apple, suggesting Eve. The *New Moon* landscape is professional, as befits a mainstream publication overseen by adults for girls. Yet readers are also encouraged to submit colorful and busy drawings and paintings for potential use as covers. The Riot Grrrls, in contrast, use irony, sarcasm, anger, and nostalgia—modes of thought less available to or appreciated in young girls—to illustrate their political messages of empowerment and sexual freedom as well as to delimit a self-absorbed, intensely personal "black and white" world.

Adults cannot join the "revolution girl-style now," but we can support it by listening to these young women and, sometimes, by telling them to be quiet to enable others (even elders) to be heard. As Sara Marcus and Kirsten Thomp-

Be an *ACTION GIRL! Don't just sit around, reading zines (well, read some), going to shows, listening to records you ordered and watching for Catwoman on old Batman reruns. Form a band with your friends! Can't write songs? Do covers! Start a zine—it doesn't matter what you write or draw, as long as you're doing it. Xeroxing is cheap! Start a label, start a club. Go to a Riot Grrrl meeting or start your own group. Do something with all that positive girl energy! Go, girl, go!* ♥, *Sarah*

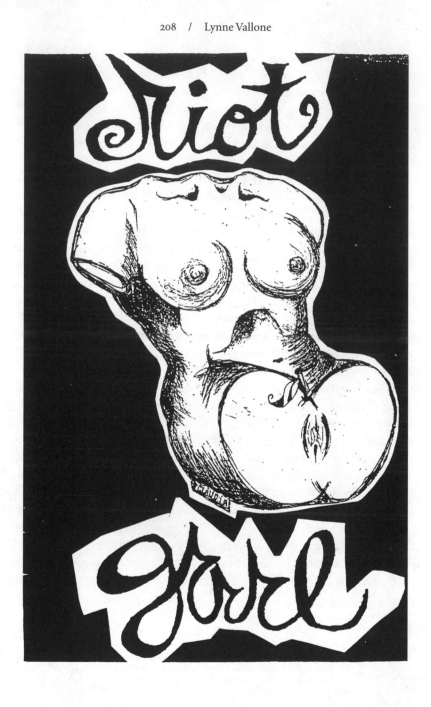

son, two high school students who helped plan the 1995 NOW Young Feminist Conference, offer, "Nobody can hear you screaming 'revolution' in an empty room" (3). To proclaim "girl power" is not to eschew the womanly, but to elevate the status and stature of the child-woman, the "ferocious child" of preadolescence (E. White 21). In fact, Riot Grrrls strongly identify with the material artifacts of children's culture (plastic barrettes, stickers, character lunch boxes), images of childhood, and "dear diary"-style confessional writing. I theorize that the Riot Grrrl movement chooses early childhood as a model in part because of a nostalgic embrace of its relative freedom from gender trouble and in part because many of the members feel they were cheated out of childhood as a result of abuse. Riot Grrrl co-opts and reinscribes the liberating and fun aspects of childhood: playing with toys, making noise, dressing oneself without regard to mother's/society's expectations, writing with magic marker all over one's body (except that they write words like *slut, rape,* and *riot grrrl*). In their refusal to put away childish things, the Riot Grrrls may seem far from their feminist "mothers." Their disavowal of the role of "daughter of the feminist," stated in the epigraph to this essay, also reminds us of the necessary otherness that age inserts into issues of identity and solidarity—even within feminism, a movement that, to its credit, has never been homogeneous.

Referring to the antic behavior of the Riot Grrrls in a pro-choice march on Washington, D.C., Emily White describes the scene thus: "The crowd gave them plenty of room, these girls getting out of hand, screeching like loose, wild birds, like kids in a schoolyard" (20). The movement is necessarily noisy, sometimes off-putting, energetic, its members at times silly or insubordinate. The revolution has the energy of *New Moon*-age girls. One commentator calls the Riot Grrrl movement "Revolution as everyday play" (Aaron 63). Girls—of any age—just wanna have necessary, important, and powerful fun.

The Riot Grrrls engender new, challenging, and perhaps unexpected understandings of the feminine and of the feminist project beyond the mainstream *New Moon.* In its abrasiveness and riotous oppositional politics, this new feminism illuminates not only the younger generation's response to feminism but also the feminist movement generally. Riot Grrrl helps to put the strong girl—not the doll—back in feminism.

An Arab Girl Draws Trouble

Allen Douglas and Fedwa Malti-Douglas

First a story, then a comic strip, "Rabâb Gives Up Drawing" owes its creation and transformations to a pair of Arab leftists, prominent Egyptian writer Yûsuf al-Qaʿîd and Syrian artist and cartoonist Yûsuf ʿAbdelkî. Its history is one of left-wing Arab politics, government censorship, and patriarchal structures. Politics, children's literature, and censorship: in the West, these are hardly strange bedfellows. Nor are they in the Arab world.

There, however, these concepts often represent different realities. To say that children's literature has a politics is no longer a daring assertion. When studies like Maria Tatar's are added to those of Ariel Dorfman and Armand Mattelart, it becomes clear that at least two types of politics are common inhabitants of children's literature in the West: the politics of the family, of parents and children, of generation and gender; and the evocation of general ideological issues, such as attitudes toward property, war, and other social phenomena. Both types are also richly represented in Arab productions for children.

There is a third type of politics that is relatively rare in Western materials for the young but very common in Arab productions for juvenile audiences. This is formal adult politics: the politics of politicians, rulers, and government policies. Such matters play a large role in children's media in the Arab states. Their presence often goes beyond the propagandistic visual ubiquity of the ruler to explicit discussions of political conflicts and potentially divisive issues (Douglas and Malti-Douglas).

How does censorship fit into all this? From the comics code of 1954, which instituted an obligatory, and draconian, moral code, through more recent attacks on alleged sex or Satanism in children's literature, censorship is certainly not foreign to Western children's literature. The Arab world, too, knows these kinds of censorship. But the presence of formal adult politics in children's media, combined with the explicit censorship that such political discussions receive in all Arab countries, means that children's literature is also powerfully affected by the nexus of formal politics and its equally formal censorship. In the Arab world, the politics of censorship weakens the boundaries between literature for children and literature for adults. The lack of clear demarcation between these two literatures thrusts the juvenile focus on gender and family into explicit connections with adult power politics. Thus, a children's comic strip of a young girl with a penchant for drawing can foreground issues of domestic and social authority, gender, politics, war, and peace.

Into all this comes the multiplicity of Arab states. The visitor to the Institut du Monde Arabe in Paris in late June 1988 was treated to a fascinating exposition of Arab political cartoons. One, instead of bearing the usual single signature, bore a dozen. Drawn by the Syrian ʿAlî Farzât, the cartoon showed an officer serving up medals from a cauldron to a bearded civilian in tatters, against the background of a bombed city. The two figures in this cartoon are both adult males. Of any women and children who might be in the civilian's family, there is no trace. We are in the masculine world of high politics.

The antimilitarism of this drawing could apply to any of a number of Arab regimes and, indeed, the absence of any specific Middle Eastern pictorial referents gives it a potentially near-universal applicability. When the Iraqi ambassador to France saw it on the walls of the Institute, however, he decided that it referred to his own country and demanded its withdrawal. Other Arab cartoonists and a number of their French colleagues rallied around Farzât, adding their signatures to his on the incriminated drawing and threatening to remove their work if his was removed. The drawing remained, serving as a visual testament to the struggle of Arab artists for freedom from censorship.

And yet Farzât had adopted a form of evasion common in the region: an abstract denunciation of oppression or injustice that does not specify the ruler or country in question. Hence, it can always be explained away as referring to another place or another time. Another option is available, however, and that is to specify the oppressor regime, especially if it is a government politically out of sorts with the state where the publication is taking place. The multiplicity of states and, therefore, of possible political referents, can be a source of problems, as it was with Farzât. It can also permit direct attacks on existing Arab governments.

These strategies for the evasion of censorship are manifested clearly in the case of the short story "Rabâb Gives Up Drawing." Written by the Egyptian al-

Qaʿîd, it was then transformed into a comic strip by the Syrian ʿAbdelkî for the children's magazine *Usâma,* published by his country's Ministry of Culture.

Elite culture and mass culture, adult literature and children's literature—these are realms that circulate both within and between Arab states. Al-Qaʿîd's story illustrates these passages, because it has crossed four borders and in the process undergone four transformations:

1. It moved from one Arab state to another, from Egypt to Syria.
2. It shifted from a verbal text to a comic strip combining visual and verbal languages.
3. It is a piece of high literature that became an item of mass culture.
4. The story has passed from adult literature to children's literature, appearing in an illustrated children's magazine.

"Rabâb Taʿtazil ʿan al-Rasm" ("Rabâb Gives Up Drawing") was published in Cairo in 1980 for informal mimeographed distribution and then in the leftist newspaper *al-Ahâlî.* It then appeared in the collection of stories *Hikâyât al-Zaman al-Jarîh,* also published in the Egyptian capital, in 1982 (al-Qaʿîd Interview). Contrary to Ceza Kassem and Malak Hashem, who provided a translation, the story did not appear in the 1980 Baghdad edition of the collection (Kassem and Hashem 197–204, 229).

This story is both about censorship and written through censorship. Rabâb is a pretty young girl whose precocious art talents are noticed by a new art teacher in her school. The teacher informs Rabâb's father of her budding genius and of the need to nurture it. Perplexed by the father's diffident reaction, the teacher enjoins Rabâb to delve into the depths of her being, to draw "with absolute freedom" and in obedience to the dictates of her heart. At home, Rabâb's father asks her to draw him. She pictures her father not as he is at home but as he is in the office, where he is Irrigation Inspector. The father then asks his daughter to fill up the pictorial workplace with a secretary and an office boy. She draws the office boy neat and smiling, as he is in truth, rather than shabby and miserable, as her father had suggested. The secretary comes out like a sex symbol from a Western movie: blonde, blue-eyed, and well built. When Rabâb's mother sees the secretary bent closely over her father, his nostrils virtually inhaling the skin on her breasts, a family quarrel ensues. Rabâb gets a spanking and the picture is torn to pieces.

Rabâb's next subject is the owner of a farm, where she and her family had spent the day. She draws him as a corpulent feudal lord. This time it is the character in the picture who makes the demands: he wants laborers, watchmen, servants. Our young artist draws these in, suitably smaller in stature. But the group soon becomes embroiled in disputes over wages and working conditions, and the commotion tears the picture to pieces.

Whom to draw next? Rabâb decides that it should be the "ruler of the country." Once drawn, he too makes demands: what is a ruler without subjects? Rabâb provides a suitably docile individual. But the ruler declares that this subject is boring; he wants one who will say yes some of the time and no some of the time—although only on inessential matters. The young artist accordingly draws a new subject, this time one with a brain, and he and the ruler agree on the rules. If the subject breaks the rules, he will be punished. Of course, break them he does. He is imprisoned and he blames Rabâb for his plight; the ruler angrily demands a new subject from Rabâb. In desperation, she tears up the picture herself.

Finally, Rabâb's brother, who wants to be an officer, asks her to draw a soldier he can lead into battle against the enemy. The soldier objects that peace has been declared, which amazes the brother since, as he puts it, the land is still occupied. Eventually the soldier, with no enemy in front of him, fires behind him, killing the brother.

For this, Rabâb is hauled into court. The fact that her brother wanted to be an officer, at a time when such types were no longer necessary, is considered a mitigating factor, and the court agrees to release her if she signs a statement never to draw again. Rabâb is willing, but her hands have disappeared. As she explains in a final declaration, she has hands only to draw and her fingers will reappear when she decides to draw again and when she will be able to draw soldiers free to make their own decisions.

The fact that the ruler is unnamed makes this a censored story about censorship. And one assumes that without this concession, the tale could not have been published in Egypt, despite the relative liberties granted (and mocked in the story) by the regime of Anwar Sadat. The concession is, however, reasonably small, since many elements in the story suggest Egypt, from the office boy's *galabiyya* (robe) to the father's position as Irrigation Inspector. Furthermore, the attack on Camp David implicit in the crack about making peace while the land is still occupied and the enemy is still at the gates points strongly toward Sadat. Nevertheless, the onomastic absences give the story a projectability and ambiguity of target that we saw with the Farzât cartoon. Like the Imam in Nawal El Saadawi's equally polemical *Suqût al-Imâm* (*The Fall of the Imam*), the ruler can be Sadat or potentially other figures (Malti-Douglas, *Men, Women* 91–117).

"Rabâb Gives up Drawing" also has cross-medium implications. True, al-Qa'îd has a daughter named Rabâb who loves to draw (al-Qa'îd Interview). But the literary medium and the far greater role that verbal discourse, compared with visual presentation, has always taken in the region would lead most readers to an allegorical interpretation in which censored drawing stands for censored writing. All art, one can conclude, is potentially subversive because of its character of social reference. Using the assumptions of social realism, the story argues that honest artists must paint what they see, with the result that the social conflicts in their work are the consequence not of their ideology but of the reality their art is obliged to reflect. Do not the landlord and his servants fight of their own accord without any help from their creator?

Equally obviously, al-Qaʿîd's narrative is based on the fourfold repetition of a structural pattern: (1) Rabâb draws a picture, (2) demands are made to add material to the picture, (3) conflict develops, and (4) the picture has to be destroyed. In each case, a male authority figure demands the presence of subordinates. This structural necessity is clearest with the brother. He is not even an adult, but he is distinguished from the artist by his gender. And despite his youth he asks not for a gun to fight for his country, but for a soldier over whom to exercise command. That such hierarchies permeate society is also implied since the four episodes form a circle, from the domestic space (the father) to the near-outside of the farm, through the farther one of the ruler, and back to the brother and domestic space again.

The narrative also moves from the real to the fantastic. In the first drawing incident, people from the real world of the text, Rabâb's father and mother, create the disturbance in reacting to the iconography of the drawings. In the two central incidents with the feudal lord and the ruler, it is the characters in Rabâb's drawings who speak, make demands, and get into arguments, without impinging directly on the reality outside their drawings. This crossing from the world of the drawing to the "real" world of the text is reserved for the last drawing incident, in which the soldier's bullets inside the drawing strike the boy outside it.

The four drawing incidents do not stand alone, however. They are framed by two other narrative sequences, based on two public institutions. The first is the school, the second, the law court. The opening and closing of the frame relate the two institutions of social control. Yet, they also contrast them. The school, the space of learning and culture, is where Rabâb receives the message of freedom and self-expression. The court, unsurprisingly, is the space that takes them away. An ambivalent society is suggested, unless we are returned to the game of ruler and quarrelsome subject. In the author's country, one might read, one is urged to democracy but punished if one takes such injunctions seriously.

The comic-strip series published in the children's magazine *Usâma* from October 1980 through February 1981 is labeled "story by Yûsuf al-Qa'îd, drawing by Yûsuf 'Abdelkî." 'Abdelkî's role was larger than this implies, for in fact he had to create a scenario before he could draw, and the result is an adaptation that has some of the qualities of a rewriting. This adaptation is 'Abdelkî's alone, since al-Qa'îd, though he is a friend of the Syrian artist, did not know of the strip based on his story until we ourselves acquainted him with it ('Abdelkî Interview; al-Qa'îd Interview).

The most obvious change is on the level of plot. The entire spat of marital jealousy in the short story is eliminated. In the comic strip, all we are told is that Rabâb drew the secretary as a pretty young woman. The picture shows her as pretty, but nothing close to the Marilyn Monroe clone suggested in the original text. Hence, even at the expense of destroying the structural pattern of the tale (with no jealousy, the incident provides no conflict and the drawing is not destroyed), the comic strip suggests that whereas politics and death are suitable subjects for Syrian children, sex and marital jealousy are not. The elimination or replacement of the sexual jealousy found in traditional materials when these are adapted for children is common in Arab comic strips (Douglas and Malti-Douglas 135–43). This bowdlerization is also similar to what the Grimm brothers practiced on their folkloric texts (Tatar, *Hard Facts*). The comic maintains the other structural elements of al-Qa'îd's story, but with some slight changes—the implications of which we return to later.

More essential is the shift from short story to comic strip. The subject matter of the story negotiated a link between written and visual codes: the written ones used to tell the story and the visual ones evoked in the story. The entire economy of such a linkage is transformed in the comic-strip medium, which itself combines written and visual, linguistic and iconic, codes of narration. This means not only that the visual (what happens in Rabâb's drawings) can be transmitted directly in the visual component of the comic strips (we go therefore from symbolic to iconic codes of signification), but that the gap between the world outside the drawings and the world inside them is collapsed, because both are represented in the visual medium of the comic strip.

The identity of narrative code presents stripological challenges: first, how to distinguish the two drawn worlds, that which is drawn in the story and that which is drawn only in the convention of the strip, and second, how to navigate the increasingly fantastic relationship between the two.

In the first installment (282), which takes place in the school, we see Rabâb's drawings as individual sheets of paper. They fit easily within the frames of the comic strip, but never compete compositionally with them, instead always remaining subordinate to the composition of the frames themselves. It is only in the third installment (285), when Rabâb draws for her father, that the drawn pictures begin to take on a visual life of their own, effectively dominating what is at the same time a frame of the strip. They are distinguished from ordinary frames by their wavy shape, which makes them look as if a breeze might lift them from the surface and carry them off into the air—from the flat world of the text to the world outside.

The same installment of the magazine includes the sequence with the landlord feuding with his peasants. Now, the pictures talk and the action is moving from the larger world to the drawn world. How do you give speech to a character in a picture? By transferring into that picture the comic-strip convention of the speech balloon. At the same time, the drawn images become the frames, and the page becomes a sequence of Rabâb's drawings. In one sense the drawings, with their wavy borders, are not frames since they are not bounded by the right-angled frame convention lines. Yet they function narratively as frames, since they are self-contained and sequential. Meanwhile, the text, having set up the drawn pictures as their own narrative sequence, has to pull the visual focus out of the drawn stories in order to show the interaction between Rabâb and the character she has just created. The simplest way to do this, of course, would

The pictures talk.

be to go back to the visual forms of the earlier episode, in which a full-sized artist dominates her modestly sized work of art.

This, however, would take the life out of the drawn reality. Thus ʿAbdelkî, in two powerful pages, develops two different forms of superposition of Rabâb's world with that of the landlord. In the first, he adopts a striking stripological procedure that we have found in other leftist Arab strips (Douglas and Malti-Douglas 32–45). The page consists of two large frames, each of which preserves both the conventional frame border and the wavy border of the drawing. Superimposed on the two-shot (or American shot, as the French call it) of these two drawings/frames is a medallion close-up of a horrified Rabâb in profile. The second page reverses the procedure, while preserving the horizontal binarism of the first, allowing the double-page layout to function as an ensemble (Douglas and Malti-Douglas 34–35; Witek 87–90). In the second page, it is Rabâb's world that is the background, and in the bottom half of the page, we see her sadly looking down at the tattered remnants of her art. The top half of the page (separated only by color and not by a frame line) shows two drawings/frames in the process of breaking apart. The absence of frame lines between the top and the bottom of the page effects the transition from the disintegrating world of the drawing to that of Rabâb.

Color and especially its intensity support the same process. The drawn images start out with pastel colors on largely white backgrounds, reflective of the girl's white sketch pad. By the time the page has disintegrated from the social conflict, however, its colors have taken on the intensity of Rabâb's reactions.

The gradual tendency, present in the original story and preserved in the strip, for drawn characters to take on a life of their own is effectively summarized in the issue cover of the second installment (283). The work of ʿAbdelkî himself, this cover illustrates Jean-Bruno Renard's point that comic-book or album covers frequently contain original compositions that, though not taken from the strips, nevertheless convey essential characteristics of the strips (196). A girl, clearly Rabâb, draws birds who take on a life of their own and fly out of the picture. At no time in the story (either prose or strip form) does Rabâb draw birds. Nonetheless, their flight conveys the idea of the coming to life of the drawn characters through the image of winged freedom.

The maximum degree of interconnection between the world of Rabâb's sketches and the larger world of the story is attained with the trigger-happy soldier. In the prose version, he merely fires from one world into the other. In the strip, ʿAbdelkî has him leap out of Rabâb's drawing, placed for this purpose on a desk so that he appears to have leapt off that object. True, Rabâb sketches him back into the drawing when she nestles his rifle in his shoulder. But the follow-

رقبأة ، قفز الجندي من الصورة ووقف أمام ربابٌ
التي تملكتها الدهشة .

The soldier leaps out of the picture.

ing frames show him again outside the drawing, in the same world as the children, as he argues with them and then shoots the brother. The fantastic becomes more physically present in the visual medium of the strip than in the written medium of the short story.

The most dramatic difference produced by the visualization of the narrative comes in the episode with the ruler and his subjects. ʿAbdelkî could have drawn a generic ruler, as he drew a generic feudal lord, but in the written story al-Qaʿîd provides no description of the ruler, as he had of the land owner. And how would a generic ruler have been pictured? Like an Arabian prince? In an officer's uniform? In a Western suit? Instead of creating a caricature combining elements of these styles (and which would have signified all Arab rulers), ʿAbdelkî, while maintaining the linguistic references to "the ruler," pictures an unmistakable Anwar Sadat.

With one stroke of the brush, the Syrian cartoonist dramatically changes the political strategy of the narrative and reshapes its anticensorship message. Yes, visual clues had already contributed to the Egyptian specificity of the story: for example, the landowner's farm, with its pigeon coop, is typically Nilotic. But drawing Sadat eliminates the projectability in al-Qa'îd's story, making the narrative much safer from the point of view of the Damascene children's periodical. The country in question cannot be Syria, and the ruler cannot be Hâfiz al-Asad or another Arab leader, since it is Anwar Sadat. Of course, it is only the fact that Rabâb has crossed state borders from Egypt to Syria that makes this change in political strategy possible. The story is no longer a censored story about censorship in the land in which the story is published but rather a story about censorship somewhere else. Unless, of course, one wishes to consider this last device the ultimate form of censorship, the removal of the home country from the class of objects being criticized.

Rulers of Arab states, especially living ones, do occasionally appear in Arab comic strips, but almost always in a positive, when not official, ceremonial guise—most commonly in the nearly ubiquitous portraiture of the head of state of the place of publication. By picturing Sadat, 'Abdelkî annexes political caricature to the visual fund of the comic strip. All the sections of the strip that deal with Sadat have much of the visual feel and wry derisive humor of good political cartooning. But how to evoke Sadat in the first place since he is not named? With a photograph. As Rabâb is thinking about drawing "the ruler of the land," we see behind her left shoulder, neither really in the frame nor out of it, an actual photograph of the Egyptian president. Not uncommon in Arabic comic strips, this device breaks with the comic-strip convention of representing real life through drawing. Its chief semiotic burden is the establishment of an absolute political reality transcending the fictional world of the strip (Douglas and Malti-Douglas 161–64).

Once he has shown us that it is the real Sadat who is in question, the comic-strip artist switches to the drawn lines of political caricature, portraying a smug benevolence. Another change: Sadat's pipe, which is on the right side of his face in the photograph, moves to the left side in almost all of his drawn likenesses. The apparent reason for this is to free his right arm to carry a riding crop, which becomes the ubiquitous pendant to his trademark pipe. This derisive scepter undercuts the gentle paternalism of the pipe, as the Sadat character threatens his subjects with it as a whip.

But just as a splash of political realism is introduced with the historical Sadat, the design of the strip moves toward symbolic, nonrealist representation. The second subject whom Rabâb creates for the ruler, the one who will sometimes say yes and sometimes say no, has alarm clocks for ears. One supposes

The ruler's subject has alarm clocks instead of ears.

that this is to establish a reference to time in an individual who knows when he can say yes and when he cannot. The clocks also replace something that Abdelkî chooses not to figure. In the short story, al-Qaʿîd's narrator explains that when Rabâb draws the quarrelsome subject for the ruler, she makes sure to draw a brain for him so that he can think. This is a superiority of writing over picturing. It is easy to say that one draws a brain. It is another matter to represent this. We are here dealing with a paradox made famous by Antoine de Saint-Exupéry in *Le Petit Prince*. If one draws a boa constrictor who has swallowed an elephant, one cannot really see the elephant. ʿAbdelkî chooses not to provide a cross-section or some conventional symbol of intelligence.

The noniconic representation becomes stronger when Rabâb is hauled before a court in the final section of the narrative. Now, everyone in the courtroom—except the heroine—is visually an Anwar Sadat. The public prosecutor is a Sadat, as is the defense attorney. Even the judge is our familiar Anwar as he sits in front of a caricature portrait of President Sadat on the wall. All sport the familiar pipe, but the riding crop has been replaced by the various accoutrements of office. Visually and intellectually, we are now completely in the world of political caricature and satire. The point, one made by other Egyptian leftists, is that all the representatives of official organs, even those specifically supposed to defend the people, are merely so many extensions of the ruler (al-Saʿdâwî; Malti-Douglas, *Men, Women* 91–117).

At the end of al-Qaʿîd's story, Rabâb finds herself without hands, in a brutal image of physical and artistic mutilation. The strip shows us no stumps. Instead, the court recorder Sadat exclaims in surprise that her fingers have become rigid. In the accompanying image, Rabâb's hands do look vaguely paralytic and the fingers are red. Only in the final frame of the strip do we see what has happened: her hands are clenched in fists which she holds out defiantly, beyond the railing that encloses her, in a classic revolutionary gesture.

In her voice balloon, Rabâb declares that when the time comes for her to draw free of tutelage, her fingers will move again to grasp the brush. She makes no mention of the freedom of the soldier, at least not in her words. This reference, which is verbal in the short story, is uniquely pictorial in the strip. Surrounding Rabâb's verbal balloon is a far larger pictorial balloon that effectively interprets her words while almost constituting a frame of its own. What is in this pictorial balloon? A scene of soldiers rushing into battle. It is clear what the free soldier will be doing: making war. In the foreground, a soldier looks backwards as he leads his men onward. The posture is reminiscent of the goddess of war in Rudé's famous *Marseillaise*. The comparison is apt, suggesting as it does revolutionary war. Finally, the militarism implicit in the strip is further strengthened by the images accompanying the title of the story in every installment. A bird, the sun, a flower, and the helmeted head of a soldier adorn a paper, as if freshly drawn by Rabâb, who is holding it. Neither sun nor flower nor bird is a significant motif in Rabâb's artistic adventures. Only the soldier echoes one of the narrative's central themes. If the structure of the story pits

Everyone in the courtroom is visually an Anwar Sadat.

artistic freedom against censorship, its thematics pit war against peace. The replacement of stumps with clenched fists does more than signal revolutionary resolve. Stumps convey mutilation and impotence; fists speak of power in reserve. The undertone of desperation in al-Qa'id's ending is replaced with a more militant optimism. Attacks on corporal integrity are not unknown in the writings of the Egyptian left, where they are associated with a feeling of desperation and hopelessness (for example, Ibrâhîm).

Ideological shifts are also explicit in the beginning of the strip. In the short story, it is a new drawing teacher who discovers Rabâb and urges her to follow her artistic spirit. In the strip it is not so simple. Rabâb draws for her regular teacher but insists, to the teacher's mounting irritation, on drawing what she wants and not what is assigned. It is the Inspector of Drawing who, on a visit to the school, explicitly contradicts the teacher, who has complained of the girl's lack of artistic docility. The Inspector then enjoins freedom upon the young artist. In both the short story and the comic strip, male authority figures stress freedom, but in the strip the female schoolteacher preaches obedience.

In the words of the short story, Rabâb is an "innocent" young girl who seeks the freedom of artistic expression only after having been pushed into it by a new teacher. In the strip, however, hers is a naturally rebellious spirit already in conflict with the resident authority. This change permits an alternate reading, not as readily available in al-Qa'id's version. Do not all of Rabâb's problems start with the original sin of disobeying her teacher? After all it is this that gets her art work noticed and sets her out on the dangerous road of social depiction, which ends up costing the life of her brother.

Thus, if personifying the ruler as Sadat makes the story in some sense safer in the Syrian strip, changing the school from a locus of freedom to one of control blurs the institutional politics of the original story. It strengthens the gender politics, however, in that it is men who lead Rabâb to the ultimately political world of drawing. In neither version do any women encourage her activities; the requests for drawings come exclusively from males.

This, however, is a piece of adult political writing made over into children's literature. How does it function in its new environment? Its political nature itself is not so extraordinary. The "Zakiyya al-Dhakiyya" series, for example, in the popular pan-Arab children's magazine Mâjid, provides frequent discussion of political issues, from underdevelopment and arms control to the Lebanese Civil War and the Arab-Israeli conflict. What is rare is the explicit treatment of inter-Arab rivalries manifested by the derisive treatment of the pictorialized Sadat. In fact, even when they are being explicitly political, and even when they are attacking a ruler or a regime, Arab strips generally occult the physical image of the ruler under attack—apparently because of the implicitly legitimizing role of the portrait of the leader in most Arab states (Douglas and Malti-Douglas 55–56). But ʿAbdelkî was led to this unusual choice at least partly by the need to take his own country's leadership out of the target area. Paradoxically, thus, it was partly the requirements of the shift to children's mass literature—where requirements for political conformity are steeper than those in adult elite literature, just as they are in other parts of the world—that produced this result, itself so unusual in children's literature.

Yet just as obviously, the Syrian artist found elements in the Egyptian story that he thought would make it suitable for children. The clearest of these is the little girl hero. But the allegorical approach chosen by al-Qaʿîd to present his political message also brings his story closer to the traditional forms of children's literature. It is not unusual, of course, for individuals writing under censorship to adopt either traditional or children's literary forms to pass on their political messages (Winock 232). Viewed as children's literature, however, these adult political issues become less important. Despite the relatively heavy politicization of material for children in the Arab world, the most important issues for the Syrian boys and girls (the strip's consumers) are those of the family and domestic sphere. And here a message that is meant to be defiantly revolutionary becomes less so.

There are elements in the original story that seek to link, in a way that we could call feminist, the domestic with the larger external political sphere. The best example is the extension of the social hierarchy so dear to the father—and to most of the males in the story—to the world of gender through the sexy secretary, linking domestic conflict with the class and political conflicts that follow. But it is precisely this incident that was removed in the comic strip. The revolutionary defiance of the female hero, of course, remains.

Yet all this takes place in a universe that is gender coded and pays homage to traditional Arab attitudes to women and the family. We have already seen how the strip for children went further than the story in turning women into images of conformity. This could be seen as a mere reflection of a social reality were it not for the fact that the women are right. Following the masculine advice to assert her individuality only brings Rabâb to grief.

Most interestingly, it brings her to grief in a way that is distinctly Arab. Though it is a girl who is rebellious, it is her brother who ends up being killed. As Hasan El-Shamy has shown, the brother-sister bond, loaded as it is with suppressed sexuality, is especially charged in Arab society (*Brother and Sister;* "The Brother-Sister Syndrome"). It certainly also plays a powerful role in Arab narratives (Malti-Douglas, *Men, Women;* Malti-Douglas, *Woman's Body*). Ordinarily, a brother is responsible for his sister's honor. This can go as far as her execution by his hand. How appropriate it is then that Rabâb's personal liberation and access to the masculine world of politics costs her brother's life. Her artistic creation literally kills him.

The story begins (this is especially clear in the children's version) with a competition between potential father figures: the biological father versus the institutional father of the schoolteacher or art inspector. Politics (and art, which in this scheme of things leads directly to politics) is a rivalry between forms of patriarchal authority: that of the family and that of the state. When the young female enters these contests, she destroys her near sexual other, her brother.

And yet this destruction does not lead to a form of liberation as it might in a feminist vision. It is not just that no significant blow has been struck against the larger patriarchy of the state. The brother is killed because his militarism is not opportune. Despite the revolutionary image of Rabâb's clenched fists, what she calls for in the final frame is a new soldier, a male like her brother who will lead the country to war. If a female can enter the masculine world of politics (albeit through the less clearly coded sphere of creative art), she can do so only in contrast to the masculine world of war.

Even in its comic-strip children's version, the story reeks of dangerous penetrations between the worlds of male and female, adult and juvenile. They function almost as a memory of the story's own history as a shift from adults' to children's literary worlds. Censorship is part of the story too, since the lack of artistic freedom pushed al-Qaʿîd to set his adult tale of adult public politics in the domestic and juvenile space of Rabâb. By crossing political borders as he crossed generic ones, ʿAbdelkî renegotiates the balance between the juvenile/domestic and the adult/public. As the audience becomes juvenile, the content becomes less so, and an unnamed ruler (such as one might find in a fairy tale) is replaced by a well-known political figure.

Nevertheless, the structural imbrication of domestic and political spheres remains in both narratives. The same patterns of authority, the same social conflicts, and, at least apparently, the same gender politics operate in all the institutions of society, from the nuclear family to the school, the workplace, the farm, and the court. Such an argument could indeed integrate feminism into a leftist critique by foregrounding the politicization of the domestic sphere.

Certainly, to most Arab leftists, picking a female artist hero is a symbolic blow for women's liberation. Successful visual artists who are women are even rarer in the Arab world than in the West. This is not primarily because women are denied professional advancement. In many ways, middle- and upper-class

Arab women enjoy better access to professional status than do their counterparts in the United States. The relative paucity of Arab female visual artists owes more to the fact that, in lands of Islamic civilization, the world of the image remains more provocative and dangerous than the more familiar universe of the word.

But a bit of al-Qaʿîd's daring was toned down by ʿAbdelkî. No marital jealousy is allowed in the children's magazine. And the birds on the cover illustration, although they figure freedom, are also in their sweetness more juvenile and feminine. As such, they call attention to the ways in which the juvenile and the feminine reinforce each other in these texts (as they do so often in the West—as Mavis Reimer argues in Chapter 3). All these changes, however, are much less ideologically significant than the transformations that many Western folktales underwent on their journey to the sanitized world of the nursery (Tatar, *Off with Their Heads!;* also U. C. Knoepflmacher in Chapter 1). This testifies to the greater accessibility of overt politics to children's literature in the Arab world than in the West.

Yet precisely because she is female, this young artist encounters problems a male might not have, particularly the problematic relationship with the brother. In these terms, the narrative moves from a problematic heterosexual relationship (clearer in the story than in the comic strip) to a problematic brother-sister relationship. This is an old story in Arab culture (Malti-Douglas, *Woman's Body;* Malti-Douglas, *Men, Women* 68–90). Whereas the first set of tensions ends in nothing worse than a marital spat, a spanking, and a torn picture, the second ends in death. Narrative collision takes place at the dangerous intersection of adult and child, male and female, public and private, fantasy and reality.

Public and private: of all Rabâb's drawings, the one with the soldier brings the most public activity, military activity, physically into the domestic space (the same room!) that she and her brother occupy. The implications of this collapsing of public into private space are most clearly visualized in the comic-strip version. Male and female are present in the brother-sister couple. We already saw how the interpenetration of drawn and "real" worlds is also maximized.

The brother's desire to be an officer collapses the social and chronological distance between childhood and the adult state. None of the other characters, whether drawn or "real," seeks to evade chronological or social states. The father asks for what is his normal due, an office boy and a secretary; the landlord, for farm workers; and the ruler, for subjects. Only the brother wants to become both an adult and an officer. With all these tensions, it is not surprising that the incident ends in homicide. True, the ending calls for new soldiers in the future, but even in the context of the leftist allegory, Rabâb remains safely on the female side of a traditional dichotomy. She must await the coming of males who will bring victory. And, in a turn that is even more traditionally Middle Eastern, her forays into the world of politics have produced only *fitna*, the social chaos created whenever women leave their appointed sphere.

Just a Spoonful of Sugar?
Anxieties of Gender and Class in "Mary Poppins"

Lori Kenschaft

> If you are looking for Number Seventeen—and it is more than likely
> that you will be, for this book is all about that particular house—you
> will very soon find it. To begin with, it is the smallest house in the Lane.
> And besides that, it is the only one that is rather dilapidated and needs a
> coat of paint. But Mr. Banks, who owns it, said to Mrs. Banks that she
> could have either a nice, clean, comfortable house or four children. But
> not both, for he couldn't afford it.
>
> —Pamela Travers, *Mary Poppins*

Both the book *Mary Poppins* (1934) and the movie "Mary Poppins" (1964) begin by inviting the reader/viewer for a walk down Cherry-Tree Lane to the
Bankses' house.[1] What we find at the end of our walk, however, differs greatly
in the two stories. The book's Mrs. Banks has chosen to have four children—
Jane, Michael, and the infant Twins—and therefore is settled into a smallish,
somewhat dilapidated home. The movie's Mrs. Banks has apparently made the
opposite choice, for her two offspring live in a grand house furnished in an op-
ulent style.

This change is one of a multitude made by the Disney studios as it transformed a collection of episodic stories about Mary Poppins and the Banks family into a more or less coherent narrative fit for a movie screen. Some of these

changes reflect the formal requirements of a film. Mrs. Banks's transformation from a middle-class mother into a well-off suffragette is not, however, simply a matter of adapting to the cinematic medium. Rather, it suggests a range of concerns around gender, family, and class that were of crucial interest to the Disney team and their (imagined) audience.

"Mary Poppins" was spectacularly successful. Although the movie was heavily promoted as a box-office splash, it exceeded all expectations by grossing $40 million, $25 million in the first year (Maltin 22). Many factors contributed to this enthusiastic reception. The movie's special effects, dance sequences, and mix of animation and live action attracted much attention, and Julie Andrews charmed viewers. But these formal characteristics do not fully explain the movie's unexpected popularity.

Fredric Jameson suggests that the drawing power of a work of mass culture comes from its ability to manage social and political anxieties successfully. This "transformational work," he explains, is both utopian and ideological: it provides a form of wish fulfillment by evoking a vision of the world as it should be, but it also legitimates the existing order by distorting and repressing those wishes. Successful mass culture, then, both arouses common anxieties and fantasies and creates a symbolic structure to contain and tame them (*Signatures* 25). Similarly, Richard Dyer argues that entertainment responds to people's real needs by promoting interpretations of those needs that fit capitalist ideology: the real problems of exhaustion and alienated labor, for example, give rise to images of unbounded energy and a fusion of work and play, which are promised as the fruits of consumerism (25). Thus, Dyer concludes, entertainment attracts not by presenting models of utopia but rather by evoking a sense of "what utopia would feel like" (18). If these theorists are correct, the popularity of "Mary Poppins" may reflect its ability to tap into and defuse or soothe anxieties that were widespread in American society in 1964.

The opening sequence of "Mary Poppins" announces that the movie is about gender and family. Film critics typically analyze musicals by contrasting a "realist" narrative that points to the way the world is, with all its problems, and the "unreal," "utopian," or "spectacle/fantasy" numbers, which promise an escape from that world (Sutton 191; Dyer 26). The first two musical numbers in "Mary Poppins," however, articulate social problems that the movie associates with Mr. and Mrs. Banks.

The song "Sister Suffragette" is a satirical spoof on Mrs. Banks and the suffrage movement. Although the lyrics seem to celebrate the suffragists, the words are undermined by the movie's choreography. The domestics are scandalized when Mrs. Banks sings of "political equality, and equal rights with men!" and pulls her skirts up, step by step, well above her knees (Sherman and Sherman 7–8). We can guess, the Disney team intimates, what sort of "equal rights" she really wants. Furthermore, although Mrs. Banks proclaims her solidarity with all women, she is blind to the flesh-and-blood women who work for her. Flighty and overdramatic, she is so wrapped up in the drama of suffragette protests that she does not see what is going on in her own household and repeatedly cuts off Katie Nanna, the exasperated nanny. Thus she is shown to be silly, self-absorbed, and oblivious of the world around her. The superficiality of her feminism is confirmed when Mr. Banks is due home and Mrs. Banks orders the maid Ellen to put away the "Votes for Women" sashes. "You know how the Corps infuriates Mr. Banks," she explains as she falls into the role of dutiful and subservient wife.

Contemporary reviewers loved the movie's rendition of Mrs. Banks. Said Ann Guerin, "The film has even improved on Mrs. Banks by making her a raging suffragette" (28). Arthur Knight called her "delightfully flibbertigibbet as the suffragette *materfamilias* who urgently needs Mary Poppins's ministrations" (30). These reviews are significant not just because they give us a glimpse of how a few viewers (professionals) interpreted the movie at the time of its release, but also—and more importantly—because they suggest the sorts of interests and concerns that collected and guided the audience. Apparently this "nutty suffragette mother" ("Mary Poppins" 6) appealed to the reviewers' images of suffrage activists—and, by extension, other feminists—as mentally unbalanced.

Mr. Banks articulates the complementary role: "I'm the lord of my castle, the sov'reign, the liege! / I treat my subjects: . . . servants, children, wife, with a firm but gentle hand. Noblesse oblige!" (12–13, ellipsis in original). He describes a home run by schedule, where order prevails and the sum total of his interactions with his children ("the heirs to my dominion") is to "pat them on the head and send them off to bed" (13). This order is illusory, of course, for Mr. Banks does not notice when his wife tells him that their children are missing ("Splendid, splendid"). Both parents thus fail to perceive the people around them, but for different reasons. Mr. Banks believes that the home should be his sovereign property, in which things and people are arranged for his comfort, while Mrs. Banks seeks drama and excitement outside the home. Both are made to look ridiculous, Mr. Banks by taking his so-called traditional gender role to an extreme and Mrs. Banks by resisting hers.

The movie's narrative line might well be titled "The Education of Mr. Banks." Indeed, one could argue that Mr. Banks is the film's protagonist: he is the only character who experiences significant external resistance, self-questioning, and personal change. Once he learns that his obligations to his chil-

Befuddled when his home doesn't match his expectations of patriarchal privilege,
Mr. Banks is not only the character most subject to slapstick head-bonkings
but also the moral center of the movie: the narrative tells of his descent,
education, and reformation as an engaged parent.

dren require his active engagement with them, the film comes to its utopic conclusion in a kite-flying scene. Mrs. Banks falls into line as she turns a "Votes for Women" banner into a tail for the children's kite: it seems that she, too, has been educated in the importance of family and childhood, though the movie does not show how this education has occurred. Mrs. Banks simply follows the lead of her husband as she subordinates her public interests to her children. In the crowning touch, Mr. Banks even gets his job back: the price of his education is effectively refunded as the bank managers join the community frolicking in the park.

In the closing scene of the movie, only Mary Poppins's bird-headed umbrella is left to voice impermissible thoughts and feelings:

Bird: That's gratitude for you. Didn't even say good-bye.
Mary: No, they didn't.
Bird: They think more of their father than they do of you.
Mary: That's as it should be.
Bird: Well, don't you care?
Mary: Practically perfect people never permit sentiment to muddle their thinking.
Bird: Is that so? Well, I'll tell you one thing, Mary Poppins: you don't fool me a bit.
Mary: Oh really!
Bird: Yes, really. I know exactly how you feel about these children, and if you think I'm going to keep my mouth shut any longer, I'm . . .

But Mary firmly closes the bird's beak, and in the last shot we see her flying off into the clouds. Nothing can be allowed to disturb the sanctity of the restored nuclear family. "That's as it should be."

The movie's narrative—parental preoccupation redeemed by the combined work of Mary Poppins and Bert—is a creation of the Disney studios. It is not even suggested by the book *Mary Poppins,* in which both parents are somewhat absentminded but genially affectionate and do not undergo any moral reformation. According to a *New York Times* preview published in 1963, this theme of parental neglect was added "to introduce a little harmless dramatic conflict" (Glenn). One must wonder, however, just how "harmless" such a symbolically and psychologically laden theme can be.

Gender conventions have long been an important marker of class status. The middle class, in particular, defined itself in the nineteenth century as the class with the financial sufficiency, but not excess, to have sharply polarized gender roles: men were to be active in the financial world outside the home, while women were to be active in the caretaking world within the home. "Mary Poppins" questions this division of labor. Mr. Banks, it suggests, cannot be a good father or a perceptive human being unless he adds caretaking to his breadwinning responsibilities. It is Bert who finally brings this lesson home to Mr. Banks, but there is no hint that Mr. Banks is declassed by his changing priorities. Rather, there is an implication that working-class people may have a secret for enjoying life that their social betters need to learn. Middle-class manhood is the focus of the movie's critique: there is no complementary suggestion that Mrs. Banks should become a breadwinner. Indeed, the movie suggests, she, too, must become more focused on the home as the center of human fulfillment.

"Mary Poppins" can even be seen as an outgrowth of the 1950s literature of conformity. Sociologists of the time often warned that the conditions of American society were depriving individuals of inner direction, willpower, and freedom. Although they used a pseudogeneric male language, their focus on the effects of life in the corporate world made it clear that they were talking predominantly about men. (Betty Friedan made the complementary critique for women.) When Bert explains to Jane and Michael that their father is caged in the bank, he is echoing a broader societal fear that American men are being deprived of their vitality, and even their virility, by their jobs: "There he is in that cold, heartless bank day after day, penned in by mounds of cold, heartless money. . . . They make cages in all sizes and shapes, you know. Bank shapes, some of them, carpets and all."

What little critical attention "Mary Poppins" has received has tended to argue that the movie's conclusion reconciles its characters and, by extension, its spectators to patriarchal and capitalist power structures. Sally Hibbin explains that Mary Poppins "reconciles husband to wife, children to parents and Michael to the dreaded bank, transforming that institution in the process. Ms. Poppins can only be a force for the status quo" (35). Leslie Donaldson analyzes the movie in terms of a polarity between order/cleanliness and disorder/dirt (a recurrent theme in Disney movies). Mary Poppins, she believes, is a "paragon of 'reverse psychology'" who brings manners and propriety to the Banks family: "She is a bulwark of reassuring conformity to conventional behavior. . . . Mary Poppins gives Jane and Michael a reassuring avenue to a fantasy life which does not endanger the security of their family, but instead restores it" (1552). Caroline Champetier discusses a similar polarity between the horizontal (the narrative realm of the family) and the vertical (the *hors-la-loi* of Mary Poppins's control over gravity), in which the children are finally restored to the realm of the horizontal (53–54). Thus all three critics see the ideological function of the movie as predominant: "Mary Poppins" reinforces the order of the powers that be. Ariel Dorfman assumes this interpretation when he quotes the line "Just a spoonful of sugar helps the medicine go down" to illuminate the enticements offered by imperial powers to their obedient colonial subjects (19).

This interpretation is certainly easy to defend, and in more ways than the critics mention. "When stands the banks of England, England stands," says Mr. Dawes senior, and the interlocking strands of imperialism, capitalism, and patriarchy pervade the movie. The bank is clearly a patriarchal institution: Mr. Dawes senior rules the bank by virtue of being a father to Mr. Dawes junior, while Mr. Banks, named after the bank, has his position because his father had it before him. The board tries to persuade Michael to follow his father into the bank by invoking "railways through Africa" and "majestic, self-amortizing canals"—the mechanisms of empire (40–41). The connections are explicit even in Mr. Banks's opening advertisement for a nanny: "A British bank is run with precision; / A British home requires nothing less! . . . / A British nanny must be a gen'ral! / The future empire lies within her hands" (14). The climax of the movie occurs when the children appear on the brink of being assimilated into the tribe of "Hottentots": dancing with the sooty chimney sweeps, they are in danger of renouncing their racial and national as well as class inheritance. Michael even tries to slip out the front door with the chimney sweeps, adopting their Cockney accent and addressing his father just as they do: "Good night, Guv'nor!" Mr. Banks, of course, grabs Michael's coat and hauls him back into the house. He cannot afford to lose his son and heir, his link to the future empire.

The whole movie is displaced into an Edwardian world that suggests unlimited wealth and comfort. The book *Mary Poppins,* published in 1934 by an Englishwoman, is set in 1930s England: Mary Poppins and her magic appear in the context of an ordinary family leading an ordinary life. The American movie, however, distances itself in both space and time by choosing to place the Banks family in London in 1910. As Larry Glenn explains, "The period was chosen because of its photogenic qualities and because the nineteen-thirties connote a degree of grimness." This "photogenic" London is itself a fantasyland, but only once (in 1973) has a reviewer commented on the disturbing distortions in the movie's highly stylized "real" world: Edwardian London, Vincent Canby notes, "was a city of terrible extremes of poverty and wealth. Yet for whom does the film shed its tears? For the bloody pigeons!" (B1). Michael's disappearance up the chimney takes on a more sinister note when one remembers that children really were used to clean chimneys and sometimes got stuck and died in the process.

This prettying up of "jolly old London" ("Have Umbrella" 114) is particularly evident in the movie's treatment of its working-class characters. Bert has the wisdom to instruct Mr. Banks in what it really means to be a father, but he would hardly be able to support children of his own. His Cockney accent persistently reminds auditors that Bert is a lower-class Other not really fit to consort with the Banks family. Dick Van Dyke's erratic delivery of the accent, repeatedly noted in the contemporary reviews, only underlines the fact that the movie was determined to portray Bert as lower class even if the actor could not consistently support that characterization.

The movie systematically erases, however, the consequences of lower-class status. Ladies in silk dresses and gentlemen in top hats are delighted to shake hands with Bert even at his sootiest. In the book, Mary Poppins joins Bert on her day off for their customary raspberry-jam cakes and tea, but Bert has only tuppence for his day's work and cannot afford to pay for tea. Nor, of course, can Mary Poppins (who in the movie ends up dropping the subject of wages altogether), so they both put on a cheery face and determine to make do without (Travers 19–24). No such hints of financial need are allowed to disturb the movie. Instead, the much-anthologized "Chim Chim Cher-ee" insists that money and status have nothing to do with happiness: "Now as the ladder of life 'as been strung, / You may think a sweep's on the bottom-most rung," explains Bert. "Though I spend me time in the ashes and smoke, / In this 'ole wide world there's no 'appier bloke" (48–49).

The movie's portrayal of working-class women is equally romanticized. The Bankses' domestics are friendly, noisy, busty, and ever-present, fulfilling their master's and mistress's wishes amid good-natured grumbling. Hibbin notes that Hermione Baddeley's "Ellen" has "provided the blueprint for many domestic characters" (35). With her middle-aged rosy cheeks and full figure and her contentment in devoting her life to nothing more than "the family" and "the master," she is the image of what the middle class wants a servant to be.

Mary Poppins herself is always a lady, which is part of why she is such a good nanny. In the United States, historically, caretakers of children who are not family members have been women marginalized either by race (southern "mammies") or by their lack of secure attachment to wage-earning men (northern nurses and governesses—and the ugly women dressed in black blown away from the Bankses' gate). Mary Poppins revivifies the nineteenth-century ideal that a woman proves her character as a lady by her actions, not by her financial or occupational status. She thus soothes the residual fear that children left to the care of social inferiors will not learn the behaviors suitable for their class, at the same time that she validates the perception that such women do not need external aids (wages, job security) as much as internal resources (strength of character, proper manners) to perform their task well.

The displacement into Edwardian England invites middle-class spectators to indulge in the nostalgia of thinking that this is what master-servant relationships really were like back then. Similarly, it allows the movie to subvert challenges to middle-class women's roles. Three years in production, "Mary Poppins" appeared about a year after Friedan's *The Feminine Mystique*, which was later credited with launching the second wave of the feminist movement. In the fall of 1964, however, this wave was only beginning to swell and few people predicted the cultural turmoil that was to occur by the end of the decade. In retrospect, 1964 seems more like 1957 than 1967. But tensions were building, and "Mary Poppins" allowed anxieties around gender to be projected onto another time. We can all chuckle when Mr. Banks pompously declaims, "It's grand to be an Englishman in 1910; / King Edward's on the throne; it's the age of men!" (12)—because men (presumably more enlightened) do not act like that any more. Mrs. Banks's suffragette enthusiasms seem similarly overblown. In an age that congratulates itself on its rationality, and would not dream of depriving women of the vote, women's suffrage seems simply a mark of the historical march of progress and modernity's broad-minded liberalism. Certainly Mrs. Banks's rotten eggs were unnecessary, along with all the rest of her emotional demonstrativeness. In our advanced age, we can be doubly sure that all that is needed, if any change is called for, is some fine tuning of women's roles.

Thus the order restored at the end of "Mary Poppins" is the order not just of family and gender but also of class and empire. The United States in 1964 was at the height of its own imperialist power, and it intervened in small countries such as those in Indochina with every expectation of success. In "Mary Poppins," set in Britain when it was still a great power, we see a reflected image that reveals and ratifies the interlocking structural and symbolic orders of nation, family, and commerce.

At least, that is one way to look at it.

If we are interested in the movie's impact on viewers and the roots of its popularity, however, the careful readings typical of literary criticism are not sufficient. A detailed analysis of narrative, language, image, and symbolism may reveal meanings and connotations that are present to a typical viewer in a vague, inarticulate, or even subliminal form, but such reconstruction is not an adequate representation of an audience's experience of a one-time (or even two-time) viewing of the movie in the theater. Certain meanings may not even be discernible unless one is viewing the movie synchronically, considering the beginning in the context of the end. Although people often do reflect on a movie after seeing it in a theater, they usually overlook many details, and even multiple viewings may not result in a totalizing narrative—perhaps especially in the case of child viewers. An interpretation that relies on seeing the movie as a whole may not, then, be the best way of understanding what most audience members see.

"Mary Poppins" was billed as a children's movie that adults would also enjoy. The reviewers' most common complaint, however, was that the movie was too long. At two hours and twenty minutes, it could give even adult viewers a case of the fidgets. Children were unlikely to sit still and silent for even a fraction of that time. When the movie was revived in Radio City Movie Hall, Canby estimated that at any given time approximately two thousand children were on their way to or from the bathroom: "The aisles were aswarm, a single file up, a single file back, creating a gentle, constant drone. It was like being inside a huge beehive" (B1). Although most theaters would not have provided such large masses of children in movement, we can hardly assume that the audiences to "Mary Poppins" were the stereotypical passive movie audience staring quietly at the screen.

Nor would many children expect to behave that way. Although parents typically try to silence their children at movies and plays, children do not automatically assume that they are not supposed to speak just because they are in an audience. (Nor, for that matter, do adults. As Lawrence Levine has documented, genteel patrons in the late nineteenth century struggled to impose silence on mass audiences.) Many parents make book reading an interactive process, encouraging their children to comment on the characters and story and pictures. That socialization may transfer to the movie theater, at least for a child's first few movies. It seems likely that parents and children, sitting next to each other in a darkened but somewhat noisy theater, would occasionally exchange comments about what is happening on the screen. The engrossment that critics tend to assume for adult spectators, in which viewers are drawn into the story and identify strongly with a character, would be unlikely in such an environment.

That kind of engrossment and identification is also directly undercut by "Mary Poppins," which insistently blurs the boundary between the "real" and the "unreal." At the very beginning, Bert looks the camera in the eye as he "answers" our question about where to find 17 Cherry-Tree Lane. Later, he again engages in conversation with an inaudible interlocutor—us. Similar blurrings between levels of reality occur repeatedly within the plane of the movie itself.

The live-action actors enter an animated world where flowers turn into butterflies and merry-go-round horses join animated horses on a racetrack. People rise to the ceiling, animated doves join the pigeons around St. Paul's, and Admiral Boom surveys the neighborhood from his literally ship-shape house. Then, of course, there is Mary Poppins's magic. All of these techniques emphasize that boundaries, including the boundary between screen and audience, are permeable. Time and again the movie impresses the audience with its technical virtuosity—its ability to make unnatural things look so natural that one cannot help wondering how the movie achieved the effect. Whether child or adult, we know that toys do not just put themselves away. Though some suspension of disbelief is expected, the procedures that make the movie entertaining also remind the viewer that the movie is a movie.

Indeed, Jim Collins suggests that musicals as a genre commonly invite the audience into the movie not through identification, but as active spectators who are "essential for the entertainment to succeed" (139). Spectatorship, in this view, is not necessarily passive. Although spectacle may construct spectators as passive recipients of a prepackaged product, it may also elicit more active forms of engagement, such as curiosity about how an effect was achieved or interaction with other members of the audience. Rick Altman argues that movie musicals are characterized by a reflexivity that highlights the film's status as film: we are expected to marvel at the film's technological tricks and to accept that the songs are motivated at least as much by the presence of the audience as by the film's narrative. This reflexivity repeatedly disrupts narrative movement, but it does not make the film radical, expose its ideological content, or diminish the audience's pleasure (6–7).

Such disruptive pressures fragment, but do not eradicate, audience identifications. One might think we are expected to identify with the title character, but the movie does not encourage that identification. Only rarely are we sutured into Mary Poppins's position by shot/reverse-shot sequences, and the only time we get privileged information about her consciousness is at the conclusion.

More frequently, we are encouraged to identify with Jane and Michael. We are repeatedly given shots of their faces as they gaze with wonder and delight at some new miracle: they, like us, are often spectators. Clearly gender coded (Jane wears a pink nightgown and rides a pink horse; Michael wears blue pajamas and rides a blue horse), they together provide every viewer with a same-sex identification. In many ways, however, they are lumped together as "the children." With the exception of the bank scene, in which Michael carries the money even though he is younger, the differences in their portrayals could be related as much to age as to gender. Jane speaks more, representing the two children to the adults in the movie, while the camera more often focuses in on Michael's face. Although the movie recognizes gender, it provides two relatively undifferentiated sites of identification.

We frequently join Jane and Michael in looking at Mary Poppins. Mary Poppins is thus "the object of the gaze," a position that many feminist critics, following Laura Mulvey, have considered indicative of women's powerlessness and passivity in a patriarchal cultural system. This gaze hardly makes Mary Poppins passive or powerless, however. Indeed, it is often her magical potency that attracts the attention, and she does not rely for her appeal on romantic or sexual allure. Disney company memos indicate that the character of the movie's Mary Poppins was highly contested. Executive Martin Kaplan explained that she needed to be "substantially more charming and affectionate than the one in the books, where she's somewhat too fastidious and vain (like her creator)" (Masters 36). Travers tried to keep any hint of a romantic alliance between Mary and Bert out of the script (Glenn). Whether she was successful is debatable, especially in the context of a movie tradition in which any adult, unmarried, heterosexual friendship is likely to be construed as romantic—and waltzes in Victorian garb don't help. But Bert's adoration of Mary is matched by that of the animated animals they encounter, and soon by Jane and Michael as well. Having the audience identify with the children certainly does not eliminate sexual overtones, but it does relegate them to second place.

The identification with the children is not, however, absolute. If we are adults, and particularly parents, our sympathies are likely to occasionally slip over to the movie's parents—especially if we feel similarly ineffective in managing a squirming youngster in the seat next to us. Because the parents are not present in large segments of the movie, this identification is unstable and parents may repeatedly return to seeing things from the children's point of view. Parents may also identify with the real-life children who are simultaneously watching the screen. Imagining their children's reactions (and seeing and hearing them) certainly affects parents' experience of the movie.

Such a viewing may produce some mixed feelings. On the one hand, simply by coming to the theater parents are doing what the movie tells them to: they are taking their children on an enjoyable outing. They may therefore feel comforted, since the movie seems to assure them that they are good parents. On the other hand, their identification with Mr. or Mrs. Banks may be disconcerting. Few parents (and especially midcentury American middle-class parents) never fear that they are neglecting their children. The standard for good parenthood in the early 1960s was high and rising. "Mary Poppins" might even seem to say that fathers as well as mothers have to subordinate all interests outside the home if they are not to fail as parents. For women, such a dictate would condemn them to the fullest form of "the problem that has no name." For men, it raises the problem, actively erased by the movie, of how to fulfill one's breadwinner responsibilities while giving one's children adequate time and attention.

According to Kathy Jackson, children in American films made before World War II tended to be represented as innocent, happy, good, and capable of solving not just their own problems but also those of adults. In the 1950s and early 1960s, however, popular films featuring children "reveal a world in which children are confused, searching, misunderstood, or deviant" and fathers in particular are "frequently absent or ineffectual." Jackson suggests that the popularity of such troubled film images of children indicates parents' fears that even the domestic world was out of their control (81, 117–18).

Parents, then, may respond powerfully to the movie's images of emotionally starved children constantly running away. While their anxieties may be soothed by the movie's resolution, in which a simple kite-flying expedition solves all the family's problems, they may also recognize the inadequacy of this solution; if nothing else, such outings would need to be repeated ad infinitum. Mothers especially may want to identify with Mary Poppins, who has the perfect touch for making children feel happy, cared for, and able to explore the world, while also enforcing discipline. But Mary has the great advantage of being able to put the nursery in order by a snap of her fingers. A mother who aspires to be Mary Poppins, like a father who defies his employers, is likely to find that the "real world" is more difficult and painful than "Mary Poppins" suggests.

All of which finally brings us to the movie's presumed primary audience: children. As Jacqueline Rose points out, the project of analyzing children's literature is highly problematic: "Children's fiction sets up a world in which the adult comes first (author, maker, giver) and the child comes after (reader, product, receiver), but where neither of them enter the space in between" (1–2). Rose concludes that a child's experience of literature is more or less inaccessible to an adult critic. I believe it is essential to heed her warnings about the distortions probable in an adult's reading of a child's reading of a cultural product, and I agree entirely with Geoff Moss that it is impossible to predict accurately the responses of "child readers in general" as if all children were the same (50). Nevertheless, I am unwilling to give up entirely the attempt to suggest how children may view "Mary Poppins." Perhaps I am simply walking in where angels fear to tread. As I argued earlier, however, "Mary Poppins" is not the closed or "readerly" text that Rose and Moss consider typical of children's literature. The movie's disruptions of "reality" mean that it does not "count absolutely on the child's willingness to enter into the book, and *live* the story" (Rose 2). Instead, it relies on a viewer's willingness to engage with a text that repeatedly emphasizes that it is a text.

"Mary Poppins" clearly draws on children's anxieties about being unloved and abandoned. At the beginning of the movie, Jane and Michael are inconveniences to their parents, both of whom would prefer to be off doing something else. Mr. Banks's comments in particular make us sympathetic to Michael's opinion that his father does not like him (though an older viewer might pause over the connection between loving one's children and liking them). By the end of the movie, however, the Banks family has become what might, in therapeutic jargon, be called "child-centered." Not only are the children welcome to spend time with their parents, but it is the parents' response to the children's interests (kite-flying) that determines the family's activities.

I suggest, however, that the overall narrative is not particularly significant in children's experience of the movie, especially among the under-ten set that is likely to be Disney's primary audience. Children are unlikely to have the patience, or the experience, or the interest, to try to comprehend the movie as a whole, especially when both the movie itself and the viewing environment encourage them to see the movie as a series of episodes rather than as a closed and coherent narrative driving inexorably toward a goal. What is more salient, then, is children's experience of individual scenes—the images and dialogue they walk away with. (Such fragmented viewing is even more significant in the 1990s, when the VCR remote enables children to control which parts of a movie they see again and again.) We can think of this as a self-constructed set of "narrative images" that represent the film in the child's mind.

Consider the bank, for example. Mr. Banks is strongly identified with the bank; he is even named after it. Susan Willis points out, however, that young children do not understand what banks do: they "see the bank as a window that dispenses cash to people whenever they run out of it" (*A Primer* 25). In a society that separates children from any form of productive labor, it takes quite a while to understand the capitalist system and banking's role in it. Songs that list "First and second trust deeds, / Think of the foreclosures! / Bonds! Chattels! / Dividends! Shares! / Bankruptcies! Debtor sales! / Opportunities! / All manner of private enterprise! / Shipyards! The mercantile! / Collieries! Tanneries! / Incorporations! Amalgamations!" (44–46) do not illuminate the issue. From a child's point of view, Mr. Banks spends his days doing something incomprehensible. But the two wardens who march Mr. Banks down the hall to the bank's darkened boardroom lend credence to Bert's explanation that

Mr. Banks is in a cage. And, while a child may not fully understand what is happening when Mr. Banks is fired, the images of the other officers tearing his flower, inverting his umbrella, and punching out his hat are quite clear. These images of threat and power convey a sense that the world of business is not a safe place.

Mark West suggests that children's senses of humor frequently turn on the tensions in their relationships with adults. Coming to consciousness and society in the context of an unequal power relationship, children enjoy jokes and stories that poke fun at adults' authority, suggest that adults are not infallibly good, or highlight the dirty and disgusting things about which adults are so squeamish (115–16). This analysis helps us understand why some children find "Mary Poppins" so funny. Although the movie is sometimes slapstick, it is a mistake to assume that this is all children see. Scenes in which everyone's clothes and faces are covered with black soot, for example, surely resonate with children's pleasures and fears around making a mess. The movie's humor repeatedly undercuts parental authority and reveals parents to be confused, foolish, and needing to listen to and learn from children. It is not so clear, then, who is reconciled to whom: the same story that can be called "The Education of Mr. Banks" can also be called "The Triumph of the Child."

In conclusion, I suggest that "Mary Poppins" stirs up in its spectators a wide range of anxieties, including those around gender, class, age, family, work, race, and nationhood. These anxieties are soothed by the narrative conclusion, which posits the middle-class nuclear family (appropriately but not excessively supported by lower-class assistants) as the site of true personal satisfaction and authentic group loyalty. The utopian vision ultimately ratified by the movie centers on this idea of family: we are all expected to feel that the movie ends well when the Banks family consolidates its ranks, Mrs. Banks symbolically gives up her suffrage activism, Mr. Banks recognizes that his most important calling is fatherhood, and Mary Poppins and Bert safely return to their marginal positions in the family/society. Along the way, however, we see glimpses of other utopian visions, such as one in which the workplace recognizes the value of sociability and play and people mingle on the basis of shared interests and pleasures, not shared age and class. The line between utopianism and romanticism is a thin one, if indeed it exists, and a utopian vision always runs the risk of resigning people to the status quo by overaccentuating the seeds of hope. Things are not so bad, mass culture often seems to say, and the problems that remain can easily be solved by embracing more of the existing system.

Nevertheless, this ideological closure is rarely complete. In "Mary Poppins," the fact that both movie and viewing conditions encourage viewers to experience the movie in an episodic fashion increases the possibility that the movie's intermittent critiques of class, capitalism, and middle-class gender and family relations may stick. There is no one way to read "Mary Poppins." When I first saw the movie, as a child, my mother leaned over after the "Sister Suffragette" line "Our daughters' daughters will adore us" to whisper what a shame it was that the mother was thinking so much about her daughter's daughters that she did not even take the time to care for her own daughter. My mother thought the movie supported her choice to interrupt her graduate work for six years to be a full-time mother. In contrast, another professional woman I know thought the movie's portrayal of Mary Poppins's and Bert's beneficial relationships with Jane and Michael supported her choice to pay another person to nurture her children during the workweek while she pursued her career.

Such contrary conclusions make it clear that what viewers bring to "Mary Poppins" greatly affects what they take away, a principle that holds for other movies and other cultural products. In her discussion of dinosaurs in Chapter 13, Susan Willis concludes that a child's images of these widespread cultural artifacts can reinforce dominant ideologies or just as easily convey utopian content. Similarly, there is no way to firmly determine whether a particular movie is "subversive" or "recuperative," whether it will provoke utopian aspirations or socialize viewers into a normative order. While the "transformational" work observed by Jameson is probably predominant in most of mass culture, the very process of raising anxieties in order to soothe them runs the risk of promoting awareness of those anxieties and provoking other answers to the questions they pose. One cannot rely on a cultural product to be, in itself, subversive or liberatory. Too much occurs during the process of interpretation for a cultural product alone, outside a tradition of critical conversation, to carry such weight. That critical tradition—be it located in a classroom, a newspaper column, a circle of friends, or a parent's whisper into a child's ear—crucially affects what people see and hear in any cultural product.

Notes

Introduction

1. For early feminist criticism of fairy tales, see, e.g., Lieberman, Lurie, Rowe, and Yolen. Zipes collects criticism and fairy tales in *Don't Bet on the Prince;* more recent discussions of gender and fairy tales include the volumes by Bottigheimer and Tatar. For early feminist criticism of picture books, see, e.g., Fisher; Nilsen; Segel, "Picture Books"; and Weitzman et al.; see also the other works cited in the essay in this book by Clark, Kulkin, and Clancy (Chapter 5).

2. As early as 1970 Lindsay published praise of Alcott in a feminist journal; for a history of criticism of Alcott, see Alberghene and Clark and also Stern. For early feminist discussions of other women writers, see, e.g., Keyser; Knoepflmacher; various essays by Myers; and Reimer's collection.

3. Literary critics working on popular culture had already addressed girls' series books (see Cadogan and Craig, Mason, J. Smith).

4. For an elaboration of the ideas in this paragraph and the next, see my "Fairy Godmothers."

5. This paragraph simply marks my most overt borrowing from Margaret Higonnet. The entire essay is informed by her telling insights.

1 / Repudiating "Sleeping Beauty"

1. When Ram Dass enters the attic room of the sleeping Sara Crewe, he assumes the role of princely awaker and also acts as a surrogate for Carrisford, the debilitated millionaire who will become Princess Sara's avuncular consort.

2. By alluding to the precedent of the Grimms in his preface to *The Pentamerone; or, The Story of Stories, Fun for the Little Ones* and by enlisting George Cruikshank as his illustrator, John Edward Taylor clearly intended to capitalize on the success of the Cruikshank-illustrated edition of the Grimms undertaken by his namesake, Edgar Taylor, in 1823–26. He invokes "Dr. Grimm" on the "philosophical character and worth" of Gi-

ambattista Basile's tales, yet adds, "At the same time, this volume will, I hope, likewise prove attractive to my younger readers, who may derive pleasure and amusement from a ramble in the Fairyland of the south" (xvi).

3. The fairy causes "everybody" in the household to fall asleep, "*except* the king and queen," who "kissed their dear child, without waking her, and left the castle," entering into a world of mutability and death (A. Johnson 9, emphasis added).

4. For discussions of Perrault's uneasy relation to D'Aulnoy and other women writers of his time, see Zipes, *Fairy Tale*, and Harries.

5. Although dramatic and cinematic adaptations of "Sleeping Beauty" often suggest that the malevolent fairy and the old woman with distaff and spindle are identical by having the same actress play both roles, there is no such identification in either Perrault or the Grimms. Basile, who stresses fortuitousness rather than fairy power, calls attention to the old woman's unwitting part in "this terrible catastrophe" and has her guiltily run away (130).

6. Burnett, as suggested above, may well have known Basile's story: Archibald Craven, who locks the garden he equates with *his* "evil fortune" and who reminds Mary Lennox of such fairy-tale figures as Perrault's Ricky of the Tuft, similarly deserts his own paralyzed offspring.

7. MacDonald reverses Perrault's emphasis in "The Light Princess" when he has the determined young princess, aided by an experienced older woman, revive the seemingly dead prince they have lugged into her bedroom. (Earlier, the immobilized prince begged his female counterpart to give him a parting kiss.) MacDonald also has fun with Perrault in "Little Daylight," both in the early scene in which the fairies give their gifts to the princess and in the final scene in which the prince kisses not a desirable young woman, but exactly the sort of wizened "mother" Perrault finds so difficult to accept.

8. "Wakeful Belles and Torpid Beasts: Retellings of 'Beauty and the Beast,'" a lecture I gave at the Northeast Victorian Studies Association and at Skidmore College, will eventually become a companion piece to this essay.

2 / Child's Play as Woman's Peace Work

1. Uniting solemn history with revisionist feminist literary study, yet omitting the child, Christina Crosby's work exemplifies the trend I protest. It is difficult to find a literature more pedophiliac than that of Victorian England, yet Crosby considers the "woman question" without reference to the child question with which it's intertwined. Crosby remarks that post-Enlightenment British thought produces history as "man's truth, the truth of a necessarily historical Humanity, which in turn requires that 'women' be outside history. . . . 'Women' are the unhistorical other of history" (1).

2. Space limitations preclude documentation for the theory and methodology that inform my approach. Contemporary work that addresses narrative structures as foundational for human learning and culture ranges from research in the "hard" sciences to postcolonial studies. Yet few premier investigators in narrative studies even notice disciplines related to children. Austen's own parodic *History of England from the reign of*

Henry the 4th to the death of Charles the 1st, "by a partial, prejudiced, and ignorant Historian," is of course scoring off pompous grown-up historians who do not recognize that they are, too (*Minor Works* 6: 139).

3. One of Edgeworth's most popular stories, "The Cherry Orchard" (part 10 of the 1801 *Early Lessons*, 51–106) was reprinted in many different forms. I refer to the first edition. The original format is reproduced in the Augustan Reprint Society's facsimile; bibliographical data are in my introduction to that volume.

4. The critique of Romantic ideology has mostly concerned revisioning gender and other issues in relation to the big six high Romantic males. For work on women writers for adults, see Stuart Curran and the anthologies edited by Carol Shiner Wilson and Joel Haefner and by Theresa M. Kelley and Paula R. Feldman. Romantic assumptions about childhood have so thoroughly conditioned later writers and critics that a critique of Romantic ideology from a juvenile perspective still needs to be argued for. Even when, refreshingly, gender is taken as constitutive in juvenile writing, differences across period are not usually taken into account, with the result that women writers contemporaneous with the Romantics come out looking pretty much the same as they did before, because the dominant "progressive" ideology of childhood remains uncontested, as in Julia Briggs's survey. When Romanticists call for "mainstreaming" women writers or detail their alternative sites of creativity and literary production (as in Haefner's essays), they think only of female cross-writers' work for grown-ups and situate Romantic women's work in relation to men's. Thus they reinforce the adultist and androcentric limits of the conventional canon even as they argue for its redefinition.

5. I am not endorsing the stereotype. Despite Ireland's reputation, the actual incidence of violence is said to compare favorably with "civilized" England's, but because violence was not confined to a particular space or time, it was perceived as a ubiquitous threat. According to many historians, however, men of all classes increasingly resorted to violence in the late eighteenth century, not only against each other individually and collectively, but also against women, for example, in forcible abduction (see James Kelly). Irish violence from the late eighteenth century on included duels; sectarian secret societies of agrarian protesters ("green" and usually Catholic) and loyalist supporters of the "Ascendancy" ("Orange" and usually Protestant); paramilitary terrorists; and revolutionists such as the United Irishmen who fomented the 1798 Rebellion and their notoriously violent opponents, the lodges honoring Protestant William of Orange's victories over his Catholic opponents at the Battle of the Boyne (1690).

6. For the obsessive involvement of children in war-related activities, see William M. Tuttle, Jr.; he notes that ideas of citizenship develop during the early school years (ch. 7).

7. Edgeworth is not being cute when she uses "wee-wee"; *Early Lessons* is printed on a child's scale, with wide margins and readable print.

8. Jürgen Habermas's notion of a body of private persons assembled to discuss matters of public concern and common interest, thus making the state accountable to society by unrestricted rational discussion of issues, has been critiqued by feminist theo-

rists for insufficient attention to gender access and for overemphasizing the role of abstract masculine rationality in communication: see, for example, Nancy Fraser on access; and Iris Marion Young's argument for affectivity and embodied knowledge in "Impartiality and the Civic Public." However idealized, Habermas's notion of an informed public opinion emergent in the late eighteenth century is important for women writers because it underlines the role of writing as social and political action.

9. "The pastoral process of putting the complex into the simple," as William Empson succinctly puts it, occasions social ideas (23), but pastoral forms in writing for children are still often dismissed as escapist.

10. For an informed overview of the masculine Romantic child-artist symbiosis, see Judith Plotz, whose argument reenacts the hegemony of Romantic assumptions.

11. "Mary" and variants such as "Marianne" have an autobiographical resonance; Edgeworth's first known letter, written when she (like the heroine) was eight, is signed "Mary."

12. Georgian women writers for children are among the first to explore the continuing problem of little boys' socialization into violence; for a recent overview, see Myriam Miedzian. Paul Fussell traces the soldier's fundamental imaginative habit of binary opposition (us versus them, self versus other, men versus women) back no further than the Great War; it has informed Irish culture and politics for centuries, however.

13. The dramatic scene also evokes the period's antiwar juvenile stories, such as those of Anna Letitia Barbauld, which Edgeworth knew well, and Wordsworth's poem "Nutting," with its similar rape of nature's riches and its very dissimilar validation of the child's passionate self-interest. Wordsworth's boy violates nature's property to establish his property in nature; Edgeworth's boy is being led not toward the masculine possession of nature, but toward the mutuality necessary to maintain culture. The two authors use the child to embody alternative notions of selfhood and its relation to the environing world.

14. As illustrated by both etymology and early writings on what has come to be called political economy, the domestic economy we tend to label "private" is the precursor and paradigm for what we now seal off as "public." Similarly, Enlightenment children's tales, like Utopian political theory, do not bracket work from play, as post-Romantic writing usually does.

15. Edgeworth uses Adam Smith's opening chapter—"Of the Division of Labour" —as the framework for Owen's clumsiness and lost time when he has to perform every step in the hat-making process himself.

16. Public-sphere theory derived from appropriation and revision of Habermas is entirely distinct from feminist theory that reads as "public" everything outside the family. Habermas's public sphere, separate from the state and the workplace, arises from within what we are more accustomed to think of as the "private." Oskar Negt and Alexander Kluge's very brief chapter titled "The Public Sphere of Children" is notable for its telling contrast between the public sphere of active child-managed play and work they desiderate, which "can be acquired only by involvement with real objects, with a

reality that is actively grasped," and the passive public sphere organized from above by public media, including educational television, which produces "precocious adults" (283–86). Fredric Jameson's "On Negt and Kluge" is especially useful for its analysis of their discussion of fairy tales, myths, and cultural narratives as collective pedagogy, which would "mean" very differently in different historical times and locales.

17. See Sara Ruddick's *Maternal Thinking*, "Notes," "Preservative Love," and "The Rationality of Care," as well as Hilary Rose.

18. Mary Field Belenky et al.'s *Women's Ways of Knowing* is among the best known of what might be called studies in feminist epistemology, which are currently revisioning models of intellectual development. Rather than privileging autonomy, independence, and abstract thought over interdependence, intimacy, nurturance, and contextual thought, such work investigates how women's connected knowing is both culturally developed and culturally functional. It is important to emphasize that connected knowing is learned rather than genetic; much of this recent work needs to be tested historically.

19. See Woolf's "Thoughts" and the last chapter of Doris Lessing's *Prisons*. I do not mean to universalize gender's effects in writing—many men have written antiwar stories for children, and no doubt some women glorify militarism in tales for the young.

20. John Aikin, Barbauld's brother, was equally adept at getting young readers to rethink the bloody events of "big" history, as in "The Price of a Victory" (maimed bodies and wasted lives), and so were many other Enlightened writers, men as well as women. My point is less to gender the "arts of peace" than to give Georgian writers of children's literature the credit that has migrated to later Romantic men. Paul A. Cantor typically asserts that their poetry "shows a new sympathy for the poor, the weak, the downtrodden, the disenfranchised, and the outcast" and credits their work with revamping poetry so that it could represent intimate details of domestic life and personal development, a familiar attribute of Georgian children's literature (706).

3 / "These two irreconcilable things—art and young girls"

1. Ann Ardis argues that the interest in aesthetics also obscured "the difficult questions raised in the debate on the New Woman novel," that is, questions about the nature of human sexuality and the relation between literature and social change (55).

2. In the revised edition of *The Pleasures of Children's Literature* (1996), Nodelman discusses didacticism in children's literature under the rubric of themes (155–59), and children's texts as idylls under the rubric of focalization (164–67). He continues, however, to emphasize that balancing oppositions is a characteristic of children's literature as a genre.

3. For a discussion of the implications of this attitude for reading and teaching children's literature, see Nodelman, *Pleasures* (1992): 7–14 and passim.

4. For a full discussion of L. T. Meade's translation of the terms of the educational campaigns into the narrative structure and strategies of her girls' school stories, see my "Worlds of Girls."

5. See, for example, the writings of Beale, Frances Mary Buss, and Emily Davies, three of the most influential pioneers of the new systems of women's education in the second half of the nineteenth century. See also Martha Vicinus's chapter, "The Reformed Boarding Schools," in *Independent Women.*

6. For a full discussion of Stead's investigation, reports, trial, conviction, and incarceration, see Deborah Gorham, "'Maiden Tribute'"; Raymond Schults; and Judith Walkowitz 81–134.

7. Cf. Sheila Jeffreys 24, whom I paraphrase in this observation. Both Gorham and Walkowitz consider Stead's conflicted stance toward women in the series, as well as in his correspondence with reformers such as Butler about the "Secret Commission."

8. Butler resigned her role as an agitator for the reform of women's education to avoid having the issue of schooling for girls tied to the danger of the streets for women. For a discussion of the theoretical continuity between her analyses of the two issues, see Barbara Caine 177–79.

4 / Romancing the Home

1. John M. MacKenzie notes that a "sharp division between boys' and girls' literature became the norm" in this period (203). For a useful discussion of boys' adventure fiction, see Martin Green, the essays by Patrick Dunae and Louis James, and the excellent collection edited by Jeffrey Richards. Edward Said and Patrick Brantlinger have contributed most interestingly to the discussion of this fiction as well. See, too, the exemplary essay on the "trajectories of desire" in imperialistic narratives by Gail Ching-Liang Low. For valuable recent discussions of the girl and the fiction of imperialism, see J. S. Bratton, Kimberley Reynolds, and Claudia Nelson. For a discussion of childhood and postimperial projects, see Lissa Paul's essay in this book (Chapter 6).

2. The full title was *Les Enfants du Capitaine Grant. Voyage autour du monde.* Contemporary English translations included a slightly abridged version of the New Zealand section (Part III), *Among the Cannibals* (1876).

3. Among others, Ballantyne's own brief history of Cook's voyages in the Pacific, *The Cannibal Islands,* makes this same point repeatedly.

4. For a brilliant discussion of these antipathetic pairs in colonialist literature, a "manichean allegory," see Abdul JanMohamed. For a bracing discussion of "colonizing women" in the Pacific, exposing similar antipathies (both acknowledged and unacknowledged) and marking the importance of "maternalism," see Margaret Jolly.

5. For a recent account of this imperial military campaign, see James Belich. Henty does not disclose his source of information, but he insists in his prefatory note that his representation of events is "all strictly in accordance with the facts."

6. Jack Stanley's fear of tattooing gives vivid expression to this anxiety, as does the peculiar note that concludes Jules Verne's *Among the Cannibals.*

7. This argument is grounded in conclusions reached by Jean Laplanche and Jean-

Bertrand Pontalis in their article on fantasy and sexuality (see especially 26). In the course of the late-nineteenth-century disputes over the value of fiction, described most cogently by Felicity Hughes, Henry James claimed that the mass audience he foresaw as the ruination of the novel looked only for "story"; Rider Haggard, although preferring romance to novel, agreed emphatically—"The story is the thing" (qtd. in Hughes 80). In her essay in this book (Chapter 3), Mavis Reimer reminds us that the typical Haggard romance excluded girls from its business no less than did the James novel. I argue, however, that the power of the kind of narrative we find in popular imperial romance is not limited to straightforwardly gendered identification with exemplary characters, but lies precisely in its capacity to construct in "story" the "desubjectivized" fantasy scene described by Laplanche and Pontalis.

8. Both novels were published immediately before the annexation of Fiji, which was sometimes associated with Benjamin Disraeli's "New Imperialism" but, apparently, was in substance the consequence of determinations made by the preceding Liberal government (Eldridge 108).

9. Kingston's attitude parallels missionary attitudes described by Christopher Herbert.

5 / Liberal Bias in Feminist Social Science Research on Children's Books

1. See, e.g., Feminists on Children's Media 5–7.

2. Furthermore, the Weitzman study cites a Modern Language Association presentation on "Women in Children's Literature" (later published in *College English*) by Nilsen in 1970. Segel argues that both Nilsen and Weitzman et al. had been alerted to the "almost incredible conspiracy of conditioning" implicit in children's books by an article by Fisher in the *New York Times Book Review* in 1970.

3. Perusal of the education literature, for instance, suggests that while much education research involving children's literature of the last twenty-five years came out of a liberal-feminist paradigm (and almost all of it cites Weitzman's study), education researchers may be in the middle of the kind of paradigm shift we advocate. Reports such as Dellman-Jenkins et al.'s 1993 essay on sex roles and cultural diversity in award-winning picture books suggest that educational researchers may not have lagged behind their sociological and psychological counterparts in the kind of work we think should emerge.

4. These are Jennings, Flerx et al., McArthur and Eisen, Koblinsky et al., Lutes-Dunckley, Ashton, and Kropp and Halverston.

5. For the former, see Jennings; for the latter, see McArthur and Eisen, Koblinsky et al., and Kropp and Halverston.

6. These are Women on Words, St. Peter, Knopp, Kolbe and LaVoie, Davis, White, Williams et al., Peirce and Edwards, Grauerholz and Pescosolido, Purcell and Stewart, Adler and Clark, Clark et al., Kortenhaus and Demarest, and Clark and Morris.

7. Education researchers may actually have such a paradigm in Dellman-Jenkins et al.

6 / Coming "to sing their being"

1. The two most striking historical examples I found of maternal literacies were Mme de Genlis (1746–1830) and Eliza Fenwick (1765–1840). Both have been lost, for the most part, in standard accounts of the history of children's literature and maternal pedagogies. Fortunately, Maria Edgeworth has been spared this fate, having been brilliantly reclaimed (in Chapter 2 in this book and elsewhere) by Mitzi Myers, to whom I owe my ability to read Genlis and Fenwick.

7 / Fictions of Difference

1. "Trapped!" appeared in 1993 and was announced as forthcoming in the author's *Danger in the Mountains,* to be published in Singapore. All quotations from the two texts are from the Indian editions.

2. See Gita Wolf's translation in *Landscapes* (in Telegu and Tamil), collected by a project called Aayana organized by the Madras Craft Foundation. See also R. K. Agnihotri et al.'s account of Eklavya, a successful experiment in primary education in Madhya Pradesh, and Anita Rampal's and Tultul Biswas's translated excerpts from *Chakmak,* Eklavya's monthly magazine, which publishes writings by children.

3. The *Panchatantra* is a collection of human and animal stories in Sanskrit, extant in the sixth century, which spread through ancient Europe and other parts of Asia. The stories deal mostly with questions of polity, celebrating shrewdness and worldly wisdom over morality.

4. Few extended discussions of children's literature in India are available. *Book Review,* however, publishes a special issue on the topic every year in November, to coincide with Children's Day.

5. Chellappa's concern with body image would speak strongly to a female reader, and this, as well as his age (old in relation to Ranjana and indeed all humans, but young in brahmarakshasha terms), makes him the mediatory figure between male and female, child and adult figures.

6. Veena Das has identified these two as the predominant explanatory frames in most analyses of the riots and proposes in their place a more narrow focus on the "local context" of every event of collective violence (160). Sudhir Kakar also points up the limitations of the "instrumentalist" theory of ethnic violence, which turns into an "instigator" theory and favors a more "social-psychological" explanation that accords significance to "primordial" attachments to cultural identity (211–15).

"Communalism" is the preferred phrase in India for the phenomenon of movements based on religious identity (which would probably be described as "ethnicity" in the West, with a greater emphasis on racial identities). The Indian State is constitutionally secular, but conflict between religious communities frequently breaks out in the form of rioting, including arson, looting, rape, and murder. The Sikh communal agitation of the 1980s and early 1990s was secessionist, demanding that a separate Sikh nation, Khalistan, be formed out of Punjab.

7. Debates about Indian secularism are widespread. See Kaushik Basu and Sanjay Subrahmanyam, especially Sen's essay.

8 / Making the Front Page

For the drift and direction of what follows, I wish to thank especially Pamela Esler, my partner and guide, who has illuminated in conversation and by her example many aspects of the issues addressed here, and my daughters, Corinna and Margaret, who have challenged me to grow up with them. Thanks are also due to Ann Bingham, Letha Deck, Geraldine Montgomery, Sarah Lawall, Catherine Mowbray, Maria Nikolayeva, Catherine Portuges, Sandra Beckett, and Maria Tymoczko, for their thoughtful counsel and cheerful encouragement at different points in the research and writing of this essay.

1. The potential application of Julia Kristeva's theory of the semiotic and symbolic to understanding the picture book has gone largely unnoticed. In brief, the image, preverbal, presymbolic, a fecund and continuous semiotic, accompanies the word, which breaks with the image, singling out, "meaning something," making a pronouncement of limited reference, saying what only symbolic language can say, Rushdie's ark on the Ocean of Notions. But the semiotic challenges again and again the finality and authority of that symbolic. The silent pictures never do stop talking.

2. Writing for children provided women with some legitimacy (if not notoriety) as early as 1685 (for example, Mlle Lhéritier, Mlle Bernard, and Mme Leprince de Beaumont). See especially Marc Soriano 190–202, 255–67. Excluding Kate Greenaway (1846–1901) and Beatrix Potter (1866–1943), few women seem to have made a career out of the production of image with text for a child audience in picture book form until after 1930. Greenaway and Potter are the only two female picture book artists Susan Meyer includes in her compilation.

3. Though storytelling has been viewed as "essentially female" (Lissa Paul, "Enigma" 156), this perspective was countered by Lucy Sprague Mitchell and Margaret Wise Brown, who at first refused to admit storytelling into the book for young children; Leonard Marcus (169) notes their subsequent change of heart.

4. Other women who wrote text for a man to illustrate include: Marjorie Flack, *The Story about Ping,* illustrated by Kurt Wiese; Else Minarik, *Little Bear's Visit,* illustrated by Maurice Sendak; Judith Viorst, *I'll Fix Anthony,* with Arnold Lobel, and *The Tenth Good Thing about Barney,* with Eric Blegvad; and Louise Fatio (Duvoisin), *The Three Happy Lions,* with Roger Duvoisin.

5. See my "Enfant terrible" for an attempt to distinguish the trickster from the enfant terrible.

6. See my "Informing Adult Readers" for more on the disjunction between image and text in George's experience.

7. One might adopt a more sympathetic reading, following Deborah Tannen. In what she calls "pragmatic homonymy," conversational partners may use sarcastic questions with the apparent intent of distance, yet "work toward a deeper effect of cama-

raderie, by drawing . . . in to emotional interaction" (166). Russell Hoban's representation of treacherous feminine discourse may ultimately effect camaraderie, but it takes more than talk to heal the wounds.

8. Among joint ventures, the d'Aulaires and Louise Fatio and Roger Duvoisin are among the few I have found to be joined in the copyright. The two Hobans and the two Lobels each hold a separate copyright for his or her part in the making of a particular picture book.

9. In "Stabat Mater," Kristeva reinvents this format; as Diane Jonte-Pace describes it, "The text intertwines two narratives in parallel columns: on the left is a series of lyrical reflections on pregnancy, childbirth, and relation with a son. . . . On the right is a discussion of the history of the cult of the Virgin Mary drawing in part upon the writings of the Fathers of the Church—the father's discourse on motherhood" (8).

10. Perhaps in her lifetime and even to this day, Flack's career has been overshadowed by those of her two husbands, the painter Karl Larsson and the poet William Rose Benêt, who, Anita Silvey reminds us, won a Pulitzer prize (244–45). I read such credits as a symptom of an editorial-husband complex.

11. For further discussion of these points of graphic order, see Molly Bang, Scott McCloud, and my "Introduction to Picturebook Codes."

12. When a picture book or comic book character is split, either via multiple images on the same page or through manifestations in different guises, each "return" may mark a diminishing of the character's control or power over the moment. See my "Introduction to Picturebook Codes." Also see Adrienne Rich 56–73.

13. Despite her "negative" qualities, it is Viola Swamp (like the big, bad wolf) who empowers daughters Lindsey and Ashley, as reported by Wolf and Heath (83, 113–14), and the girls' mother! Having just shown us how she used Swamp's persona to fight daughter Ashley's "literary fire" with her own, Wolf (the mother) describes Swamp as "a notorious substitute teacher with a commanding voice and black fingernails" (114).

14. The picture books I examine here generally feature the white female within an environment of white males and white children. I must let others tell the story of feminist resistance on the part of women who are black and other disenfranchised minorities within the covers of the picture book. bell hooks provides a useful starting point, as do Clark, Kulkin, and Clancy in Chapter 5 in this book.

9 / Discourses of Femininity

1. The intertextual relationships operate in complex ways. A reader need not have a detailed knowledge of *The Tempest* because pertinent elements of the play are recapitulated in the novel: the focalizing character engages directly with ideas generated by that text. In contrast, *The Ebony Tower* (for which *The Tempest* is also a pre-text) presents an intertextual effect that may be actualized by readers: it is not directly invoked in *In Summer Light*, but the two works are oriented toward a shared cultural phenomenon and have common events and character configurations. Readers familiar with the Fowles novella will summon it from their repertoire of possible intertexts, and it will be used,

as Owen Miller puts it, "as a supplement brought by the reader to facilitate additional meanings of the text, to which the text lends itself" (35). This intertextuality is, in Jonathan Culler's formulation, "less a name for a work's relation to particular prior texts than a designation of its participation in the discursive space of a culture" (103). Such relationships are different again from the use of the Rapunzel story in *The Tower Room*, which is a specific allusion readers are invited to recognize.

10 / Taking Over the Doll House

1. Freud analyzes E.T.A. Hoffmann's "The Sandman" in a famous essay concerned largely with fears of castration aroused in young boys by the *unheimlich*. Several toy narratives I do not examine in this essay partake strongly of the uncanny in other ways (see my *When Toys Come Alive* ch. 7).

2. Such doll houses were often built with panels that swung open and locked like cabinet doors and were the wrong size for most dolls (A. Fraser 171). Some miniatures had an adult commercial purpose to begin with: advertising full-sized goods by the same craftsman.

3. F. Armstrong in "Gender and Miniaturization" finds that images of the miniature such as Dickens exploits in his "little" women are a complex and ambiguous matter in their import for female subjectivity, since, although miniaturization tends to diminish women, women writers have nevertheless managed to subvert "belittlement" in several ways. In "The Dollhouse as Ludic Space, 1690 1920," Armstrong discusses accounts that suggest that little girls have persistently played with doll houses in ways that may subvert adult wishes for domestication of the female child.

4. However, Formanek-Brunell indicates that doll making developed into a means for women to enter the commercial arena, employ other women, and exploit "a maternalistic style [that] blurred the boundary between home life and the marketplace" (63).

5. The longing to have one's own home rather than serve in another's has special racial as well as class considerations in the United States, as Lorraine Hansberry's play *Raisin in the Sun* (1966) demonstrates. For an account of changes in feminist thinking on this subject that parallels mine, see Clark, Kulkin, and Clancy's essay (Chapter 5) in this book.

6. Rahn suggests that Potter, in a belated initial rebellion, makes the doll house a symbol for her parents' home, in which she was virtually incarcerated, and portrays herself and her fiancé (also her publisher), Norman Warne, as the mouse couple.

7. Both Myers, in her ongoing revisionist studies of Regency and Georgian women writers (including Chapter 2 of this book), and Nelson, in discussing nineteenth- and twentieth-century boys' books, emphasize the power of ideals associated with the feminine embodied in didactic and/or religious literature from the late eighteenth century almost to the end of the nineteenth century. B. Smith's investigation of bourgeois women of northern France in the nineteenth century emphasizes their conservative social power. Vallone gives a chilling account of how the concept of "home" permeated and masked the structures of power in Victorian women's prisons (*Disciplines* ch. 1).

8. It is haunting to read in Golden's *The Women Outside* of the homeless bag lady who rejected the constrictions of a shelter yet "created several living spaces . . . in various vacant lots." Golden states that one of these makeshift sites "had a well-kept homeyness" (49).

9. At least one branch of feminism, which celebrates matriarchal as opposed to patriarchal heritage, would find this lineage (which in doll house stories often skips one generation to go from grandmother to granddaughter) significantly empowering.

10. The analysis of "home" in children's literature continues to hold a central place. Bachelard has influenced many critics besides me to see "home" as "felicitous space" in children's literature. Other more feminist theorizing is also ongoing. In the unpublished abstract of her presentation, Bixler contrasts home as depicted by male and female authors; in the "'Golden Age' children's classics . . . female writers typically portray the home itself as a pastoral oasis when presided over by a nurturant female." In contrast, Paul, in an unpublished paper, discusses two children's books about girls and women in which the theme of escape from home is dominant: Maud Reuterswaard's *A Way from Home* (published in Swedish in 1979) and Jane Gardam's *Through the Dolls' House Door* (1987).

11. Again, I want to emphasize that this text, like other toy narratives, may be interpreted at a racial level. I have elsewhere treated this subject in texts where reference to race is blatant (*When Toys Come Alive* ch. 6).

12. It strikes me that my own advocacy of doing away with assigned familial roles can be questioned. The older I get, the more I find these roles tiresome and limiting, but I realize that my willingness to make this declaration comes from the fact that I have experienced and often enjoyed all of the familial roles traditionally available to my gender (as well as professional roles not easily available to women in the past) and I have never been asked to give up any of them. I cannot speak fairly, therefore, to the longing of those who have not had these experiences or have been deprived of them against their will. From one feminist perspective, I do know that women have been far too often asked to assume and maintain these familial roles if they want any shelter at all for themselves. Significantly, the role of the bag lady has been connected with the rejection of these roles (see Golden, for instance).

11 / Comforts No More

1. See Jesse Jackson's speech at the Democratic National Convention in 1988, in which he uses the quilt as a metaphor for national unity (qtd. in Showalter, *Sister's Choice* 169) and the growing literature on the NAMES Project Quilt, especially Showalter 169–74, Elsley, Hillard, and Hawkins.

2. For more on the Harriet Powers quilt, see Fry; for more on other African-American story quilts, see Benberry, esp. 43–47, 57–73.

3. See, particularly, Ferrero et al. and Showalter 148–50. It is important to note that these traditions were not all encompassing. Many women quilted alone rather than collaboratively, and many women were unaware of the tradition of a dowry chest filled with

quilts. Moreover, research shows that early patchwork quilts were not, as tradition would have it, always testimonies to household economy; rather, the middle and upper-middle classes often purchased bolts of cloth specifically to be cut into pieces and sewn into a pattern.

4. In this era, the distinction between an adult and a child audience was not yet firmly fixed (see Brodhead 85).

5. For example, in Alice Walker's much-anthologized short story "Everyday Use," the mother, Mrs. Johnson, "reads" two family quilts: "In both of them were scraps of dresses Grandma Dee had worn fifty and more years ago. Bits and pieces of Grandpa Jarrell's Paisley shirts. And one tiny faded blue piece, about the size of a penny matchbox, that was from Great Grandpa Ezra's uniform that he wore in the Civil War" (720).

6. The 1840s were the heyday of the Egyptology craze in America. In 1842, George Gliddon, former American vice consul in Cairo, gave a series of lectures on ancient Egypt to a Boston audience, which conceivably could have included some girls who worked in the Lowell mills (or members of their families). He toured for the next two years, frequently attracting audiences of two thousand and selling twenty-four thousand copies of the book he published on the subject in 1843 (Irwin 4).

7. Interestingly, the opportunities that mill work offered women at the outset of the enterprise were promising: company housing and wages were good, and opportunities for self-education were plentiful. By the 1840s, conditions had deteriorated, as suggested by the growth of the Ten Hour Movement. Girls were responsible for working a seventy-five-hour week and tending three and four machines. Overseers, now paid bonuses for the production on their shift, were encouraged to harass slower workers, whose pay was docked if they could not keep up (Eisler 37–38). The last issue of *The Lowell Offering* was published in 1845, the year Annette's "Patchwork Quilt" appeared.

8. Although I do not want to push the point too far, it is worth noting Aunt Pen's use of the adjective "queer." Her maiden aunt status, the implications of her intellectual pursuits (countered, of course, by her quilting experience), and Alcott's own sure knowledge of the Boston marriage tradition suggest possibilities for a queer reading of this tale.

9. For a discussion of the shift in the philosophy and sociology of art from an understanding of art as produced by individuals to something produced by communities, see Wolff.

10. See the African-American folktale "The People Could Fly," in Hamilton 166–73.

11. The quilt is part of the collection of the Solomon R. Guggenheim Museum, which might be read as co-optation by the hegemonic discourse of patriarchal institutions. It remains, however, an inalienable possession of Ringgold's family, for, like other fabric gifts that participate in a woman's economy, it can be authenticated in terms of its maker and thus does not lose power with shifting ownership.

14 / Grrrls and Dolls

My thanks to Amy Earhart, Susan Bolet Egenolf, Howard Marchitello, Beverly Lyon Clark, and Margaret Higonnet for their comments.

1. See, however, the following studies in literary and cultural criticism, which begin to map the power imbalance between adult and child: Jacqueline Rose, *The Case of Peter Pan: or the Impossibility of Children's Fiction;* Peter Hunt, *Criticism, Theory, and Children's Literature;* and James Kincaid, *Child-Loving: The Erotic Child and Victorian Culture.* See also Mitzi Myers, "The Erotics of Pedagogy"; Beverly Lyon Clark, "Fairy Godmothers"; and the essays in this book by Lori Kenschaft, Mitzi Myers, Mavis Reimer, and Susan Willis.

2. On this topic see also the works by Carol Gilligan and Lyn Mikel Brown, the psychologist Mary Pipher, the educators Myra and David Sadker, and the sociologist Deborah Tolman.

3. Of course, the need to fight against the current political climate and the recent attacks on *Roe vs. Wade* and reproductive freedom might galvanize young women to feminist activism.

4. The second conference, held in April 1995 in Arlington, Virginia, and titled the NOW Young Feminist Summit Against Violence, was organized almost entirely by young feminists.

5. *Sassy* magazine (which "claims a readership of three million" [Chideya 86]), an early supporter and promoter of the Riot Grrrl movement and girl bands such as Bikini Kill and Babes in Toyland, briefly reviewed (and reviled) *The Morning After* in the October 1993 issue: "This sucky little volume purports to be an examination of feminism on campus. . . . As for encouraging us to stop overreacting and 'transform everyday experience back into everyday experience,' hello, Katie dearest, harassment *is* everyday experience! That's the real problem" (40).

6. Although Riot Grrrl enlarges the category of "girl" beyond its usual parameters—some members are college age or even older—the network can credibly be called a youth movement, or a girls' movement, in that its members consciously position themselves in opposition to adults while valorizing a preadolescent girlhood most of them have grown out of. In this essay, however, I have quoted teenaged Riot Grrrls whenever possible. Many members joined Riot Grrrl in their middle or later teens and have remained in the movement as they have grown. At this point, it is impossible to say how old one can become and viably be called a Riot Grrrl. All quotations of youth writing are transcribed exactly as written.

7. Kathleen Hanna, lead vocalist of Bikini Kill, is probably as close to a spokesperson as Riot Grrrl has had. See, for example, the interview with Hanna by Denise Shepard in *Ray Gun.* For a short interview with a member of Riot Grrrl LA that sheds light on the movement's organization and structure, see "hey there, riot grrrl!" Riot Grrrl Jessica Rosenberg with *Signs* Program Assistant Gitana Garofalo gathered a number of Riot Grrrls together and discussed through conference calls and e-mail the Riot Grrrl movement. This fascinating and illuminating conversation was published in the "Feminisms and Youth Cultures" issue of *Signs*, unfortunately too late for me to incorporate into this essay. See also Klein.

8. Charles Aaron, for example, quotes *Girl Germs* to end his *Village Voice* piece on

Riot Grrrl. Although he does not overinterpret the selection—which would be inappropriate—he introduces it with a patronizing attitude: Riot Grrrls "sneer, you know, *compassionately,* and spit in the pale, male face of the Generation X cliché, possessed by a radical spirit to 'do' something. Who knows exactly what?" (66).

9. The Internet has now become a hotbed of accessible Riot Grrrl activity through webpages, homepages, discussion groups, and e-mail.

10. In her zine *Hangnail,* Lee Ann reprints her angry letter to *Seventeen* in response to their May 1993 article "It's a Grrrl Thing": "I am really upset, very pissed off inside. . . . For twenty years I have struggled hard and now, all over the country my life is taking on some trendy 'I wanna-be helped' concept" (4).

11. See Joanne Gottlieb and Gayle Wald's insightful essay on Riot Grrrl and the independent music scene. For a good, brief overview of women in alternative music, but a dismissive view of Riot Grrrl music, see Rachel Felder.

12. As Heavens to Betsy implied, the majority of Riot Grrrl members are white and privileged (Carlip 39).

13. The term comes from the title of an early Bikini Kill cassette (Kim 53).

14. *USA Today,* ABC News, Maria Shriver, and Maury Povich have also been interested in reporting (exploiting?) the Riot Grrrl movement, Emily White notes (18). She adds that after this fervor Riot Grrrl instituted a "press block" to avoid misrepresentation by the media and burgeoning jealousy among the chapters or group members. White believes this "isolationism" will ultimately be harmful to the movement (18). However, in 1993 the alternative music magazine *Fiz* reported a documentary in the making about Riot Grrrl—*Not Bad for a Girl,* written and produced by Lisa Apramian, a Los Angeles clinical psychologist (Apramian 60–64). And yet, the press block seems to have worked: I have found little on Riot Grrrl in the mainstream press published after 1993.

15. The September/October 1994 issue of *New Moon* indicated, in response to a reader's query, that the editors are considering publishing a magazine for older teens. They also publish a bimonthly guide for adults entitled *New Moon Network: For Adults Who Care About Girls.*

16 / Just a Spoonful of Sugar?

1. To facilitate distinguishing between the book and the movie, I italicize the title of the book and place the title of the movie in quotation marks. All film lyrics are quoted as they appear in Sherman and Sherman's *Songs from Walt Disney's "Mary Poppins."* All other quotations from the movie were transcribed from the video.

Works Cited

Aaron, Charles. "A Riot of the Mind." *Village Voice* 2 Feb. 1993: 63+.

ʿAbdelkî, Yûsuf. Telephone Interview with Fedwa Malti-Douglas. 9 Apr. 1995.

ʿAbdelkî, Yûsuf, and Yûsuf al-Qaʿîd. "Rabâb Taʿtazill ʿan al-Rasm." *Usâma* 282–90 (Oct. 1980–Feb. 1981).

Adler, Emily Stier, and Roger Clark. "Adolescence: A Literary Passage." *Adolescence* 26 (1991): 757–68.

Agnihotri, R. K., et al., eds. *Prashika*. New Delhi: Ratna Sagar, 1994.

Ahmad, Aijaz. *In Theory: Classes, Nations, Literatures*. London: Verso, 1992.

Alberghene, Janice M., and Beverly Lyon Clark. Introduction. *"Little Women" and the Feminist Imagination*. Ed. Janice M. Alberghene and Beverly Lyon Clark. New York: Garland, 1999. xv–liv.

Alcott, Louisa May. "Happy Women." 1868. *Alternative Alcott*. Ed. Elaine Showalter. New Brunswick: Rutgers UP, 1988. 203–6.

———. "Patty's Patchwork." *Aunt Jo's Scrap-Bag: My Boys, etc.* Boston: Roberts, 1872. 193–215.

Allard, Harry, and James Marshall. *Miss Nelson Is Missing*. Boston: Houghton, 1977.

Altman, Rick. Introduction. *Genre: The Musical*. Ed. Rick Altman. London: Routledge, 1981. 1–7.

Amiel, Barbara. "Feminism Hits Middle Age." *National Review* 24 Nov. 1989: 32–35.

Annette. "The Patchwork Quilt." *The Lowell Offering*. Ed. Benita Eisler. 1977. New York: Harper, 1980. 150–54.

Antrobus, Helen. "Revolution Girl-Style Now!" *Utne Reader* Mar./Apr. 1993: 17–18.

Anzaldúa, Gloria. *Borderlands/La frontera: The New Mestiza*. San Francisco: Spinsters-Aunt Lute, 1987.

Apramian, Lisa. "Not Bad for a Girl." Interview with Fran Miller. *Fiz* Dec. 1992/Jan. 1993: 60–64.

Ardis, Ann L. *New Women, New Novels: Feminism and Early Modernism.* New Brunswick: Rutgers UP, 1990.

Armstrong, Frances. "The Dollhouse as Ludic Space, 1690–1920." *Children's Literature* 24 (1996): 23–54.

———. "Gender and Miniaturization: Games of Littleness in Nineteenth-Century Fiction." *English Studies in Canada* 16 (1990): 403–16.

Armstrong, Isobel, ed. *New Feminist Discourses: Critical Essays on Theories and Texts.* London: Routledge, 1992.

Armstrong, Nancy. *Desire and Domestic Fiction: A Political History of the Novel.* New York: Oxford UP, 1987.

———. "The Occidental Alice." *differences* 2 (Summer 1990): 3–40.

Ashcroft, Bill, Gareth Griffiths, and Helen Tiffin. *The Empire Writes Back: Theory and Practice in Post-Colonial Literature.* London: Routledge, 1989.

Ashton, Eleanor. "Measures of Play Behavior: The Influence of Sex-Role Stereotyped Children's Books." *Sex Roles* 9 (1983): 43–47.

Auerbach, Nina, and U. C. Knoepflmacher. "Refashioning Fairy Tales." *Forbidden Journeys: Fairy Tales and Fantasies by Victorian Women Writers.* Ed. Nina Auerbach and U. C. Knoepflmacher. Chicago: U of Chicago P, 1992. 11–20.

———, eds. *Forbidden Journeys: Fairy Tales and Fantasies by Victorian Women Writers.* Chicago: U of Chicago P, 1992.

Austen, Jane. *Minor Works.* Vol. 6 of *The Works of Jane Austen.* Ed. R. W. Chapman. 1954. London: Oxford UP, 1963.

———. *Northanger Abbey and Persuasion.* 1818. Vol. 5 of *The Novels of Jane Austen.* Ed. R. W. Chapman. 3rd ed. 5 vols. London: Oxford UP, 1959.

Bachelard, Gaston. *The Poetics of Space.* Trans. Maris Jolas. New York: Orion, 1964.

Baker, Houston A., Jr., and Charlotte Pierce-Baker. "Patches: Quilts and Community in Alice Walker's 'Everyday Use.'" *Southern Review* 21 (1985): 706–20.

Ballantyne, R. M. *The Island Queen; or Dethroned by Fire and Water. A Tale of the Southern Hemisphere.* London: Nisbet, 1885.

———. *The Cannibal Islands; or Captain Cook's Adventures in the South Seas.* London: Nisbet, n.d.

Bang, Molly. *Picture This: Perception and Composition.* Introd. Rudolf Arnheim. Boston: Beacon, 1992.

Barbauld, Mrs. [Anna Letitia], and Dr. [John] Aikin. *Evenings at Home; or, the Juvenile Budget Opened, Consisting of a Variety of Miscellaneous Pieces for the Instruction and Amusement of Young Persons.* 1792–96. 2 vols. in 1. Philadelphia: James Kay, n.d.

Basile, Giambattista. "Fifth Diversion of the Fifth Day: Sun, Moon, and Talia." *The Pentamerone of Giambattista Basile.* Trans. Benedetto Croce. Ed. N. M. Praeger. Vol. 2. London: Lane, 1932. 129–32.

Basu, Kaushik, and Sanjay Subrahmanyam, eds. *Unravelling the Nation: Sectarian Conflict and India's Secular Identity.* New Delhi: Penguin, 1996.

Baudelaire, Charles. *The Flowers of Evil.* Trans. James McGowan. Oxford: Oxford UP, 1993.

Beale, Dorothea. *A Few Words to Those Who Are Leaving.* London: George Bell, 1881.

———. *History of the Cheltenham Ladies' College, 1853–1904.* Cheltenham: "Looker-On" Printing Works, [1919].

———. "Schools of To-Day." *Atalanta* 3 (1889–90): 315–17.

———, ed. *Work and Play in Girls' Schools.* London: Longmans, 1898.

Belenky, Mary Field, Blythe McVicker Clinchy, Nancy Rule Goldberger, and Jill Mattuck Tarule. *Women's Ways of Knowing: The Development of Self, Voice, and Mind.* New York: Basic, 1986.

Belich, James. *The New Zealand Wars and the Victorian Interpretation of Racial Conflict.* Harmondsworth: Penguin, 1988.

Bell, Florence. "The Sleeping Beauty in Four Scenes." *Fairy Tale Plays and How To Act Them.* London: Longmans, 1908. 109–38.

Benberry, Cuesta. *Always There: The African-American Presence in American Quilts.* Louisville: Kentucky Quilt Project, 1992.

Berger, John. *Ways of Seeing.* New York: Penguin, 1977.

Bhabha, Homi. "The Ambivalence of Colonial Discourse." *October* 28 (1984): 125–33.

Bikini Kill. Interview with Denise Shepard. *Ray Gun* Dec./Jan. 1993: n. pag.

———. "Rebel Girl." *Yeah, Yeah, Yeah, Yeah.* LP. Kill Rock Stars, 1992.

Bixler, Phyllis. "The Child in the Female Pastoral World: Houses as Images of Nurturance in Early Twentieth-Century Children's Books by Women." Children's Literature Association Conference. Trinity College, Hartford, CT. June 1992.

Blain, Virginia, Patricia Clements, and Isobel Grundy, eds. *The Feminist Companion to Literature in English: Women Writers from the Middle Ages to the Present.* New Haven: Yale UP, 1990.

Blake, William. *Songs of Innocence.* 1789. *William Blake: A Selection of Poems and Letters.* Ed. J. Bronowski. Harmondsworth: Penguin, 1958.

Bloom, Harold. *The Western Canon: The Books and School of the Ages.* New York: Harcourt, 1994.

Bodichon, Barbara Leigh Smith. *Women and Work.* 1857. Rpt. in *Barbara Leigh Smith Bodichon and the Langham Place Group.* Ed. Candida Ann Lacey. Women's Source Library. New York: Routledge, 1986. 36–73.

Bottigheimer, Ruth B. *Grimms' Bad Girls and Bold Boys: The Moral and Social Vision of the Tales.* New Haven: Yale UP, 1987.

Bowlby, Rachel. *Just Looking: Consumer Culture in Dreiser, Gissing, Zola.* New York: Methuen, 1985.

Brantlinger, Patrick. *Rule of Darkness: British Imperialism, 1830–1914.* Ithaca: Cornell UP, 1988.

———. "Victorians and Africans: The Genealogy of the Myth of the Dark Continent." *Critical Inquiry* 12 (1985): 166–203. Rpt. in *"Race," Writing, and Difference.* Ed. Henry Louis Gates, Jr. Chicago: U of Chicago P, 1986. 185–222.

Bratmobile. "Brat Girl." *The Real Janelle.* LP. Kill Rock Stars, 1994.

Bratton, J. S. "British Imperialism and the Reproduction of Femininity in Girls' Fiction,

1900–1930." *Imperialism and Juvenile Literature.* Ed. Jeffrey Richards. Manchester: Manchester UP, 1989. 195–215.

Briggs, Julia. "Women Writers and Writing for Children: From Sarah Fielding to E. Nesbit." *Children and Their Books: A Celebration of the Work of Iona and Peter Opie.* Ed. Gillian Avery and Julia Briggs. Oxford: Clarendon, 1989. 221–50.

Brodhead, Richard H. *Cultures of Letters: Scenes of Reading and Writing in Nineteenth-Century America.* Chicago: U of Chicago P, 1993.

Browne, Anthony. *Piggybook.* New York: Knopf, 1986. N. pag.

Browne, Malcolm. "A Dinosaur Named Sue Divides Fossil Hunters." *New York Times* 21 July 1992: C1.

Buchsbaum, Herbert. "Revolution, Girl Style." *Scholastic Update* 12 Mar. 1993: 22–23.

Burnett, Frances Hodgson. *A Little Princess.* 1905. London: Penguin, 1984.

———. *The Secret Garden.* 1911. New York: Dell, 1977.

Buss, Frances M. *Leaves From the Notebooks of Frances M. Buss, Being Selections From Her Weekly Addresses to the Girls of the North London Collegiate School.* Ed. Grace Toplis. London: Macmillan, 1896.

Butler, Josephine. *The Education and Employment of Women.* 1868. Rpt. in *The Education Papers: Women's Quest for Equality in Britain, 1850–1912.* Ed. Dale Spender. Women's Source Library. New York: Routledge, 1987. 69–89.

Cadogan, Mary, and Patricia Craig. *You're a Brick, Angela! A New Look at Girls' Fiction from 1839 to 1975.* 1976. Rev. as *You're a Brick, Angela! The Girls' Story, 1839 to 1985.* London: Gollancz, 1986.

Caine, Barbara. *Victorian Feminists.* Oxford: Oxford UP, 1992.

Canby, Vincent. "Mary's Poppin' Up Again." *New York Times* 10 June 1973: B1, B16.

Cantor, Paul A. "Stoning the Romance: The Ideological Critique of Nineteenth-Century Literature: An Afterword." *South Atlantic Quarterly* (Special Issue on Contemporary Perspectives on Romanticism) 88 (1989): 705–20.

Carlip, Hillary. *Girl Power: Young Women Speak Out!* New York: Warner, 1995.

Carpenter, Humphrey, and Mari Prichard. *Oxford Companion to Children's Literature.* Oxford: Oxford UP, 1984.

Carroll, Lewis. *The Annotated Alice: Alice's Adventures in Wonderland and Through the Looking Glass.* Ed. Martin Gardner. 1960. New York: New American Library, 1974.

Carter, Angela. *Sleeping Beauty and Other Favourite Fairy Tales.* London: Gollancz, 1982.

Certeau, Michel de. *The Practice of Everyday Life.* Trans. Steven Rendall. Berkeley: U of California P, 1988.

Chambers, Aidan. Letter to Lissa Paul. 30 Dec. 1994.

Chambers, Aidan, and Jan Mark. "The *Signal* Poetry Award." *Signal* 59 (May 1989): 75–92.

Champetier, Caroline. "Mary Poppins." *Cahiers du Cinema* 283 (Dec. 1977): 53–54.

Chideya, Farai. "Revolution Girl Style." *Newsweek* 23 Nov. 1992: 84–86.

Ching-Liang Low, Gail. "His Stories? Narratives and Images of Imperialism." *New Formations* 12 (1990): 97–123.

Chodorow, Nancy. *The Reproduction of Mothering: Psychoanalysis and the Sociology of Gender.* Berkeley: U of California P, 1978.

Christian-Smith, Linda K. *Becoming a Woman through Romance.* New York: Routledge, 1990.

Clark, Beverly Lyon. "Fairy Godmothers or Wicked Stepmothers? The Uneasy Relationship of Feminist Theory and Children's Criticism." *Children's Literature Association Quarterly* 18 (1993–94): 171–76.

Clark, Roger, and Heidi Kulkin. "Toward a Multicultural Feminist Perspective on Fiction for Young Adults." *Youth & Society* 27 (1996): 291–312.

Clark, Roger, Rachel Lennon, and Leanna Morris. "Of Caldecotts and Kings: Gendered Images in Recent American Children's Books by Black and Non-Black Illustrators." *Gender & Society* 7 (1993): 227–45.

Clark, Roger, and Leanna Morris. "Themes of Knowing and Learning in Recent Novels for Young Adults." *International Review of Modern Sociology* 25 (1995): 105–23.

Clausen, Christopher. "Home and Away in Children's Fiction." *Children's Literature* 10 (1982): 141–52.

Collins, Jim. "Toward Defining a Matrix of the Musical Comedy: The Place of the Spectator within the Textual Mechanisms." *Genre: The Musical.* Ed. Rick Altman. London: Routledge, 1981. 134–46.

Collins, Patricia Hill. *Black Feminist Thought: Knowledge, Consciousness, and the Politics of Empowerment.* New York: Routledge, 1990.

———. "Learning from the Outsider Within: The Sociological Significance of Black Feminist Thought." *Social Problems* 33 (1986): S14–32.

Coontz, Stephanie. *The Way We Never Were: American Families and the Nostalgia Trap.* New York: Basic, 1992.

Craik, Dinah Mulock. *The Fairy Book: The Best Popular Fairy Stories Selected and Rendered Anew.* London: Macmillan, 1863.

Cranny-Francis, Anne. *Feminist Fiction.* Cambridge, Eng.: Polity, 1990.

Crosby, Christina. *The Ends of History: Victorians and "The Woman Question."* New York: Routledge, 1991.

Culler, Jonathan. *The Pursuit of Signs.* Ithaca: Cornell UP, 1981.

Curran, Stuart. "Altering the 'I': Women Poets and Romanticism." *ADE Bulletin* 88 (Winter 1987): 9–12.

———. "Romantic Poetry: The I Altered." *Romanticism and Feminism.* Ed. Anne K. Mellor. Bloomington: Indiana UP, 1988. 185–207.

Dabydeen, David. "On Not Being Milton: Nigger Talk in England Today." *The State of the Language.* Ed. Christopher Ricks and Leonard Michaels. London: Faber, 1990. 3–14.

Das, Veena. "The Spatialization of Violence: Case Study of a 'Communal Riot.'" *Unravelling the Nation: Sectarian Conflict and India's Secular Identity.* Ed. Kaushik Basu and Sanjay Subrahmanyam. New Delhi: Penguin, 1996. 157–203.

d'Aulaire, Ingri, and Edgar Parin d'Aulaire. *Pocahontas.* Garden City: Doubleday, 1946.

Davies, Emily. *Thoughts on Some Questions Relating to Women, 1860–1908*. Ed. E. E. Constance Jones. Cambridge: Bowes, 1910.

Davis, Albert. "Sex-Differentiated Behaviors in Nonsexist Picture Books." *Sex Roles* 11 (1984): 1–15.

DeBold, Elizabeth, Marie Wilson, and Idelisse Malave Reading. *Mother-Daughter Revolution: From Betrayal to Power*. Reading: Addison-Wesley, 1993.

Dellman-Jenkins, Mary, Lisa Florjancic, and Elizabeth Blue Swadener. "Sex Roles and Cultural Diversity in Recent Award Winning Picture Books for Young Children." *Journal of Research in Childhood Education* 7 (1993): 74–82.

Dhareshwar, Vivek. "Caste and the Secular Self." *Journal of Arts and Ideas* 25/26 (1993): 115–26.

Doane, Janice, and Devon Hodges. *Nostalgia and Sexual Difference: Resistance to Contemporary Feminism*. New York: Methuen, 1987.

Donaldson, Leslie. "*Mary Poppins*." *Magill's Survey of Cinema: English Language Films*. Second Series, Vol. 4. Ed. Frank N. Magill. Englewood Cliffs: Salem, 1981. 1550–53.

Dorfman, Ariel. *The Empire's Old Clothes: What the Lone Ranger, Babar, and Other Innocent Heroes Do to Our Minds*. Trans. Clark Hansen. New York: Pantheon, 1983.

Dorfman, Ariel, and Armand Mattelart. *How To Read Donald Duck: Imperialist Ideology in the Disney Comic*. Trans. David Kunzle. New York: International General, 1975.

Douglas, Allen, and Fedwa Malti-Douglas. *Arab Comic Strips: Politics of an Emerging Mass Culture*. Bloomington: Indiana UP, 1994.

Doza, Christine. "bloodlove." *Ms.* May/June 1995: 37–41.

Dunae, Patrick. "Boys' Literature and the Idea of Empire, 1870–1914." *Victorian Studies* 24 (1980): 105–21.

DuPlessis, Rachel Blau. *Writing Beyond the Ending: Narrative Strategies of Twentieth-Century Women Writers*. Bloomington: Indiana UP, 1985.

Dyer, Richard. *Only Entertainment*. London: Routledge, 1992.

Eby, Cecil Degrotte. *The Road to Armageddon: The Martial Spirit in English Popular Literature, 1870–1914*. Durham: Duke UP, 1987.

Edgeworth, Maria. *Early Lessons*. 10 parts. London: J. Johnson, 1801.

———. *A Memoir of Maria Edgeworth, with a Selection from Her Letters by the Late Mrs. [Frances] Edgeworth*. Ed. by Her Children. 3 vols. London: privately printed Joseph Masters and Son, 1867.

———. *Works of Maria Edgeworth*. Vol. 13 containing *Early Lessons*. Boston: Samuel H. Parker, 1825.

Eisler, Benita. Introduction. *The Lowell Offering: Writings by New England Mill Women (1840–1845)*. Ed. Benita Eisler. 1977. New York: Harper, 1980. 12–41.

Eldridge, C. C. *Victorian Imperialism*. London: Hodder, 1978.

El Saadawi, Nawal. *The Fall of the Imam*. Trans. Sherif Hetata. London: Methuen, 1988.

El-Shamy, Hasan. *Brother and Sister Type 872*: A Cognitive Behavioristic Analysis of a

Middle Eastern Oikotype. Folklore Monographs Series 8. Bloomington: Folklore Publications Group, 1979.

———. "The Brother-Sister Syndrome in Arab Family Life, Socio-Cultural Factors in Arab Psychiatry: A Critical Review." *International Journal of the Sociology of the Family* 11 (1981): 313–23.

Elsley, Judy. "The Rhetoric of the NAMES Project AIDS Quilt: Rereading the Text(ile)." *AIDS—The Literary Response.* Ed. Emmanuel S. Nelson. New York: Twayne, 1992. 187–96.

Emma. "What Riot Grrrl Means to Me." *Riot Grrrl NYC* Mar. 1993: n. pag.

Empson, William. *Some Versions of Pastoral.* 1935. Norfolk, CT: New Directions, 1960.

Engelhardt, Tom. "The Morphing of the American Mind." *New York Times* 24 Dec. 1994: 25.

Faludi, Susan. "Whose Hype?" *Newsweek* 25 Oct. 1993: 61.

Felder, Rachel. "The Girls in the Band: A Profile of Women in Alternative Music." *Antaeus* 71/72 (1993): 197–203.

Feminists on Children's Media. *Little Miss Muffet Fights Back.* New York: Feminists on Children's Media, 1974.

Fenwick, Eliza. *Visits to the Juvenile Library; or Knowledge Proved to be the Source of Happiness.* London: Tabart, 1805.

Ferree, Myra Marx, and Patricia Yancey Martin. "Doing the Work of the Movement: Feminist Organizations." *Feminist Organizations: Harvest of the New Women's Movement.* Ed. Myra Marx Ferree and Patricia Yancey Martin. Philadelphia: Temple UP, 1995. 3–23.

Ferrero, Pat, Elaine Hedges, and Judy Silber. *Hearts and Hands: The Influence of Women and Quilts on American Society.* San Francisco: Quilt Digest, 1987.

Fetterley, Judith. *The Resisting Reader: A Feminist Approach to American Fiction.* Bloomington: Indiana UP, 1978.

Fisher, Elizabeth. "Children's Books: The Second Sex, Junior Division." *New York Times Book Review* 24 May 1970: Children's Books sec., 6, 44.

Flack, Marjorie. *Angus and the Cat.* Garden City: Doubleday, 1931. N. pag.

Fleming, Anne Taylor. "Younger Women Are Sisters, Too." *New York Times Magazine* 19 June 1988: 16–17.

Flerx, Vicki, Dorothy Fidler, and Ronald Rogers. "Sex Role Stereotypes: Developmental Aspects and Early Intervention." *Child Development* 47 (1976): 998–1007.

Forde, H. A. *Across Two Seas: A New Zealand Tale.* London: Wells Gardner, 1894.

Formanek-Brunell, Miriam. *Made to Play House: Dolls and the Commercialization of American Girlhood, 1830–1930.* New Haven: Yale UP, 1993.

Foster, Shirley, and Judy Simons. *What Katy Read: Feminist Re-Readings of "Classic" Stories for Girls.* Iowa City: U of Iowa P, 1995.

Fowles, John. *The Ebony Tower.* London: Cape, 1974.

France, Kim. "Grrrls at War." *Rolling Stone* 8–22 July 1993: 23–24.

Fraser, Antonia. *A History of Toys.* Frankfurt am Main: Delacorte, 1966.

Fraser, Nancy. *Unruly Practices: Power, Discourse, and Gender in Contemporary Social Theory.* Minneapolis: U of Minnesota P, 1989.

Freud, Sigmund. "The 'Uncanny.'" *The Standard Edition of the Complete Psychological Works of Sigmund Freud,* Trans. James Strachey. Vol. 17. London: Hogarth, 1955. 217–52.

Fry, Gladys-Marie. "Harriet Powers: Portrait of an African-American Quilter." *Stitched from the Soul: Slave Quilts from the Ante-Bellum South.* New York: Dutton, 1990. 84–91.

Frye, Northrop. *Anatomy of Criticism: Four Essays.* Princeton: Princeton UP, 1957.

Fussell, Paul. *The Great War and Modern Memory.* New York: Oxford UP, 1975.

Genlis, Madame Stéphanie de. *Letters on Education; Containing All Principles relative to three different plans of Education; to that of Princes, and to those of Young Persons of both Sexes.* London: Bathurst, 1783.

Geras, Adèle. *The Tower Room.* 1990. London: Lions, 1992.

Gilbert, Sandra M., and Susan Gubar. *The Madwoman in the Attic: The Woman Writer and the Nineteenth-Century Literary Imagination.* New Haven: Yale UP, 1979.

Gilligan, Carol. *In a Different Voice: Psychological Theory and Women's Development.* Cambridge: Harvard UP, 1982.

Gilligan, Carol, and Lyn Mikel Brown. *Meeting at the Crossroads: Women's Psychology and Girls' Development.* Cambridge: Harvard UP, 1992.

Gilligan, Carol, Nona P. Lyons, and Trudy J. Hanmer, eds. *Making Connections: The Relational Worlds of Adolescent Girls at Emma Willard School.* Cambridge: Harvard UP, 1990.

Girls Editorial Board. Editorial. *New Moon.* July/Aug. 1995: 2.

Glenn, Larry. "Percolating 'Poppins.'" *New York Times* 11 Aug. 1963: B7.

Godden, Rumer. *The Dolls' House.* 1947. New York: Viking, 1949.

———. *Impunity Jane.* New York: Viking, 1954.

Golden, Stephanie. *The Women Outside: Meanings and Myths of Homelessness.* Berkeley: U of California P, 1992.

Gorham, Deborah. "The Ideology of Femininity and Reading for Girls, 1850–1914." *Lessons for Life: The Schooling of Girls and Women, 1850–1950.* Ed. Felicity Hunt. Oxford: Blackwell, 1987. 39–59.

———. "The 'Maiden Tribute of Modern Babylon' Re-Examined: Child Prostitution and the Idea of Childhood in Late-Victorian England." *Victorian Studies* 21 (1978): 353–79.

Gottlieb, Joanne, and Gayle Wald. "Smells Like Teen Spirit: Riot Grrrls, Revolution and Women in Independent Rock." *Microphone Fiends: Youth Music and Youth Culture.* Ed. Andrew Ross and Tricia Rose. New York: Routledge, 1994. 250–74.

Gould, Stephen Jay. "A Biological Homage to Mickey Mouse." *The Panda's Thumb.* New York: Norton, 1982. 95–107.

———. "Dinomania." *New York Times Review of Books* 12 Aug. 1993: 51–56.

Graff, Gerald. *Professing Literature: An Institutional History.* Chicago: U of Chicago P, 1987.

Grauerholz, Elizabeth, and Bernice Pescosolido. "Gender Representations in Children's Literature: 1900–1984." *Gender & Society* 3 (1989): 113–25.

Green, Martin. *Dreams of Adventure, Deeds of Empire.* New York: Basic, 1979.

Greene, Vivien. *English Dolls' Houses of the Eighteenth and Nineteenth Centuries.* 1955. New York: Scribner's, 1979.

Greer, Germaine. *The Obstacle Race: The Fortunes of Women Painters and Their Work.* New York: Farrar, 1979.

Grimm, [Jakob and Wilhelm]. *The Complete Grimms' Fairy Tales.* Introd. Padraic Colum. Commentary by Joseph Campbell. New York: Pantheon, 1972.

———. *Grimms Märchen.* Ed. Carl Helbling. Zürich: Manasse Verlag, n.d.

———. *Grimms' Tales for Young and Old.* Trans. Ralph Manheim. London: Gollancz, 1979.

Griswold, Jerry. *Audacious Kids: Coming of Age in America's Classic Children's Books.* New York: Oxford UP, 1992.

"GRRRL Talk." *Glamour* May 1993: 134.

Guerin, Ann. "Poppins with Snap and Crackle." *Life* 25 Sept. 1964: 28.

Habermas, Jürgen. *The Structural Transformation of the Public Sphere: An Inquiry into a Category of Bourgeois Society.* Trans. Thomas Burger and Frederick Lawrence. 1962. Cambridge: MIT P, 1992.

Haefner, Joel. "(De)Forming the Romantic Canon: The Case of Women Writers." *College Literature* 20 (June 1993): 44–57.

———. "The Romantic Scene(s) of Writing." *Re-Visioning Romanticism: British Women Writers, 1776–1837.* Ed. Carol Shiner Wilson and Joel Haefner. Philadelphia: U of Pennsylvania P, 1994. 256–73.

Hallberg, Kristin, and Boel Westin, eds. *I bilderbokens värld: 1880–1980.* Stockholm: Liber, 1985.

Hamilton, Virginia. *The People Could Fly: American Black Folktales.* New York: Knopf, 1985.

Hanna, Kathleen. Interview with Denise Shepard. *Ray Gun* Dec./Jan. 1993: n. pag.

Haraway, Donna. "A Manifesto for Cyborgs: Science, Technology, and Socialist Feminism in the 1980s." *Socialist Review* 80 (1985): 65–107. Rev. and rpt. as "Cyborg Manifesto and Fractured Identities." In *Social Theory: The Multicultural and Classic Readings.* Ed. Charles Lemert. Boulder: Westview, 1993. 597–604.

Harries, Elizabeth Wanning. "Simulating Oralities: French Fairy Tales of the 1690s." *College Literature* 23 (June 1996): 100–115.

"Have Umbrella, Will Travel." *Time* 18 Sept. 1964: 114.

Hawkins, Peter S. "Naming Names: The Art of Memory and the NAMES Project AIDS Quilt." *Critical Inquiry* 19 (Summer 1993): 752–81.

Hearts and Hands: A Social History of Nineteenth-Century Women and Their Quilts. Prod. Pat Ferrero and Julie Silber. Ferrero Films, 1987.

Heavens to Betsy. Liner Notes. *Calculated.* LP. Kill Rock Stars, 1993.

———. "Terrorist." *Calculated.* LP. Kill Rock Stars, 1993.

———. "White Girl." *Calculated*. LP. Kill Rock Stars, 1993.

Hedges, Elaine. "'The Needle or the Pen': The Literary Rediscovery of Women's Textile Work." *Tradition and the Talents of Women*. Ed. Florence Howe. Urbana: U of Illinois P, 1991. 338–64.

Henty, George. *Maori and Settler: A Story of the New Zealand War*. 1890. London: Blackie, 1911.

Herbert, Christopher. *Culture and Anomie: Ethnographic Imagination in the Nineteenth Century*. Chicago: U of Chicago P, 1991.

"hey there, riot grrrl." Interview with Fran Miller. *Fiz* Dec./Jan. 1993: 65.

Hibbin, Sally. "Reissue/ *Mary Poppins* (1964)." *Films and Filming* 333 (June 1982): 34–35.

Higonnet, Margaret Randolph. "Diffusion et débats du féminisme." Colloque: Ecriture féminine et littérature de jeunesse. Institut Charles Perrault, Eaubonne. 19 March 1994.

———. "La politique dans la cour de récréation: la critique féministe et la littérature enfantine." *Culture, texte et jeune lecteur*. Ed. Jean Perrot. Nancy, France: PU de Nancy, 1993. 109–25.

Hillard, Van E. "Census, Consensus, and the Commodification of Form: The NAMES Project Quilt." *Quilt Culture: Tracing the Pattern*. Ed. Cheryl B. Torsney and Judy Elsley. Columbia: U of Missouri P, 1994. 112–24.

Hoban, Russell. *A Bargain for Frances*. Illus. Lillian Hoban. New York: Harper, 1970.

———. *The Mouse and His Child*. New York: Harper, 1967.

———. "'The Mouse and His Child': Yes It's A Children's Book." *Books for Your Children* Winter 1976: 3.

Holcombe, Lee. *Victorian Ladies at Work: Middle-Class Women in England and Wales, 1850–1914*. Hamden: Archon, 1973.

Honig, Edith. *Breaking the Angelic Image: Woman Power in Victorian Children's Fantasy*. New York: Greenwood, 1988.

hooks, bell. *Feminist Theory: From Margin to Center*. Boston: South End, 1986.

———. "Representations of Whiteness." *Black Looks: Race and Representation*. Toronto: Between the Lines, 1992. 165–78.

———. *Yearning: Race, Gender, and Cultural Politics*. Boston: South End, 1990.

Hopkinson, Deborah. *Sweet Clara and the Freedom Quilt*. Illus. James Ransome. New York: Borzoi-Knopf, 1993. N. pag.

Hughes, Felicity A. "Children's Literature: Theory and Practice." *ELH* 45 (1978): 542–61. Rpt. in *Children's Literature: The Development of Criticism*. Ed. Peter Hunt. London: Routledge, 1990. 71–89.

Hulse, Michael, David Kennedy, and David Morley, eds. *The New Poetry*. Newcastle-on-Tyne: Bloodaxe, 1993.

Hunt, Peter, ed. *Children's Literature: The Development of Criticism*. London: Routledge, 1990.

———. *Criticism, Theory, & Children's Literature*. Oxford: Blackwell, 1991.

————, ed. *Literature for Children: Contemporary Criticism*. London: Routledge, 1992.

Ibrâhîm, Sunʿ Allâh. *Al-Lajna*. Cairo Matbûʿât al-Qâhira, 1982.

Ingelow, Jean. *Mopsa the Fairy*. 1869. *Forbidden Journeys: Fairy Tales and Fantasies by Victorian Women Writers*. Ed. Nina Auerbach and U. C. Knoepflmacher. Chicago: U of Chicago P, 1992. 215–316.

Irwin, John T. *American Hieroglyphics: The Symbol of the Egyptian Hieroglyphics in the American Renaissance*. New Haven: Yale UP, 1980.

Jackson, Kathy Merlock. *Images of Children in American Film: A Sociocultural Analysis*. Metuchen: Scarecrow, 1986.

Jacques, Faith. *Tilly's House*. New York: Atheneum, 1979.

Jaggar, Allison, and Paula Rothenberg Struhl, eds. *Feminist Frameworks*. New York: McGraw-Hill, 1978.

Jaggar, Allison, and Paula Rothenberg, eds. *Feminist Frameworks*. 2nd ed. New York: McGraw-Hill, 1984.

————, eds. *Feminist Frameworks*. 3rd ed. New York: McGraw-Hill, 1993.

James, Henry. "The Art of Fiction." 1884. *The House of Fiction: Essays on the Novel by Henry James*. Ed. Leon Edel. London: Hart-Davis, 1957. 23–45.

James, Louis. "Tom Brown's Imperialist Sons." *Victorian Studies* 17 (1973): 89–99.

Jameson, Fredric. "On Negt and Kluge." *The Phantom Public Sphere*. Ed. Bruce Robbins. Cultural Politics 5. Minneapolis: U of Minnesota P, 1993. 42–74.

————. *Signatures of the Visible*. New York: Routledge, 1992.

JanMohamed, Abdul R. "The Economy of Manichean Allegory: The Function of Racial Difference in Colonialist Literature." *Critical Inquiry* 12 (1985): 59–87. Rpt. in *"Race," Writing, and Difference*. Ed. Henry Louis Gates, Jr. Chicago: U of Chicago P, 1986. 78–106.

[Jeffrey, Francis]. Rev. of *Tales of Fashionable Life*, by Maria Edgeworth. *Edinburgh Review* 14 (July 1809): 375–88.

Jeffreys, Sheila. "'Free From All Uninvited Touch of Man': Women's Campaigns Around Sexuality, 1880–1914." *The Sexuality Papers: Male Sexuality and the Social Control of Women*. Ed. Lal Coveney, Margaret Jackson, Sheila Jeffreys, Leslie Kay, and Pat Mahony. London: Hutchinson, 1984. 22–44.

Jennings, Sally. "Effects of Sex Typing in Children's Stories on Preference Recall." *Child Development* 46 (1975): 220–23.

Johnson, A. E., trans. *Perrault's Fairy Tales*. New York: Dover, 1969.

Johnson, Pauline. *Feminism as Radical Humanism*. St. Leonard's, Austral.: Allen, 1994.

Jolly, Margaret. "Colonizing Women: The Maternal Body and Empire." *Feminism and the Politics of Difference*. Ed. Sneja Gunew and Anna Yeatman. St. Leonard's, Austral.: Allen, 1993.

Jonte-Pace, Diane. "Situating Kristeva Differently: Psycho-Analytic Readings of Woman and Religion." *Body/Text in Julia Kristeva: Religion, Women, and Psychoanalysis*. Ed. David Crownfield. Albany: State U of New York P, 1992. 1–22.

Kakar, Sudhir. "The Construction of a New Hindu Identity." *Unravelling the Nation: Sec-*

tarian Conflict and India's Secular Identity. Ed. Kaushik Basu and Sanjay Subrahmanyam. New Delhi: Penguin, 1996. 204–35.

Kake. "Who is Choking and Dying?" *Riot Grrrl NYC* Mar. 1993: n. pag.

Kamen, Paula. *Feminist Fatale: Voices from the "Twentysomething" Generation Explore the Future of the "Women's Movement."* New York: Fine, 1991.

Kaplan, Cora. "Pandora's Box: Subjectivity, Class and Sexuality in Socialist Feminist Criticism." *Making a Difference: Feminist Literary Criticism*. Ed. Gayle Greene and Coppélia Kahn. London: Methuen, 1985. 146–76.

Kassem, Ceza, and Malak Hashem, eds. *Flights of Fantasy: Arabic Short Stories*. Cairo: Elias Modern Publishing House, 1985.

Keating, Peter. *The Haunted Study: A Social History of the English Novel, 1875–1914*. London: Fontana-Harper Collins, 1989.

Keen, Suzanne. "Narrative Annexes in Charlotte Brontë's *Shirley*." *Journal of Narrative Technique* 20 (1990): 107–19.

Kelley, Theresa M., and Paula R. Feldman, eds. *Romantic Women Writers: Voices and Countervoices*. Hanover: UP of New England, 1995.

Kelly, James. "The Abduction of Women of Fortune in Eighteenth-Century Ireland." *Eighteenth-Century Ireland* 9 (1994): 7–43.

Kermode, Frank. *The Genesis of Secrecy: On the Interpretation of Narrative*. The Charles Eliot Norton Lectures 1977–78. Cambridge: Harvard UP, 1979.

Keyser, Elizabeth Lennox. "'Quite Contrary': Frances Hodgson Burnett's *The Secret Garden*." *Children's Literature* 11 (1983): 1–13.

Kim, Tahee. "Capitalism Indie-Style." *Option* Mar./Apr. 1993: 49+.

Kincaid, James R. *Child-Loving: The Erotic Child and Victorian Culture*. New York: Routledge, 1992.

Kingston, William H. G. *Mary Liddiard; or The Missionary's Daughter*. London: Gall, 1873.

———. *Millicent Courtenay's Diary; or The Experience of a Young Lady at Home and Abroad*. London: Gall, [c. 1873].

———. *Waihoura; or The New Zealand Girl*. Edinburgh: Gall, [c. 1873].

Klein, Melissa. "Duality and Redefinition: Young Feminism and the Alternative Music Community." *Third Wave Agenda: Being Feminists, Doing Feminism*. Ed. Leslie Heywood and Jennifer Drake. Minneapolis: U of Minnesota P, 1997. 207–25.

Knight, Arthur. "It's Supercalifragilisticexpialidocious!" *Dance Magazine* 3 (Oct. 1964): 30–32.

Knoepflmacher, U. C. "Little Girls Without Their Curls: Female Aggression in Victorian Children's Literature." *Children's Literature* 11 (1983): 14–31.

Knopp, Sharon. "Sexism in the Pictures of Children's Readers: East and West Germany Compared." *Sex Roles* 6 (1980): 189–205.

Koblinsky, Sally, Donna Cruse, and Alan Sugawara. "Sex Role Stereotypes and Children's Memory for Story Content." *Child Development* 49 (1978): 452–58.

Kolbe, Richard, and Joseph LaVoie. "Sex-Role Stereotyping in Preschool Children's Picture Books." *Social Psychology Quarterly* 44 (1981): 369–74.

Kortenhaus, Carole, and Jack Demarest. "Gender Role Stereotyping in Children's Literature: An Update." *Sex Roles* 28 (1993): 219–32.

Kristeva, Julia. *Revolution in Poetic Language.* Trans. Margaret Waller. New York: Columbia UP, 1984.

———. "Stabat Mater." Trans. Leon S. Roudiez. *The Kristeva Reader.* Ed. Toril Moi. New York: Columbia UP, 1986. 160–86.

Kropp, Jerri, and Charles Halverston. "Preschool Children's Preferences and Recall for Stereotyped Versus Nonstereotyped Stories." *Sex Roles* 9 (1983): 261–72.

Krull, Kathleen. "Faith Ringgold: A Quilt Tells a Story." *Publishers Weekly* 15 Feb. 1991: 61–62.

Kuhn, Thomas. *The Structure of Scientific Revolutions.* Chicago: U of Chicago P, 1970.

Kuznets, Lois. *When Toys Come Alive: Narratives of Animation, Metamorphosis, and Development.* New Haven: Yale UP, 1994.

Lamm, Nomy. "It's a Big Fat Revolution." *Listen Up: Voices From the Next Feminist Generation.* Ed. Barbara Findlen. Seattle: Seal, 1995. 85–94.

Lanes, Selma G. *The Art of Maurice Sendak.* 1980. New York: Abradale-Abrams, 1984.

Langland, Elizabeth. "Nobody's Angels: Domestic Ideology and Middle-Class Women in the Victorian Novel." *PMLA* 107 (1992): 290–304.

Lanham, Richard A. *Literacy and the Survival of Humanism.* New Haven: Yale UP, 1983.

Laplanche, Jean, and Jean-Bertrand Pontalis. "Fantasy and the Origin of Sexuality." *Formations of Fantasy.* London: Methuen, 1986. 5–34.

Lauretis, Teresa de. *Technologies of Gender: Essays on Theory, Film, and Fiction.* Bloomington: Indiana UP, 1987.

Lee Ann. *Hangnail* (Pennsylvania) 3 (n.d.): 1–22.

Lemert, Charles, ed. *Social Theory: The Multicultural and Classic Readings.* Boulder: Westview, 1993.

Lessem, Don. *Dinosaurs Rediscovered.* New York: Simon, 1992.

Lessing, Doris. *Prisons We Choose To Live Inside.* CBC Massey Lectures. Montreal: CBC Enterprises, 1986.

Levine, Lawrence. *Highbrow, Lowbrow: The Emergence of Cultural Hierarchy in America.* Cambridge: Harvard UP, 1988.

Lieberman, Marcia. "Some Day My Prince Will Come: Female Acculturation through the Fairy Tale." *College English* 34 (1972): 383–95. Rpt. in *Sexism and Youth.* Ed Diane Gersoni-Stavn. New York: Bowker, 1974. 228–43.

Lindsay, Karen. "Louisa May Alcott: The Author of *Little Women* as Feminist." *Women: A Journal of Liberation* 2 (Fall 1970): 35–37. Rpt. in *Sexism and Youth.* Ed Diane Gersoni-Stavn. New York: Bowker, 1974. 244–48.

Lobel, Arnold. *The Rose in My Garden.* Illus. Anita Lobel. New York: Greenwillow, 1984. N. pag.

Lord, Deane. "By George! A Curious Monkey's Creator Reflects on 50 Furry Years." *Boston Globe Magazine* 22 Nov. 1987: 40–42+.

Lowry, Lois. *A Summer To Die.* New York: Houghton, 1977.

Lurie, Alison. "Witches and Fairies: Fitzgerald to Updike." *New York Review of Books* 2 Dec. 1971: 6–11.

Lutes-Dunckley, Candida. "Sex-Role Preferences as a Function of Sex of Storyteller and Story Content." *Journal of Psychology* 100 (1978): 151–58.

Lüthi, Max. *Once Upon a Time: On the Nature of Fairy Tales.* Trans. Lee Chadeayne and Paul Gottwald. 1970. Bloomington: Indiana UP, 1976.

MacKenzie, John M. *Propaganda and Empire: The Manipulation of British Public Opinion, 1880–1960.* Manchester: Manchester UP, 1984.

MacLeod, Anne Scott. *American Childhood: Essays on Children's Literature of the Nineteenth and Twentieth Centuries.* Athens: U of Georgia P, 1994.

Mainardi, Pat. "Quilts: The Great American Art." *Feminist Art Journal* 2 (Winter 1973): 1, 18–23.

Maitland, Sara. "'I Believe in Yesterday'—An Introduction." *Very Heaven: Looking Back at the 1960s.* Ed. Sara Maitland. London: Virago, 1988. 1–15.

Malkin, N. "It's a Grrrl Thing." *Seventeen* May 1993: 80–82.

Malti-Douglas, Fedwa. *Men, Women, and God(s): Nawal El Saadawi and Arab Feminist Poetics.* Berkeley: U of California P, 1995.

———. *Woman's Body, Woman's Word: Gender and Discourse in Arabo-Islamic Writing.* Princeton: Princeton UP, 1991.

Maltin, Leonard. *The Disney Films.* New York: Crown, 1984.

Mansfield, Katherine. "The Doll's House." *The Silent Playmate: A Collection of Doll Stories.* Ed. Naomi Lewis. London: Gollancz, 1979. 179–92.

Marcus, Leonard. *Margaret Wise Brown: Awakened by the Moon.* Boston: Beacon, 1992.

Marcus, Sara, and Kirsten Thompson. "Young Feminist Summit Empowers New Activists." *National NOW Times* May/June 1995: 3.

Marquis, Claudia. "The Power of Speech: Life in *The Secret Garden.*" *AUMLA* 68 (1987): 163–87.

Marryat, Emilia. *Amongst the Maoris: A Book of Adventure.* London: Warne, 1875.

Mary Poppins. Dir. Robert Stevenson. With Julie Andrews, Dick Van Dyke, David Tomlinson, and Glynis Johns. 1964. Videocassette. Walt Disney, [1993].

"Mary Poppins." *Variety* 2 Sept. 1964: 6.

Mason, Bobbie Ann. "Nancy Drew: The Once and Future Prom Queen." *The Girl Sleuth: A Feminist Guide.* Old Westbury: Feminist, 1975. 48–75.

Masters, Kim. "Hell's-a-Poppins." *Premiere* 3 (Apr. 1990): 36–37.

Maynard, Mary. "Privilege and Patriarchy: Feminist Thought in the Nineteenth Century." *Sexuality and Subordination: Interdisciplinary Studies of Gender in the Nineteenth Century.* Ed. Susan Mendus and Jane Rendall. London: Routledge, 1989. 221–47.

McArthur, Lelie Zebrowitz, and Susan Eisen. "Achievement of Male and Female Storybook Characters as Determinants of Achievement Behavior by Boys and Girls." *Journal of Personality and Social Psychology* 33 (1976): 467–73.

McCallum, Robyn. "Metafictions and Experimental Work." *International Companion*

Encyclopedia of Children's Literature. Ed. Peter Hunt. London: Routledge, 1996. 395–407.

McCloud, Scott. *Understanding Comics.* Northampton: Kitchen Sink, 1993.

McRobbie, Angela. *Feminism and Youth Culture: From "Jackie" to "Just Seventeen."* Boston: Unwin, 1991.

———. "Just Like a Jackie Story." *Feminism for Girls: An Adventure Story.* Ed. Angela McRobbie and Trisha McCabe. London: Routledge, 1981. 113–28.

———. "Shut Up and Dance: Youth Culture and Changing Modes of Femininity." *Cultural Studies* 7 (1993): 406–26.

Meade, L. T. *A World of Girls: The Story of a School.* 1886. Chicago: Donohue, n.d.

Meyer, Susan. *A Treasury of Great Children's Book Illustrators.* New York: Abrams, 1983.

Miedzian, Myriam. *Boys Will Be Boys: Breaking the Link Between Masculinity and Violence.* New York: Doubleday, 1991.

Miller, Owen. "Intertextual Identity." *Identity of the Literary Text.* Ed. Mario J. Valdes and Owen Miller. Toronto: U of Toronto P, 1985. 19–40.

Millett, Kate. *Sexual Politics.* Garden City: Doubleday, 1970.

Mitchell, Sally. *The New Girl: Girls' Culture in England, 1880–1915.* New York: Columbia UP, 1995.

Moebius, William. "The *enfant terrible* Comes of Age." *Notebooks in Cultural Analysis.* Ed. Norman Cantor and Nathalia King. Vol. 2. Durham: Duke UP, 1985. 32–50.

———. "Informing Adult Readers: Symbolic Experience in Children's Literature." *Reading World Literature: Theory, History, Practice.* Ed. Sarah Lawall. Austin: U of Texas P, 1994. 309–27.

———. "Introduction to Picturebook Codes." *Word and Image* 2 (Apr./June 1986): 141–58. Rpt. in *Children's Literature: The Development of Criticism.* Ed. Peter Hunt. London: Routledge, 1990. 131–47.

Mohanty, Chandra Talpade. "Under Western Eyes: Feminist Scholarship and Colonial Discourses." *Third World Women and the Politics of Feminism.* Ed. Chandra Talpade Mohanty, Ann Russo, and Lourdes Torres. Bloomington: Indiana UP, 1991. 51–80.

Moore, George. *Literature at Nurse, or Circulating Morals: A Polemic on Victorian Censorship.* 1885. Ed. Pierre Coustillas. Hassocks, Eng.: Harvester; Atlantic Highlands: Humanities, 1976.

Morgan, Genevieve Sanchis. "Katherine Mansfield's House of Fiction: The Intersection of the Domestic and the Artistic in 'The Doll's House.'" Toys in the Attic Conference. CSU Dominguez Hills. 17 Sept. 1993.

Rev. of the *The Morning After: Sex, Fear, and Feminism on Campus,* by Katie Roiphe. *Sassy* Oct. 1993: 40.

Morris, Pam. *Literature and Feminism.* Oxford: Blackwell, 1993.

Moss, Anita. "Feminist Criticism and the Study of Children's Literature." *Children's Literature Association Quarterly* 7 (Winter 1982): 3.

Moss, Geoff. "Metafiction and the Poetics of Children's Literature." *Children's Literature Association Quarterly* 15 (Summer 1990): 50–52.

Mulvey, Laura. "Visual Pleasure and Narrative Cinema." *Screen* 16 (1975): 8–18. Rpt. in *Issues in Feminist Film Criticism.* Ed. Patricia Erens. Bloomington: Indiana UP, 1990. 28–40.

Myers, Mitzi. "The Erotics of Pedagogy, Historical Intervention, Literary Representation, the 'Gift of Education,' and the Agency of Children." *Children's Literature* 23 (1995): 1–30.

———. "Impeccable Governesses, Rational Dames, and Moral Mothers: Mary Wollstonecraft and the Female Tradition in Georgian Children's Books." *Children's Literature* 14 (1986): 31–60.

———. Introduction. *Early Lessons, Part 10.* 1801. Augustan Reprint Society Nos. 263–264. UCLA: William Andrews Clark Memorial Library, 1990. iii–xiii.

———. "Romancing the Moral Tale: Maria Edgeworth and the Problematics of Pedagogy." *Romanticism and Children's Literature in Nineteenth-Century England.* Ed. James Holt McGavran, Jr. Athens: U of Georgia P, 1991. 96–128.

Negt, Oskar, and Alexander Kluge. "The Public Sphere of Children." *Public Sphere and Experience: Toward an Analysis of the Bourgeois and Proletarian Public Sphere.* Trans. Peter Labanyi et al. 1972. Minneapolis: U of Minnesota P, 1993. 283–88.

Nelson, Claudia. *Boys Will Be Girls: The Feminine Ethic and British Children's Fiction, 1857–1917.* New Brunswick: Rutgers UP, 1991.

Nesbit, E. *The Enchanted Castle.* 1907. London: Penguin, 1994.

———. *The Phoenix and the Carpet.* 1904. Harmondsworth: Penguin, 1959.

Nichols, Grace. "The Battle With Language." *Caribbean Women Writers: Essays from the First Interactional Conference.* Ed. Selwyn R. Cudjoe. Wellesley: Calaloux, 1990. 283–89.

———, ed. *Can I Buy a Slice of Sky: Poems from Black, Asian and American Indian Cultures.* London: Knight, 1993.

———. *Come on into my Tropical Garden.* London: Black, 1988.

———. *The Fat Black Woman's Poems.* London: Virago, 1984.

———. *Give Yourself a Hug.* London: Black, 1994.

———. *i is a long memoried woman.* London: Karnak, 1983.

———. *Lazy Thoughts of a Lazy Woman.* London: Virago, 1989.

———. "My Black Triangle." *Lazy Thoughts of a Lazy Woman.* 1989. Rev. and rpt. in *Culture Shock.* Ed. Michael Rosen. Harmondsworth: Puffin, 1991. 74–75.

———, comp. *Poetry Jump-up: A Collection of Black Poetry.* 1988. Harmondsworth: Puffin, 1990.

———. *Whole of a Morning Sky.* London: Virago, 1986.

Nilsen, Alleen Pace. "Women in Children's Literature." *College English* 32 (1971): 918–26.

Noble, Andrea. Letter. *New Moon* May/June 1994: 5.

Nodelman, Perry. "Children's Literature as Women's Writing." *Children's Literature Association Quarterly* 13 (Spring 1988): 31–34.

———. "Interpretation and the Apparent Sameness of Children's Novels." *Studies in the Literary Imagination* 18 (Fall 1985): 5–20.

———. *The Pleasures of Children's Literature.* New York: Longman, 1992.

———. *The Pleasures of Children's Literature.* 2nd ed. New York: Longman, 1996.

———. *Words About Pictures.* Athens: U of Georgia P, 1988.

Oates, Joyce Carol. "Celestial Timepiece." *Celestial Timepiece: Poems by Joyce Carol Oates.* Illus. Paula George. Dallas: Pressworks, 1980. 24–25.

Oneal, Zibby. *In Summer Light.* 1985. London: Gollancz, 1988.

Orenstein, Peggy (in association with the American Association of University Women). *SchoolGirls: Young Women, Self-Esteem, and the Confidence Gap.* New York: Doubleday, 1994.

Panchatantra. Trans. Franklin Edgerton. UNESCO Collection of Representative Works. Translation Collection, UNESCO, Paris. London: Allen, 1965.

Paola, Tomie de. *Strega Nona's Magic Lessons.* New York: Harcourt, 1982. N. pag.

Patmore, Coventry. *The Angel in the House.* 4 vols. Boston: Ticknor, [1854–1862].

Paul, Lissa. "Away from Home Through the Dolls' House Door." Unpubl. ms. 1993.

———. "Enigma Variations: What Feminist Theory Knows About Children's Literature." *Signal* 54 (1987): 186–201. Rpt. in *Children's Literature: The Development of Criticism.* Ed. Peter Hunt. London: Routledge, 1990. 148–64.

Peirce, Kate, and Emily Edwards. "Children's Construction of Fantasy Stories: Gender Differences in Conflict Resolution Strategies." *Sex Roles* 18 (1988): 393–404.

Perrault, Charles. *Contes de Perrault.* Ed. Gilbert Rouget. Paris: Editions Garnier Frères, 1967.

Pipher, Mary. *Reviving Ophelia: Saving the Selves of Adolescent Girls.* New York: Ballantine, 1994.

Plotz, Judith. "The Perpetual Messiah: Romanticism, Childhood, and the Paradoxes of Human Development." *Regulated Children/Liberated Children: Education in Psychohistorical Perspective.* Ed. Barbara Finkelstein. New York: Psychohistory, 1979. 63–95.

Polacco, Patricia. *The Keeping Quilt.* New York: Simon, 1988. N. pag.

Poovey, Mary. *Uneven Developments: The Work of Gender in Mid-Victorian England.* Chicago: U of Chicago P, 1988.

Potter, Beatrix. *The Tale of Two Bad Mice.* London: F. Warne, 1904.

Pratt, Mary Louise. "Criticism in the Contact Zone: Decentering Community and Nation." *Critical Theory, Cultural Politics and Latin American Narrative.* Ed. Steven M. Bell, Albert H. LeMay, and Leonard Orr. Notre Dame: U of Notre Dame P, 1993. 83–102.

———. *Imperial Eyes: Travel Writing and Transculturation.* London: Routledge, 1992.

Purcell, Piper, and Lara Stewart. "Dick and Jane in 1989." *Sex Roles* 22 (1990): 177–85.

al-Qaʿîd, Yûsuf. "Rabâb Gives Up Drawing." Trans. Nadia El-Kholi and Hoda El-Sadda. *Flights of Fantasy: Arabic Short Stories.* Ed. Ceza Kassem and Malak Hashem. Cairo: Elias Modern Publishing House, 1985. 197–204.

———. "Rabâb Taʿtazil ʿan al-Rasm." *Hikâyât al-Zaman al-Jarîh.* Cairo: Dâr al-Thaqâfa al-Jadîda, 1982.

———. Telephone interviews with Fedwa Malti-Douglas. 9 and 15 Apr. 1995.

Rahn, Suzanne. "Tailpiece: The Tale of Two Bad Mice." *Children's Literature* 12 (1984): 78–91.

Rampal, Anita, and Tultul Biswas. "Children Voice Concern." *Seminar* 443 (July 1996): 21–29.

Rana, Indi. *The Devil in the Dustbin.* 1989. New Delhi: Penguin, 1992.

———. *The Roller Birds of Rampur.* London: Bodley Head, 1991.

Reimer, Mavis, ed. *Such a Simple Little Tale: Critical Responses to L. M. Montgomery's "Anne of Green Gables."* Metuchen: Children's Lit. Assn. and Scarecrow, 1992.

———. "Worlds of Girls: Educational Reform and Fictional Form in L. T. Meade's School Stories." *Re-Presenting Power: British Women Writers, 1780–1900.* Ed. George Kucich and Donelle R. Ruwe. New York: Gordon, in press.

Reinharz, Shulamit. "Experiential Analysis: A Contribution to Feminist Research." *Theories of Women's Studies.* Ed. G. Bowles and R. Duelli Klein. London: Routledge, 1983. 162–91.

Renard, Jean-Bruno. *Bandes dessinées et croyances du siècle.* Paris: Presses Universitaires de France, 1986.

Rey, Hans A. *Curious George.* Boston: Houghton, 1941.

Rey, Margret, and Hans A. Rey. *The Complete Adventures of Curious George.* Boston: Houghton, 1995.

Reynolds, Kimberley. *Girls Only? Gender and Popular Children's Fiction in Britain, 1880–1910.* Philadelphia: Temple UP, 1990.

Rich, Adrienne. *Of Woman Born: Motherhood as Experience and Institution.* 1986. Rev. ed. New York: Norton, 1995.

Richards, Jeffrey. Introduction. *Imperialism and Juvenile Literature.* Ed. Jeffrey Richards. Manchester: Manchester UP, 1989. 1–11.

———, ed. *Imperialism and Juvenile Literature.* Manchester: Manchester UP, 1989.

Ringgold, Faith. *Tar Beach.* New York: Scholastic, 1991. N. pag.

"Riot Grrrl is . . ." *Riot Grrrl NYC* 2 (n.d.): n. pag.

Riot Grrrl Press Catalogue. N.p., 1994. N. pag.

Robbins, Trina. *A Century of Women Cartoonists.* Northampton: Kitchen Sink, 1993.

Röhrich, Lutz. *Folktales and Reality.* Trans. Peter Tokofsky. Bloomington: Indiana UP, 1991.

Rose, Hilary. "Thinking from Caring: Feminism's Construction of a Responsible Rationality." *Love, Power, and Knowledge: Toward a Feminist Transformation of the Sciences.* Bloomington: Indiana UP, 1994. 28–50.

Rose, Jacqueline. *The Case of Peter Pan: or the Impossibility of Children's Fiction.* 1984. Philadelphia: U of Pennsylvania P, 1993.

Rosenberg, Jessica, and Gitana Garofalo. "Riot Grrrl: Revolutions from Within." *Signs* 23 (1998): 809–41.

Rossetti, Christina. *The Complete Poems of Christina Rossetti: A Variorum Edition.* Vol. 1. Baton Rouge: Louisiana State UP, 1979.

Rowe, Karen E. "'Fairy-born and human-bred': Jane Eyre's Education in Romance." *The*

Voyage In: Fictions of Female Development. Ed. Elizabeth Abel, Marianne Hirsch, and Elizabeth Langland. Hanover: UP of New England, 1983. 69–89.

———. "Feminism and Fairy Tales." *Women's Studies* 6 (1979): 237–57.

Ruddick, Sara. *Maternal Thinking: Toward a Politics of Peace.* Boston: Beacon, 1989.

———. "Notes Toward a Feminist Peace Politics." *Gendering War Talk.* Ed. Miriam Cooke and Angela Woollacott. Princeton: Princeton UP, 1993. 109–27.

———. "Preservative Love and Military Destruction: Some Reflections on Mothering and Peace." *Mothering: Essays in Feminist Theory.* Ed. Joyce Trebilcot. Totowa: Rowman, 1983. 231–62.

———. "The Rationality of Care." *Women, Militarism, and War: Essays in History, Politics, and Social Theory.* Ed. Jean Bethke Elshtain and Sheila Tobias. Savage, NJ: Rowman, 1990. 229–54.

Rushdie, Salman. *Haroun and the Sea of Stories.* London: Granta-Viking Penguin, 1990.

Rustin, Margaret, and Michael Rustin. *Narratives of Love and Loss.* London: Verso, 1987.

al-Saʿdâwî, Nawâl. *Suqût al-Imâm.* Cairo: Dâr al-Mustaqbal al-ʿArabî, 1987.

Sadker, Myra, and David Sadker. *Failing at Fairness: How Our Schools Cheat Girls.* New York: Simon, 1994.

Said, Edward W. *Culture and Imperialism.* London: Vintage, 1994.

———. "An Ideology of Difference." *Critical Inquiry* 12 (1985): 38–58. Rpt. in *"Race," Writing, and Difference.* Ed. Henry Louis Gates, Jr. Chicago: U of Chicago P, 1986. 38–58.

Scarry, Elaine. *Body in Pain: The Making and Unmaking of the World.* New York: Oxford UP, 1985.

Schama, Simon. *Landscape and Memory.* London: Harper, 1995.

Schults, Raymond L. *Crusader in Babylon: W. T. Stead and the Pall Mall Gazette.* Lincoln: U of Nebraska P, 1972.

Secret Weapon 1 (1993): 1–24.

Segel, Elizabeth. "'As the Twig Is Bent . . .': Gender and Childhood Reading." *Gender and Reading: Essays on Readers, Texts, and Contexts.* Ed. Elizabeth A. Flynn and Patrocino P. Schweikart. Baltimore: Johns Hopkins UP, 1986. 165–86.

———. "Picture Books and Princesses: The Feminist Contribution." *Proceedings of the 8th Annual Conference of the Children's Literature Association.* Ed. Priscilla Ord. Boston: Children's Literature Association, 1982. 77–83.

———. "Picture Book Sex Roles Revisited." *School Library Journal* 28 (May 1982): 30–31.

Seiter, Ellen. *Sold Separately: Parents and Children in Consumer Culture.* New Brunswick: Rutgers UP, 1993.

Sen, Amartya. "Secularism and Its Discontents." *Unravelling the Nation: Sectarian Conflict and India's Secular Identity.* Ed. Kaushik Basu and Sanjay Subrahmanyam. New Delhi: Penguin, 1996. 11–43.

Sendak, Maurice. *Where the Wild Things Are.* n.p.: Harper, 1963. N. pag.

Senner, Wayne M. "Theories and Myths on the Origins of Writing: A Historical

Overview." *The Origins of Writing.* Ed. Wayne M. Senner. Lincoln: U of Nebraska P, 1989. 1–26.

Seth, Vikram. *Beastly Tales from Here and There.* New Delhi: Viking, 1991.

Sharp, Evelyn. *The Making of a Schoolgirl.* 1897. Introd. Beverly Lyon Clark. New York: Oxford UP, 1989.

Shavit, Zohar. *Poetics of Children's Literature.* Athens: U of Georgia P, 1986.

Sherman, Richard M., and Robert B. Sherman. *Songs from Walt Disney's "Mary Poppins."* Buena Vista: Wonderland Music, 1963.

Showalter, Elaine. "Feminist Criticism in the Wilderness." *Critical Inquiry* 8 (Winter 1981): 179–205. Rpt. in *The New Feminist Criticism: Essays on Women, Literature and Theory.* Ed. Elaine Showalter. New York: Pantheon, 1985. 243–70.

——. *A Literature of Their Own: British Women Novelists from Brontë to Lessing.* Princeton: Princeton UP, 1976.

——. *Sexual Anarchy: Gender and Culture at the Fin de Siècle.* New York: Viking-Penguin, 1990.

——. *Sister's Choice: Tradition and Change in American Women's Writing.* New York: Oxford UP, 1991.

Silvey, Anita, ed. *Children's Books and Their Creators.* Boston: Houghton, 1995.

Sims, Rudine. "Strong Black Girls: A Ten Year Old Responds to Fiction about Afro-Americans." *Journal of Research and Development in Education* 16 (Spring 1983): 21–28.

"Six reasons why riot grrrl press is important right now, bi Marika." *Riot Grrrl Press Catalogue.* N.p., 1994. N. pag.

Smith, Adam. *An Inquiry into the Nature and Causes of the Wealth of Nations.* Ed. R. H. Campbell and A. S. Skinner. The Glasgow Edition. 2 vols. 1976. Indianapolis: Liberty Classics, 1981.

Smith, Bonnie. *Ladies of the Leisure Class: The Bourgeoisie of Northern France in the Nineteenth Century.* Princeton: Princeton UP, 1981.

Smith, Dorothy. "Sociological Theory: Methods of Writing Patriarchy." *Feminism and Sociological Theory.* Ed. Ruth Wallace. Newbury Park: Sage, 1989. 34–64.

Smith, Dorothy E. "Femininity as Discourse." *Becoming Feminine: The Politics of Popular Culture.* Ed. Leslie G. Roman, Linda K. Christian-Smith, and Elizabeth Ellsworth. London: Falmer, 1988. 37–59.

Smith, Jane S. "Plucky Little Ladies and Stout-Hearted Chums: Serial Novels for Girls, 1900–1920." *Prospects* 3 (1977): 155–74.

Soriano, Marc. *Les Contes de Perrault: Culture savantes et traditions populaires.* Paris: Gallimard, 1968.

Spivak, Gayatri Chakravorty. *In Other Worlds: Essays in Cultural Politics.* London: Routledge, 1988.

Srivatsava, Sigrun. "Trapped!" *Book Review* 17 (Nov. 1993): 17–18.

Stacey, Judith. "Can There Be a Feminist Ethnography?" *Women's Studies International Forum* 11 (1988): 21–27.

Stallybrass, Peter, and Allon White. *The Politics and Poetics of Transgression.* Ithaca: Cornell UP, 1986.

Stead, W. T. "The Maiden Tribute of Modern Babylon." *Pall Mall Gazette* 6 July 1885: 1–6; 7 July 1885: 1–6; 8 July 1885: 1–5; 10 July 1885: 1–6.

Steedman, Carolyn. "True Romances." *Patriotism: The Making and Unmaking of British National Identity: Vol. 1, History and Politics.* Ed. Raphael Samuel. London: Routledge, 1989. 26–35.

Steig, Michael. *Stories of Reading: Subjectivity and Literary Understanding.* Baltimore: Johns Hopkins UP, 1989.

Stephens, John. *Language and Ideology in Children's Fiction.* London: Longmans, 1992.

———. "Gender, Genre and Children's Literature." *Signal* 79 (1996): 17–30.

Stern, Madeleine, ed. *Critical Essays on Louisa May Alcott.* Boston: Hall, 1984.

Stevenson, Robert Louis. *A Child's Garden of Verses.* 1885. Illus. Charles Robinson. 1896. La Jolla: Green Tiger, 1975.

———. "A Gossip on Romance." 1882. *Essays by Robert Louis Stevenson.* Ed. Will D. Howe. New York: Scribner's, 1892. 220–34.

Stewart, Susan. *On Longing: Narratives of the Miniature, the Gigantic, the Souvenir, the Collection.* Baltimore: Johns Hopkins UP, 1984.

St. Peter, Shirley. "Jack Went Up the Hill . . . But Where Was Jill?" *Psychology of Women Quarterly* 4 (1979): 256–60.

Sutton, Martin. "Patterns of Meaning in the Musical." *Genre: The Musical.* Ed. Rick Altman. London: Routledge, 1981. 190–95.

Tannen, Deborah. *Gender and Discourse.* New York: Oxford UP, 1994.

Tatar, Maria. *The Hard Facts of the Grimms' Fairy Tales.* Princeton: Princeton UP, 1987.

———. *Off With Their Heads! Fairy Tales and the Culture of Childhood.* Princeton: Princeton UP, 1992.

Taylor, Charles, et al., eds. *Multiculturalism: Examining the Politics of Recognition.* Princeton: Princeton UP, 1994.

Taylor, John Edward. Preface. *The Pentamerone; or, The Story of Stories, Fun for the Little Ones.* 2nd ed. London: Bogue, 1850.

Thorne, Barrie. "Re-Visioning Women and Social Change: Where Are the Children?" *Gender & Society* 1 (1987): 85–109.

Tolman, Deborah. "Doing Desire: Adolescent Girls' Struggles For/With Sexuality." *Gender & Society* 18 (1994): 324–42.

Tompkins, Jane. *Sensational Designs: The Cultural Work of American Fiction, 1790–1860.* New York: Oxford UP, 1985.

———. "Sentimental Power: *Uncle Tom's Cabin* and the Politics of Literary History." *Glyph* 2 (1978). Rpt. in *The New Feminist Criticism: Essays on Women, Literature, and Theory.* Ed. Elaine Showalter. New York: Pantheon, 1985. 81–104.

Touchstones: A List of Distinguished Children's Books. West Lafayette: Children's Literature Association, [1985].

Travers, Pamela L. *Mary Poppins*. 1934. New York: Harcourt, 1962.

Tuttle, William M., Jr. *"Daddy's Gone to War": The Second World War in the Lives of America's Children*. New York: Oxford UP, 1993.

Vallone, Lynne. *Disciplines of Virtue: Girls' Culture in the Eighteenth and Nineteenth Centuries*. New Haven: Yale UP, 1995.

Verne, Jules. *Among the Cannibals*. London: Ward, [c. 1876].

Vicinus, Martha. *Independent Women: Work and Community for Single Women, 1850–1920*. Women in Culture and Society. Chicago: U of Chicago P, 1985.

————, ed. *A Widening Sphere: Changing Roles of Victorian Women*. Bloomington: Indiana UP, 1977.

Walker, Alice. "Everyday Use." *Norton Anthology of Literature by Women*. Ed. Sandra M. Gilbert and Susan Gubar. New York: Norton, 1985. 2366–74.

Walkowitz, Judith R. *City of Dreadful Delight: Narratives of Sexual Danger in Late-Victorian London*. Chicago: U of Chicago P, 1992.

Warner, Marina. *Managing Monsters: Six Myths of Our Time*. The 1994 Reith Lectures. London: Vintage, 1994.

Waugh, Patricia. *Metafiction: The Theory and Practice of Self-Conscious Fiction*. London: Methuen, 1984.

Weiner, Annette B. *Inalienable Possessions: The Paradox of Keeping-While-Giving*. Berkeley: U of California P, 1992.

Weitzman, Lenore, Deborah Eifler, Elizabeth Hokad, and Catherine Ross. "Sex-Role Socialization in Picture Books for Preschool Children." *American Journal of Sociology* 77 (1972): 1125–50. Rpt. in *Sexism and Youth*. Ed. Diane Gersoni-Stavn. New York: Bowker, 1974. 174–95.

West, Mark I. "The Grotesque and the Taboo in Roald Dahl's Humorous Writings for Children." *Children's Literature Association Quarterly* 15 (Fall 1990): 115–16.

White, Allon. *The Uses of Obscurity: The Fiction of Early Modernism*. London: Routledge, 1981.

White, Emily. "Revolution Girl-Style Now: Notes From the Teenage Feminist Rock n' Roll Underground." *The Reader* (Chicago) 25 Sept. 1992: 8+.

White, Hedy. "Damsels in Distress: Dependency Themes in Fiction for Adolescents." *Adolescence* 21 (1985): 251–56.

Williams, Allen, Joetta Vernon, Martha Williams, and Karen Malecha. "Sex-Role Socialization in Picture Books: An Update." *Social Science Quarterly* 68 (1987): 148–56.

Williams, Dawn. *Function* (California) 6 (n.d.): 1–42.

Willis, Susan. *A Primer for Daily Life*. New York: Routledge, 1991.

Willmott, Don. "Abort, Retry, Fail?" *PC Magazine* 23 Jan. 1996: 350.

Wilson, Alexander. *The Culture of Nature: North American Landscape from Disney to the Exxon Valdez*. Toronto: Between the Lines, 1991.

Wilson, Carol Shiner, and Joel Haefner, eds. *Re-Visioning Romanticism: British Women Writers, 1776–1837*. Philadelphia: U of Pennsylvania P, 1994.

Winock, Michel. *Histoire Politique de la Revue "Esprit," 1930–1950*. Paris: Editions du Seuil, 1975.

Witek, Joseph. *Comic Books as History: The Narrative Art of Jack Jackson, Art Spiegelman, and Harvey Pekar*. Jackson: UP of Mississippi, 1989.

Wolf, Gita, trans. *Landscapes: Children's Voices*. Madras: Tara, 1996.

Wolf, Shelby Anne, and Shirley Brice Heath. *The Braid of Literature: Children's Worlds of Reading*. Cambridge: Harvard UP, 1992.

Wolf, Virginia L. "From the Myth to the Wake of Home: Literary Houses." *Children's Literature* 18 (1990): 53–67.

Wolff, Janet. *The Social Production of Art*. New York: St. Martin's, 1981.

Women on Words and Images. *Dick and Jane as Victims: Sex Stereotyping in Children's Books*. Princeton: Central New Jersey NOW, 1972.

Women's Action Alliance. *An Annotated Bibliography of Nonsexist Picture Books for Children*. New York: Women's Action Alliance, 1973.

Woolf, Virginia. *The Diary of Virginia Woolf: Vol. 5, 1936–1941*. Ed. Anne Olivier Bell and Andrew McNeillie. San Diego: Harcourt, 1984.

———. "Professions for Women." *Collected Essays*. Vol. 2. New York: Harcourt, 1953. 284–89.

———. "Thoughts on Peace in an Air Raid." *The Death of the Moth and Other Essays*. 1942. New York: Harcourt, 1974. 243–48.

———. *Three Guineas*. 1938. New York: Harcourt-Harbinger, 1966.

The World Almanac and Book of Facts 1995. Mahwah: Funk, 1994.

Yolen, Jane. "America's Cinderella." *Children's Literature in Education* 8 (1977): 21–29.

Young, Iris Marion. "The Ideal of Community and the Politics of Difference." *Feminism/Postmodernism*. Ed. Linda J. Nicolson. New York: Routledge, 1990. 300–323.

———. "Impartiality and the Civic Public: Some Implications of Feminist Critiques of Moral and Political Theory." *Feminism as Critique*. Ed. Seyla Benhabib and Drucilla Cornell. Minneapolis: U of Minnesota P, 1987. 57–76.

———. *Throwing Like a Girl and Other Essays in Feminist Philosophy and Social Theory*. Bloomington: Indiana UP, 1990.

Zipes, Jack. *Breaking the Magic Spell: Radical Theories of Folk and Fairy Tales*. Austin: U of Texas P, 1979.

———, ed. *Don't Bet on the Prince: Contemporary Feminist Fairy Tales in North America and England*. New York: Methuen, 1986.

———. *Fairy Tale as Myth/Myth as Fairy Tale*. Lexington: U of Kentucky P, 1994.

———. *Happily Ever After: Fairy Tales, Children, and the Culture Industry*. New York: Routledge, 1997.

Zolotow, Charlotte. *Mr. Rabbit and the Lovely Present*. Illus. Maurice Sendak. New York: Harper, 1962.

Contributors

Liam Clancy was a double major in dance and sociology at Rhode Island College, where he worked with Roger Clark on status changes among aged men and women from a cross-cultural perspective. He now performs with a dance company in New York City.

Beverly Lyon Clark teaches English at Wheaton College in Massachusetts. She has published books on fantasy, on tutoring, on Lewis Carroll, and on school stories, as well as an edition of Evelyn Sharp's *The Making of a Schoolgirl* and a coedited collection called *"Little Women" and the Feminist Imagination.* Her work has appeared in *Children's Literature, Philological Quarterly, New Literary History, Profession,* the *Chronicle of Higher Education,* and the *Women's Review of Books.*

Roger Clark is a professor of sociology at Rhode Island College, where he teaches, among other things, feminist approaches to sociological theory, research methods, and family. In recent research he has looked at gender relations from a cross-cultural perspective. Clark has published about three dozen research articles in *Gender & Society, Sociological Quarterly, Social Science Quarterly, Aging and Human Development, Adolescence, Youth & Society,* and other journals.

Allen Douglas is a professor of West European studies, history, and semiotics at Indiana University. His books include *From Fascism to Libertarian Communism: Georges Valois Against the Third Republic* (1992) and, with Fedwa Malti-Douglas, *Arab Comic Strips: Politics of an Emerging Mass Culture* (1994). He is currently completing a book on the *Canard Enchaîné.*

Margaret R. Higonnet, professor of English and comparative literature at the University of Connecticut, is a former editor of *Children's Literature.* Her essays on children's literature have appeared in *Children's Literature, Children's*

Literature Association Quarterly, Poetics Today, Enfance, La revue des livres pour enfants, and several collections of essays. Her current focus is the interplay between formal experiment and critical assumptions. Volumes she has edited include *Borderwork: Feminist Engagements with Comparative Literature* (1995), *Antifeminism in the Academy* (1996), and *Nineteenth-Century British Women Poets* (1996).

Lori Kenschaft received her Ph.D. in American Studies from Boston University in 1999. She is currently working on a young adults' biography of Lydia Maria Child, which will be published by Oxford University Press, and writing a "biography" of one of the very first dual-career marriages: between Alice Freeman Palmer (first female president of a liberal arts college and one of the founding faculty members of the University of Chicago) and George Herbert Palmer (professor of philosophy at Harvard University).

Karen Klugman is a photographer residing in Guilford, Connecticut, whose work has appeared in national exhibitions and is included in museum collections. She also writes and teaches about the interaction between photography and cultural issues. Her most recent work includes a series of large-scale color photographs of people at the beach entitled "Under the Influence of the Sun & Advertising" and photo essays about Disney World for the book *Inside the Mouse.*

U. C. Knoepflmacher, the Paton Foundation Professor of Ancient and Modern Literature at Princeton University, is the author of four books and many articles on Victorian literature. He has coedited collections of essays on Mary Shelley, George Eliot, and other subjects, as well as a collection of fantasies and fairy tales by Victorian women writers; with Mitzi Myers, he coedited a special issue on "Cross-Writing Child and Adult" for *Children's Literature* (1997). His new book on gender and Victorian children's literature is *Ventures into Childland: Victorians, Fairy Tales, and Femininity* (1998).

Heidi Kulkin was a double major in psychology and sociology at Rhode Island College, where she worked with Roger Clark on bringing multicultural feminist theoretical perspectives to bear on adolescent fiction. She has since completed a master's degree in social work at Tulane University and has published articles in *Youth & Society* and *Pediatrics.*

Lois R. Kuznets is a professor emeritus from San Diego State University, where she taught British medieval literature and children's literature. A former president of the Children's Literature Association, she has written a number of articles in the field, centered on fantastic and realistic novels for children of middle years, as well as a study of Kenneth Grahame (1987). Her study *When Toys Come Alive: Narratives of Animation, Metamorphosis, and Devel-*

opment (1994) won the Children's Literature Association Book Award for 1994 and the first International Research Society for Children's Literature Award for distinguished research in the field.

Fedwa Malti-Douglas, winner of the 1997 Kuwait Prize for Arts and Letters, is the Martha C. Kraft Professor of the Humanities in the College of Arts and Sciences at Indiana University. She has written numerous books on cultural and gender studies of the Middle East and North Africa. Her novel, *Hisland,* appeared with SUNY Press in 1998.

Claudia Marquis was born in St. Lucia, West Indies, and emigrated to Canada when she was ten years old. She received her university education at Concordia University, Montreal, and then at McMaster University, Hamilton, Ontario, where her postgraduate studies focused on nineteenth-century literature. Since 1979 she has lived in Auckland, New Zealand, where she teaches Renaissance and Victorian literature in the Department of English at the University of Auckland. She has published a number of articles on children's fiction, especially that written by New Zealand authors, and introduced children's literature into Auckland's master-of-arts program. Her present writing interests include fantasy and nineteenth-century colonial fiction written for children.

Robyn McCallum, associate lecturer in children's literature at Macquarie University, Sydney, wrote a doctoral dissertation entitled "The Dialogical Construction of Subjectivity in Adolescent Fiction." She has published several articles about children's literature, is turning her dissertation into a book, and, with John Stephens, is cowriting *Retold Stories: Metanarratives and Reversions in Children's Literature.*

William Moebius, professor and chair of the Department of Comparative Literature at the University of Massachusetts at Amherst, has published articles on children's literature in *Word and Image, Notebooks in Cultural Analysis,* and *Reading World Literature.* His "Room With a View: Bedroom Scenes in Picture Books" won the 1993 Children's Literature Association Article Award.

Mitzi Myers teaches writing, children's literature, and young adult and adolescent literature at the University of California, Los Angeles. She has published extensively on historical literature for the young and historical pedagogy and has held fellowships from the National Endowment for the Humanities, the American Philosophical Society, the American Council of Learned Societies, and the John Simon Guggenheim Memorial Foundation. Her specialties are women writers of the later eighteenth century, including Maria Edgeworth, Mary Wollstonecraft, and Hannah More; Irish studies; women's fiction; and cultural criticism. She has guest-edited special issues of several academic journals concerned with these topics, including *Children's Literature*. She is the co-editor of the Pickering and Chatto twelve-volume reprint of Maria Edgeworth's selected works with special responsibility for four volumes, including the adult novel *Belinda* (1801), *Practical Education* (1798), and the tales for children and young adults. She is also finishing a critical study of Edgeworth and progressing on a literary life of Edgeworth.

Lissa Paul, professor at the University of New Brunswick in Canada, teaches children's literature, literary theory, and feminist theory. Her work appears primarily in *Signal*. She has also collaborated with Pam Nason on *Reading Otherways*, a "maternal literacies" project on facilitating schooled literacy development through the recognition of what the maternal brings to the institutional.

Mavis Reimer is an assistant professor of English at the University of Winnipeg in Canada, where she teaches children's literature and Victorian studies. She has edited a collection of essays on L. M. Montgomery's *Anne of Green Gables*, entitled *Such a Simple Little Tale.*

John Stephens, associate professor in English at Macquarie University, Sydney, is the author of *Language and Ideology in Children's Fiction* (1992), two books about discourse analysis, and approximately fifty articles. With Robyn McCallum he is cowriting *Retold Stories: Metanarratives and Reversions in Children's Literature.*

Rajeswari Sunder Rajan has taught in both India and the United States. She has published a book of essays, *Real and Imagined Women: Gender, Culture, and Postcolonialism* (1993), and has edited *Lie of the Land: English Literary Studies in India* (1992). Her essays in cultural critique and Victorian studies have appeared in *Signs*, the *Yale Journal of Criticism, Social Scientist,* and collections. She is preparing a critical study of Dickens entitled "The Novel Subject: Subalternity and Realism in Dickens's Fiction."

Cheryl B. Torsney, professor of English at West Virginia University, writes most frequently on late-nineteenth-century American fiction, but she is also interested in children's literature and literary theory. She has coedited (with Judy Elsley) *Quilt Culture: Tracing the Pattern* (1994), a volume of essays about the quilt as metaphor in literature, history, and philosophy.

Lynne Vallone, associate professor of English at Texas A&M University, is the author of *Disciplines of Virtue: Girls' Culture in the Eighteenth and Nineteenth Centuries* (1995) and the coeditor (with Claudia Nelson) of *The Girl's Own: Cultural Histories of the Anglo-American Girl, 1830–1915* (1994). She is currently writing a book about Queen Victoria's girlhood.

Susan Willis is an associate professor at Duke University, where she teaches literature and culture. She is the author of *Specifying: Black Women Writing the American Experience* and *A Primer for Daily Life* (1991) and coauthor of *Inside the Mouse: Work and Play at Disney World* (1995). She is married and has five children. As a Marxist intellectual, she is committed "to quickening the utopian imagination, and resisting the professionalization of public life and the compartmentalization of experience."

Illustration Credits

Page 208   By Claudia Von Vacano. *Riot Grrrl NYC* 1 (Mar. 1993): n. p. Reproduced
by permission of *Riot Grrrl NYC*.

Page 230   © The Walt Disney Company.

Index

Library of Congress Cataloging-in-Publication Data

Girls, boys, books, toys : gender in children's literature and culture /
    edited by Beverly Lyon Clark and Margaret R. Higonnet.
        p.   cm.
    Includes bibliographical references and index.
    ISBN 0-8018-6053-9 (alk. paper)
    1. Children's literature—History and criticism.   2. Sexism in
literature.   3. Girls—Books and reading.   4. Boys—Books and
reading.   5. Play—Social aspects.   6. Toys—Social aspects.
7. Sexism.   I. Clark, Beverly Lyon.   II. Higonnet, Margaret R.
PN 1009.5.S48G57   1999
305.3'09—dc21   99-22652
                                                                        CIP